The Concept of Order

THE CONCEPT
OF ORDER

Edited by Paul G. Kuntz

Published for Grinnell College
by the University of Washington Press
SEATTLE AND LONDON

Copyright © 1968 by the University of Washington Press
Library of Congress Catalog Card Number 68-26736
Printed in the United States of America

Foreword

In 1963 Carnegie Corporation awarded fifty thousand dollars to Grinnell College to support several programs of curriculum experimentation. One of these was the "Interdisciplinary Seminar on Order," directed by Professor Paul G. Kuntz, who at that time was a member of the Grinnell College faculty.

The seminar was designed to "focus attention of students and faculty . . . on a single basic concept" over an extended period of time so as to foster interdisciplinary communication and enhance the sense of intellectual community. During the 1963–64 school year, Grinnell brought to its campus more than twenty distinguished scholars representing various academic disciplines: philosophy, history, religion, psychology, political science, philology, literature. These eminent visitors participated in seminars and panel discussions, led meetings of regular classes, conversed informally with students and faculty; and each of them presented a paper on some aspect of the "Concept of Order" as grasped from within his own discipline.

Since the seminar was also intended to make a "lasting contribution to the understanding and interpretation of order," Professor Kuntz readied the papers for publication. He collected and edited those which had been presented during the seminar, oversaw their revision and refinement, and supplemented them with additional essays from other scholars. The present volume is the fruit of this persistent and earnest labor by Professor Kuntz and the scholars who devoted their constructive thinking to the central concept of "Order."

HOWARD R. BURKLE
Chairman, Department of
Philosophy and Religion
Grinnell College

Acknowledgments

The editor wishes to thank the authors of the following papers for their unfailing kindness. The seminar at Grinnell College would have been impossible without the help of secretaries, both those who issued the invitations and those who typed the papers: Mrs. Warren Beaty, Mrs. J. Michael Young, and Mrs. Richard Cole, and Mrs. H. A. Meacham who ran thousands of sheets through the multilith machine. Mrs. Susan Livingston aided in the final stages of editing the copy. The editor is grateful to many students who listened patiently and questioned eagerly, and especially to the translators, Jean Scanlon and J. Michael Young. Without Mr. Young's help the editor could not have learned to see the set of papers as a whole, and would not have been compelled to inquire into the many meanings of order revealed in corresponding opposites. Without the editorial help of Lynn C. Richman the index could not have been prepared.

The editor is deeply indebted to President Howard R. Bowen for the beginning of this cooperative enterprise, to Dean James H. Stauss for its continuance, to President Glenn Leggett for its completion. This published account may be the beginning of many such endeavors. The editor expresses his profound thanks to Carnegie Corporation of New York for making it possible.

PAUL G. KUNTZ

Grinnell College
July, 1966
Emory University
February, 1967

Contents

Introduction

I. FORMULATING THE PROBLEM

From many discussions in the past emerged a desire to probe into what leading scholars meant by "order." I began in 1959 to call attention to the centrality of the category "order" in American philosophy, and I found such a wealth of alternatives that an adequate treatment required the full time of a course. From this emerged a bibliography that grew summer after summer and during the academic year. I was encouraged in my desire to invite leading scholars to Grinnell College by President Howard R. Bowen. Among the scholars who had written considerably about order are not only those who have contributed, but also the mathematician Norbert Wiener, the physicist Harlow Shapley, and the biologist Paul Weiss. Leading men in the humanities also gave moral support; among them are Austin Warren and Lewis Mumford.

With the aid of Carnegie Corporation came the opportunity to probe with two dozen leading scholars into the meanings of order. As director of the Seminar on Order I proposed to focus attention on order at Grinnell College during the year 1963–64 in the interest of an education that would transcend the gulf between the "two cultures," for "order" is relevant to all the disciplines of the liberal arts and to all the sciences. This book is more than a record of a year of excitement. It may implement in other colleges and universities the investigation of concepts shared by the sciences, the arts, and the humanities.

A philosopher's interest is naturally in concepts of highest generality, what are called categories. Clearly, if a term is used in every art and science, it is a candidate to rank with being, truth, quality, quantity, space, time, cause, and so forth. The editor's speculation about order as a category can be seen in the statement of 1962 submitted to Carnegie Corporation and to scholars who were invited to participate in the seminar:

Central in modern mathematics is the concept of "ordering relation"; in statistics and probability the central contrast is between randomness and order. Randomness is a concept used by physicists; there are applications of the concept in statistical mechanics and in thermodynamics where it appears as entropy. Chemistry and biology disclose atomic, molecular, and macro-orders. Social and political thought, dealing with culture and civilization generally, use concepts of "social order," "law and order," both of these in contrast to "anarchy," or "lawlessness." There is a contemporary political dialogue between those who desire greater social cohesion and those who desire less cohesion through the state. There are logical and psychological orders; we speak of "ordered" as opposed to "muddled" minds. There is an order of inference and of proof; there are orders of scientific investigation; methods order inquiry and require that the subject matter reveal law and regularity. Religion and metaphysics are concerned with the source of order and the necessity of order. The traditional belief in God implied an orderly nature. The question must now be put: are there other faiths that could sustain the search for unknown orders and the achievement in human life of the new orderliness? That man can bring order out of chaos is central to artistic composition: eliciting "form," "style," and "pattern."

Students and scholars together are to engage in a search for a common element in the diverse uses of "order," if there is one; otherwise, for reasoned distinctions between "the orders," in the case that they are not reducible to one type. There are new technical tools that scholars in every field have borrowed from logic and mathematics in clarifying concepts. Therefore, we hope for significant scholarly advance by bringing together those knowledgeable in mathematics and logic with those in other fields.

Many people complain that philosophers do not communicate with men in other fields, but care only to communicate with each other, and the way of interdisciplinary work is important whereas the way of intradisciplinary inquiry is not only trivial but progressively trivial. The editor need not agree with the judgment of critics of philosophy to allow that his conception of philosophy is that of participating with men of any profession and those of no profession in getting their ideas clear. It was Dewey who turned philosophers from exclusive attention to the problems of philosophy to the problems of men. More than a third of the contributing scholars hold chairs of philosophy, but each of these philosophers has some strong interest in another field or fields. Perhaps the most wide-ranging of these philosophers are James K. Feibleman and Paul Weiss. Each is the author of a system of metaphysics and has applied his principles to human organizations, to the arts and religion, to literature, and to science. Monroe Beardsley has concentrated his interests in aesthetics and thus has dealt with all the fine arts. Charles Hartshorne, Herbert Spiegelberg, and W. Donald Oliver have had a special interest in psychology. Richard Cole has been especially concerned with foundations of logic and mathematics in the general area of philosophy of science. Ernan McMullin was trained in physics and has contributed much to the history of science and to logic. Peter Caws also was trained in physics and is eminent both in philosophy of science and in educational administration. Helmut Kuhn has contributed to the history of philosophy, especially of aesthetics. No summary such as this can do justice to the ways in which these philosophers have made their very abstract reflections pertinent to concrete fields. For example, Charles Hartshorne has no peer among contemporary American philosophers who have influenced theology, specifically toward revising the traditional doctrines of God. Two of the most distinguished philosophers of law, who have studied in law schools and taught jurisprudence, are Iredell Jenkins, who is also an aesthetician, and Samuel Stumpf.

These philosophers' papers are distributed, in the table of contents, among subject matter fields because, for the most part, they deal with specific areas of order: order in history; order in literature and the fine arts; order in religion and ethics; order in the sciences; order in language, learning, and personality; order in human society.

Language and literature are represented by Kenneth Burke, Joshua Whatmough, and John Crossett. History is represented by two of the great speculators about the destiny of mankind, Arnold Toynbee and Eric Voegelin, and by an American historian, an authority on Andrew Carnegie, Joseph Wall. Religion is represented by Joseph Kitagawa, Edward Conze, and Hans Hofmann. Kitagawa and Conze have great interest in Buddhism, one by birth and the other by conversion. Hans Hofmann has combined psychiatry with the career of a theologian.

Science is represented by a geologist who is also a historian of science, Cecil Schneer. Ernan McMullin is a philosopher who deals with Aristotelian and modern physics. John Greene is a specialist in Darwin and Darwinism; R. S. Westfall is a specialist in Newton and seventeenth-century science and theology. Thus the history of science is represented.

The social sciences are represented by eminent theoreticians: Carl Friedrich and Stanley Hoffmann in political science, and Talcott Parsons in sociology.

These authorities, it must be noted, were selected because each had already written about order, and had secured a distinguished place in the bibliography of the subject.

To these men the general problems of order were presented, and each endeavored to answer with special reference to his area of competence. I shall now present a historical approach to the problem of order in a perspective that tries to synthesize the angles of vision from which our authors see order.

II. HISTORY OF THE PROBLEM: MYTHICAL, ANCIENT HEBREW AND GREEK, BUDDHIST, MODERN, AND OUR POST-MODERN PROBLEMS

The history of the concept of order is as long and widespread as mankind, and as intricate as the arts and sciences themselves. Many of these papers begin with a primitive myth of order. How did the order of nature and the order of society begin? In the beginning, we are told in Genesis, the earth was "without form and void," and the principle of order is God, who separated light from darkness, day from night, and appointed the habitation of sea to fish, earth to serpents and four-footed animals, sky to birds, and over all placed man. To bring order out of chaos is divine, and the human role in nature and in society is to abide by God's commandments. The powerful tie between man and God is a relation of faithfulness called the covenant. After the Flood, a punishment for sinful men, especially those corrupters of the flesh, comes the guarantee of the order and constancy of nature: "While the earth remaineth, seedtime and harvest, and cold and heat, and summer and winter, and day and night shall not cease" (Genesis 8:22).

The emphasis of these papers, when they pay attention to mythical and ancient conceptions on order, is to ask whether this prehistorical and historical material has validity today and is relevant to us. The dominant answer is affirmative. Kitagawa argues, as does his associate Mircea Eliade, that we may in our modernity, unless we attend to myth and ritual, miss the sacred dimension. Burke, Voegelin, and Hofmann show how Biblical language can be used in very different ways to solve problems in literature, history, and psychiatry. One paper differs strongly: Peter Caws rejects the question of the origin of order; the important point is its use and enjoyment however it came to be.

Paul Weiss calls our attention to two aspects of the Hebrew myth of order: first, that the order does not seem to be necessary, and, second, that order is said to be imposed on the world. But this seems, according to Weiss, a mistake, because even if events happen by chance, and are not designed, there would emerge, as from the tossing of a penny, a sequence of heads and tails, which could not fail to have an order, that is, some definite arrangement, although not necessarily a cyclical alternation between the two sides of a coin (p. 15).

Other writers do not so boldly confront the ancient Hebrew myth with a twentieth-century theory. Probably the historian of religion, Joseph Kitagawa, would think such a confrontation ahistorical: Kitagawa puts the creation myth in a context of its own, "primitive religion," and connects the myth with rituals in which men symbolically return to chaos and experience a rebirth of order (pp. 270–75). The importance for life of the sacred story is that it orients man in dependence upon a celestial model of order.

Hans Hofmann, a theologian, insists on the wisdom in ancient myths. He differs from Kitagawa in regarding the concept as a polar pair, order-and-chaos, for the world cannot be without both, just as in Greek philosophy a concrete thing requires both form and matter.

The critic Kenneth Burke and the historian Eric Voegelin stress the use of Biblical metaphor in understanding man and his history. Burke used the Biblical notion of covenant to oppose modern mechanism. Voegelin uses the Biblical notion of the Exodus to oppose the modern notion of man creating his own destiny.

Often a consideration of myths of order is limited to the heritages of Israel and Greece. Edward Conze's paper, however, includes a full treatment of the Buddhist concept of Dharma. Conze's paper challenges us to think of likenesses and differences. It is especially instructive to see that the Sanskrit and Pali equivalent in Hindu culture has the same ambiguity as the Western concept of order. We moderns seek for different words for the cosmic order, the social order, and the personal moral order. Can all these realms of concern be guided by a single principle? One of the attractions of such an ancient philosophy and religion as Buddhism is evidently a need to unify the realms.

Just as the Hebraic vision of order is challenged by Weiss, so the Hellenic vision of order is challenged by Charles Hartshorne. Weiss's quick refutation of the belief in a Creator imposing order upon an otherwise orderless world is based upon the observation that events occurring in random sequences produce orderly results. Hartshorne's quick rejection of the cosmic order of the Greeks is based upon the observation that their doctrines of order left no room for accidents or real chance. Various authors who have considered Greek philosophy on order and disorder would challenge Hartshorne, for, argue Feibleman and McMullin, Aristotle allowed for accident or contingency in his conception of the cosmos.

The influences of ancient Israel and Greece are nowhere more evident than in the thinking of Arnold Toynbee about order, and specifically the order of human history, which he calls here "pattern." The question is raised by Plato and Polybius: What sequence of constitutions can we discern, or which class of men rules in succession? With Voegelin, Toynbee has been concerned with Gibbon's pattern of rise and fall and with Thucydides' problem of learning from the failure of his own generation how to pass on wisdom to the succeeding generation so that it might not fall into futile disorder. Toynbee's work is, by his own account, also deeply rooted in the Biblical response. First, man is challenged by God and is free to respond, as did Jonah, with a "no" rather than a "yes." The results of a challenge are not predictable or determined (pp. 46, 47, 57). Second, the concern of man should be with the salvation of the whole human race. The philosophy of history that Toynbee has been preaching is distinctly a prophetic call to men to turn from their wickedness to serve the true God of all mankind.

Concepts of order developed by the ancient Greeks are compared in Ernan McMullin's "Order in Plato and the Aristotelian Tradition." The concept of order that dominated ancient Rome is presented in John Crossett's "Love in the Western Hierarchy." These essays complement each other because one, by a philosopher of science, concerns the order of nature; the other, by a humanist, concerns the order of society. One deals with the good order (*euta-*

xia) that ought to prevail in relations between and among persons. The other deals with how things are arranged (*taxis*) .

Order according to ancient thinkers was inseparable from purpose; ends or goals are higher than the means used to attain ends, and ends are themselves on different levels. Hence the order of nature and society rests on an order of forms that is teleological and hierarchical.

Neither Crossett nor McMullin, authorities on ancient classical thought, ignores the fact that ancient Greece and Rome produced a variety of views of order. The contrasts between Plato and Aristotle provided, for succeeding pagan, Jewish, Moslem, and Christian thinkers, alternative doctrines which might be either opposed or reconciled. For example, it is well established that one cannot lump together Plato and Aristotle on form and matter as "the Greek view" because one conceived of forms apart from matter, the other of forms with matter. Plato in his *Timaeus* requires a Demiurge or workman god to explain how form and matter are brought together. But, if they are already together, no Demiurge is required, and Aristotle does not argue for one.

Some symposiasts devoted much attention to the primitive and ancient concepts of order, but seemed eager to rush to the "modern world," as Whitehead called the conceptions that became forceful from about 1600. Thus the medieval preparation for the modern world was neglected. However, John Crossett connects Virgil with St. Augustine and St. Thomas Aquinas, all of them stressing a hierarchy of virtues quite different from modern ethical opinion and, Crossett argues, very superior to hedonism. The editor has tried to show elsewhere that between St. Augustine and Galileo was a development that made great progress in clarifying the concept of order.[1] An order, as St. Thomas was accustomed to define it, is a relation of priority or posteriority between terms according to a principle. We must always specify, to be clear, whether the priority of one to another is temporal, spatial, causal, of value, of social rank, and so forth.

The distinctive notion of order of the modern world is, according to Richard S. Westfall, that of "a set of necessary relations capable of exact mathematical description" (p. 78). Among thinkers of the seventeenth century there was no doubt that the cosmos is ordered,

[1] Paul G. Kuntz, "Order" in *The New Catholic Encyclopedia* (New York: McGraw-Hill, 1967) , X, 720–23.

and this belief is one of the keys to Newton's work. The critical point concerns the kind of order. Whereas Aristotelian order was based on qualities—such properties as wet, dry, hot, cold—the new science was quantitative. The concept of a mechanical order is that the real properties of things are size and shape: the nature of aggregates depends on the nature of the parts, the qualities sentient beings perceive such as color and sound are but secondary or merely subjective. These are points shared by Galileo, Descartes, and Newton. Points that divide the moderns are whether the order is grasped as necessary or whether it is learned from experience and is therefore contingent. Newton's empiricism opposes Decartes' rationalism. Yet another paper, Cole's "The Causal Order and the Logical Order," calls our attention to the similarity of Newton and Descartes, by contrast to the radical empiricism of David Hume.

Science of the seventeenth century was not sharply divided from metaphysics. As we are reminded by Westfall, the cause of order in nature, which Newton investigated, meant on one hand "physical principles," but, on the other hand, the order and beauty we see in the world proclaim the source of all regularity, God (pp. 79–81).

The Newtonian world served as a model for the works of man. Of this we are reminded by Rudolf Arnheim's "Order and Complexity in Landscape Design." Arnheim contrasts the formal French garden to the English informal garden, and also to the seemingly irrational Zen garden. In the classical garden, the elements are sharply defined and relations are completely controlled by geometrical principles. The simpler the principle, such as a straight line and a regular curve, the greater the conformity to rational order (p. 158). Two further principles of order made visual in the formal garden of the classical period were axial symmetry and hierarchy. Space can be divided so that two halves are in balance. And things can be arranged in a pyramid, so that, for example, height and size are covariants; that is, "with increasing height the horizontal sections get smaller" (p. 162).

It is an old story with us that the sciences continued to regard the order of nature as quantitative and to seek everywhere for necessary laws, whereas the postclassical romantic arts exalted spontaneity, and sometimes irrationality; our artists also complain that classical order lacks romantic variety. Although there is no paper *ex professo* on the romantic revolt, the editor claims that such papers as Arnheim's could not have been written today without the influences of such poets and thinkers as Goethe. Elsewhere the editor has tried to show precisely what the issues are with respect to order and chaos.[2]

Evidence for the above statement about the continuity of science, in spite of the revolt of the poets, is found in John C. Greene's "The Concept of Order in Darwinism." Darwin and the Darwinians did not dissent from the Newtonian faith in "a law-bound system of matter in motion" (p. 89). Whereas Westfall's account of Newton is of unqualified intellectual triumph, the progress of Darwinian evolutionary theory is crossed with perplexity about its first principles. Darwinism survives as a general philosophy in Sir Julian Huxley today, marked, as Greene notes, by "the same linking of cosmic, biological, and cultural evolution in a single continuum of progressive development, the same naturalism in the concept of man, the same search for analogies between biological and social evolution, the same confidence in science and its power to create an ever new and better future for the human race" (p. 103). But at every point of certainty, there is doubt conveyed by ambiguity of terms or wavering of doctrine.

The first paradox of Darwinian order is that, if nature is only a "a law-bound system of matter in motion," how could it be "a framework of contrived structures fitted as a stage for the activities of intelligent beings?" Newton had derived the latter principle from Christian natural theology, but the two views are incompatible. In the former view, no state of the system could be regarded as initial or final, as required by the latter view of divine creation in the beginning, redemption in the end. Yet evolution is an attempt to explain the progress of species mechanistically.

The second paradox of Darwinian order is that the "law-bound system" is of necessary laws, yet the mechanism of evolution requires not only "universal mutability" but chance. How could there be "random variation" in a Newtonian world? (pp. 90–92). The third paradox is that the mechanistic process is conceived as blind and indifferent to value, yet the notion of evolutionary progress is evaluative, that is, the more evolved is better than the less evolved. Spencer said progress was "not an accident, not a thing within human control, but a beneficent necessity." (pp. 93–94). T. H. Huxley disallowed Spencer's effort to derive ethics from biology (pp. 94–95), an attempt of a type made notorious by G. E. Moore

[2] Kuntz, "Quality vs. Quantity: The Qualitative World of William Blake vs. The Quantitative World of Isaac Newton," unpublished.

as the "naturalistic fallacy." The fourth paradox is that the concept
of order implicit in evolutionary theory is sometimes that of providential teleology, sometimes that of statistical regularity, but neither of these is compatible with mechanical regularity, or either
concept with the other (pp. 97–99).

Greene's critical analysis of the philosophy of Darwinism is most
instructive because of its negative results. It also serves to introduce
us to various problems not yet solved within the context of our
modern theory of order. These problems are:

1. *How far can the mathematical analysis be pushed?* Joshua
Whatmough endorses the application of statistical analysis to the
structure of language. Monroe Beardsley tries information theory in
the analysis of aesthetic order but finds it seriously deficient.

2. *How far can the order of nature be discovered by empirical
observation?* Richard Cole is dissatisfied with the Humean account
of our knowledge of natural law and attempts a doctrine of necessary causal connections. Cecil Schneer is dissatisfied with the empiricist account of scientific knowledge and prefers the idealistic account of the mind's activity in creating natural order.

3. *Can there be real chance if nature is a deterministic order?*
Three papers bear upon the reality of chance, those of Weiss,
Feibleman, and Hartshorne.

4. *How can we conceive of the free agency of men, a personal
order, if our idea of order is deterministic, that is, of laws external
to agents?* Herbert Spiegelberg and W. Donald Oliver consider
persons in moral relations to each other and defend the autonomy
of the moral order. That is, they deny such a form of reduction of
agency to motion, a great point also in Kenneth Burke's essay. Also
in league with the defense of the moral as irreducible is Samuel E.
Stumpf's attack on the reduction of the moral order to the legal
order as in legal positivism or sociological jurisprudence.

5. *Finally, how do the modern philosophies of order connect the
human realms of choice and value with rational order?* Iredell
Jenkins' case against modern philosophies is that they deal at best
with the two modes, possibility and necessity, but can make no sense
of man or the world without purposiveness. Helmut Kuhn's account
is a dialectical defense of the doctrine of hierarchical order.

The editor has placed Helmut Kuhn's "The Case of Order in a
Disordered Age" penultimate in the sequence of essays. One reason

is that its vast scope and critical approach can best be appreciated after such a survey as I have sketched. Another reason is that Kuhn shows the contemporary crises: he was forced into American exile by a dictator who appealed to order as his justification. Although, as Caws argues, order and value are almost synonymous, we seem to confront orders, as in the state exemplified by the Führer's *Ruhe und Ordnung,* that are by no means necessarily good. The editor's grappling with the concepts of order began with the consideration that in the political realm a new order is often a new disorder.[3] A fine final affirmation of order, in spite of the disruptions of war, is Joseph Wall's "The Historian's Approach to Reality."

All these five areas of conflict are vital to a new philosophy of order for which thinkers now seem to be reaching. Contemporary science, although continuing on the same basis as Newton, has in some areas, such as evolutionary theory, revised its methods radically when confronted with different kinds of order. Also, the mechanistic philosophy (in its view of man's knowledge and purposes)[4] does not satisfy philosophers in areas of aesthetic and moral value.

The editor has argued elsewhere that the present crisis of man's understanding of himself and the world has great bearing upon practical affairs.[5] In the area of society, politics, and international relations are three essays by social scientists: Talcott Parsons, Carl J. Friedrich, and Stanley Hoffmann. Toynbee and Voegelin have argued as historians that the division of the soul requires some new orientation to restore human integrity. In the same way, Friedrich, Hoffman, and Wall are making recommendations about the institutions of the future.

Parsons' "Order as a Sociological Problem" would indicate that societies are functioning quite well in getting individual members to internalize the rules and to abide by them. Friedrich indicates great hope that men can balance the claims of freedom against the claims of order. That is, in a federal system of government, men can avoid the extremes of anarchy or of tyranny. But how to bring

[3] Kuntz, "Ruhe und Unordnung," *The Haverfordian,* LV (March, 1936), 105–6.

[4] Kuntz, "Mythical, Cosmic, and Personal Order," *The Review of Metaphysics,* XVI (June, 1963), 718–48.

[5] Kuntz, "Meanings of Order," "Order, Chaos, and the Arts," and "Is Talk about Order Talk about God?" unpublished; "Religion of Order and Religion of Chaos," *Religion in Life,* XXXV (Summer, 1966), 433–49.

together sovereign states into viable relations, avoiding mutual destruction by war, is an outstanding problem to which Stanley Hoffmann addresses himself. For most of us the lack of even a minimal world order is the most pressing problem of our generation. Wall confronts us with the horror of the chaos we could produce by nuclear war so that we may deal moderately and cautiously in international relations.

Regarding the new philosophy of order for which thinkers are now reaching, we need to ask whether we should try to recover the wisdom of the mythical and metaphysical views of the Hebrews, Greeks, and Romans. The following dialogue provides an example of the problem that results in contemporary society when a classicist and his ancient theory of order conflicts with a modernist who is reaching for a new philosophy of order.

III. THE PROBLEM

Perhaps the reader has been present when his friends, in a reflective or argumentative mood, fell to challenging one another's definitions and theories of order. This must be so common that, in relating a recent dialogue, I am probably reminding the reader of some experience of his own. One speaker is a musician and aesthetician, the other a poet and classicist. The announced topic was, "Is *Avant-Garde* Art Antihumanistic?"

Whatever the subject may be, "order" and its opposite, "chaos," are terms that may emerge in the discussion. For they are always just beneath the surface, unless the discourse is overtly theoretical or philosophical. In the following I report, as the dialogue in fact took place, how each side developed a characteristic position. The modernist and the classicist each came to see in the other a thesis that must be opposed. Those who came to hear the announced topic discussed were at first disappointed. But in the end a bigger issue was opened up than "Is *Avant-Garde* Art Antihumanistic?"

"Art," said the classicist, "is essentially didactic. Art teaches man about human nature, which is but one of the many fixed essences only partly revealed in the concrete and transient mode of this visible world. Beyond this visible world is the invisible divine Order. In contrast to our imperfect copy is the original, the perfect divine Order. The right relation is the subordination of the transient to the eternal, the copy to the archetype. Art can serve, with religion, philosophy, morality, to order man to the ultimate principle of Order."

"Do we listen to music to learn of a perfect order?" inquired the modernist. "Each work of art, even each rendition of each composition, has a *unique* order. One cannot rank the works of art according to the fixed degree to which one reveals a *single* Order more than another. A symphony is not "about" this single Order any more than it is about the order of society under Napoleon or about the order of nature according to Linnaeus. There is no need for the conception of an ultimate Order 'behind' all the particular orders, and, moreover, the concept of a perfect Order is nonsense."

"Far from nonsense," responded the classicist, "for perfect Order alone makes sense, if anything does."

"What do you mean by 'order' apart from your Christian and Platonic Theory?"

"Order," said the classicist, "is sameness opposed to difference. It can be symbolized by an all-black painting or any one given quality where no part is distinguishable from any other part."

"Rubbish," said the modernist; "that all black painting is not an order at all. For order rests upon relation between different things. If there is but one thing, there is no order."

"Would there also be no disorder if there were only one thing?" queried the classicist.

"Or disorder—right. Moreover," replied the modernist, "there is a meaning of 'order' that rests upon difference in energy, implying that even distribution of energy throughout an area is the very opposite of order. The more perfectly distributed, the more disordered."

"Oh, yes, entropy according to thermodynamic theory," the classicist declared.

"Well, then you know that work can be done by a machine only so long as there is energy to be converted, as in the heat engine, by a difference in pressure. If we had equal pressure and no difference between steam and condensed water, which follows from your definition of order, there would be only disorder," argued the modernist.

"First you accused my meaning of 'order' of being neither order nor disorder, and now of being only disorder. Come now, can I be guilty of both those opposites? Or are you playing with different meanings of order, different both from mine and from each other?" questioned the classicist.

The modernist: "The opposite of an orderly arrangement is a random distribution. When the elements fall by chance, then they are most unlikely to be in a sequence such as 1, 2, 3, 4, where the ordering relation is 'successor of by 1.' "

"A series is a kind of order, but it is not perfectly orderly because there is a difference between the elements," added our classicist friend.

"Would you call orderly a mere repetition, such as 1, 1, 1, 1?"

"No: the most perfect order is Unity itself, the One, beside which there can be no other. A series, like any imperfect order, is a unity in plurality. The plurality is a defect."

"But all ordering is of elements that are related in some way or other, and would you say that one thing can be related at all?" continued the modernist.

"By identity—related to itself. This is perfect in its symmetry."

"And I have chosen an order, the series, beginning 1, 2 or better 0, 1, < 2 and $0 < 1$, where there are ordered pairs, 1, 2, and 0, 1 as the mathematicians say," asserted the Modernist.

"Yes," says the classicist, "that is *your* order. I make 'order' synonymous with 'unity,' and there are degrees of orderliness as we approximate perfect unity."

"How useless an order that is, and, may I add also, how dull," retorted the modernist.

"What *use* is order put to? And what *interesting* order can you be thinking of? The number series is *useful* but not *interesting,* and the sequence of episodes in a story is *interesting,* but not *useful.* I enjoy the concept of perfect unity, and use I never think of. . . ."

"Very well," interrupted the modernist, ready to take up the gauntlet, "I respond to your challenge. The diatonic scale is an ordering of sounds that is both *useful* to the correlating of notation and instrumental in producing music, and is also a source of delight in organizing the sound for the hearer. It is an order in the precise sense of a series, for the relation 'higher than in pitch' orders sounds in an asymmetrical way. We go up the scale by going higher, and we come down the scale by going lower. The converse relation is lower than in pitch."

"Oh, very well, a scale, which literally is a ladder, has equal intervals. You see, order means an identity of some sort," said the classicist, smiling.

"Yes, the musical scale is not simply order by the relation 'higher than in pitch,'" agreed the modernist, "but, 'higher than to a similar degree.' I had not disallowed an aspect of unity in any order of this sort—it is *you* who have called the diversity, or difference, or plurality a deficiency of order. . . ."

"What is *chaos,* then?" asked the classicist.

"*Tohu va bohu,*" shouted the modernist, using a bit of Hebrew, "more familiar in the King James Version of the creation story from Genesis as 'without form and void.' Before the Lord God *separated* light from dark, or earth from water, when earth was undifferentiated, then there was chaos. Just as I tried to say, without separated elements, there is no order, because relations are between different things, and if there is no relation, there is no order."

"What is chaos?" repeated the classicist.

"The absence of relation altogether, neither likeness nor difference, would be chaos," answered the satisfied modernist.

The classicist pushes his question, "Then chaos is neither orderly nor disorderly?"

"Exactly," responded the modernist, "because any array of elements that is orderly must also be disorderly."

"What a contradiction! You accused me of calling disorder order—now you yourself fall into nonsense," said the classicist pointing an accusing finger.

"No, not nonsense," said the modernist, "only a paradox, a seeming contradiction. For every relation is of a specific sort. What is orderly in one way cannot be orderly in all ways. Let me ask you, what is the order of 1, 2, 3, 4 . . . ?"

"Obviously, magnitude."

"Is 4, 3, 2, 1 . . . also orderly?" asked the modernist, now taking over the questioning.

"Yes, in the opposite way." answered the classicist.

"Minitude?"

"If you wish."

"But neither magnitude nor minitude is the order of 1, 3 . . . and 2, 4 . . ."

"Oh," interrupted the classicist, "all the odd numbers and all the even numbers together related by 'greater than by 2 (or less than by 2),' no?"

"But either magnitude or minitude is a rhythmic order, say odd, even, odd, even, odd, even, odd, even, etc." stated the modernist.

"You are making your point of kinds of order. Have you a place for symmetry?" asked the classicist.

"Of course," responded the modernist, "a sequence symbolized by *a, b, c, b, a* would be symmetrical."

"Have you even a place for fluctuating order?" continued the classicist.

"Yes, symbolized perhaps by *a, b, c, b, c, a, c, b, d, c, a, b* . . ."

"If that's order, then any arrangement of elements is an order."

"Yes," agreed the modernist, "any arrangement: some are familiar as magnitude (and the reverse or converse order, 'minitude') , symmetry, but others have not yet been identified and named."

"But then there is no one meaning of order, or no one model of order by which all orders can be judged and ranked?" asked the perplexed classicist.

"No, no one model," assured the modernist.

"I've been trying to save the concept of Order, and you have been content to leave us with only a 'set' of loosely related concepts of order. Perhaps with only a 'family resemblance' between them, if so much!" accused the classicist.

"I do not deny the accusation. Rather you have seen exactly what I mean by the plurality of orders."

"You have given up the concept of the great chain of being, which is an order of orders?"

"Yes," continued the modernist, "in the sense that there is a ranking of beings from God through angels to men and through animals to plants and nonliving things, if you mean that each higher thing attracts the lower and each lower thing strives to be like the higher on the scale of being. In this pyramid of being there is supposed one simple unity like a point at the peak of being, and, as we descend, one finds strictly correlated multiplicity, evil, ugliness, confusion, falseness, and nonbeing."

"Are you saying that you have more confidence in your 'plurality of orders' than in the 'great chain of being'?"

"Of course," says the modernist; "I take it for granted that we have outgrown the view of the universe as a hierarchy from the pure being of God down to sheer nothingness."

"Would you, like Lovejoy, put evolution in its place?" questioned the classicist.

"Evolution as a unitary order, with everything going upward and onward? Not that either," corrected the modernist, "because just as it is not necessarily true that a thing is good, true, and beautiful to the extent that it has more being in the scale, so it is not necessarily true that a thing is good, true, and beautiful to the degree that it is more evolved."

"You would refute both the chain of being and the philosophy of evolution with the same argument," said the classicist smiling.

"Most seriously, there is no final or perfect Order," stated the modernist.

"Can you *prove* that?" said the classicist.

"A perfect order would be orderly in every aspect and to every point of view. But how can that be? Think of my examples."

"With God all things are possible," retorted the classicist.

"Yes," said the modernist agreeing in his own sense, "it would have to be another world in which order could be perfect."

"But the order of this world, imperfect as it is, cannot be without that divine Order," said the classicist very positively.

"Sure it can—we don't need the concept 'perfect Order,' and we can't think of 'perfect Order,' " said the modernist.

"Do you have any way to explain the unity of the universe?" questioned the classicist.

"The multiverse, you mean?" corrected the modernist.

The debate ended with a basic disagreement between the classicist and our modernist. The chairman had to intervene, for the time of adjournment had passed. The supposed topic of humanism and art was lost in the discussion of order that seemed of greater urgency. Although this debate ended in disagreement, each thinker had changed his position somewhat by clarifying his earlier view. Let us now look at some other conflicting views of order provided by various thinkers included in the Seminar on Order.

IV. ALTERNATIVE SOLUTIONS

Questions about order spring from every art and science, and therefore, to settle our question about the meaning of order, what better technique than to allow various scholars to speak their minds on the topic?

One way to clarify the alternative solutions is suggested by White-head in *Science and the Modern World:*

. . . The mentality of an epoch springs from the view of the world which is, in fact, dominant in the educated sections of the communities in question. There may be more than one such scheme, corresponding to cultural divisions. The various human interests which suggest cosmologies, and also are influenced by them, are *science, aesthetics, ethics, religion*. In every age each of these topics suggests a view of the world. Insofar as the same set of people are swayed by all, or more than one, of these interests, their effective outlook will be the joint production from these sources. But each age has its dominant preoccupation; and during the past three centuries in question, the cosmology derived from science has been asserting itself at the expense of older points of view with their origins elsewhere. Men can be provincial in time as well as in place.[6]

At the very least we should be able in these papers to recognize the divergences among men of different quadrants of culture: religion, ethics, aesthetics, and science. In this section I shall try to bring out the differences and the disagreements. In the next section I shall try to evoke from the contributions a synthetic view, a philosophy of order that seems historically to be called for in the contemporary crisis. Whitehead has neatly characterized this endeavor as philosophy relevant to all the other disciplines:

Philosophy, in one of its functions, is the critic of cosmologies. It is its function to harmonise, refashion, and justify divergent intuitions as to the nature of things. It has to insist on the scrutiny of the ultimate ideas, and on the retention of the whole of the evidence in shaping our cosmological scheme. Its business is to render explicit, and—so far as may be—efficient, a process which otherwise is unconsciously performed without rational tests.[7]

Since our several essays, all on order, are from the four quadrants of religion, ethics, aesthetics, and science, let us inquire whether there are meanings of order characteristic of each.

Order in the religious context regularly refers to an ultimate principle of order, impersonal with the Buddhists, personal with the Jews and Christians. Whether the Buddhist Dharma or the God of the Bible, and we may suppose the Moslem Allah, the Hindu and Zoroastrian and Confucian supreme principles also, there is one principle that accounts for all other orders. Religion is a powerful drive toward metaphysical unification beyond the appearance of multiplicity and confusion. Order in the religious sense refers to the right ordering of human thought and action, and is therefore regu-

---

[6] Alfred North Whitehead, *Science and the Modern World* (New York: Macmillan Co., 1926) p. ix; italics added.

[7] *Ibid.*, pp. ix–x.

larly a teleological concept. Put another way, order in a religious context is coupled with purpose. To subordinate man to Dharma or to God, would not, however, be to enslave man, according to the proponents of religious order, but to liberate man from his own ways which do not lead to salvation or ultimate bliss. This can be so because a man identifies his very being with Dharma or with God, or finds himself truly in dependence upon or in identity with the ultimate source of order. To be so ordered to the ultimate source of being and goodness is to be truly free (not free in the sense of doing as one pleases, which by contrast seems being wayward or capricious). A concept of religious order is often questioned on the grounds that it deprives man of his free choice between goals, that it fills him with despair contemplating the infinite qualitative difference said to exist between the human and the divine order, and that it is not basically a very clear concept of the order that man needs.

Many such critics of religious order would miss their mark in criticizing the essays in this collection. The grounds of faith are laid in human experience rather than in proofs of the existence of God. Indeed, quite remarkable by its absence is any argument from the order and harmony of the world to a divine creator. Such a topic would have been almost automatic up to a few generations ago. Moreover, the concern of religious thinkers Hofmann, Kuhn, Hartshorne, and Kitagawa is not to protect the divine omnipotence and omniscience but to present a conception in which man can be free. Hence the problem of evil is no longer the stumbling block in conceiving of the moral relation between God and man. With this shift away from transcendent majesty, the difference between Christianity and Buddhism has become less drastic. And all this is much to the liking of Toynbee, whose *Religion of an Historian* is intended to prepare us for a genuine "world religion" to replace continental pretenders to that title.

Order in the moral context regularly deals with the right relations between persons. In this broad sense we study the moral order not only in ethics, which is formally represented in Herbert Spiegelberg's study of rules, but in three studies of concepts of man, by Kenneth Burke, John Crossett, and W. Donald Oliver; in a study of jurisprudence, by Samuel Stumpf; in the historians' essays, by Eric Voegelin, Arnold Toynbee, and Joseph Wall; in studies of society and institutions, by Carl J. Friedrich, Talcott Parsons, and Stanley Hoffman.

There emerges a consensus among authorities. No one of them considers the moral order derivative from the natural order. Neither by causal relation nor by logical deduction do these thinkers assert that we can begin with gravitational force, chemical bonds, or DNA molecules and end with obligation of person to person. In a word, they all defend the autonomy and irreducibility of the moral order. Further, the moral order can be possible because the natural order is not one of deterministic necessity.

A degree of free choice is possible because present facts are compatible with alternative futures. The meaningfulness of "it ought to be *A* rather than *B*" is grounded ontologically in the compatibility of either *A* or *B* with present conditions. The moral order is a normative order, that is, there are standards by which we judge the rightness and wrongness of acts. Our authors tend toward moral objectivism, claiming that some kinds of acts can be known to be intrinsically wrong, and that this kind of truth is universal. Many kinds of obligations are conventional only. For instance, Stumpf and Spiegelberg except legal statute from universality. But something must be independent and nonarbitrary to give us the basis for judging and condemning unjust laws. The moral order finally is an ordering of acts done to attain certain ends. It is dynamic because it is purposeful. Man the moral agent is an orderer of his own acts, and consequently reflexive. He is responsible for the consequences, and, because he has said yes or no, he is to be praised or blamed for his acts.

There are no very severe critics of these aspects of the moral order, at least among our scholars. Perhaps Peter Caws would say that the moralists had ignored the value aspects of science. Certainly two ideas are questionable. John Crossett supports the idea of a rather rigid hierarchical ordering of duties. Our critics of rigidity, whether from an aesthetic or a psychiatric point of view, might ask whether this kind of morality takes account of the variety of human circumstances. Certainly our romantics in aesthetics, extending their principles to conduct, would justify some spontaneity. Also, our social scientists see a great variety of good orders among humankind. There is, notes Carl Friedrich, no hierarchy of rights discoverable in the Bill of Rights. The courts must decide where one limits the other or takes precedence. Hence the relation between them is one of dialectical tension.

Order in the aesthetic context regularly deals with arrangements of sensuous qualities, at least if we speak of the papers by Rudolf Arnheim and Monroe Beardsley. If we include also John Crossett's study of Virgil, poetry from the aesthetic field, and Joshua Whatmough's study of the order of language, the component of intellectual order becomes dominant rather than recessive.

The artist, we are reminded often throughout the series, is an arranger of materials, an orderer who brings order out of relative disorder, said also (by implicit analogy to the Creator God) to bring order out of chaos. What is the order of works of art?

Aesthetic order is, like moral order, normative. We are considering whether results of ordering are more or less satisfactory. The artist has begun with natural orders, his materials of color and shape, sound and temporal duration, and uses such existent order to produce better order. About this process a number of aspects seem clear. First, there is no one kind of patterning or style of patterning. Some styles exalt symmetry, others asymmetry; some define the parts clearly, others leave parts as aspects of wholes; some define relations rationally, as geometrical figures, others prefer the organic order of growth that cannot be easily defined.

Nor does order in the aesthetic sense exclude disorder. The moral order may be conceived as better if all wrong, crime, sin, evil, and so forth were excluded, but certainly aesthetic order requires disorder. At least if order is design, then unintended or chance effects may make the work better. Simplicity is required, but so is complexity. Too much simplicity bores us, as too much complexity confuses.

Both of our aestheticians agree that a work of art can be analyzed as to part or as to whole. There are small-scale orders, for example, the texture of a rug, and large-scale orders, for example, the proportions of a house. Hence, we can study how orders are ranged hierarchically, for example, how the rug fits the room, the room the suite of rooms, the suite the whole house, the house the landscape, and so on.

There have been attempts to make the aesthetic order supreme. One interesting argument is that the aesthetic order is fundamental to human experience and the moral order is derivative. Although no paper argues this explicitly, Kenneth Burke argues against it. The artist qua artist may dissociate himself from social obligation, as does James Joyce's Stephen Dedalus, who decides he will not serve his nation, his church, or his family *(non serviam)*. Hence, argues Burke, the aesthetic approach to order neglects responsibility of a moral sort. It has sometimes been argued that, since the artist does not care whether his order corresponds to real order, he is also unfit intellectually. Thus we pass to the order that is expected to be true to the structure of nature.

Order in the scientific context regularly deals with observable phenomena corresponding to laws, preferably of an exact and therefore mathematical sort, and, because these are predictive laws, they are testable by future phenomena.

Three papers from historians of science, Ernan McMullin, R. S. Westfall, and John C. Greene, deal with specific contributions to the scientific order. Half a dozen papers deal with determinism, necessary causation, and mechanistic models of explanation, all of them troubled by reconciling human freedom of choice with a scientific account. Richard Cole's paper defends causal necessity, while Charles Hartshorne stresses chance in the natural order. Cole is troubled by a Humean picture, according to which anything might happen. Hartshorne is troubled by a Laplacian view, according to which nothing may happen other than what an omniscient mind might deduce from knowledge of the laws plus facts at any time in the process. They seem to be arguing opposite positions, and it is notable, as mentioned earlier, that what is called "science" contains incompatible presuppositions about the natural order. So John Greene argues brilliantly about Darwinism (pp. 90–93), but the disagreements about what science suggests about the order of things are even less capable now of easy solution.

What is a "chance" event? The common deterministic view, presuming perfect mechanical order or sufficient reason for every event, is an event for which we do not know the causes. This is a common view, propounded today for example by Harlow Shapley, who also denies, as an article of scientific faith, the possibility of real disorder or chaos. A chance event was in Plato's account, according to McMullin, an example of the recalcitrant and stubborn aspects of things, unintelligible, nonpurposive, unreasoning (pp. 66–67). Did Aristotle mean that a chance event was an exception to the normal in the sense that it could be defined statistically as something that rarely happens (pp. 71–72)? No, he answers, a chance event for Aristotle was something unplanned. But if we do not hold a theological view of nature, now progressively abandoned after

Newton and Darwin, how are we to conceive a chance? Evolutionary theory depends upon "random variation" (p. 93).

Many of our authors turn to thermodynamics and gas theory for concepts of disorder. Whereas commonly the crystal is a model of order (p. 146), a gas is the model of disorder. None of our authors mentions the interesting middle case between solid and gas, the liquid, about whose order the late J. D. Bernal of London made such interesting contributions. The state of entropy is considered by Whatmough, Schneer, and Feibleman, among others. To call it "complete random distribution" is to define the unknown by the unknown, for what is randomness? Is it a property of a method of sampling (p. 8)? This will scarcely do for a theory based on real chance events. Functionally the state is reached when there is no usable energy in a closed system, and this is the state of equilibrium, as of even temperature (pp. 143–46). This is also odd, because then perfect chaos would be order, and the distinction order/disorder would break down (p. 11).

Clearly this is an area of excitement not only because of paradox, but because of new techniques, like information theory, investigating the stochastic series in which what has happened in a series allows some prediction as to future events. Whatmough applies this to language, Beardsley to musical notes. The world appears rather —to Feibleman, Weiss, and Hartshorne, as it did to C. S. Peirce—a rich disorder yielding regularities. The order of the universe is a disorder, the matrix of all limited orders (p. 000).

Can this new cosmology lead us to avoid the conceptual contradictions of Darwinism? Or are we trading one set of well-known puzzles for another set of less-known puzzles?

Now that we have sketched the consensus of views about religious order, moral order, aesthetic order, and scientific order, what are we to make of the cosmos, if we can still call it such, and of man?

One general conclusion, from a geologist, Cecil Schneer, is that the order of science owes just as much to the scientist as to nature, and that, in this respect, the scientific order is no less a creation of man than is history or music. Schneer's book called *The Search for Order*, which is a history of physical science, might then serve as the title of the history of any discipline. Schneer does not, as did Kant, explain the agreements between men as to structure on the basis of universal categories rather than on the basis of correspondence. Doubtless the idealistic alternative would appear to nearly every other contributor as no less difficult than realism. For example, Caws wishes to maintain the distinction between order discovered and order created.

Certainly most authors other than Conze are order-pluralists in the sense that they distinguish one kind of order from another without appeal to any common principle. Conze's question would be about the interdependence of the natural order and the moral, as well as their independence. Or, what of moral and aesthetic orders? Or the order of knowing (*ordo cognoscendi*) and the order of being (*ordo essendi*)? There are happily good models, such as Oliver's consideration of the thesis that what is meant by "mind" and "matter" are two ways of relating neutral stuff (William James). A model of careful work is Stumpf's "Moral Order and Legal Order." In the next section we shall try to continue the tendencies of Weiss and Jenkins to conceive the modes of being as orders of the complex world.

What of the order of orders? There are many references to traditional structures. Not only the *hierarchical* (the great chain of being), but also the *analogical* (microcosm-macrocosm) and the *evolutionary* (from incoherent homogeneity to coherent heterogeneity) are mentioned, but no one seems to trust these very far. Weiss and Feibleman leave the whole a disorder, a matrix whence by selection we may derive any order. This merits further work, and the conclusion will be a reflection of the world as many orders together.

A generation or so ago there was confidence that in passing from order in religion, ethics, aesthetics, through science, one arrived at last at the very form of order itself. The definition of order in the theory of relations of Russell and of Whitehead is "a relation transitive, asymmetrical and connected." No one quarrels with this as a major clarification of the idea of serial order. What is dubious is whether this does what Russell (and others such as Royce) thought it did, namely, illuminate the nature of every order whatsoever. The fact that no author of the twenty-eight represented here offers the definition may not be traced to ignorance of relational logic. The mistake of Russell and Royce was to think of serial order as the type and essence of all order. A formal definition is deficient because it omits consideration of the stuff ordered and the process and purpose of ordering. And there are many formal orders, some symmetrical, as referred to in Arnheim's essay, and hence not asymmetrical at all.

Also the transitive relationship, $A > B$, $B > C$, $A > C$, requires at least three members. But a symmetrical pair, ⌊ ⌋ or ⌋ ⌊, having but two members, has an order. The third limitation is that, if serial order is taken as the type of order, then the philosopher is tempted to force relation between persons called "the moral order" into a chainlike mold. Royce conceived of the moral order as a "chain of command," as though the army were the model for persons! [8]

One thing is achieved by the analysis of order in the theory of relations and the analysis of order from the four perspectives of religion, ethics, aesthetics, and science. This is stated neatly by Whitehead: " 'Order' is a mere generic term: there can only be some definite specific 'order,' not merely 'order' in the vague." [9] We must always specify which type of order and which kind of order if we would avoid ambiguity. Therefore it follows that it is true of any assemblage that it must be disorderly in some respect if it is orderly in another respect. It is then no necessary contradiction to say of any assemblage that it is both orderly and disorderly.

Now that we have examined various solutions to the problem of order, let us attempt to look at how these different answers may be understood in relation to each other and in relation to the whole of human understanding.

V. RESOLUTION: ORDER AND ITS OPPOSITES

1. Generic order, "a relation of definite sort"; *opposite:* nothing.

Out of the complexity of human culture, with striking divergences among meanings of order in religious, moral, aesthetic, and scientific contexts, emerges a generic meaning of the category. "Order is a relation of definite sort." This definition is deliberately so general that it characterizes everything there is, so long as it has enough complexity to be distinguished into parts of some sort; among these there must be some relation (the search for the least part has left the notorious "atom" with complexity and structure). We then say what definite relations there are, on the basis of relations which may be symmetrical or asymmetrical or nonsymmetrical, transitive or atransitive or nontransitive, connected, and so

---

[8] Josiah Royce, "Order," from Hastings' *Encyclopedia of Religion and Ethics,* reprinted in *Royce's Logical Essays,* edited by Daniel S. Robinson (Dubuque, Iowa: Wm. C. Brown Co., 1951), p. 224.

[9] Alfred North Whitehead, *Process and Reality* (New York: Macmillan Co., 1929), p. 128.

forth. We must have an infinite number of order types because part of the definition of an order is the number of terms related. Since there is no greatest number, the number of formal order types is innumerably many.

This definition of order, because it is so minimal, satisfies the need for meaning that covers all differences; but when order applies everywhere, then we are left with nothing except nothing in contrast to generic order. Let us consider Arnheim's example, a rubbish pile. Could it be an order in this generic sense? There are complexes with no "relations of a definite sort" that we grasp between the qualities, the origins, the functions of things. The rubbish pile would not seem in these senses at all orderly. But that the refuse is together spatially is one such definite order, and that the debris has been discarded as worthless is another. "Order" then becomes a most general term, like "being" in some philosophies.

2. Order a relation of some formal type (e.g., series); *opposite:* order of another formal type (e.g., a symmetrical rather than an asymmetrical relationship).

In speaking of order of some formal type we can use an example such as "serial order," which means an order like 1, 2, 3, etc. or $\triangle$, $\square$, $\bigcirc$, etc., where there is a direction or sense called asymmetry. In this serial order the relation of first to second and second to third gives us the same kind of relation as that of first to third ("more than" in some respect, in these cases). When we have all of the above along with the same relation to any whole number or plane figure with a number of sides, then we are contrasting serial order to other types of order. The series 1, 2, 1, and $\triangle$, $\square$, $\triangle$, are symmetrical. Each can be read the same way backward or forward. In general, one formal type of order contrasts with another formal type. When we say that orders may be asymmetrical or symmetrical we distinguish two types; we add nonsymmetrical because some relations are said to be sometimes one or sometimes the other, or symmetrical in one respect but asymmetrical in another.

3. Order of a material kind (e.g., temporal order of events); *opposite:* order of another material kind (e.g., spatial order between things).

Order may be specified by the relating characteristic of events or things related. Because ignoring them yielded us the abstract or formal types of relations, we might well call these concrete or material kinds of order. When we say that events are in temporal order such as "before" or "after," we may then contrast the ordering to spatial ordering, "to the right of" or "to the left of"; or a logical ordering of "premise of an argument" or "conclusion of an argument"; or a causal ordering, "condition or cause" and "consequence or effect."

4. Order of a world, a categorial order; *opposite:* chaos or the undifferentiated, the state of things to which categories do not apply.

If every ordering is not only of a formal type but also of some nonformal or material kind, to what are we contrasting the collectivity of relations which we can so categorize? The answer of myth is *tohu va bohu,* the precreation state without light or dark or wet or dry, and probably also without before or after, up or down, cause or effect. This state is the undifferentiated. Notably, we must conceptualize chaos by negation of order which we now take for granted. Chaos is then only a hypothetical state. We may introduce "chaos" by supposing the undifferentiated consciousness of the infant to be "a blooming, buzzing confusion." But the evidence seems to be that the infant does differentiate its mother from the rest of the world. So "chaos" is hardly even then experienced; we have only a hypothesis of the state of affairs to which categories do not apply. Theoretically this is not nothing, for there are relations, but not of specifiable kinds; and since relations are all of kinds as well as types, we may not hope ever to experience chaos. For one thing, probably no sentient being could survive long enough in chaos to know what had happened to it in this state.

5. The correlation of orders; *opposite:* disorder, that which in the lack of such correlation, by following some ordering principle, we may set in order. Note, disorder is the uncoordinated which we can coordinate, whereas chaos is the undifferentiated which we cannot differentiate.

What we commonly call "chaos" is only a case of disorder, and now we may inquire about the contrast of order to disorder.

What we usually mean by an orderly house, or a business in good order, or an orderly legal system is not conveyed formally by such a type of order as a series or a kind of order such as temporal order. These are surely included in such household, business, and legal orders; for example, each of these now requires a calendar to represent the days of the year, classified into seven-day weeks and grouped into twelve months of approximately equal duration. The temporal series is symbolized by correspondence to a spatial series. The calendar is a complex order in which two principles are coordinated. "Earlier than" characterizing May 1 related to May 2 as well as Monday to Tuesday is represented spatially by areas on the left and right in the printed representation $\boxed{\begin{array}{c}\text{Mon.}\\1\end{array}}$ and $\boxed{\begin{array}{c}\text{Tues.}\\2\end{array}}$. What would "disorder" be? If the calendar of this May should show $\boxed{\begin{array}{c}\text{Mon.}\\1\end{array}}$ and succeeding it $\boxed{\begin{array}{c}\text{Tues.}\\3\end{array}}$ or $\boxed{\begin{array}{c}\text{Wed.}\\2\end{array}}$, we should note the lack of coordination. The interesting thing about disorder is that we are aware of the failure to follow out a principle, and we therefore know how to put things in order. A disorderly state, is, as Bergson once noted, frustrating because we expect certain kinds of relations. He illustrated these kinds as organic and mechanical: to expect one kind and to meet with the other leaves us without ability to carry through our plans. What is called "disorder" is therefore either objectively a state of uncoordinated orders, or subjectively our lack of coordination with what we encounter.

We have therefore distinguished between "chaos" (the undifferentiated) and "disorder" (the uncoordinated). Chaos is close to nothing, because where there is nothing other than anything else, there can be no relation of one thing to another. But there must be relationship of thing to thing for there to be uncoordination. Hence, disorder may be, and indeed often is, as Paul Weiss points out, too many orders. For the individual an orderly state of coordination must be and must seem unified. We may fail to grasp the unifying principle and mistakenly call order "disorder." However, learning may allow us to say at a later stage, as of a work of art, that although at first it appeared disorderly because of its richness and complexity, only later did its ordering principle become evident.

6. A "realm" or "regime" or "mode of being," sometimes called an order, is a complex with certain formal types of relations, certain material orders, and categorial orders and correlation of orders; *opposite:* some other realm, also multidimensional, hence not simply contrasted.

Only now are we prepared to consider what some of our authors call "realms," or the orders called "natural," "historical," "legal," "social," "spiritual," "logical," and so forth. It is with these realms that religion, morality, art, and science deal, but there is much overlap among these orders. Can we specify a relationship of a definite sort to distinguish the historical from the natural? Both employ temporal ordering. The historical and the social realms are both composed of persons who make decisions and act. The logical realm is more distinctive because of implicative relations between propositions.

We cannot have the kind of formal clarity here that we attained between formal types of order, or among categories, space, time, cause, and so forth, or the kinds of coordination that specify the organization of households or businesses.

Our authors show us probably the best we can attain. We may, with Stumpf, compare and contrast the moral and the legal order, showing that one cannot be reduced to the other, and that the moral is the basis of the legal and the standard by which we judge the legal. The relationship is complex, just because the two orders are multidimensional and partially overlap.

7. An order of orders, or a world hypothesis, such as hierarchical, processlike, dialectical synthesis of opposites, etc.; *opposite:* some other world hypothesis.

We are here engaged in asking about the relationship between relationships, or the ordering of orders. Although this sounds alarming, a few examples will show us familiar instances. A person is sometimes said to have a world or to be in a world, and the parallel of the person to the world is called the microcosm of the macrocosm. We are all now familiar with the pattern of the relevance of the model to understanding the planetary system in the atom. Another example is to view the nation as a great household, a parallel we think of in the word "economy" and in the metaphorical reference to a "father of his country."

It would be convenient if the orders could be ranged hierarchically. In distinguishing "lower" from "higher," some hierarchical systems call the "natural" the lower, the "spiritual" the higher, and put the others—"historical," "social," "legal"—in between, on the basis that the natural provides the conditions, the historical the implementation, the spiritual the fulfillment of the ultimate ends of man. When Pascal distinguished three orders, one dealt with mathematically, the second empirically, and the last by *l'esprit de finesse,* he probably had some such religious interpretation of the realms in mind.

Paul Weiss built his metaphysical system on no hierarchical principle but on the basis of equal importance of realms. Given four that are ways of ordering, each applies to the whole of reality, and we can make any perspective in turn dominant, interpreting the others.

The crucial question seems, therefore, how many realms of being are there? Are there only four, and these four? Are there only three, as Iredell Jenkins says: necessity, possibility, and purposiveness?

Questions of the number of realms are perhaps not answerable or perhaps not even crucial. These order-realms or modes of being are themselves complex and may be distinguished further. For example, Weiss's "actuality" probably covers both Stumpf's moral and his legal orders. Surely Jenkins' "purposiveness" covers both Weiss's "actuality" and his "ideality." The important matter is not to try to reduce one order to another, but to respect differences, and then to discern the relations between orders.

Is there a single world order, or a single principle of order? One thing we can know: the efforts to find one have failed. Is the whole a mechanistic system? Or is the whole to be an organism? Or is the whole a formal system? Or is the whole a contextual process? Adequate as each formulation is when consistently carried out, none has succeeded in doing justice to all the data. Each system has points of absurdity, where it fails to convince those who hold an alternative world hypothesis, and each seems to the relatively dispassionate to be weak on certain points, as mechanists are in dealing with qualities and with free choice, and so on.[10]

The way of Weiss and Jenkins seems sound: consider the world as many orders together. If we do not succeed in one of the simple views of the world that makes it all into matter in motion or ideas in the mind of God, so let it be. We can construct views more complex to do justice to the variety of things and the multiplicity of relations, to the modes of being.

And so this interdisciplinary seminar points toward a vision of the world yet in the making—the world in process, including the view and the changing of the view, therefore inevitably but deliberately being altered to fit new knowledge and human needs.

[10] Stephen C. Pepper, *World Hypotheses: A Study in Evidence* (Berkeley: University of California Press, 1961).

Some may express surprise that the analysis of order in an interdisciplinary inquiry of this sort, based on a concept that has been analyzed in symbolic logic, leads to speculative philosophy. Can analysis end in metaphysics? The editor's answer is that analysis is strong in discrimination of differences, and therefore a very present help in the case of ambiguity, but that the task of discerning orders is metaphysical inevitably and constructive necessarily. The world is many orders together. Analysis helps us perceive the *manyness* of orders. Metaphysics is required to see the *togetherness*.

Analysis of the Concept of Order

JAMES K. FEIBLEMAN

Disorder

I

The general notion of order is prevalent in many disciplines where it functions as an undefined primitive, but disorder has aroused less interest.

Intuitively, order has always been understood in terms of law, a law that consists in a similarity among disparate elements, often combined with the property of compulsion. The clearest and earliest statement is that of Heraclitus. Law (or *logos*) is the element or arrangement common to all things [1] and responsible for the orderly process of change.[2] The law "steers all things through all things" and is why "all things are one." [3]

JAMES K. FEIBLEMAN has taught philosophy for twenty-seven years at Tulane University in his native New Orleans. Chairing the department has been only one of several lines of work which include a five-year business career, a literary productivity almost unmatched among American philosophers, and lectures on psychiatry at the School of Medicine of Louisiana State University. In philosophy his indebtedness has been to Charles Sanders Peirce, to Whitehead, and the early Bertrand Russell. His most considerable work is *Ontology* (1951).

[1] G. S. Kirk and J. E. Raven, *The Presocratic Philosophers* (Cambridge, Eng.: Cambridge University Press, 1957), p. 187.

[2] Kathleen Freeman, *The Pre-Socratic Philosophers: A Companion to Diels Fragmente der Vorsokratiker* (Cambridge, Mass.: Harvard University Press, 1947), p. 116.

[3] Kathleen Freeman (ed.), *Ancilla to the Pre-Socratic Philosophers: A Complete Translation of the Fragments in Diels Fragmente der Vorsokratiker* (Cambridge, Mass.: Harvard University Press, 1948), Fragment 50 of Heraclitus.

This conception of order as law has prevailed until almost modern times. Existing elements have some common property which combines them. But the elements so combined must be different elements, for identical elements cannot be ordered. 5, 6, 7, 8, for instance, is an order, while 5, 5, 5, 5 is not. Order seems to require some similarity among differences. Order, then, can be identified with similarity and disorder with differences.

Is this an acceptable definition of order: similarity among differences? If so, then order has the limitation that it cannot be total. The distribution of the terms is crucial. For total order would be order among all the elements and not merely among some as required by the definition. But if order is not total then disorder is required in any total account, and so disorder becomes as important as order. Disorder from this description would seem to be a larger domain, a point to which later it will be necessary to return.

The conception of order as lawfulness is perhaps older than that of disorder, but disorder is not an entirely new idea. Under other names it has been widely recognized by philosophers. Three examples should suffice to support this contention, and for the purpose I will choose from the work of Aristotle, Leibniz, and Peirce.[4]

Aristotle discussed disorder as fortituousness or contingency. Fortuitousness means that reality may issue in either of two opposite directions.[5] The discussion of contingency occurs in connection with possibility and necessity as one of the modalities.[6] For Aristotle, contingency follows from the proposition "it may be"; for what is necessary is also possible, but what is possible may not be necessary, and what is possible but not necessary is contingent.[7] In general it seems fair to claim that the evidence of the modalities is in favor of the existence of disorder as a factor to be reckoned with in the constitution of the world.

Leibniz, employing the same set of modalities, recognized the distinction between necessary and contingent truths. He argued that

---

[4] Professor Turquette relies upon the same three philosophers to describe the elements of disorder which he hopes "can be captured by means of a 3-valued logic." See Atwell R. Turquette, "Modality, Minimality, and Many-Valuedness," *Acta Philosophica Fennica*, Fasc. 16 (1963).

[5] Aristotle *De Interpretatione* 18b8, in *The Works of Aristotle*, trans. W. D. Ross (London: Oxford University Press, 1928).

[6] *Ibid.* 22a10–20 and 21a34.

[7] *Ibid.* 22a15. See also the discussion in W. and M. Kneale, *The Development of Logic* (Oxford: Clarendon Press, 1962), p. 85.

"if certain possible things never exist, existing things cannot always be necessary." [8] "A truth is *necessary* when the opposite implies contradiction, and when it is not necessary it is called *contingent*.[9] Necessary truths are "truths of reason," while contingent truths are "truths of fact." [10] Moreover, the "degree of likelihood" can be obtained "from the data." [11] Thus we see that Leibniz, like Aristotle, accepted the existence of real objective contingency: "truths of fact" or "likelihood."

Real objective disorder for Peirce was called chance. His name for it was "tychism," the "doctrine that absolute chance is a factor in the universe." [12] He gave four reasons for accepting the principle. Two of these are the phenomena of growth and feeling, both of which are opposed to the conservation of energy. The third gave the fact of the prevalence of variety in the universe as evidence for chance, and the fourth pointed out that the explanation of law has to be in terms of nonlaw, and nonlaw is chance.[13] Peirce specifically called out and rejected the subjective view of chance, which as existing can be responsible for other elements in the real world.[14]

Presumably it has been supposed that if order is understood, disorder can be accounted for in two ways: formally as the negative of order and materially as the absence of order. But does this give a true picture of disorder? Can it be that, despite the etymology of the term, disorder is nothing positive?

Before attempting to answer these questions it might be instructive to examine some empirical problem in one of the sciences in which the concept of order-disorder is specifically involved.

II

It will be best to choose for this purpose a typical pair of conflicting theories: entropy and evolution. Let us begin by stating them.

[8] L. E. Loemker (ed.), *Philosophical Papers and Letters* (Chicago, Ill.: University of Chicago Press, 1956), I, 405.

[9] P. P. Wiener (ed.), *Leibniz: Selections* (New York: Charles Scribner's Sons, 1951), p. 480.

[10] G. W. Leibniz, *The Monadology and Other Philosophical Writings,* trans. R. Latta (Oxford: Clarendon Press, 1898), p. 33.

[11] Weiner (ed.), *Leibniz: Selections,* p. 82.

[12] C. Hartshorne, P .Weiss, and A. W. Burks (eds.), *Collected Papers of Charles Sanders Peirce* (Cambridge, Mass.: Harvard University Press, 1935–58), Vol. VI, par. 201.

[13] *Ibid.,* par. 613.

[14] *Ibid.,* pars. 102, 322.

First, entropy: the second law of thermodynamics, derived from the work of Clausius on the heat engine, states in effect that in an isolated system heat never flows from cold to hot bodies, or that in such a system natural processes result in an increase in entropy by tending toward an equilibrium in which the entropy is maximum.[15] Entropy means that in an isolated system the direction of development in time is from order to disorder.

Second, evolution: the theory of organic evolution, derived from the work of Darwin, is in its current form "a two-state phenomenon: the production of variation and the sorting of the variants by natural selection." [16] The production of variation is due to selection pressures from the environment. Evidently, this is a process involving a large element of chance, but it clearly indicates a tendency to move from disorder to order, or from the simpler organization to the more complex. Animals with all of their cortical complexity have developed from simpler organisms.

A comparison of entropy with evolution discloses an immediate conflict. Entropy calls for the development of disorder from order, and evolution for the development of order from disorder. Assuming that all life is a small part of the universe, which all present evidence indicates it to be, then entropy has a far wider application than organic evolution. But it seems inevitable that both entropy and evolution must apply to some of the same systems. Entropy is said to hold for all isolated systems, and evolution is said to hold for *some* isolated systems. To the isolated systems to which evolution applies, namely, living organisms, entropy should apply also.

Entropy and evolution are specified for isolated systems, not for the universe. But perhaps the difficulty can be pointed up by applying both theories to the universe.

The entropy theory requires that the unavailability of energy is on the increase and tends toward the equalization of temperatures (the so-called "heat-death"). When the maximum entropy of the universe has been reached there will be a total disorder of the particles it contains.

The evolution theory applied to the universe bears another name and has another sponsor. It is called "agapism" and was also the

---

[15] See, for example, Max Planck, *Treatise on Thermodynamics,* trans. A. Ogg (New York: Dover Publications) , p. 100.

[16] Ernst Mayr, *Animal Species and Evolution* (Cambridge, Mass.: Belknap Press of Harvard University Press, 1963) , p. 8.

work of Peirce. Peirce supposed that the universe had its origins in chaos but that gradually order developed and is on the increase.[17] He contended that because of the action of random dispersion disorder is self-defeating, that, in short, chance begets order.[18] By means of a process akin to habit-taking, a generalizing tendency in the original chaos will grow, and complexity will inevitably increase.[19]

The conflict of these two theories is clear. The law of entropy (assuming it can be applied to the universe) calls for increasing cosmic disorder. The law of agapism calls for increasing cosmic order. Entropy will have reached its maximum when the random distribution is complete. Agapism will have reached its maximum when complete order has emerged from disorder. The universe began in perfect chaos (agapism) ; the universe will end in perfect chaos (entropy) . Order is increasing (agapism) ; order is decreasing (entropy) . Both cannot be true, but both could be false if, for instance, the present proportions of order and disorder were fixed in a steady state.

If the understanding of the distinction between order and disorder must hang upon the facts of cosmological origins or on the nature of teleological destiny, then we are indeed in a very bad way. Verification in either case is impossible to come by. Entropy is expected to apply to all isolated systems, but we do not know whether the universe can be considered an isolated system because we do not know whether it has a boundary. Agapism requires that the universe will reach perfect order at the end of time. Neither entropy nor agapism can be extended without qualification to the universe as a whole. But agapism makes a kind of order out of disorder, while entropy makes disorder necessary as a limiting case of order. We shall see that this distinction allows for a solution to the problem of the nature of disorder.

III

Attempts to resolve the difficulty presented by the need to discover the proper relations between order and disorder—assuming that disorder is positive—have taken several forms. One of these is

---

[17] Hartshorne, Weiss, and Burks (eds.) , *Collected Papers of Charles Sanders Peirce*, Vol. I, par. 411; Vol VIII, par. 317.

[18] *Ibid.*, Vol. VI, pars. 287–317.

[19] *Ibid.*, Vol. I, par. 409; Vol. VI, par. 58.

the theory of probability; another has occurred under the names of chance and law.

The whole discipline of statistical probability, with its rules of procedure, its design of investigations, its established methods and measures for sampling distributions, its statistical tests and measures of deviations, and in particular its standardization of errors, marks the attempt to bring disorder within the domain of order by widening the domain.

The theory of probability might be described here as the attempt to construct an order which, in contrast with other types of order, would adequately represent disorder. However, probability theory does not include a definition of disorder. Disorder is crucial to the theory and is represented there by randomness. But randomness is a property of the *method* of sampling, not of the sample itself.[20] Random dispersion is examined by the method of random sampling. And random sampling is then interpreted as representing an indefinitely large population where by "indefinitely large" is meant unknown in extent and possibly infinite. In connection with the encounters of an individual in a population, there can be an element of uncertainty that does not extend to the whole population. There is no evidence that the constancy of any rate that applies to a collection must be maintained by any particular member of it or even that the constancy is inalienable, only that the collection manifests it.

Events are accounted for by the encounters between elements of order and those of disorder, the attraction of elements that belong together and the repulsion of elements that do not. This is purely statistical, and the statistical averaging of these encounters constitutes the history of any segment of the actual world.

It is evident from probability theory that neither order nor disorder entirely prevails. At the outset of this study we noted that order has usually been understood in terms of law. Since law and chance are inevitably associated, we have now to state the terms of their association.

Chance is the intersection of causalities. Such encounters are bound to occur under the crowded conditions prevailing in the population of orderly relationships.

The concept is not exactly a new one. It has simply never found

[20] W. A. Wallis and H. V. Roberts, *Statistics: A New Approach* (Glencoe, Ill.: Free Press of Glencoe, 1960).

favor. The victories have been won by absolutists on both sides. Cournot may be credited with the clearest statement, if not with the first, of the position founded on an intermediate choice. He attributes chance to the independence of each causal series and includes every possible permutation and combination among the many series, each of which operates in complete independence of the others,[21] a principle recognized by Russell also as the postulate of separate "causal lines" according to which it is possible to infer from an event that is a member of a causal series something about the other members regardless of events that are simultaneous but not in the series.[22] Thus all contact between any of the individual members of a causal series of events and any of the individual members of another series is purely fortuitous, that is to say, it occurs by chance.

Let us suppose, for example, that two men are running toward the gates to trains in a busy railroad station. The gates are set in walls that are at right angles, and the two men in their haste collide. In the course of the consequent confusion they miss their trains. Each was engaged in an orderly procedure according to well-understood rules of behavior. But there was, as it happened, the additional event of an accidental encounter where segments of the two procedures intersected. Laws always apply, but they are never absolute. There is present in every application a measure of discrepancy. Chance occurs as the last decimal place, or as the extenuating circumstances that mitigate against full application.

Matters of fact are not logically necessary, at least in their totality, because the whole of existence is not. That is to say, perhaps the universe is necessary but we have no logic to provide for it. But what is not rational is not thereby proved irrational. For the forgotten element in the consideration is that contradiction is part of logic. The logical is the domain of consistency and inconsistency. What is contradictory is inconsistent, but it is not thereby nonlogical. It is true, of course, that reason expands its area of relevance as more and more of the universe becomes amenable to our understanding of order and our knowledge of natural laws. Thus what is deemed irrational today may be found to be rational tomorrow. But

[21] A. A. Cournot, *An Essay on the Foundations of Our Knowledge,* trans. M. H. Moore (New York: Liberal Arts Press, 1956), chap. iii, esp. p. 44.

[22] Bertrand Russell, *Human Knowledge* (New York: Simon and Schuster, 1948), chap. v, esp. p. 459.

then what is the irrational in itself, if not a certain kind of relation to rationality, a minimum remnant that functions to keep things moving? The point is that disorder accounts for existence. Existence depends upon movement and opposition; but with order completed there would be no such activity. This state will never occur, however, for chaos is primeval and eternal, the matrix of permanent possibilities of order.

It is not a far step from this conception of disorder to the original conception of chaos from which order emerges. Chaos is the sum of all orders, the matrix from which particular orders are derived. That it must remain a chaos and not become itself a kind of superorder is required by Gödel's theorem. Chaos cannot therefore be defined as order in the sense of "all orders," for if it contains all orders it cannot itself be an order. But it can be chaos, or disorder in the positive sense defined. And the chaos can be infinite only in the sense of the infinite defined in the Cantor-Dedekind Axiom.

IV

It is time now to draw some conclusions. If our discussion has been helpful, it should lead us to a positive definition of disorder, for that is what from the beginning we have been endeavoring to discover.

The first conclusion to which we seem bound is that order is applicable not to the universe but only to some proper part. For instance, life is an isolated phenomenon in which there is a tendency to order (evolution) at large in a world of disorder (entropy). The ordering relation would have to be outside the domain so ordered.

The second conclusion is that the distinction between order and disorder tends to disappear when the domain of both is the universe. Perfect chaos has a uniformity about it that renders it perilously close to order. Total order and total disorder may prove to be the same thing. But such identification blurs a genuine distinction that discriminates between elements recognizably real in the universe, and explanation for this reason rejects it. At the same time, however, we must recognize that we are appealing to orderly explanation in the rejection.

What, then, is disorder?

Disorder is a term with both a negative and a positive definition. The negative definition of disorder given at the beginning of this paper as the absence of order is the common one, but it is possible to construct a new positive definition. We can arrive at it, perhaps, by the expedient of converting the terms in the definition of order. Order was defined earlier as the similarity between differences. Disorder, then, would be equivalent to the difference among similarities. If we consider the positive aspect of disorder as meaning the extent to which the elements of a given order are distributed outside that order among the elements of other orders, constituting in this way an additional and separate order, then disorder becomes another kind of order, namely, the order that requires a rich interpolation of the elements of other orders. The essence of my thesis is that disorder depends upon the random dispersion of limited orders: the degree to which the elements of a particular class are scattered.

Disorder, then, may be defined as the extent to which the elements of a given order are distributed outside that order among the elements of other orders.

The concept of disorder may be enlarged by showing for the positive definition that if repeated for many orders the consequent expansion will develop a difference in the elements of order distributed, and a difference also in the type of distribution of the elements, but a similarity in the consequent disorder. It betrays a uniformity, surprisingly enough. For disorder is disorder: there is only one kind. When disorders are widespread, disorder itself is only extended. The limiting case of the spread is akin to classical Hilbert space, with its infinity of variables.[23]

In disorder it is understood that the scattered elements are tagged: they are the elements of order—out of order. Thus, although disorder is related to order, the relation is not one of simple negation. A good example would be the disorder $\rightleftharpoons$ order transitions of the constituents of alloys. Evidently, electrical resistance to semiconductors is a function of disorder. Dis-order is a misnomer, for the property we are endeavoring to identify by means of the term is positive. Disorder is not the mere absence of order, although it is that, too. It is in fact total order. Order depends upon symmetry of proportion, disorder upon chance variation. Order prevails over disorder in an isolated system when the elements of order exceed those of disorder. Disorders of the properly large types have matrix properties.

[23] M. H. Stone, *Linear Transformations in Hilbert Space* (New York: The American Mathematical Society, 1932).

As David Bohm has indicated, each is meaningless except in contrast with the other.[24] Order-and-disorder share an essential affinity, similar to that shared by permanence-and-change, or by similarity-and-difference. I add that order-disorder are idem-level polarities; that is to say, they are complementary but only on the same analytical level.

Disorder is nothing less than the order of the universe. It is reasonable under this analysis to consider disorder the wider concept and order a special case. Disorder is always wider than order, a rich matrix replete with orders from which limited orders arise.

V

The larger the combinations of matter, the greater the fortuitous element. This follows from the fact that the more events there are, the more contingencies are possible. Aristotle made something of the same point in connection with the population of a city when he said that "law is order; but a very great multitude cannot be orderly." [25] There is very little room for arbitrariness within the atom because the range of nuclear events is small. This increases, however, with every increase in the number of atoms. And it increases also with combinations of atoms, for every integrative level provides its own occasions for chance encounters. Thus contingency must increase still more with combinations of molecules. With the comparatively large size of genes contingencies occur noticeably, as for instance in mutations. Contingencies in the macroscopic world are many, as evidenced by human life. Such contingencies must be still larger in the states of affairs that prevail among galaxies.

Events contain some of the structures of logic fragmented by the effects of the additional element of contingency, which is not anything in itself but simply the product of colliding necessities and impossibilities. Thus existence is a condition in which order fares only partly well because mixed with disorder. That the world of matter discloses many logical systems suggests, however, that contingency is fundamental, as fundamental to material existence as necessity and impossibility are to logical structures. If it were not for the element of disorder, the universe of matter could be reduced to

[24] David Bohm, "Problems in the Basic Concepts of Physics," Inaugural Lecture delivered at Birkbeck College, University of London, 1963.
[25] Aristotle *Politics* 132a30.

that of logic. But in fact it cannot, and it is this fact which preserves the distinction.

We began with the notion of order, and we saw there that it requires disorder. Logically speaking, the concepts are not absolutely separable. The isolated systems to which order applies have proved to be temporary segments of the more enduring flux of the universe of disorder. Order is consistency in logic; disorder is completeness among events. And at this point the distinction between logic and events is clear, as well it must be if logic is applicable at all.

Some Paradoxes Relating to Order

I

The problem of order is beset by a number of very serious paradoxes. If we focus on these paradoxes and find the solutions to them, we will, I think, become clearer regarding the nature of the basic idea.

Order does not seem necessary. (Genesis, for example, starts off as if there were no order at all, and takes order to be imposed on the world.) Others say that the world must be under the control of a God, because chance could not have produced what is today. Both views are mistaken. The second can be easily shown, and this in turn will show that the first view is also mistaken. If one took a coin and tossed it up a hundred times the probability of getting a hundred tails would be one half to the hundredth power $(\frac{1}{2}^{100})$. The probability of getting a heads-tails-heads-tails-heads-tails . . . sequence would also be one half to the hundredth power. Any

PAUL WEISS, Sterling Professor of Philosophy at Yale since 1962, is widely known as a teacher, author, and editor. With others he founded the Metaphysical Society of America and edited the *Review of Metaphysics* from 1947 to 1964. His wide interests include painting and acting, sports, travel, education, and religions. *Modes of Being* is his system, now interpreted and amended in *Philosophy in Process,* a diary showing tremendous energy and boundless trust in rendering all being intelligible. He has been president of the American Philosophical Association and received the degree L.H.D. from Grinnell College in 1960.

possible sequence of a hundred throws, no matter what it is—fifty heads and then fifty tails, or a hundred heads, or a hundred tails, whatever the sequence—that particular sequence would have the probability of only one half to the hundredth power. It is impossible in this case of a hundred throws to have sequence having a higher probability value than one half to the hundredth. The reason why we commonly overlook this is that there are more cases of sequences in which there are fifty heads and fifty tails distributed somehow or other. More generally, no matter what one did, no matter how a particular sequence came about, any particular sequence has a definite probability value.

We can make this point another way. If one were to take a blackboard and throw on it a thousand dots, then superimpose on them a Cartesian coordinate system and draw a line from one dot to another, an algebraist could provide a formula for it.

It is impossible to have a situation in which there would be no order at all. 1. *Though any given order seems to be contingent, some order is inescapable.*

An order of some kind seems to be inescapable. This conclusion leads to two questions:

a. Can there be an order which has nothing to order?

b. Could there be an order which excludes all disorder?

a. If there is to be an order, there must be something which is ordered; otherwise the order would be nothing more than an idea of order, a possibility, not a structure. A structure, a genuine order, requires something which it is to structure; otherwise it would collapse into a mere idea. An order without anything that is ordered is not possible. (Order makes no sense unless there is something to be ordered. This must have a different order or be without order. But that is only to say that order, if it is to be meaningful, requires that there be some thing which, relative to the order in question, is disorderly.)

b. For an order to have something to order, there would have to be something in relative disorder. But if there must be something which is in a relative disorder, there can be no order which excludes all disorder. 2. *Although whatever is, is inevitably ordered, if there is to be order there must be that which is relatively without order.*

3. *We want and work toward order in the sciences and logic, in our homes and in our lives; nevertheless we defy it as being too constraining.* We cherish spontaneity, rebellion, novelty, creativity,

and the breaking of the burdens and restraints to which we are subject. Every order is a tissue of internal relations, where things are involved one with another. In desiring order our ultimate ideal is to have everything in some kind of a structure, involving internal relationships. But we also want to preserve the independence and freedom of items, for otherwise they will lose their individuality and power. Each order is in some sense restrictive. We give up one order and move on to another as a consequence of the fact that the first neglected certain factors.

The ultimate ideal is somehow to have everything in some kind of a structure, but we find that at every moment the structure we have denies the genuine individuality of the things that are ordered. Order is at once desirable and undesirable.

Though we impose order upon the world in the process of knowing, the world has an order of its own, limiting and constraining our freedom to impose orders. We learn by making scientific experiments, by adventuring, by studying, thereby discovering what kinds of orders things have. Yet the orders that we come to know are those we ourselves impose. The choice of one order rather than another would then seem to be largely arbitrary. Yet this does not seem to be the case. We once thought that the space-time world was Euclidean, but were finally forced to give up that idea. According to the contemporary cosmological astronomers, the spatio-temporal world is essentially non-Euclidean. Our freedom to impose a geometric order upon the world is limited by the nature of the world itself. The nature of things made us give up the order that we had been trying to impose.

Order is a product of creativity, but we are creative only when we reject some order. Hence we have a fourth paradox: 4. *Creativity, though it both produces and possesses order, denies the building power of any order.*

II

Can these paradoxes be overcome? If they can we will gain not only an insight into the nature of order, but an insight into the nature of the universe, of which order is only one facet.

An essential clue to the solution of these paradoxes is the nature of disorder. Disorder is an excess of order; it occurs when there are too many orders imposed upon a set of entities. Like the contradiction, something is both a cat and not a cat, it faces us not with nothing, but with too much.

Order is selective and restrictive; it provides a channel through which to move from one entity to another; it helps to organize things in such a way that they can be understood. Disorder instead provides too many channels through which to move from one entity to another, too many alternative ways in which to understand.

A case of disorder would be a heap, a miscellany, a heterogeneity of entities which are not similar in color, origin, shape, place, meaning, or value. These entities logicians call members of a class; mathematicians say that they make up an aggregate or a set. Though distinct, they are sufficiently joined to be together in one group. But the ways in which they can be related are too many. It is a disorder, contrasting with the usual arrangement of the positive integers, 1, 2, 3, 4, 5 . . . , which offers only one way to move from one number to another.

Our first paradox is resolved with the recognition that while no particular order is necessary, it is necessary that there be some order or other. A particular order is a means by which we can move clearly and easily from one entity to another. If we get rid of all particular orders we are left with a set of aggregated elements which can be interrelated in an endless number of ways. Our first paradox points up the fact that we are interested in order because it is a way of making selective use of a multiplicity of things.

The second paradox can be overcome, by recognizing that one imposes order upon that which, relative to the order, is disordered. Though all entities are ordered, though there is even some sort of order in any aggregate, from the standpoint of a particular order which we are to impose, that on which we impose it is relatively disordered.

Order enables us to make selective use of a multiplicity of things. Why is it, then, that we fear it? Why do we reject it, rebel against it, try to fight against it? Why do we always try to find new ways of organizing things, why do we want spontaneity? I think it is because we take two positions with respect to any set of entities. We look at them from the standpoint of ordering structure and from the standpoint of the entities to be ordered. We rebel against an order out of consideration for the entities ordered. We want them to stand in some independence of one another, so as to be able to express themselves fully. We want some way of relating various items, but not to the exclusion of all spontaneity, or the possibility of discovering other ways of relating the entities on which the order is imposed.

To order is to subordinate, to encompass from a particular perspective: it is to restrict entities in a definite way. Order allows one to systematize them, and hence to understand and control them. But it also limits and prevents us from seeing new, fresh, different ways in which they might be ordered. Our third paradox is thus resolved; order is desirable, but not absolutely, for it does deny individual freedom to some degree.

In our knowledge of the spatio-temporal world, we seem both to impose order and to discover order. This paradox disappears, I think, with the realization that the world of space-time is an aggregate of various entities, i.e., that there is an excess of order in the world. When we impose an order we in effect select one of the many orders that were there originally; we pay attention only to this and ignore the others. The order one tries to impose is an order that is present in the original conglomeration of orders. The imposed order is selected out of the indefinitely many that are present.

We must distinguish between a prescriptive order and a descriptive order. A prescriptive order is imposed, subordinating something else. A descriptive order is discovered. Every situation contains a descriptive order—even the most chaotic, produced by so-called "random" activities. If I wish to assign numbers to a group of people, I can do it by first counting the women and then the men, by first counting the people under eighteen and then the ones over eighteen, or I can do it by row, or by columns, or by height, and so forth. If I start off with the group of people as an aggregate, I have all these different descriptive orders open to me. The creative process is to be understood in a somewhat similar way. He who is engaged in a creative act faces an aggregate of materials, tools, and perhaps subject matters. The outcome of the act, though in part controlled by a prescriptive order, yields a descriptive order. The creative act in one sense simply shows us what there is, at the same time it gives us a new way of looking at what there is.

Some historians and students of creativity look at creative works to see if they can find a single order in them all. They come up with the Golden Section, the serpentine line, the principles of harmony, and so on, telling us that all art should exhibit these. But the orders they find are simply summaries of what has been found in past creative works. They ignore the fact that the creative artist produces new ways of looking at what already exists. He defies order as it is ordinarily seen, to present us with a new descriptive order.

III

We can now profitably ask ourselves, What are the basic ways of ordering things? There are just a few.

The things of the world are related in time and space. They are contemporaries or predecessors and stand in extended relations to one another. This order is objective, allows for some degree of predictability, and has a certain "cosmic stretch." Yet, from one perspective, this ordered space-time world appears to be a disorder, a chance gathering of things. It is one of the achievements of science to make evident the structures and laws which dominate the spatio-temporal world, and which therefore enable us to make some kind of intelligible sense out of it. The scientifically known world is a world basically ordered that we can know, express, or identify.

Mathematicians look outside the scientific world to entities ideally structured and related. They study formal ways in which entities are related, without paying attention to the entities as they are in space and time. The mathematical results are applied by engineers to the concrete data of everyday life. The scientist stands somewhere in between the two, utilizing the work of the mathematician to approach the world of the engineer, and thereby getting an abstract expression of it. He selects certain mathematical formulas for his purposes and then tries to see whether the world itself will answer to these. The scientist does not arbitrarily impose an order. If he did, he would not need to look to the world at all. Though there are alternative types of geometry, the world has only one. The task of the scientist is to find that geometry which enables him to make the best possible rational account of what is in fact occurring in this world.

Both the scientist and the mathematician look away from the everyday world and its ordinary space and time in order to catch that basic structure which is most intelligible. Knowing this, they know better than would otherwise be possible what is in fact occurring in the daily world.

God is often said to be the omniscient absolute judge, which is to say that he sees all things in their ultimate meaning. So far as he is concerned with the world, he understands the whole of it. The order which comes from him is essentially an order of evaluation, not from the standpoint of man, or as merely here and now, but of values, and to a final eternal standard of value.

In the philosophy of *Existenz* an attempt is made to look at the world from the position of man. It offers a basic human mode of ordering. Let us look at death from these various perspectives. For the existentialist it is the topic of one's basic anxieties, in terms of which we are to understand everything else, and in terms of which, therefore, we are to subordinate and order all other things. If one looks at death from the standpoint of biological science, it is seen to be a significant but not all-significant event: the death of a man is similar in kind to that of a cat or a cockroach. It does not then have the dominant meaning that it has for the *Existenz* philosophers, being simply one of a number of relatively important occurrences. Growth and decay, degeneration and birth are then equally significant. From the standpoint of a mathematician death does not even enter the picture, since his ideas are essentially about what is, frozen crystal clear in eternity. And for many a religious man death is nothing more than a prelude to another life, and is certainly not an object of anxiety.

From different perspectives, different things stand out in prominence and other things fall away. One perspective need not be better than another. All are equally basic and are equally significant for different objectives. Each subordinates the others from its own position. Each is ultimate and has a value that the others do not have, and each gains by being subordinated to the others. They are all equal in ultimacy, but they do different things. Depending upon where one starts, one has a distinct way of ordering the entities comprising the world.

But, if there is no best or right way of ordering, how are we going to have all of them at once, together? To get beyond all of them, or to speak of all of them, we must somehow stand away from them all. Does that mean that there is a higher order? I do not think so. To look at all basic ways of ordering things we must stand in one of these ways and talk in a very abstract way of it and the rest.

Order in History

Configurations of History

I. INTRODUCTION

When one talks about philosophy of history there is always an assumption, deeply rooted in the philosophies of history of the nineteenth century, that the person who talks about such a subject is presenting a position or wishes to defend a position; now nothing of the sort is happening here. There is a science that investigates the questions of pattern in history. This science, like any other, is progressing; and if any present solution to problems is taken in a doctrinaire manner, as giving an ultimate truth about history, this is one of the gravest misunderstandings possible. I am reminded of this when I think back to the last time Professor Arnold Toynbee and I were together at a wonderful meeting in Normandy, where we had frequent luncheon discussions. At that time I asked Professor Toynbee, who was under attack by various critics, what he thought of these attacks and criticisms. He confessed to me candidly, "Well, you

ERIC VOEGELIN is professor in the University of Munich and director of the Institute for Political Science. He has held many posts in the United States, among them Boyd Professor at Louisiana State University from 1942 to 1958. He is best known for his monumental *Order and History*, which shows learning and scope comparable to Gibbon's *Decline and Fall*. One of the most interesting phases of his life work is the attack upon ideology. Just as Toynbee regards communism as a Judeo-Christian heresy, so Voegelin regards all the political "isms" as mistakes about the moral nature of man: the root of chaos is to believe that values are only man-made.

see I wrote these things twenty-five years ago, and I have almost forgotten what they are, and now I must defend them." So please do not
hold me to anything that I have written previously, because science
progresses and things change. Do not take too seriously, or in an
absolute sense, what I have to say today, because these problems as
I present them today are again subject to change, and perhaps in
two years I will have found other things which will demand a very
different answer.

The problem of change is implied even in the title of this paper,
"Configurations of History." Now what is meant by "configuration"? Just twenty years ago discussion centered almost exclusively
on the meaning of history; and just the change in language from
"the meaning of history" to "structure" or "patterns," or "a totality
of patterns making the configuration of history," indicates a considerable change in the theoretical problem. When one speaks of the
meaning of history, in the sense of the great philosophies of history
of the eighteenth and nineteenth centuries, it is already assumed that
history is the sort of thing of which one can know the meaning.
History happens not to be such a thing, because a thing must be
given as finite in time, and history quite obviously extends into an
unknown future. Therefore history is incomplete and is not a thing.
What the meaning of history is, no one knows or ever will know, so
long as we exist in time. It is of course impossible to pronounce on
the meaning of history. Whether one does so in the sense of progressivist philosophies of the eighteenth century; or of the positivist
interpretation of history, such as Comte's in the nineteenth century;
or of the Marxist interpretation, makes little difference. All these
interpretations, which pretend to tell you what the meaning of
history is, presume that one can know history as a complete thing.
To put the matter in technical language, history is considered *modo
futuri exacti,* in the mode of a perfected future, as if one knew what
the end would be.

In fact one does not know what the end will be, and therefore any
pronouncement on the meaning of history is impossible. Nevertheless, we are concerned about such a meaning; and we are concerned
because, so long as we have both history and a consciousness of
history, people will pronounce on the meaning of history. In this
sense, then, the meaning of history (now used in a different sense)
is a permanent occupation of the human mind. People are concerned about the meaning of history, and hence one can very well

have an empirical science of the opinions that have been pronounced at one time or another on the meaning of history. The
meaning of history is thus something that actually happens in
history; it is part of, occupation with, and pronouncement on,
history. In that sense, for example, there is a book by Karl Löwith,
which has become quite famous, on the meaning in history—not the
meaning *of* history, but meaning *in* history. What is meant here is
that within history people express themselves on its meaning, and
the series of expressions on meaning are themselves very meaningful
sequences, about which one can make empirical statements. This,
then, would be another meaning of history.

Neither of these two meanings is the one that enters into the
concept of configuration. "Configuration" refers to more than the
patterns that are observable in history, such as sequences of institutions. In various high civilizations we know that we begin with
certain types of political organization, usually of a monarchical or
an aristocratic type, and that democratic types always come rather
late in the course of a civilization. Such sequences would be patterns
that can be empirically observed. But this is not all, because conceptions of order in a civilization are always accompanied by the
self-interpretation of that order as meaningful, that is, the persons
living in an order have opinions about the particular meaning that
order has. In this sense, self-interpretation is always part of the
reality which we live. This is the reality of order, of political order,
or, as we might say, of history. A configuration considers all of these
aspects, not only the institutional aspects, but also the self-interpre-
tations—the opinions expressed concerning meaning.

If one now wishes to set off the concept of configuration from the
concept of the meaning of history, it must be said that the term
"meaning of history," in the sense in which people pronounce
opinions on the meaning of history, is associated with the peculiar
ideologies of the eighteenth and nineteenth centuries. There are the
progressivist opinions of the meaning of history, like those of Condorcet or of Kant; the positivistic opinions, like those of Comte and
of various modern positivists in the social sciences; the Marxist
interpretations of the meaning of history; and so on. "Meaning" is
thus an ideological term. But if one includes opinions concerning
the meaning of the reality, and then looks for patterns of history
that embrace both institutions and these expressions of meanings,
then one gets the problem of configuration. In looking for configu-

rations one does not express an opinion on the meaning of history, but rather considers the meaning of history as something on which people express opinions, and these expressions of opinion are then part of the reality being examined.

This, then, is just a preliminary expression of what is meant by configuration; one takes into account the expressions of opinion concerning the meaning of history, without one's self offering an opinion concerning the meaning of history. This clarification, however, is just preliminary; it leaves the question open, whether patterns in history can be discovered at all. Now we must be skeptical about this, all the more so because we have an imposing body of literature on patterns of history. Recall, for example, Professor Toynbee's *Study of History,* with its twelve enormous volumes concerning patterns that can be discerned empirically in history.

What I wish to discuss here is not the enormous number of patterns that can be discerned in history, but rather certain theoretical questions: How can one discern such patterns with a minimum of error? Can one arrive at certain general propositions today? Of course every science is progressing, and what we can achieve today will be superseded tomorrow, but something may nevertheless be possible even today. My intention here is to present some selected problems about which one can make comparatively definite pronouncements even now.

II. THE ECUMENIC AGE

The first topic with which I shall deal is the distinction of a period in history, which is circumscribed by certain definite phenomena forming a pattern in the total configuration of history. I shall call this period the *ecumenic age.* I use this title because the period in question is that critical period in the history of mankind when (1) ecumenic empires were founded, (2) a theory of ecumenic empires was developed, and (3) it was realized that ecumenic empires were not the solution to organizing mankind as a unity.

This period extends from approximately the eighth century before Christ to the eighth century after Christ, at which time it had run its course and new problems had arisen. The factors that enter into the complex, and that we shall discuss, are three in number: (a) the historiographic events of the time, (b) the founding of ecumenic empires themselves, and (c) certain spiritual outbursts. I shall deal most extensively with the spiritual outbursts, but first I must comment on historiography.

Historiography is something that we today take for granted. We write history about almost anything, even about things that do not have a history. We just call it history. But historiography had definite beginnings in the history of mankind. In fact, there were three such beginnings, which we shall now discuss. These took place, counting from West to East, in Hellas, in Israel, and in China. All three beginnings of historiography occurred at approximately the same time, within a period of two or three centuries; and, so far as we know, there were no cultural influences connecting the three, but rather they sprang up independently of one another. If we now look at the beginnings of historiography in these three cases (it is obviously an interesting problem, since on these occasions there was an intense consciousness of history), we find something very peculiar. The earliest comprehensive historiography in Hellas is the history written by Herodotus. The largest part of the historiography contained in the Old Testament is the so-called Deuteronomic history of Kings. It ends with the fall of Jerusalem, and therefore was probably written after the fall of Jerusalem, some time after the exile. Here again we have the history of the kingdom, beginning with the Davidic foundation and ending with the fall of Jerusalem in the clash with the empires of Assyria and Babylonia. Finally, taking the great Chinese historiographic work of Ssŭ-ma Ch'ien, begun by his father, one again finds that it was written in the period from the second to the third century B.C., and that it deals with the history of classical China: the three dynasties and their downfall to the empire of King Ch'ien, Shih Hung Ti of the Ch'ien dynasty and the rise of the Han dynasty, under which Ssŭ-ma Ch'ien and his father wrote. Thus, in each of these three appearances of historiography, the subject matter which seems to be worthy of commemoration, that which motivates the writing of historiography, is the clash of some sort of order with the order of an empire—more specifically, of an ecumenic empire. One might even say that this clash with the order of an empire is the original subject matter of historiography. The clash between an order that is not imperial with one that is, and the problems arising from that situation, provides the starting point for the writing of historiography.

Taking this as a starting point, we might propose the general rule that whenever there is a clash of a nonimperial order with an imperial order, someone will start writing historiography. But this is not acceptable. Generalizations do not come so easily. It happens in these three instances, but there are numerous counterexamples in which all sorts of societies and orders have clashed with empires, were destroyed by empires, and yet nothing happened in the way of historiography. It happened only under certain circumstances, which means that we must introduce further factors to determine more closely the complex pattern that evolves here.

Obviously the historiographer must be in possession of some means of discretion, some criteria by which he judges the clash of that one order with an imperial order to be worthy of interest. Furthermore, in the opinions of the historians we have mentioned, it is the order of the ecumenic empire that is considered less valuable, while the order destroyed in its clash with the imperial one is considered to be more important and more valuable. Presupposed in the writing of historiography, then, are clear conceptions of what an order is, and what the standards of right and true order are.

This introduces the third factor: whenever we have the phenomenon of historiography, and wherever we have ecumenic empires, we also have spiritual outbursts. These assumed the form of philosophy in Hellas, of prophetism in Israel, of Buddhism in India, of Confucianism and Taoism in China, and of Zoroastrianism in Persia. Spiritual outbursts thus form a part of the pattern. But this still does not give the whole story, since one now might think that wherever spiritual outbursts and ecumenic empires occur, this combination will invariably lead, in the event of a clash of orders, to the writing of history. But in fact this is not so; there were the definite spiritual outbursts of Zoroastrianism in Persia, and there was the magnificent Persian Empire, founded by Cyrus and continued by Darius, yet no historiography was ever written in the period of the Achaemenid Empire itself. Persian historiography became fertile only at a much later period, at the time of the clash with Islam. Nor does one find historiography in India. There is the spiritual outburst of the late Upanishads, and also of the *Mahābhārata* and of the Buddhist scriptures, and there are definitely empires (e.g., the Persian Empire, the Alexandrian Empire, and the empire of Mahmud, which developed in the wake of the Alexandrian Empire), yet no Indian has ever written history. The historical knowledge that we have from Indian sources is extremely thin and very difficult to unravel, coming from the Purāṇa type of literature, which is definitely not historiography.

We might go on to ask such questions as why, when the factors of spiritual outburst and of ecumenic empire were present, as in the cases of Persia and India, still no historiography developed. I shall not go into this, for to do so would involve us in highly complicated technical details. I simply wish to draw your attention to the problem that because of such counterexamples one cannot make the generalization that wherever there are spiritual outbursts and ecumenic empires, and clashes between orders, historiography is invariably written.

But certainly in the three cases mentioned first (in the cases of the Hellenic, the Israelitic, and the Chinese historiography) these three factors are present, and are of importance in the phenomenon of historiography. Here, then, is a very interesting complex, which illustrates a pattern, a definite configuration in history. We find not only a configuration of these three phenomena (outburst, ecumenic empire, and historiography), but also a very interesting pattern in history, insofar as these three instances (the Hellenic, the Israelite, and the Chinese) occur at about the same time. There is thus a sort of horizontal pattern running through history. At the same time, in three various civilizations, similar developments occur independently of one another, thus yielding a parallelism of such occurrences or a chronological parallelism in the absolute time of history.

Questions of the type just raised, which can be solved only by showing necessary connections and patterns of the type indicated, have not escaped attention. I should like to mention at least two constructions of history that start from the partial observation of such phenomena. One of these is the observation that the occurrences of spiritual outbursts are generally parallel in time. This parallelism in time of prophetism, Zoroastrianism, Taoism, Buddhism, and philosophy has been called the "axis time of history" by Karl Jaspers, in his book on the *Origin and Goal of History,* because all of these phenomena occurred somewhere between the eighth and the second century B.C. Jaspers thus considers this a decisive period in history. But Professor Toynbee has, in Volume VII I believe, criticized Jaspers very severely for playing havoc with history, since spiritual outbursts also occur at times other than the period between 800 and 200 B.C. For instance, there was a man named Moses

in the thirteenth century B.C., and there was a man named Jesus
after 200 B.C., and there were further such developments which
would compel us, were we to attend to all these spiritual outbursts,
to consider a period from approximately the thirteenth century B.C.
to about the tenth century A.D., when this period of spiritual outburst ended.

So you see now why determination by a plurality of factors is
necessary if we are to discover a legitimate, critically tenable pattern
in history. The isolation of one of these factors yields a striking
parallelism and suggests that whenever these spiritual outbursts
occur there is an axis time of mankind. But this is to ignore the fact
that there are other constellations with spiritual outbursts, both
earlier and later, and that these specific outbursts which Jaspers has
in mind gain meaning only when put into the context of the two
other factors. It is thus a complex of three phenomena which really
makes a pattern, while any one factor in isolation does not form a
pattern. The same problem arises when one isolates the factor of
empire, as was done earlier. This sort of inadequate consideration of
factors took place even as early as the Apocalypse of Daniel. You
will recall the symbolism of the image with the head of gold, then
silver, which would break the feet of clay and then become the
kingdom of God, filling the whole world. The four empires indicated by the metals in the image were interpreted as being the
Assyrian, Persian, Greek, and Roman empires. The four empires in
question were to be ended, by a decisive act of God, and a fifth
empire was then to fill the earth. This was an accepted philosophy
of history right into the seventeenth century, determining Jacques
Bossuet's conception of history in 1683.

This construction of history in terms of empires had a long
history after the Apocalypse of Daniel. It was resumed, for example,
by Hegel. In Hegel's *Philosophy of History* there is what might be
called an imperial apocalypse, insofar as Hegel did not assume the
state to be the ultimate unit in history, and history to be a sequence
of states, but rather the sequence of units that forms history was for
Hegel a sequence of empires. There were the Chinese Empire, the
Indian Empire, the Persian Empire, the medieval empire, and the
empire of Napoleon. These empires were for Hegel both the carriers
and the intelligible units of history, in much the same sense that
civilizations are the intelligible units for Professor Toynbee. Thus
imperial units, much in the style of the apocalypse, though includ-

ing such new units as the Chinese and Indian empires, were still the basic units out of which history was constructed.

But such constructions do not work. They are possible only by ignoring everything in history that is not an empire. Take, for example, Hegel's chapter on the Persian Empire. The Persian Empire can be considered a unit in history only because Hegel considers the Persian Empire to include everything conquered by the Persians, including Egypt, Babylonia, Assyria, the kingdoms of the Medic Empire, the kingdoms of Israel and Judah, and so on. A period of three thousand years of Near Eastern history is nicely telescoped by Hegel into the Persian Empire, which comes at the end and conquers all else. But the whole structure of history preceding the Persian Empire in the Near East is simply not discussed by Hegel. Thus empires alone are not sufficient. This principle of construction again shows that certain spectacular events, like spiritual outbursts or empires, practically invite the construction of history about them. What is really necessary is the gathering of sufficient empirical material to find the complexes that really belong together, and that, being without an *instantia contraria,* will be truly valid.

With the occurrence of a complex of factors at a critical juncture in history, the likelihood of inaccurately describing such patterns is greatly increased. For example, whenever one finds a complex of three such factors, the temptation might be to consider this a confirmation of Jaspers' concept of axis time. Adding the other factors we have discussed, one finds a horizontal structure in history, running from the West to China, all in approximately the same period—from the fifth to the second century B.C. But at the same time one finds that this imperial period of the ecumenic empires is preceded, for example, by a whole structure of Near Eastern history before the ecumenic empires—the history of Egypt, Sumer, Babylon, Assyria, the kingdoms of Israel and Judah, and so on. There is not only a horizontal structure of elements in chronological parallelism, but also a further vertical structure of elements. There is a vertical line in time, which starts at approximately 2000 B.C. and runs through about the eighth century B.C., when it branches out into the civilizations of Hellas, Persia, China, and India. It then moves along parallel lines until it again branches out, this time covering the whole globe. Beginning with the eighth century, then, we find entirely new civilizations, such as the independent Islamic, the

Western, and the Byzantine civilizations, which did not even exist in the period of the ecumenic empires.

The pattern of history appears to be not simply a question of the parallel and the axis time of Jaspers. We have also recognized a vertical line, which one might call the main line, running through Near Eastern history and through the numerous branching-out phenomena, which can be identified by the complexes of phenomena indicated above.

This is one way of getting at things, but it involves all sorts of presuppositions. I now want to discuss some fundamental categories that must be used in judging the importance of historical phenomena.

III. CATEGORIES

The first of these categories I take from what we have called the main line of history in the Near East, starting early in the second millennium around 2000 B.C. This is the category of *exodus,* used in the Biblical sense. When a society gains a new insight into the true order of personal and social existence, and when it will abandon the larger society of which it is a part when it gains this insight, this constitutes an exodus. When such a higher insight is gained, the group that gains it will establish itself as a separate entity, outside the confines of the society within which it had previously dwelt. In this sense one might say that the exodus of Abraham from Ur is the first formal exodus of which we have any knowledge. The second one is, of course, the great exodus of the Israelites under Moses from Egypt, the events by which the people of Israel was established outside the confines of Egypt, and ultimately in the promised land. These are the models of exodus. This type of exodus, however, is now a prominent phenomenon in history. Whenever a new insight into order is gained, there is always the question whether to emigrate from the present order into a situation in which the new order can become socially dominant and relevant for the society that has gained the insight.

We also find in the history of Israel and Judah, in their relation to the exiled Hebrews in Babylon, the development of a conception of an exodus of Israel from itself. In the sixth century Isaiah put forth the idea that one must start spreading the gospel of the true order under God, and the missionary meaning of the exodus is to make this conception valid for all mankind. The completion of this idea occurs in Christianity, in which this conception of the exodus has become a fundamental category, playing a determining role in the philosophy of history of St. Augustine. I want to give you St. Augustine's formulation of the problem of exodus, for it very probably will never be surpassed. It is philosophically perfect, and hence it is still a valid category today.

He gives this formulation in the narrations on the Psalms, which are sermons on the Psalms of a popular nature; but their popularity does not mean that the formulation is therefore relaxed. On the contrary, it is more exact and more precise than in the *City of God*. According to St. Augustine, in man, in the soul, there are organizing centers. The two principle centers are the love of self and the love of God; these are the emotional orienting centers in the soul. Between these two centers there is continual tension: man is always inclined to fall into the love of self and away from the love of God. On the other hand, he is always conscious that he should orient himself by the love of God, and he tries to do so in many instances. Exodus is defined by St. Augustine as the tendency to abandon one's entanglements with the world, to abandon the love of self, and to turn toward the love of God. When the tension is strongest toward the love of God, then we find an exodus from the world. Here is a passage from the *Sermons on the Psalms:* "Incipit exire, qui incipit amare. Exeunt enim multi latenter, et exeuntium pedes sunt cordis affectus; exeunt autem de Babylonia." ("They begin to depart who begin to love. Many there are who depart and not know it. For their walk of departure is a movement of the heart. And yet they depart from Babylon.") [1]

Now let us establish a connection between this passage and our discussion of exodus. "They begin to love. Many there are who depart and not know it." It is a subconscious process at first, for the walk of departure, the manner in which they abandon the world, is a movement of the heart toward the love of God. And even if it is so subconscious that perhaps they do not even know it themselves, they nevertheless depart from Babylon, and are engaged in an exodus toward the heavenly Jerusalem. The existential tension of departure, the walk of departure, is a movement of the heart—this is the definition of exodus. The problem is reduced to what today we

---

[1] St. Augustine, *Enarrationes in Psalmos,* Psalm No. LXIV, 2:42–44. Another English translation appears in *Expositions on the Book of Psalms* (Oxford: J. H. Parker, 1849) , III, 252.

would call a philosophy of existence. St. Augustine speaks of a fundamental tension, which all can experience; and, so far as the formulation is concerned, one cannot go beyond that. So you see, it is a perfect formulation of the problem. It is not only perfect philosophically, it is also extremely beautiful.

This tension, I should say, is central to the interpretation of history. Wherever changes in the existent order occur, they are changes in the direction of the exodus mentioned. Wherever this tension is understood, new insights into order occur, and then the actual pattern of an exodus appears. We have concrete examples in the exodus of the Israelites from Egypt, and in the exodus of the Pilgrims from Holland and England. The tension between the established order and the new insight yields a new order of higher validity.

Here, then, is just one of the categories that must be used. Before I discuss the further implications of this category, I must first clarify some issues for the benefit of nonphilosophers. What is so magnificently expressed here by St. Augustine will ordinarily be objectified by most people. They are not familiar with this tension toward God, nor with faith in the existential sense, as expressed in Hebrews 11:1: "Faith is the substance of things hoped for and the proof of things unseen." People do not ordinarily live with this tension, yet they still want to immigrate into the kingdom of God. This pole of the tension will be objectified by various imageries into a kingdom of God, depicted in very definite colors and incidents.

Thus there are various possibilities for objectification, among which there are two fundamental possibilities. One is to project the kingdom of God into the future, that is, to assume that somehow the structure of history, in which we are living and in which we experience this tension toward God, will actually be replaced, in history, by a perfected kingdom of God. This is the escape by objectification, which is usually called apocalyptic, as in the Apocalypse of Daniel, telling of that which is to come with the fifth monarchy, or as in the Apocalypse of St. John, telling of a millennium, or as in the modern apocalyptic visions of the perfect realm of reason, the perfect realm of positivist science in the Comtian sense, or the perfect realm of Marxist communism. Here we have types of apocalyptic visions by which that one pole of the tension, the love of God, is projected into an event in history, in which the structure of history or society is changed into perfection. This is the apocalyptic escape.

There is also another type of objectifying escape, which is not into a future time, but rather into the beyond, into perfection in a spiritually understood eternity beyond this world. This escape into the beyond, with various means of escaping the structure of this world of society and history, is what was called in antiquity *gnosis*. The various gnostic movements advise man how to escape from the structure of the world into the spiritual, pneumatic existence beyond this world. This is not a future in history, but the end of all history, the escape from history into spiritual perfection, into the pleroma beyond history.

These, then, are the two fundamental possibilities: escape into eternity or escape into future time. These two fundamental possibilities of escape, objectification into gnostic eternity or into an apocalyptic future, provide fundamental categories for the interpretation of history.

Of course there are many differences. For example, in the period of the classical apocalypses, the period from Daniel to Baruch, cryptic events are always introduced as the intervention of God, while in modern apocalypses, which are progressivist and revolutionary in type, the actions involved are those of men. These are very important differences and subdivisions, of course. But the fundamental categories for the escapes from the exodus are still the two we have named.

Of course there is one genuine solution which, in the wake of the apocalyptic beginnings, is that adopted by Christianity: the acceptance, one might say, of the apocalyptic imagery of something that happens in the future. Christ himself, for example, in Mark 13, has a perfectly classical apocalypse in the Jewish sense. And immediately after pronouncement of the apocalypse follows the story of the passion, the beginning of the apocalyptic events in time. The transformation of these apocalyptic beginnings into an eschatology, which means that they are projected now into a future out of time, is a very curious intermediate conception. It depends upon neither the gnostic eternity here-and-now, nor upon the apocalyptic future, but rather upon something that will happen in time, but that, when it happens, will be beyond time. It is a very curious mixed form, a compromise between the two extremes. And, so long as one adheres to this view closely, he avoids the danger of falling into the extremes, either apocalyptic or gnostic. Of course there is always a considerable number of Christian side movements, sectarian movements, and, today, secularist movements, which do not observe the wisdom of the view, and which thus fall back into the classic type of apocalypse and hence recede from rationality.

Now again I have given you a group of categories which immediately attach to the fundamental category of exodus as developed by St. Augustine: the two categories that describe possible objectifications of that tension into conceptions of eternity or of the future. But there is also a third way in which one may stray from the rational path, namely, by the establishment of empire. In the desire to attain a perfect order for all, here and now, one might organize all persons into an overwhelmingly strong power, thus determining for everyone what order is, and then enforcing it. This would be an ecumenic empire. Now this ecumenicism of empire, which attempts to establish an order here and now, embracing all known mankind, is a phenomenon which also occurred in that period in which the questions of spiritual existence became topical. It belongs with the other phenomena we have observed. The ecumenic empire is one solution, in the sphere of power, for obtaining the perfect order for mankind.

Empirically, of course, these empires are limited in number, because of their great size. And, if means of communication are ineffective, there may be several such empires contemporaneously, each hearing only faintly of the others. As a matter of fact, around 200 B.C. there was such a series of empires, extending from the Atlantic to the Pacific: in the West the Roman Empire, then the Hellenistic empires in the Middle East, then the Mauryan Empire in India, and finally the Han Empire in China. There was thus an active chain, tending from western Europe to eastern Asia, but with very little communication between the various empires then existent. But in the same civilizational area there cannot be several empires simultaneously, and hence in the West we find a temporal sequence of empires. The earliest of these was the Persian Empire, then came the Alexandrian conquest and the succession of empires, which were finally swallowed up by the Roman Empire in the west and the Sassanian Empire in the Middle East. The only ones that existed near one another in the entire period were the Roman Empire and the Sassanian Empire. Their contact along mutual borders led to a number of problems, and the structure of each was influenced by the other.

In the wake of the rise of the Roman Empire, the theory of the ecumenic empire was developed, and in particular the very peculiar theory of the historian Polybius. It is interesting to note that Polybius was a contemporary of the author of the Apocalypse of Daniel. In the Apocalypse of Daniel we find the Jewish reaction to the phenomenon of empire. In Polybius' history we find the reaction of a conquered Greek to the Roman Empire.

The conquered Greek Polybius, who in the Roman eyes was a social aberration, gives a very curious account of the problem of empire. First, he sees that the empire is an inevitability in history. As the political situation was, there had to be an empire. It was the Roman Empire, one might say, which fulfilled the purpose of history by conquering the lands where the former Persian and Alexandrian empires had failed. Empires were the order of the day, and the Romans thus fulfilled the demand of their time. So there was a sort of inevitability in the course of history then, just as today it is inevitable that smaller, formerly natural units can no longer exist. We must have political units of a certain order and magnitude in order to realize the possibilities of the industrial revolution, and therefore we must have a common market in Europe, rather than an unorganized collection of national states.

In contradistinction to modern imperialists, however, Polybius was a philosophically cultivated person. His thought about the phenomenon of empire went beyond the mere inevitability of history, and he asked himself the question, If the whole world has in fact been conquered by that expanding Roman Empire, so what? And this great "so what?" found splendid expression in the famous scene of the Roman general Scipio Africanus the Elder after the conquest of Carthage. As Scipio stood on the hill overlooking the flaming ruins of the conquered Carthage, his older friend Polybius noticed tears running down Scipio's cheeks and asked him: "In this hour of victory over that splendor, why do you cry? What is the cause of your tears?" And Scipio answered, "When looking down on Carthage I think of the day when the same will happen to Rome." I only wish some of the conquerors of today would entertain similar ideas.

Exemplified here is the complete consciousness that nothing under the sun will endure forever—that the orders established by the great victories of the time will one day fall to another, stronger power. Polybius thus understood, even at the beginning of that great Roman Empire, that if it were established, still nothing of real importance would have been accomplished. That idea seems to have been very popular, since it was, indeed it had to be, presupposed as the background for very peculiar features in the Gospels and in the letters of St. Paul. With the appearance of Christ it was the task of the apostles, and especially of Paul, to penetrate that *oikoumenē* (inhabited world) with the Gospel. When that was done, and when the whole known world (which the Romans had by that time imperially organized) was penetrated by the gospel, then the second coming of Christ would occur. In the terminology of Polybius, then the *telos*, the purpose of history, would be fulfilled. So the *telos* that was questioned by Polybius, the *telos* of empire (and Polybius was certain that the establishment of such an empire fulfilled nothing) —this question of the *telos*, of the purpose, was taken up by St. Paul. The telos would be fulfilled when that whole *oikoumenē* was penetrated by Christianity, and then would come the apocalyptic end. Then the last things would happen, the prophecy of Christ, the branding of the arm.

In Paul's expansion of the problem of meaning beyond the power sphere and into the spiritual sphere, we can see what is defective about the whole idea of empire. It lacks the factor of the spirit. It is one of the great achievements of the later church to have found the balance between spirit and power, and to have seen that while social organization of a sort is necessary, it is certainly not the end of things, unless it is penetrated by the substance of spiritual order.

Let us dwell for a moment on this aspect of the life of St. Paul. Our view explains quite a number of peculiar things in the biography of St. Paul: his missionary urgency, his insistence on traveling through every province of the Roman Empire and on establishing there a center from which the gospel could then be spread further, his plan to travel even to Spain (perhaps he was actually there, though the matter is not settled) before going back to Rome to suffer martyrdom there. And this also explains St. Paul's urgency: he believed that he could accomplish this in his own lifetime, and that even in his lifetime Christ would make his second coming.

The solution here, as in the former case of objectification, lies in establishing a balance between the order within the world and the spiritual order, without lapsing into a pure empire of power or into a sterile apocalyptic or gnostic attitude. The church was, one might say, the cement that reintroduced rationality through this necessary balance between secular and spiritual order.

I shall discuss one further category, and then I shall come to my conclusion. This final category is that of *representative humanity,* which always appears in connection with the configuration of history. We must accept as a fact of our history that, for reasons unknown (which might be said to be the mystery behind the configuration of history), not all men are endowed equally with spirituality; and, even when they are endowed with spiritual sensitivity, insights into order develop only gradually in the course of time. Every new insight begins with a single person, who receives it, one might say, as a representative of the whole of humanity. As a matter of fact, the very idea that there *is* a humanity, that there *is* a mankind, and that one can generalize about man, appears only when certain revelatory insights occur. These are spiritual outbursts. We now recognize that man is that being who is capable of insight into true order, the order of true existence and of God, which can only be understood through the orders actually existent in history. That would be the definition of man from which all ideas of a general conception of man must begin. Before such spiritual outbursts, no general conception of man is possible. In the Egyptian hieroglyphs, for example, the hieroglyphs for Egyptian and for man are identical. So a man is only an Egyptian, and whoever cannot be designated as an Egyptian cannot be designated as a man at all. Only when spiritual insights are attained does man become defined as that being who receives his orders through existence from God. There is therefore a tremendous importance attaching to these spiritual outbursts and insights. The recipients of such insights act as representatives of humanity, with the obligation to communicate their insights to all mankind. Every prophet, every philosopher, every enlightened person like a Buddha, a Confucius, a Lao-tse with his doctrine of *Tao,* the Way, comes as an element of disorder in his society, because he has received an insight into the true order, which is different from the established order. Thus, every new insight into order is the beginning of a revolution of more or less considerable dimensions.

This element of representative humanity is a real factor, not only in these outbursts of ancient times (this "axis time," in Jaspers' term), but also in the present day. If we look, for example, at Vico in the eighteenth century, we find very curious elaborations of the problem. He sets as his absolute representative the intellectual of his own period. He must then recognize, of course, that all men have not yet reached the level of the intellectual, and that most people do not even know what that is. He then introduces the concept of humanity, the total mass of mankind, for whom representatively certain insights are received by men of the type of Vico, so that a man like Vico becomes a type of the representative man, substituting for Plato or for Christ. In the theory that succeeded Vico's in the nineteenth century, Comte actually does this. In 1854, Comte is introducing the era of Comte and replacing the era of Christ. It is the element of representativeness that gives momentum to all of the modern ideological movements. The representatives or leaders of such movements feel themselves to be the representatives of mankind, and they feel that everyone must be converted to the representative type of truth. The category of representative humanity thus runs from antiquity down to the modern era, to the contemporary political mass movements, conducted by sectarians like Comte and his positivist movement, the progressivists, and so on.

IV. CONCLUSION

There are other such categories which might be discussed, but these are sufficient for our purposes. In conclusion I want to present a problem. I have pointed to a large number of patterns in history. Just think of the vertical patterns running through the history of mankind from the second millennium B.C. to the present. Or think of a parallel series of ecumenic empires running from the Atlantic to the Pacific, about 200 B.C. Or consider the beginning of this general process in the eighth century B.C. Now if we formulate general propositions, and assume that they are true, the question is, Of what do we predicate all these predicates? Of what do we say all these things? Usually one speaks of history as a subject; we call these patterns in history, for example. Or, as I have put it in the title, we call this the configuration of history. But, if you think for a moment, you will see that such language is misleading: this is not a configuration of history, because history is itself nothing but this configuration. It is identical with it. Insofar as we have history, we have it only to the extent that we can discern such patterns. The patterns are thus identical with history.

And this raises a further question: Who is the subject of this history? Obviously it is not single human beings. Obviously it is not single concrete societies, like the Roman Empire, since these patterns apply to India and to China as well. Obviously it is not simply civilizations. The only possible answer seems to be that it is mankind. Mankind has history, and in mankind appear such configurative patterns. But this will not do either, since, as I mentioned before, the idea of man is only an idea, and not a reality. Mankind is not a given thing. Mankind stretches back into the past toward unknown beginnings. It moves into the future toward unknown times. What we call mankind is simply an idea, which arises on the occasion of certain experiences of revelation or illumination, and which is then extended to all other people who do not have such insights. We include within mankind, for example, all Africans, yet in all Africa there never was an insight that would have enabled an African tribe to conceive the idea of man or of mankind. There simply was no such thing. These are Western, or at least largely Western, ideas—classical and Christian ideas.

Therefore mankind does not exist, and cannot be the subject of history. It is not an empirical object. This would suggest, therefore, that ultimately the subject can only be Being in the most general sense, Being itself; that everything that happens and which we call history, including our idea of mankind, is a happening in Being itself, which is behind all specific things and all specific happenings. This means that the subject matter, the matter in which all these formal elements occur, is not a datum, and that the classical metaphysical categories of form and matter do not apply at all. But in this way the subject disappears, and we have left only relations.

Now this opens very interesting possibilities, and suggests comparisons, because we are in a similar situation in physics today. In theoretical physics we also have all sorts of relational discoveries, which are so thoroughgoing that the subject matter, the terms of the relations, disappears. We do not know what matter is in which this or that happens. We know only the relations, and we have no matter aside from these relations, as for example in nuclear physics.

Once again, then, the subject which in physics is called "matter" is on the point of disappearance, if indeed it has not already disappeared (the more radical theories would say it is gone, and that we have only the relations) . We have found a similar problem in the theory of history: the subject to which all these things happen is disappearing, and we have thus come back practically to a cosmology, a philosophy of the cosmos. And in this philosophy of the cosmos all sorts of things happen, yet we are unable to describe, to define, or to delineate a subject to which they happen. They are simply events in Being.

ARNOLD TOYNBEE

Indivisibility and Unpredictability of Human Affairs

In beginning this paper, I think I ought to raise the question, "Is there such a thing as the philosophy of history?" because I suppose a majority of living historians would say that there is not. They would say it is such a nebulous idea, so confused, in fact such philosopher's stuff that it is not real. In all countries in, anyway, the western world, at the present time—even in Scotland and Germany, which are, I suppose, the most philosophical of all western countries —I suppose the majority of historians would condemn the philosophy of history. In my own country, England, certainly a majority are very vehemently against there being such a thing, and if we did have in England a committee on un-English activities—of course if the committee were staffed by congressmen, I mean by members of Parliament, it would not matter because they would not care about whether there was a philosophy of history or not—but if it were staffed by historians and I found myself at that time in England, I

ARNOLD J. TOYNBEE was long director of studies at the Royal Institute of International Affairs, London. Writing his *Study of History* occupied him during the years 1934–61, but not to the exclusion of an annual *Survey of International Affairs* for about half those years, and a series of similar studies. Professor Toynbee's view of history as "a vision . . . of God revealing Himself in action to souls that are sincerely seeking Him" is much debated, as is his view that a genuine world religion must replace nationalism if mankind is to survive.

should have to run to the border and take asylum in Scotland, because I should probably be called up and tried and condemned as a heretic.

I think historians have two objections to the philosophy of history. I have mentioned one, the feeling that it is something vague, nebulous, and unreal. That is rather a good objection, because it puts it up to people like Professor Voegelin and myself to demonstrate not only that there is such a thing as philosophy of history, but that this is important and in fact that one cannot study history more than superficially without going into the philosophy of history as well as into history itself, if indeed the two are distinguishable.

The historians' second objection is one that they talk about less, I think, and it is probably not so good an objection. I think it is that if they once admitted that the philosophy of history was a reality and was important, they themselves would have to begin to think about it, and they do not want to do that. They want to go on studying the facts of history and, if possible, to keep themselves clear of philosophy. As I say, that is not such a good objection because it may mean, if Professor Voegelin and I are right, that the unphilosophic historian is limiting himself to a rather superficial view of what history is and what the nature of historical facts is.

Historians are given some justification for their disbelief in the philosophy of history by the actual looseness with which the term "philosophy of history" has been used. It has been used up to date in a number of quite different meanings, some of which do not really apply at all.

A philosopher, of course, might also question whether there is such a thing from his point of view. He might say that everything in the universe is a philosopher's concern, so philosophy is, of course, concerned with history among many many other things. But, he might say, there is no such thing as a separate philosophy of history. There is just philosophy, which is all-comprehensive, and history is just one of the things that philosophy deals with incidentally because it deals with everything that there is. That is perhaps a rather good point of view, and I think a historian who approaches the philosophy of history will have to realize that he is committing himself to approaching philosophy in general. He cannot limit his philosophical outlook when once he has come onto philosophical ground at all.

Some people, when they speak of "philosophy of history," are using a rather pretentious title to mean merely a comprehensive view of history itself as a whole—a panoramic view, as opposed to the detailed view of the specialist who concentrates on some particular piece of history.

I am certain, myself, that a comprehensive view of history is necessary, though, of course, it is equally necessary to do detailed microscopic work on history as well. I think the comprehensive view is necessary because I believe that without it there can be no understanding of history. But this is not philosophy; this is just the study of history taken, as it should be taken, as a whole, and seen within the widest possible framework.

There is a third meaning that is sometimes given to the term "philosophy of history." Some people mean by that the analysis of the structure of history. Is history just chaotic? "Just one damned thing after another?" as somebody said. Or does it have a discernible pattern in it? And, if history has a pattern, is this pattern progressive? Is it a one-way street, or is it repetitive? Is it a circle in which you go round and round? Or is it two different rhythms that one could conceive of, I suppose, in the movement of human affairs? But there might be some kind of combination of the two rhythms. After all, in any wheeled vehicle, the wheels go round and round, but the vehicle itself, thanks to the wheels going round and round in a repetitive way, goes along a definite course from one point to another. So there might be a possible combination of the two rhythms in that way. Then, let us suppose that history is partly repetitive, though the repetitive element in it might not be the main movement. Suppose that the repetitiveness is a subordinate movement in the rhythm of history. Then we must ask ourselves: Are there classes of events, or classes of institutions, whose representatives have enough in common with each other to make a comparative study of them first of all possible, and secondly illuminating and therefore valuable?

Let us think of some possible objects of comparative study. Of course, far the most fundamental and important is the individual human being. Every human personality is in some sense unique. Even the most primitive human beings have personal names. Being labeled with a personal name implies that one is in some sense unique among all mankind, and that is true of every human being to some extent. At the same time, if we did not have something in common, and a very, very great deal in common, we could not recognize each other as human beings, and the study of history would then be impossible. The only human beings whom we know by direct experience are, first of all, oneself, and, second, the people whom we happen to meet in our very brief life on this earth. We can never meet the generations of men who are already dead, and these are the majority of the human race up to date. As you know, on Roman gravestones one of the phrases for someone dying is that he has migrated *ad plures,* to the majority; he has joined the majority; he has joined the dead who are the majority over the living. And, if we are really going to have two thousand million years more of human life on this planet, then the generations still unborn will vastly outnumber, to an incredible extent, all the human beings who have so far lived and died. Now the only way in which we can get into touch with either the unborn or the dead is by analogy with our knowledge of the living, and therefore, if comparison between individual human beings were not possible, if there were not something that we call "the uniformity of human nature" underlying the individuality of each human personality, then each human being would be sewn up in his own personality; there would be no human communication, and certainly no knowledge of the past. Thus the comparative study of individual human beings is fundamental to all history and, in fact, fundamental to all human affairs. Because man is a social animal who does not know how to live except in community with his fellow men, he must, therefore, have some understanding of them, and he can have this only by analogy, by the comparative method, outside the very narrow circle of people that he knows personally.

Then, of course, one can make a comparative study of various human institutions. One can compare different kinds of states, city states, nation states, federal states, and empires. Each of these subdivisions of the category "state" can be studied in a comparative way. One could make comparative studies of constitutions and perhaps find the thing that Professor Voegelin alluded to in his paper, a typical succession of constitutions—say from oligarchy to democracy. The ancient Greek philosophers busied themselves very much with this question of the different types of constitution, classifying them, seeing which constitutions fit into which class, and Plato, followed by the historian Polybius, went on to sketch out what he believed to be a necessary inevitable series of political stages, starting with monarchy, going on to aristocracy, then to plutocracy, then to democracy, and finally to tyranny, perhaps coming round in a circle from tyranny to monarchy again. So constitutions are obviously a subject for comparative study.

Then there are declines and falls. There is Gibbon's famous history of the decline and fall of the Roman Empire; and there have been other empires and other declines and falls. It is instructive to compare the decline and fall of the Roman Empire with the declines and falls and then rises again of, say, the Chinese Empire, or with the decline and fall of the ancient Persian Empire, or of the ancient Egyptian Empire, and so on. Some people have written comparative studies of revolutions, which is also an instructive thing to do. Others have written of civilizations, which, when one is discussing units of study, is to take a unit more useful than that of nations or states. One could make a comparative study of renaissances; one could make a comparative study of religions, classifying religions into different kinds—monotheistic, polytheistic, primitive or more advanced—or into missionary religions and ethnic religions. A comparative study of the three historic missionary religions, Christianity, Islam, and Buddhism, is, I think, a fruitful subject.

We come now to the point that Professor Voegelin raised in his paper, the comparative study of what he calls "configurations," meaning a cluster or group of some of these elements of human history. The obvious value of finding repetitions or recurrences of configurations is that they are much less likely to be accidental and thus due to chance recurrences of individual factors. If A recurs a number of times or B recurs a number of times, this may be just accidental. If the cluster ABC occurs and there is another cluster ABC—well, the more elements there are in the cluster which all recur on some other occasion or occasions, the less likely this is to be due to chance, and the more likely there is to be some reason for it.

Let me pause for a moment on the particular configuration that Professor Voegelin used as his illustration: the connection between some would-be universal empires and would-be world states, an outburst of historiography, and an outburst of religion. A question was raised about how Thucydides fits into the picture in the case of the Greek historians and the Persian Empire. I would suggest that the underlying link between the rise of a great empire and an outburst of historical writing is something very fundamental to human nature, namely, curiosity. Of course we are not the only animals that have curiosity. Every farmer knows that a cow has curiosity about the pasture in the next field just the other side of the fence, whether it has better grass than she is eating at the moment or worse; and, if she can get through the fence, she will find out what the grass is like on the other side. But a cow's curiosity is very limited compared to our human curiosity. In fact, our curiosity is so much greater than that of any other animal that we know of that it is really a difference in kind; and I would say that curiosity, like freedom of choice, is one of the distinguishing characteristics of human nature as against the nature of other forms of life on this planet. Any striking and apparently important political event will arouse curiosity, and this curiosity will move some people to try to make a record of the event, to write the history of it; and one of the most striking political events possible is the rather sudden rise of a great and widespread empire, especially if it is very sudden and if the people who build that empire are people who up to this moment have been rather obscure and in fact almost unknown. I think that what struck Herodotus' imagination about the Persian Empire was that, until about the middle of the sixth century B.C., i.e., until about a century before Herodotus' time, the Persians were really unknown. They came from the province of Fars in the southern corner of Persia (Iran), away from the main routes, the main highways, of southwest Asia, and in one generation they conquered the greater part of the western end of the civilized world of the day, except for European Greece, from Asiatic Greece to Egypt on the west, and to what is now western Pakistan on the east. That an unknown people should put together this vast empire was naturally something that struck historians' imaginations.

The question of how Thucydides comes in is answered by the fact that it is not only the rise of a great empire that is a striking political event. What set Thucydides off was the outbreak of a great and, as it turned out, disastrous war between the two leading states of independent European Greece at the time, Athens and Sparta. Thucydides divined that this was going to be a fateful war for the Greek world and for Greek civilization. It was that striking event that moved him to write his history. As Professor Voegelin said, it is not only the rise of a great empire that leads people to write history, and, conversely, the great empire may rise and fall without anybody being inspired to write the history of this. Yet certainly the sudden rise of a great empire is one of the things that sets historians off thinking and writing. It is no accident that two of the greatest of the ancient Greek historians, namely, Herodotus and Polybius, whom Professor Voegelin also mentioned, were inspired by the rise of a great empire: Herodotus by the rise of the Persian Empire, and Polybius by the rise of the Roman Empire. A third, Procopius, a very great historian who lived in the sixth century of the Christian era, was inspired to write by the attempt of the Roman imperial government at Constantinople to reconquer the western provinces of the Roman Empire, where it had at that time collapsed and had been overrun by barbarians. The Roman Empire did reconquer North Africa, Italy, and a bit of Spain, at ruinous cost to itself. As you see, this third great ancient Greek historian was also inspired by something to do with the rise and fall of empires.

As for the interconnection between empires and outbursts of religion or philosophy, I would suggest that this goes back to another fundamental thing in human life, and that is man's love of liberty and his determination to have some freedom in some sphere of life. The price of world unity, even partial world unity, in a so-called and would-be world empire, is the giving up of liberty in the political and perhaps to a certain extent in the economic field. It was not for nothing that these partial world empires arose in the past. They arose as solutions to the problem that confronts us today, the problem of either having unity and peace or bringing upon oneself and on one's world and on the human race as a whole some indescribable castastrophe. But everything has to be bought at a price, and world peace and order have to be bought at the price of the loss of local sovereignty and political liberty, and perhaps of a great deal of economic liberty as well. And, since people are determined to have liberty in some sphere, when they are barred out from exercising that liberty in the political field or the economic field, the religious field is the one to which they turn. So it is not accidental that, in the time of the Roman Empire, the true history of creative and active life in the Roman Empire was the history of the competition of the various religions from the east, including Christianity, which were competing for the conversion of the Greeks and Romans. In similar fashion, the true history of the first phase of the Chinese Empire was the entry of Buddhism into China and the conversion of China to that religion.

We come now to yet another meaning, a fourth meaning, of the

phrase, "philosophy of history," a meaning which Professor Voegelin brought up at the conclusion of his paper. By "philosophy of
history" some people mean the use of history as an approach for
peering into the mystery of the universe. This is sometimes called,
not "philosophy of history," but "metahistory," on the analogy of
Aristotle's term "metaphysics." As you know, when Aristotle had
studied physics, *physika* (which in Greek means literally "study of
the growth of things" and was limited to apply to the study of the
growth or evolution of material nature) he found that, in the
course of studying physics, he had raised questions that did not lie
within the physical field. Because the scrolls were after those of the
physics, they were called "after the physics," *ta meta ta physika,*
which then acquired the sense of being "beyond" physical questions.
On that analogy one might call this peering into the mystery of the
universe, which is the surrounding of human life on earth, *ta meta
ta historika,* "what is beyond human history."

Now this meaning of "philosophy of history," or "metahistory" if
we may call it that, is an important one, because, after all, all the
great religions have looked at history from this point of view. That
is how St. Augustine, whom Professor Voegelin mentioned, looked
at history. They looked at it in terms of something beyond this life
on earth. Christianity, Judaism, and Islam have in common a view
of history which begins with the Creation and goes on through the
Fall and the Redemption to the Last Judgment. Buddhism has a
view of history which takes the individual out of the world of
personality and desire into the state of extinguishedness (nirvana),
but they all alike lead one's mind beyond the confines of this visible
and material world into something of an essentially different, spiritual dimension. So this metahistorical meaning of the phrase "philosophy of history" is, I would say, a very important one.

We come now to some of the words in my rather portentous title,
the indivisibility of human affairs. The universe as a whole does
seem to be indivisible. At least, whenever we try to pick out of the
universe some piece of it, some portion of the phenomema which in
general, in their totality, we call "the universe," in order to study
this piece in isolation, we always find that we have to break out of
the arbitrary and artificial boundaries that we have drawn about
this little fragment that we have marked out to study. The questions
raised within that artificially limited area always force us to look

outside the area to something beyond, and, however wide we make the area that we delimit, there is always something beyond that we find we must study in order to understand what lies inside that limited area. This suggests that the universe is really indivisible, and probably infinite as well.

If the universe as a whole is indivisible, so, a fortiori, must be the human portion, or human aspect as we say, of the universe. The universe seen in its physical aspect flows, as the physicists tell us, through a continuous channel of space-time. In his physical aspect, man is part and parcel of this space-time continuum which is the physical universe. Conversely if man, who also has a spiritual aspect, is part and parcel of the whole universe, I suppose that implies that the whole universe has in it something analogous to, corresponding with, or akin to, the spiritual side of human nature. Anyway, human nature is part of the universe as a whole. If one tries to extricate human nature and human affairs from the rest of the universe, he will to that extent distort the picture of what human affairs and human life are like.

We human beings have been endowed, I suppose, with good enough minds to know just how bad our minds are. That means that we have minds good enough to know that they are bad, in the sense of being imperfect. But they are very inadequate indeed for studying the universe—as we discover the moment that we try to study even a fragment of the universe. The radical defect of human minds is, I suppose, that they cannot take in the universe as a whole in a single act of all-embracing and instantaneous comprehension; and, if the universe is an indivisible whole, I suppose that would be the only way of seeing the universe as it really is. But of course we can not begin to do that. The way in which our minds operate is, as we know, to comprehend ("comprehend" means to grasp, to pick up, to seize) bits of the universe, handfuls of the universe, piece-meal; and, when we have grasped one bit and another bit and another bit, then we try to arrive at the universe as a whole by piecing these bits together. This mental picture of the universe, arrived at by first dissecting the universe into artificial pieces and then trying to glue these pieces together—this is the way in which our minds work—must be really a very misleading patchwork. It cannot be anything like the true picture of the indivisible reality of the universe. However, owing to the imperfection of human intellectual powers, we cannot avoid partitioning our mental map of the universe into what academic people call "disciplines," i.e., various branches of learning.

Human affairs as a whole is just one discipline among a number, the other disciplines covering the whole of the nonhuman part of the universe, and human affairs is of course a fairly wide discipline. Yet human affairs cannot be understood properly except as being an inseparable part of this indivisible universe which includes all the nonhuman phenomena as well. Like other living creatures, man is inseparable from his total environment, and neither his acts nor his experiences are intelligible if they are not studied in man's environmental setting. Now how far does man's environment extend? We come back to the fourth meaning of "philosophy of history" that I suggested to you, the metahistorical meaning, the way in which history is approached in the great religions of the world—a way that carries one outside the confines of this world into another world, or other worlds. That is all part of man's environment. That means that we must study history in a very large field, which includes the whole field of the most philosophic and theological-minded of the religions. Of course, looking now downward instead of upward, the study of human affairs, in its turn, is broken up into a number of what one might call subdisciplines: psychology, theory of knowledge and logic, anthropology, sociology, economics, political science, history, and so on. History is really a way of looking at all these other aspects of human affairs from a particular point of view. It is a point of view from which they are seen in movement through time —an important point of view because we live in the time dimension and it is impossible to be conscious except in the time dimension. So history, insofar as it sees human affairs moving through time, sees them, I think, in an aspect which is part of their reality.

Owing to the limitations of human thinking, we cannot avoid dividing human affairs into these compartments and concentrating on some single department at a time, but we must never let ourselves take the dividing lines between the so-called disciplines seriously. This partitioning into disciplines has happened in a very accidental, haphazard way; it is very unsystematic and irrational. It is full of terms and labels that do not really describe the thing to which they are eventually attached, and it is full of cross divisions. History and economics are cross divisions of the others, because there is an economics of primitive society and every kind of institution and every individual human being who has every lived. I do not know why the study of the social life and culture and manners and customs of primitive people is particularly called "anthropology." It implies that only primitive people are human and that when you become more civilized you cease to be a subject for anthropology, which means literally "a study of human beings." Whether people like us are superhuman or subhuman, I do not know. Nor do I know why sociology is limited to the manners and customs of peoples who believe themselves to be more advanced, because as a matter of fact the more primitive peoples, peoples like the Hopi Indians or the Apaches, and so on, have a tighter social organization in many cases than the so-called more advanced peoples. Sociology should certainly apply to the primitive as well as the more advanced peoples, though conventionally the label is applied to the study of the manners and customs of the more advanced peoples. I do not see what the difference between sociology and anthropology really is. Then, psychology—the title would imply that it is concerned with the whole of the human psyche, including the conscious and volitional top level of it as well as the unfathomable subconscious or unconscious depths of it; but in practice the psychologists so far (I say "so far" because it is a young science so far) concentrate on the subconscious part, so that psychology really ought to be called the study of the subconscious part of the human psyche. As for theory of knowledge, epistemology—this really applies to the conscious and volitional part, but that part is inseparably bound up with the subconscious part, and the distinction between the two is really an artificial one.

Even if the "disciplines" were rationalized, which I think would be very difficult—there is some kind of academic vested interest in keeping them as they are—the mere division of human affairs into these artificial compartments would be an obstacle to understanding. We ought to be very ready to shift the partition walls about, moving them here and there, according to whichever arrangement is more convenient for the advancement of knowledge and understanding. Probably a number of you in this room have been in a Japanese house and have noticed how it differs from a Western house. In our Western houses the internal compartments forming the different rooms are, as we know, fixed; they are part of the rigid and permanent structure of the house. But that is not so in a Japanese house. Inside a Japanese house the different rooms are divided from each other by movable screens. In a few seconds, in a Japanese house, you can rearrange the whole interior organization by moving those screens about. If we must have disciplines, and if we must have partitions between them, we ought to proceed on the system of the Japanese house, where the internal partitions are recognized as being temporary, provisional, and readily movable, not on the principle of the Western house, where they are fixed once and for all until the house falls down.

We ought to try to study the universe as a whole all the time. And yet, with our human limitations, this is very difficult to do. One thinks here of C. P. Snow's famous account of the division between the two cultures, the culture of the nonhuman sciences and the culture of the humanities. I think of my own education. I was educated in one of the best preparatory schools, I suppose, in England, but in England, as you know, compared to this country, we specialize to extremes. We specialize at a very early stage. After having been given an introduction to chemistry which was really beneath contempt, at the age of about sixteen I was given the following choice: "Now that you have climbed up the lower rungs of mathematics as far as trigonometry, would you like to embark upon the calculus, or would you like to say good-bye forever to mathematics and read a lot more Greek and Latin authors?" Unfortunately I chose to read a lot more Greek and Latin authors—a wrong choice because, having already learned Latin and Greek, I could have done that any time later in life, whereas I could not go back and learn the calculus. Owing to this specialization, combined with freedom of choice, at an early age, I, like many other people in the humanities side of study, am excluded from that other world of mathematical understanding of the universe. This is a very great and serious limitation.

We ought to try to study the universe as a whole all the time, and to gain at least a glimpse of other aspects of it than the aspect on which we ourselves, in one short life, have to concentrate.

What I have to say now might be written off by the scientists as being the mere prejudice of a humanist, but I would say that, since we are human beings, the humanities do have the first call on us. I think that "the proper study of mankind is man," in the sense that the first business on the agenda of every human being is to live with himself—a difficult thing to to—and the second is to live with his fellows. If we fail in this human task, we cannot succeed in anything else, because in human life the ultimate source of all energy, all creation, all power comes out of human nature itself. We have largely extended the material drive of our power by the ingenious physical tools that we have invented, but they would be nothing, they would have no effect, if there were not human beings to use them. So human nature comes first, and human affairs matter supremely to us, because they are *our* affairs.

Also, human nature is more difficult than nonhuman nature for human minds to understand, and, as far as we can understand, to control. Science together with the application of science to technology has been mankind's great success, as we know. Self-knowledge and the application of self-knowledge to social, cultural, and spiritual relations have, I suppose we must confess, been mankind's great failure up to date. You will remember a famous passage in one of Plato's dialogues in which Socrates, one of the characters in the dialogue, is describing his own intellectual history. He tells how, as a young man, he had been fascinated by the physical science of the Greek scientists from the Asiatic part of Greece on what is now the western coast of Turkey, but how, when he had become more mature, he had turned away from studying astronomy and physics and all that to the study of truth and falsehood, right and wrong, good and bad—the things that really concern human life. And there is a story that Socrates once visited the shrine of Delphi, which was the greatest religious center in Greece; it is tucked away in a rather remote and backward part of European Greece. At the shrine of Delphi, as you know, there were written over the entrance the Greek words, *Gnothi seauton*. "Know yourself." Know *yourself*, because that is the entrance to all knowledge and understanding. And what Socrates was really saying was that this precept of the Delphic oracle was one that he had taken to heart and was the one that had determined his direction in philosophy.

Because science has been such a success and because our relations with each other have been such a failure so far, science today has great prestige as compared with human studies, and this has tempted humanists to try to express human affairs in scientific terms, which have been coined for describing nonhuman nature. This pseudoscientific approach in human affairs is, I would say, not illuminating to the study of human affairs. So far from being illuminating, it is misleading. The aspects of the universe that science studies are fundamentally the impersonal or abstract aspects, but human nature is fundamentally personal. Human affairs are very personal, and personal affairs cannot be understood by trying to transpose them into impersonal terms. You only get further away from them, instead of nearer to an understanding of them, if you try to express them in an impersonal way.

Science, dealing with nonhuman affairs, correctly uses deterministic terms of cause and effect. But a human being's relations with himself and with his fellow human beings are not cause-and-effect relations, in the sense that they are not rigidly determined; it is not absolutely necessary, and therefore predictable, that one human action should follow another. The distinctive feature in human nature, besides curiosity, is, I should say, consciousness and free will, at least a glimmer of consciousness and free will. I believe, and this is an act of faith, that consciousness and free will are realities and not illusions, as some thinkers have supposed them to be.

In so far as there is reflection, planning, choice, there is neither predetermination nor predestination. I therefore think that a formula such as "challenge and response" is a more realistic approach to the study of human affairs—an approach that better conveys the reality of human relations—than the cause-and-effect formula of the scientists. This works marvelously when scientists are considering nonhuman nature, but it does not work when considering human affairs. I supposed that I had invented the phrase "challenge and response," but afterward I found that I had got it when I was a child from the poet Robert Browning. There is a poem by Browning called "Master Hughes of Saxe-Gotha" in which the lines occur:

—O who may challenge them, not a response
Get the church-saints on their rounds.

These two words, "challenge" and "response," had sunk into my mind and had then come out again, with me thinking that they were mine.

This notion that human relations work by challenge and response is, as you will see, rather like the Hegelian and the Marxian notion of a thesis with an antithesis set up against it, and then a synthesis that is a resolution of the contradiction or clash between the thesis and the antithesis. The Hegelian-Marxian formula is put in a rather limited intellectual form. I think that "challenge and response" has the advantage of covering the emotional and volitional side of human action, as well as the purely intellectual. I have sometimes been challenged myself as to the relation of my notion—or, really, of Robert Browning's notion—of challenge and response to the Hegelian notion of thesis, antithesis, and synthesis. I know what the answer is. It is that each of these variations on the same idea is derived independently from what is the ultimate source of so very much of our Western thinking, and that is the Old Testament. The Old Testament is at the back of a very great deal of our thought, even though we are not conscious of what the origin is. The books of the Old Testament are a collection of separate books, written by different men, and I suppose the extreme limits of the dates are about a thousand years apart; but there is, I think, a common theme that runs through all the books of the Old Testament giving it the unity that it has. This theme is God's successive challenges to a series of human beings. God challenges Adam and Eve not to eat of the fruit of the tree of knowledge, He challenges Noah to build the Ark before the flood comes, He challenges Abraham to make his exodus from Ur of the Chaldees, He challenges Moses to lead the children of Israel out of Egypt, He challenges Samuel to devote his life to the service of Yahweh, and He challenges Jonah to go and preach in Nineveh—which would be like asking a member of the John Birch Society to go and preach his gospel in Moscow today. As you well know, when Jonah received that challenge from God he fled. He took passage on a ship from some Phoenician port in the opposite direction and tried to get to the western end of the Mediterranean, but found in the end that it was worse for him if he did not give a positive response, an affirmative response, to God's challenge, and go and preach to the people of Nineveh. The point of this idea of challenge and response is that there is no determinism here. The challenged individual is free, free of course at his peril, as Jonah was free at his peril, as Adam and Eve were free at their peril, to refuse to do what God asks of him. At his peril and at his risk of loss, he is free to disobey God's demand on him.

This is a very different relation, as you will see, from cause and effect, because a cause can have only one effect. A single cause must have a single uniform effect every time that this cause comes into operation. But a challenge may have at least two responses, I will or I won't, and it may have quite a number of variations on those. This, I believe, is the nature of the relation between human actions, and, as I say, it is quite a different relation from that of cause and effect. If the nexus in human affairs is not cause and effect but challenge and response, this means that in human affairs, unlike astronomy, for instance, the future is unpredictable, because, at every encounter between God and a human being and between one human being and another, there is not a predetermined result but rather a freedom of choice which is unpredictable by nature. However much you know about the previous situation, if human freedom of choice is geniune, as I believe it to be, then any amount of knowledge about the previous situation will not enable you to predict with certainty what choice the human being is going to make when he is challenged.

Human history is full of the unexpected. As you remember, before the Second World War, statisticians in this country made magnificent calculations of what the birth rate in the United States was going to be. These calculations were based, as they had to be, on the birth rate and the movement of the birth rate for the past twenty years, fifty years, one hundred years. Then the American people made fools of the statisticians by suddenly changing their habits about the size of family that they chose to have, and all those calculations were wasted. It was quite unpredictable that the American people were going to change their habits about the size of family, but they did so, and that made nonsense of the statisticians' predictions.

Who, round about the year A.D. 200, could have foreseen the conversion of the emperor Constantine to Christianity only a century later? Well, one man in the second century A.D., Celsus, did foresee it and wrote a book called *About the Truth* to confute Christianity before it was too late. It was the kind of book people write nowadays in Western countries about communism. But, on the whole, people did not foresee the victory of Christianity until the time when this overtook them.

How could the rulers of the Roman and the Persian empires, when they were fighting each other, have foreseen that Mohammed's followers were going to conquer both their empires within a few years? And who, in 1923, could have foreseen that Hitler was going to become the ruler of Germany and was going to come near to conquering the world? At that moment my wife and I were just setting out to write a current history of international affairs, and we had a great deal of material to get into a limited number of pages. I had written a small snippet on Hitler's abortive *Putsch* in Bavaria in 1923, and we were discussing what we could leave out. The chairman of our publications committee said: "What is this non-sense about this man called Hitler who has made this futile attempt at a *Putsch?* Cut it out!" So we cut it out, and, naturally, I was very sorry afterward that we had.

Such unexpected events show that in human affairs we cannot predict the future. On the other hand, when we look back over our records of the past, we do find regularities and recurrences. In fact, we do find something like a pattern. One has to ask oneself how one can reconcile a patterned past with an unpredictable future.

I will say something about this very briefly in conclusion. My guess is that patterns in the past, insofar as they are real—and, though this is very controversial, I believe them to be real—are patterns due to a certain amount of uniformity, of regularity, in the working of the subconscious part of the human psyche, whereas the element of unpredictability, which I think is the dominant element, comes from the freedom of choice that we have on the conscious and volitional level of our minds. But sometimes our wills, by opposing each other, cancel each other out, and then the subconscious and the emotional side of life gets its own way. Human life is a perpetual struggle of the consciousness and the will to try to keep their control over the subconscious and emotional part of the psyche, and to extend their control over it in order to make life more rational and more purposeful than it is. That is perhaps the essential underlying nature of human life.

So I would say that the element of pattern in human life that is revealed by our records of the past is genuine, though it is not the dominant element in life. The dominant element is, I think, the unpredictability of the future, and this arises, I believe, from the fact that there is a genuine thing called freedom of will.

Order in the History of Science

ERNAN McMULLIN

Cosmic Order in Plato and Aristotle

My task is to open a discussion of three successive views of cosmic order by giving an outline of the earliest of these, the one that characterized the thinkers of ancient Greece. Hopefully, what I have to say will allow the reader to appreciate better the significance of the Newtonian and Darwinian "revolutions." My first problem is that there was no single "Greek" concept of order, and that to understand the thought of any major Greek philosopher on this topic one would have to trace the entire dialectic of Greek cosmological speculation. My second problem is that cosmic order for the Greeks depended upon moral order; in some sense the two were ultimately one. The order that exists in the visible cosmos, for Plato in particular, is a sort of image of the order that exists in the life of a good and reasonable man. Cosmology and moral philosophy cannot, therefore, properly be separated. But in the scope of this brief paper I shall have to confine myself somewhat artificially to

ERNAN McMULLIN was born in Donegal, Ireland, the son of a lawyer-father and a physician-mother. He took degrees in both physics and divinity in his native land and studied philosophy at Louvain. Father McMullin's work in the philosophy of science has included notable conferences at Notre Dame that have led to the many-authored books *The Concept of Matter* (1963) and *Galileo, Man of Science* (1967). Father McMullin has been president of the American Catholic Philosophical Association and is chairman of the Department of Philosophy at the University of Notre Dame.

cosmic order, and for practicality to Plato and Aristotle, leaving aside their great predecessors.

The notion of order is one of the central clues, perhaps the central clue, to Plato's thought. Throughout his work, Plato was concerned with the search for intelligibility in things; indeed, his whole philosophy must be seen as a search for the immutable, unchangeable forms, which he supposed could give the most profound kind of knowledge. Two things seem to have impressed Plato. First, he was convinced of the availability of certain knowledge; geometrical knowledge is certain, and perhaps some moral truths are known with certainty also. The second thing that struck him was that the number of the certain truths is very small, and that their attainment is a very laborious affair. These two facts led him to make his famous distinction between the work of reason and the work of sense. This distinction had been made before, but Plato brought the dichotomy to a point that none of his predecessors had, and that few of his successors were to do. The contrast between the world of form or objects of reason on the one hand, and the world of sense or changing objects on the other hand, became the central theme in all of the Platonic dialogues.

In trying to build toward an understanding of Aristotle we must see him against the background of this Platonic view. Consequently, I propose to discuss Plato's development of this contrast between reason and sense, particularly in the context of one of his latest works, the *Timaeus*. I could just as easily have chosen one of the other works, such as the *Republic,* or the *Sophist,* or the *Philebus,* but for the purposes of this discussion it seems most profitable to take a cosmological work, in fact the only cosmological work Plato wrote.

The first part of the *Timaeus* is concerned with the problem of how reason is carried through in the universe. Plato sees the work of reason all around him, although he sees this work not clearly, but rather as the images on the wall of a cave, to use the famous metaphor from the *Republic.* Yet the work of reason is there, and so Plato tries in this cosmological myth, this likely story as he calls it, to understand the formation of the universe from the point of view of reason. He tries to discover how, so far as we can trace, reason would act, how reason would form the kind of world that we have.

In this part of the myth, and in the myth in general, Plato is concerned with becoming or change, but from two quite different points of view. First he wants to ask how the objects of sense, the natural objects of the visible world, have come to be. How is it that there are sensible objects? It is by no means obvious to him that there should be such objects; he requires an explanation. The first kind of becoming, the first kind of change or making with which he is concerned, is the making by which the sensible objects themselves come to be. The second, which is of a quite different sort, is the kind of change or becoming undergone by the sensible objects once they have been formed. When the sensible object has been launched, so to speak, on its career, it then undergoes changes in itself. And he has to inquire what kind of law or what kind of order governs that change. These are two quite different questions, and there are two quite different sorts of order for which he is looking. One, if you like, is the order imparted by creation; the other is the order that subsequently discloses itself in the activity of the created objects.

The second part of the *Timaeus* is perhaps the more interesting for our present topic. In it Plato goes on to show the negative side of the concept of order, attacking the question from a different point of view. This approach has good reason. If we take a very general concept like order, it seems to be hard to get hold of it. Order seems to be everywhere, like being, and it is a bit thin somehow; one wonders how he is to get inside the concept. As has often been pointed out, notably in recent times by Karl Popper, the most profitable way to get inside a concept like this is to ask where order is not present. Look for the negative instances, in other words, as a clue to the meaning of order itself. Neither Plato nor Aristotle defines very clearly what he means by order, and indeed this would be difficult to do. But both men do say quite a bit about disorder, so perhaps we can trace what they mean by order by looking at the negative side of the picture and asking what for them is disorder, and where it comes from.

In the second part of the *Timaeus,* Plato takes up the point, obvious to him, that the world is not entirely ordered, and that in fact the world shows much disorder. In some of his earlier works, for example the *Republic,* he represents the sensible world as an image of the world of form. Here, however, the stress is somewhat differ-ent. He asks the question, What is the source of the disorder in the sensible world? When form is imaged in the sensible order, why does it turn out so imperfectly?

He answers this question in a number of different ways, and these are important, especially for an understanding of Aristotle. He points out, first of all, that to have sensible objects at all there must be some sort of ground for them, some sort of field, so to speak, within which they exist. This ground or field must provide two things. First, it must allow the forms to be multiplied; it must allow many triangles, for example, instead of a single form of triangle which is perfect and beautiful, and about which geometers may reason. Instead of a single form of triangle, in the sensible order there are many triangles—wooden triangles, bronze triangles, and so forth—all of them realizing, to a greater or lesser extent, the form of triangle. What is it that permits that kind of multiplicity, that kind of manyness? Second, there must be something that allows things to change their form, to become less of an image, or more of an image, or a better image of the form itself. What is it that allows such changes to take place?

Plato gives the same answer to both of these questions. He describes the famous receptacle, the matrix of becoming, which he seems to identify with space in some sense, with a sort of perceptual space in which the images come to be. This matrix, this mother of all becoming as he calls it, can be instantiated in many different ways; and it also makes it possible for things to move from one place to another, which is the simplest kind of change. In this way, then, the receptacle is absolutely necessary if Plato is to explain how there can be multiplicity or change. The receptacle is quite independent of the realm of the forms, and if there were no such receptacle there would be nothing but forms. But there is something besides the realm of the forms—namely, the sensible world; and so Plato postulates something that is independent of and set over against the realm of forms, and this is the receptacle.

When it is said that the receptacle is set over against form, this is meant quite literally; we must understand the receptacle by contrast with form, and form by contrast with the receptacle. The receptacle is the unintelligible, that which cannot be understood in terms of form. It does not change, and hence it is in some sense immutable, but it cannot be studied by reason, because reason can operate only through the forms or ideas. Space is a precondition for there to be things, but the mind cannot directly grasp it until it is specified in some fashion by the forms. Space, or the receptacle, which is the second agency required for there to be sensible objects, is, so to speak, set over against reason. It is independent of reason and form.

When Plato begins to talk of the receptacle he uses another term, which is very difficult to understand and which is extremely important for an understanding of Aristotle, and for an understanding of the relation between Aristotle and Newton: namely, the term "necessity." The use of the term in this context is misleading to the modern reader, as has often been pointed out. When we today think of necessity we tend to think of regularity. We think of things that always act in the same way, we think of hypothetical sentences, and so forth; in other words, we relate necessity with intelligibility. It is important to see that for both Plato and Aristotle, though not in quite the same way, necessity is almost the opposite of this. Necessity does not mean the same thing as regularity, and Plato tries to show that in fact it implies irregularity. That which is necessary, as Plato and Aristotle use the term, does not always act in the same way.

What does he mean, then, by necessity, "blind necessity," as he calls it? Why does he call it "necessity"? Since he associates the term with the receptacle, I think it is perfectly obvious that he means the factor which is over against reason. Since he stresses purpose so much in this context, I also think it clear that he means the unreasoning, the unpurposive aspect of things. He means that aspect of things which is not entirely controlled by mind. At the beginning of the passage in which he discusses this, he says that reason, when it attempts to work upon the receptacle, upon necessity, is not entirely successful. It tries to persuade necessity, but can never do so with complete success. Although commentators on Plato have disagreed about the implications of this statement, they would in general agree that the sense here is that reason, operating in the universe, can never entirely overcome the element of nonpurposiveness. This element of nonpurposiveness acts throughout the universe and is associated with space, with the ground of all becoming which is independent of form, and owes nothing to form.

Another part of this section is devoted to the myth of the demiurge, which is also very difficult to interpret. The demiurge is the maker, the craftsman, and the difficulty comes in trying to decide whether Plato understands by the demiurge someone who is apart from or outside of his work, as ordinarily a craftsman would be. He does use the word "god" to describe the demiurge, but this does not mean very much. Does he mean by this a being who is in some sense outside the work that he makes, or does he mean a reason that works through and inheres in the universe itself—a pantheistic reason, to use a much later term? It seems to me that Plato deliberately leaves this point open. In fact I think that this is one of the most important parts of the myth, as F. M. Cornford, who has written a great deal on this point, argues. It seems to me that this was deliberately left vague by Plato, as an important lesson to be learned from the myth itself. There is a great difficulty in establishing whether the reason or purpose that we see working through the universe indicates a being outside the universe, or a reason which is inherent in the universe itself, taken in some sense as a living being, as of course Plato takes it to be. This question, I think, is left unanswered.

But for our purposes this does not matter so much as the question, What is the relationship between reason and the demiurge himself? The craftsman operates with reason upon a material that is given him, and that does not depend on him; this much is clear. The material is just as independent in its existence, so to speak, as is the craftsman himself. The craftsman can only operate with this material up to a point; it acts over against him, and in a certain sense it is itself a source of irregularity, where irregularity is seen as a kind of disorder in the universe itself.

This means that when we ask about disorder, in the context of this passage we must give two kinds of answer. First of all, Plato seems to be saying that when the demiurge makes sensible objects, when he brings them into being, the material upon which he is acting is somehow recalcitrant; it acts against him, it is stubborn, and so it does not come out the way that he intended it to. Hence in that becoming which is the making of things themselves there is an element of defect or lack, and the source of this element, the source of this disorder, is not in our minds but in the receptacle. Professor A. E. Taylor, one of the great commentators on Plato, has tried to suggest that the source of disorder here is simply a lack of understanding on the part of the knower; but this, it seems to me, is not very plausible. There is in fact a lack of intelligibility on the part of the object itself, due to the material in which the form can be realized, only defectively.

That, then, is the first kind of defectiveness. The second kind appears in the behavior of the being itself. When an animal, for example, has offspring, some of these offspring turn out to be monstrosities—a point which Aristotle will discuss more fully. How are we to understand this irregularity in the order of becoming? Here, once again, Plato seems to suggest that the source of this irregularity is some kind of active power of resistance within the material itself. There is somehow a stubborness about it which, when a being comes to act, cannot be altogether overcome.

In a certain sense I am reading something into Plato at this point, because he does not separately discuss this second kind of becoming. He is so much impressed by the idea of static mathematical form that biological forms, it seems to me, are not as adequately treated by him as they are by Aristotle. If one had asked Aristotle about becoming, he would have answered immediately that becoming is itself the clue to understanding all things. It was clear to him that we understand a thing in terms of its behavior. For Aristotle, one comes to know the form of a thing, the essence of a thing, by studying how it behaves—i.e., how it changes, for behavior is a form of change.

With Plato, however, since the primary kind of form for him is mathematical, not biological, one sometimes gets the impression that any kind of change at all is a departure from intelligibility. This, of course, is not true, and Plato himself presumably does not mean that; it is simply a defect in the analogy at this point. Nevertheless, one does sometimes get the impression that mutability of any kind is considered by Plato a kind of defect in intelligibility; and this certainly needs correction in the biological realm, and in fact in any realm but the mathematical.

Before finishing with this discussion of Plato, I should like to cite a passage from the *Timaeus*, because I think that it summarizes many of the points I have just made. He is speaking of the work of the demiurge, and he says:

Taking thought, therefore, he found that, among things that are by nature visible, no work that is without intelligence will ever be better than one that has intelligence, when each is taken as a whole, and moreover that intelligence cannot be present in anything apart from soul. In virtue of this reasoning, when he framed the universe, he fashioned reason within soul and soul within body, to the end that the work he accomplished might be by nature as excellent and perfect as possible. This, then, is how we must say, according to the likely account, that this world came to be, by the god's providence, in very truth a living creature with soul and reason.[1]

Plato is saying here, and he emphasizes this passage, that no work that is without intelligence will ever be better than one which has intelligence. He says elsewhere in the *Timaeus* that this is a key point, namely, that intelligibility and the good are closely related; whatever is good is intelligible, and whatever is intelligible is good. Whatever is less intelligible is less good. Hence, if the demiurge is a good being, which Plato, of course, assumes, he presumably will try to realize intelligibility insofar as he can—he will try to make his realm understood insofar as he can. Thus, when we look at some aspect of nature and find within it intelligibility, it is Plato's key point that this is not only the object of intelligence, but also the product of intelligence as well. This is of course a mighty assumption, and in it we find a striking contrast between Greek and modern thought. Plato is saying here that, if we find something in the universe which can be understood, this is not only the object of the mind, which of course it obviously is, but also the product of mind in some fashion.

In addition to this point, which is heavily stressed, he also brings out a second point, which perhaps I have not made clear: namely, that intelligence cannot be present in anything apart from soul. Now by "soul" he means the principle of life. There cannot be intelligence in anything without a principle of life. This is rather important in the context of the *Timaeus,* for later on he will ask where movement comes from, and he will argue that movement always comes ultimately from the soul. There is a certain difficulty here, for he seems to suggest that before the work of the demiurge in infusing soul into body or matter there is some kind of disorderly motion; nevertheless, it seems safe to say, and most commentators agree, that Plato holds in the last analysis that all forms of motion in the universe must ultimately derive from life principles. And since all things move, all things must therefore have some form of "life," however rudimentary.

This, then, gives us a brief look at the main strands of Platonic thought. There is a common theme in all this: in accounting for the intelligibility of the things of the sensible world, one looks

[1] Francis MacDonald Cornford, *Plato's Cosmology: The "Timaeus" of Plato Translated with a Running Commentary* (London: Routledge and Kegan Paul; New York: Humanities Press, 1952), pp. 33–34.

first of all to the realm of the things which do not change, and then to the realm of the good. The identification of the realm of the intelligible and the realm of the good then allows one to give what we would today call a teleological analysis of the universe. It is "teleological" because it is an analysis in terms of purpose, and the purpose is seen as imposed upon the material by the work of a craftsman, rather than being inherent to the material itself. The material is over against the craftsman, entirely lacking in good and in intelligibility, so that the purpose and the good come from the craftsman. Therefore, when we try to understand things, when the speculative intelligence looks at the universe, the work of an intelligence must be projected upon the universe, seeing order as the work of intelligence and disorder as the product of matter or, to use the more Platonic term, of space, upon which the intelligence has attempted to work. Space is taken in a rather "stufflike" sense, but at any rate it is the agency that is over and against intelligence. We need not concern ourselves here with the question of whether the soul imposed upon the universe has some irrational motions or not. The main outline of the Platonic teleology seems to be clear.

I have spent this much time on Plato because one can understand Aristotle much better against this background. In one sense Aristotle appears as a postscript to this trend of thought, and I think that this is the way he viewed himself. The commonplace remark, of course, is to say that Aristotle rejects the Platonic philosophy of extrinsic, immutable forms outside of the sensible universe; he wants to say that there is no evidence for this sort of doctrine. Aristotle, with his theory of abstraction, wishes to show that the Platonic argument for the reality of these separate forms is invalid, and that the forms can be adequately explained as being within each sensible object. He argues that every sensible being—a man, or an animal of any sort—realizes or is an instance of some particular form, and that this form is perfectly realized in that being.

Once one supposes that the form, the ground for intelligibility, is within beings themselves, there follows a profound consequence for the notion of order and for the whole teleological approach. This consequence is perhaps more far-reaching than Aristotle realized. It follows from this approach that Aristotle is denied a craftsman, since for him natures have always been. He can and does discuss becoming, but only one kind of becoming—the kind that is proper to the nature itself once given. He cannot ask who made these natures, where they came from, or why they are as they are. He has excluded these questions almost by definition. Aristotle's natures have always been there, just as Plato's forms were always there; but Aristotle's natures, which are the sensible objects, have been changing. They come and go, they are generated and corrupted. They are themselves the realm of the changeable, and within the changeable itself Aristotle has found the ground of immortality. He does not seek it outside the sensible world. Although Aristotle does not put it in this way, I think it is fair to say that he finds the ground of immortality and immutability in the species. He declares the species, the essential form, to be the object of science and philosophy. Although, in the tradition of Greek thought, science must be concerned with the immutable order (and this is an assumption that Newton will question radically), and although the order of change must therefore be transcended, Aristotle accomplishes this not by going outside the order of change, but rather by taking the species as his subject matter. Individual men may come and go, but the species, man, is always the same. The nature is always the same, and so it is an adequate object of science. One can have a science of men because there is always man, and man does not change. This is the major reason that Aristotle must at all costs exclude an evolutionary point of view. Such a point of view would have required a very fundamental modification within the teleological scheme he was proposing.

In any case, Aristotle has the forms within the objects. The effect of this, as I have indicated, is to deny him the supposition of a craftsman like the Platonic demiurge. Without a craftsman, however, one cannot see the individual natures as products of purpose, so that teleology here will take on a very different meaning. In looking at giraffes and elephants and horseflies and so on, one cannot say that each of these was fashioned by an intelligence for a particular purpose. Aristotle might have liked a "strong" teleology of this kind, since after all he was a pupil of Plato; nevertheless, it is difficult to find a ground for it in his own system, since he has no craftsman and no reason working at the beginning, upon which form will depend. There is, after all, a profound difference between a demiurge and an unmoved mover.

The demiurge is responsible for the kinds of things there are, as any craftsman is. The unmoved mover is simply responsible for motion of the natures which themselves are already there. It is true that the motions are the clue to these natures, so that there is a profound sense in which the natures themselves do depend upon the unmoved mover. Nevertheless, at first sight at least, it does seem that what has become dependent upon the first cause is simply the movement within the universe, and not the kinds of things that exercise this movement. These kinds are given.

This being the case, then, I suggest that for Aristotle teleology had to be quite different from what it had been for Plato. The passage in which he attempts to define it occurs in the Second Book of the *Physics*.[2] Here he discusses the negative concepts which, as I suggested, are usually the clue to the positive concept; he discusses the varieties of disorder or, as he calls them, chance and spontaneity. For him a chance event is the opposite of the ordered, it is that which is set over against order, where order seems to mean something imposed upon behavior, upon change. Consider a case of biological chance, where the outcome of some process departs from the normal order—for example, an animal produces an offspring that is not quite like the parent or is abnormal in some way or other. Just because it is outside the normal order, Aristotle maintains that it demands a special explanation, one which is in no way derivable from our knowledge of the *telos* of the being itself. Only consequences that *are* derivable from the *telos* (ultimately from the form of the being) can be understood teleologically. This, then, is how Aristotle understands teleology: it arises in the tendency of the being to reproduce, or in general to behave, in the normal way.

What is the evidence for teleology? I would suggest, although this is admittedly not the view of many Aristotelians, that the evidence of teleology for Aristotle is simply and solely regularity of behavior. The fact that it is regularity considered as in some sense "good" does not weaken this claim. I would also like to suggest (although I can do no more here than suggest it) that by adopting this position Aristotle has already taken a giant step to the views of Newton and Darwin, who dismissed teleological forms of explanation, not as invalid, but as scientifically irrelevant. In a sense the Greeks had their Newton and their Darwin in Democritus and Empedocles. Consequently it is very instructive to see, in the passage I mentioned in the *Physics*, the very uneasy way in which Aristotle handles these

[2] Richard McKeon (ed.), *The Basic Works of Aristotle*, the Oxford translation under Sir W. D. Ross (New York: Random House, 1941). The crucial passage from the *Physics*, 2.5.195b31, is found on pp. 243–47.

two thinkers. He feels bound to reject both the atomism of Democritus and the evolutionism of Empedocles as no more than a blind mechanism which can never produce good things. In this kind of context, Aristotle is still a Platonist. When he criticizes Democritus in this famous passage, he criticizes him in just the way that Plato did, and in almost the same words. The difficulty is, however, that Aristotle no longer held the Platonic principle that had made Democritus' position previously seem untenable. Plato could have argued quite consistently against Democritus: we have in the universe about us the evidences of reason and intelligence; how can you possibly hold that the regularities, the intelligibilities, the reason working through the universe, come from the blind (and the word "blind" is important) concourse of atoms? But Aristotle could not use this argument. Democritus after all did suppose that the atoms moved in a regular way, so there was no question about regularities. In Aristotle's own terms, there was no disagreement about formal cause between them, since Democritus admitted formal cause just as much as did Aristotle. The point at issue was not the regularity of the motions of the atoms, but rather whether one could discern reason working through these motions.

Plato held that in fact one had to see this regularity as the work of reason itself and not as something that could issue from the blind. And in the Platonic position, as I have tried to show, this was coherent. But in the Aristotelian world view this is a considerably more difficult thesis to maintain. It seems to me that if Democritus and Aristotle had actually argued this, Aristotle's argument could have been shown to depend rather strongly upon the Platonic presupposition that he himself had questioned. In this particular paragraph Aristotle seems to jump from one idea of disorder to another in a somewhat questionable way. The chance event is defined by him in two ways that at first sight seem only slightly different, but which are, in fact, not easily correlated at all. Sometimes it is represented as something that happens rarely—as the rare event, an irregularity, something outside the ordinary, something that happens for the least part. If that were what is meant by a chance event, it would come very close to some modern definitions of chance in the context of statistics. But this definition of the chance event will not do for a criticism of Democritus, for Democritus is not talking about things that happen for the least part. This is not his meaning of chance at all. What Democritus clearly has in mind here is rather the kind of blind necessity that Plato spoke about: it is simply the result of the workings of a blind agency and has nothing to do with regularity. This is an altogether different notion of disorder: it is the unplanned rather than the rare. One cannot readily move from this sense to the other. And there are, in consequence, two different conceptions of cosmic order implicit in this passage also.

Let me summarize by saying that Aristotle is taking form to be intrinsic to the sensible object instead of outside it. As a general rule, this object acts in a regular way, although occasionally it acts irregularly. This occasional irregularity is attributed to the influence of matter. Why matter should produce irregularity is a very difficult question, and one which I cannot develop in the space allotted me. In brief, though, I should like to suggest that the reason why matter produces irregularity for Aristotle is not at all what it was for Plato. Matter is not an active source of defect, it seems to me, for Aristotle; matter is simply the context, the source of potentiality, to use his own phrase, within which things can happen that alter the natural behavior of material things. If, for example, an acorn is put by itself, say in the drawer of a table, it will always stay an acorn. But if the acorn is put in a pigpen it will not stay an acorn very long. The occurrence of the irregularity, which is the pig eating the acorn—after all, pigs do not usually eat acorns, or if they always did there would not be any oak trees—is due to the fact that the acorn is within a material context; it is, so to speak, in a place where something can happen.

I think that there is an important disagreement or difference of emphasis here between Aristotle and Plato. One is saying that matter is an active source of disorder; the other is saying that matter is a kind of generalized context within which beings can act upon one another and therefore prevent each other from attaining their normal goals. There is also a second point of difference, which I hope can be developed in later discussion. Since for Aristotle teleology or purpose can be *identified* only in terms of normality, it seems to be difficult for him to identify purpose within the natural order other than by regular behavior. Since this is the case, then it becomes quite difficult for Aristotle to exclude the atomistic doctrine of mechanism, even though he does very much want to exclude it. I do not say that it is impossible for him to handle the problem, but he must have a very sophisticated way of doing so. Mechanism, after all, is regular, and if a being always acts toward an end, then we can understand it in terms of this end, whether that being be a Newtonian atom, or a corpuscle, or an Aristotelian animal. Thus there seems to be a kind of slippage within the Aristotelian position toward a view in which an identification of the cosmic order with the good will be both vague and difficult to ground. One is already partway to the rejection of teleology as a significant and irreducible category of natural explanation. The cosmic order of Aristotle, the empiricist, can thus be viewed as somewhere halfway between the teleological order of Plato, consciously directed to the good, and the mechanistic cosmic order of the Newtonians, where considerations of the good are no longer scientifically relevant.

RICHARD S. WESTFALL

Newton and Order

I will not begin with the obvious statement that Isaac Newton based
his work in science on the fundamental conception that nature is an
ordered whole. That assumption he shared with every scientist of
his day and indeed with every educated man. The concept of an
ordered cosmos is a fundamental aspect of our heritage from Greek
thought. The problem, then, is not to establish Newton's conviction
that nature is ordered, since on that plane of generality we can say
nothing that will distinguish him from other men, but to examine
the particular form in which he conceived the order in nature.
When we examine Newton in this way, we discover that his basic
contributions to science were the direct products of his peculiar
conception of order in nature and its relation to the goals of science.
We find, moreover, that his conception of order is a common thread
running through all his work. At first glance his two great books,
the *Principia* and the *Opticks,* present different aspects—the one
abstract and theoretical, the other concrete and experimental. If we
examine the two from the point of view of order, we perceive at
once a fundamental unity of outlook. There is no single key to

RICHARD S. WESTFALL trained at Yale, taught in Iowa for ten years, largely at
Grinnell College. His present work on Sir Isaac Newton grows out of his noted
study *Science and Religion in 17th Century England.* He is now professor in the
Department of History and Logic of Science at Indiana University.

Newton's work. It can be illuminated from a number of angles, each one of which offers a different insight. Among them the concept of order provides one unique and revealing perspective.

Newton was convinced that order in nature presents itself to observation as a set of necessary relations capable of exact mathematical description. The work of science is to uncover these relations. Let us examine this conception of order in comparison to certain others. With seventeenth-century science as a whole it shared a quantitative conception of order on which the possibility of mathematical science rested. Aristotelian science, in contrast, had been qualitative. The properties by which the four elements were defined, for example, were wetness, dryness, heat, and cold; these were ultimate properties which could not be referred to others yet more fundamental. The possibility of quantitative treatment was ruled out by the grouping of qualities in pairs of opposites; both wetness and dryness, both heat and cold, both lightness and heaviness were considered as positive qualities forming the two ends of a scale. On such a scale, which lacked a fixed point, measurement was impossible. The mechanical philosophy of the seventeenth century reacted against Aristotle to assert that only the quantitative properties of a body, its size and shape, and with Newton its mass, are real; other qualities, the secondary qualities, are the responses of sentient beings to the motion of particles endowed merely with size, shape, and mass. The secondary qualities, moreover, were conceived not as opposites but as different quantities of the same thing. Cold, for example, ceased to be considered as a positive quality and became merely a small quantity of heat. No body was positively light, but some were less heavy than others. Aspects of Newton's work are best seen in this light—his scale temperatures, for example, and, more importantly, his conclusions about colors. With the discovery of the composition of white light he demonstrated that every sensation of color is associated with a ray having a unique index of refraction. As Newton remarked in his first paper, the science of colors was now found to be as mathematical as any part of optics.

The quantitative, mathematical aspect of Newton's conception of order distinguished it from the Aristotelian. The extent to which he carried mathematical description distinguished it from others of the seventeenth century. Before Newton, Galileo had revolutionized the science of mechanics with the concept of inertia. To achieve it he had abstracted his thought from the world of physical reality to an ideal world in which perfectly round balls roll on perfectly smooth planes. In this ideal world of abstract mathematical relations he successfully deduced the mathematical equations that describe uniform and accelerated motion. The ideal world, moreover, gave the key to understanding motion in the physical world, which approaches the ideal but fails to realize it completely because of the grossness and imperfection of matter. Newton carried Galileo's work a step further. Not only does the abstract world of mathematical relations define the ideal case of motion, but the extent to which motion in the physical world fails to realize the ideal is itself subject to mathematical treatment. Galileo's perfectly round balls and perfectly smooth planes do not exist, but the friction between Gilbert's cloth untrue and Sullivan's elliptical billiard balls can be measured and entered in the equation for the ideal case. Galileo had discovered that projectiles in a vacuum trace out parabolas. Real projectiles are retarded by the air, but its resistance can be measured and the deformation of the parabola described. In the ideal case of perfect elasticity, a body rebounds from a solid obstacle with the normal component of its velocity exactly reversed; no body is perfectly elastic, but its index of elasticity can be computed. In Newton's conception of order the ideal case, as used by Galileo, became as it were the first term of an infinite series. By adding corrective terms, mathematical physics could extend its description to any chosen degree of precision.

A second feature of Newton's conception of order was its implicit assertion of the uniformity of nature. From the Greek point of view the eternal truths of mathematics had been applicable primarily to the immutable heavens; manifestly they did not describe the constant change and corruption of the mundane world. Hence Aristotle had divided the cosmos at the sphere of the moon; the perfection and changelessness of the celestial realm required even a different matter, a fifth element or quintessence, distinct from the four elements of the corruptible world. Again Newton was not unique in asserting the uniformity of nature. Before him both Galileo and Descartes, to name no others, had affirmed it. Galileo had preceded him in applying the geometry of the heavens to terrestrial motion. The unique feature of Newton in this respect was his application of terrestrial mathematics to the heavens. The ideal case of motion, we have said, is only the first term of an infinite series. This is true of the heavens as well. Where astronomers before him had sought the perfect figure to describe orbits—the circle and, with Kepler, the ellipse—Newton showed that this is only the first term to which a multitude of inequalities, all subject to mathematical treatment, must be added to increase precision. The elliptical orbit of the moon is an ideal figure. In the second edition of the *Principia* Newton calculated five inequalities that deform the ellipse. Thus all of nature follows a uniform pattern, not of ideal mathematical relations, but of mathematically computable deviations from the ideal relations.

In so far as the mathematical definition of order is concerned, Newton was distinguished from his contemporaries by the rigor with which he applied it. He was distinguished from them still more by the contention that order thus defined is the proper object of scientific investigation. Such an ideal of scientific study is so readily accepted today that it is difficult to realize its novelty in the seventeenth century. It is difficult to understand that it is readily accepted today primarily because of the example of Newton, although it should be added that here again he followed a path earlier indicated by others, notably Galileo. Let us look back again briefly to the Aristotelian ideal of science, an ideal that prevailed until well into the seventeenth century.

To Aristotle a scientific demonstration was the demonstration of effects from necessary causes. The object of scientific investigation was not merely order but causes, although of course he held that causes form an ordered hierarchy. The two best known theoreticians of scientific method in the seventeenth century, Francis Bacon and René Descartes, both accepted the Aristotelian ideal of demonstration through necessary causes. Descartes, with whom one cannot avoid comparing Newton, was obsessed with the problem of certainty. In his famous exercise of systematic doubting he tried to state the problem in the most extreme form. In the search for something absolutely certain, he resolved to doubt everything for which he could find any reason to doubt. Let me assume, he said, that the universe is governed by an evil genius dedicated to deceiving me. Can I in this case, can I with the whole cosmos as it were working against me, find some immovable foothold of certainty? His answer was the famous *"cogito,"* which he used in a manner analogous to a geometric axiom. From a certain premise, by a process of reasoning modeled on geometry, he must arrive at certain conclusions. Descartes was impressed by geometry; in that science alone past ages had built something secure. The problem was to rebuild philosophy, including natural philosophy, with the instrument of mathematics. Descartes believed in order. He believed in mathematical order, and he tried to bring certainty into science by equating it with mathematics. Thus matter was equated with extension, that is, with geometrical space, and in his treatise *Le Monde* he undertook to show that, given matter and motion, a universe such as ours must result. Note that the verb is "must," not "might." In an early version of the *Discourse on Method* he discussed a problem facing optics in his age, a problem he later solved triumphantly. Spherical lenses do not refract light to a perfect focus; what is the shape of a lens that will do so? To solve the problem, Descartes said, we must first know the law of refraction. To learn the law of refraction we must first know the manner in which light traverses transparent media; to know this we must know the nature of the action of light, which in turn requires that we know what a natural potency is in general. When we know the first term, we can retrace the series and arrive at the shape of the lens. Here is the Cartesian ideal of science —to start with necessary principles from which effects can be deduced with certainty. Cartesian science was a priori. Descartes distrusted the information of the senses. Reason alone, working from certain principles, could arrive at truth, demonstrating phenomena from necessary causes.

Newton's position was far more empirical. Science begins with observation and confirms its conclusions by observation. Such a procedure cannot lead to the certainty that Descartes desired. We are not gods, and the imperfect certainty of observation is the best that our human condition allows. Since nature is quantitative, her phenomena are quantitatively related. The work of science is to discover these relations and to state them with such rigor that mathematical demonstration lends its precision to the empirical facts supplied by observation. Mathematical order rigorously demonstrated constitutes science. From Newton's point of view such order is a demonstrated conclusion rather than a necessary cause. Order itself must have a cause. Perhaps it stems from physical principles; perhaps it is the direct product of the will of God.

Newton was not in the least opposed to investigating the cause of order. In the Queries attached to the *Opticks* he detailed a program of research for science:

What is there in places almost empty of Matter, and whence is it that the Sun and Planets gravitate towards one another, without dense Matter between them? Whence is it that Nature doth nothing in vain; and whence arises all that Order and Beauty which we see in the World? To what end are Comets, and whence is it that Planets move all one and the same way in Orbs concentrick, while Comets move all manner of ways in Orbs very excentrick; and what hinders the fix'd Stars from falling upon one another? [1]

The passage goes on to assert Newton's opinion that God is the source of the regularities mentioned. In other places he ascribed gravity to the workings of an aether. In either case, however, demonstrated order is a fact independent of its cause, and the first task of science is to discover order.

The famous quarrel between Newton and Robert Hooke as to who discovered the law of gravity hinges on this conception of science. Years before the *Principia* appeared, Hooke had suggested in print that the orbits of the planets were to be explained by an attraction from the sun. He had even suggested the inverse square law in a letter to Newton. When the *Principia* was submitted to the Royal Society, Hooke thought he had been robbed; and, since he was not a shrinking violet, he said as much. The scorn with which Newton greeted this claim is a thing wonderful to behold—absolute and devastating. What? Did Hooke think science was a collection of bright ideas? Bright ideas were cheap enough, and he could have them as readily as Hooke. The force of his work lay in the mathematical demonstrations. He had demonstrated that a centripetal force acting under an inverse square law would hold a planet in an elliptical orbit. He had shown that under an inverse square law a spherical body attracts bodies external to it as though its mass were concentrated at its center. Therefore the force of gravity at the surface of the earth, removed from the center by the earth's radius, could be compared to the force holding the moon, at its distance from the center, in its elliptical orbit. Order thus demonstrated with mathematical rigor constituted science. Hooke, it might be added,

---

[1] Isaac Newton, *Opticks,* based on the fourth edition (New York: Dover Publications, 1952), p. 369.

never understood what Newton was saying; he apparently went to his grave convinced that Newton had plagiarized from him.

The law of gravity brings us to Newton's central contribution, as it appears to me, to physics—the concept of force. Force, to Newton, is the name attached to one type of mathematical order. To understand the Newtonian idea of force let us turn back again to Descartes, since the idea of force is part of Newton's reaction to Descartes. In so far as vague ideas of force had appeared in natural philosophy before him, Descartes rejected them as one aspect of the human tendency to project subjective sensations onto physical nature. Virtues, sympathies, forces—they are all rejected by Cartesian physics under the disdainful label of occult qualities. In the physical world there is merely matter in motion, and every phenomenon is ultimately caused by the impact of one moving particle of matter upon another. Consider the explanation of gravity. The earth is the center of a small vortex of whirling matter. Circular motion always produces a centrifugal tendency, but nature is a plenum so that all matter cannot fly away from the center. Those bits with a superior centrifugal tendency will make their way outward by forcing those with less toward the center. What we call weight is merely a deficiency in centrifugal force. Again, consider his explanation of magnetic attraction, perhaps the supreme achievement of Cartesian ingenuity and one that always leaves me undecided whether to gasp in amazement or merely to laugh. Matter exists in three different forms: gross particles of which physical bodies in the ordinary use of that term are composed; air, which consists of tiny perfect spheres; and what he calls the first element, which, to be brief about it, fills up all the chinks. Between the spherical particles of air there are continuous passages, and in these the first element sometimes congeals into long corkscrew-shaped pieces with a sort of concave triangular cross section—his channeled pieces, *parties cannelées*. Some materials, notably iron, have pores of identical shape, and magnetic attraction is caused by the motion of the *parties cannelées* through the corkscrew pores. Very well, you may say, but which way are these corkscrews going to turn—with a left-hand thread or a right-hand thread? Suppose both types of *parties cannelées* get produced—then what? To which Descartes replies: Exactly; there are two types of *parties cannelées;* and are there not two types of magnetic poles, which we label north and south?

From these two examples we can see the inherent contradiction never eliminated from Cartesian physics. Descartes wanted to mathematize physics, but he could never bring particular phenomena under mathematical treatment. Since the ultimate term of a Cartesian explanation was the motion of a particle which by definition could not be observed but only imagined, his physics always ended in the qualitative description of imaginary microscopic machines. The only exception was his successful enunciation of the law of sines in optics, which unlike the rest of his physics was simply the statement of a mathematical relation. Even here he felt obliged to justify it by a spurious mechanical explanation.

The central feature of Newtonian physics is the deliberate cutting through the fabric of qualitative description to attain the end that Descartes himself desired, a quantitative science. The concept of force was a deliberate abstraction that moved the investigation onto a new plane. Whenever a body is accelerated, whenever its constant motion in a straight line is changed in any way, force is exerted. Earlier in the seventeenth century Galileo had defined acceleration. For a given acceleration, Newton said, force is proportional to the mass of the accelerated body. It was not by accident that both the concept of mass and the concept of force first emerged clearly in the *Principia*. Force was a mathematical relation that avoided the question of cause. The concept of a universal force, the force of gravity, rested on the mathematical order of nature. Because the acceleration of a falling apple could be correlated with the deviation of the moon's orbit from a straight line, because the acceleration of Mercury could be correlated with those of the other planets, Newton could postulate a universal force of gravity.

Cartesian physicists found the concept of force impossible to accept. When the Dutch scientist Christian Huygens heard that Newton was publishing a theory of the universe, he wrote to a friend that he hoped it would not include any suppositions such as attraction. Alas, it did, and the Cartesians were horrified. The idea that matter had a power of attraction was a return to occult qualities of scholastic science. Newton replied to their accusation in the General Scholium which he added to the second edition, and in the Queries of the *Opticks*.

"The hypothesis of vortices," he began, "is pressed with many difficulties." The difficulties can be summed up in one phrase, mathematical inconsistency. The laws of vortical motion require certain relations that do not correspond to those actually observed in the solar system. This was to slay Cartesianism with the weapon of its own choice, mathematical order.

To tell us that every species of things is endowed with an occult specific quality by which it acts and produces manifest effects is to tell us nothing, [he continued in the Queries,] but to derive two or three general principles of motion from phenomena, and afterward to tell us how the properties and actions of all corporeal things follow from those manifest principles, would be a very great step in philosophy, though the causes of those principles were not yet discovered, and therefore I scruple not to propose the principles of motion above mentioned [that is, attractive forces], they being of very general extent, and leave their causes to be found out.[2]

Perhaps nothing reveals the difference between the ideals of Newtonian and Cartesian science more clearly than certain letters written by Leibniz after the *Principia* appeared. Leibniz was not prepared to reject the vortex; it explained something that Newton's law could not explain—the fact that all of the planets revolve about the sun in virtually the same plane. By Newton's law they could be in any plane; the fact that they are all in one plane seemed to require a vortex to carry them along. Leibniz, in other words, was not satisfied when Newton presented mere mathematical order. He demanded a cause.

Leibniz' letters suggest the other objection of Cartesian science to Newton. If force is not an occult quality, what is it? To this demand the General Scholium replied, *"Hypotheses non fingo"* (I do not frame hypotheses). In one sense the statement is manifestly false. Newton did frame hypotheses—and on the very question of gravity. Gravity was either the direct result of the action of God, or it was the result of an aethereal medium. Nevertheless, Newton's phrase is an accurate statement of his conception of science. Gravity was an observed mathematical order in the universe, and the fact of order was a valid and useful conclusion apart from the designation of the cause of order. "I do not need to frame hypotheses," might have been a better statement of Newton's position. "I can frame them; I do frame them; but I do not need to frame them." The discovery of order is itself the proper goal of science. More than that, to frame a hypothesis is to pollute demonstration with speculation. The mathematical relation called gravity has been demonstrated with the maximum rigor that science allows. At the moment we cannot speak

[2] *Ibid.,* pp. 401–2.

with any certainty of the cause of gravity. The rigor of science then demands either that we do not frame hypotheses, or at least that we separate our hypotheses clearly from conclusions that are not speculative.

If we turn to Newton's work in optics we find that the same conception of mathematical order is its distinguishing feature. The central point of Newton's *Opticks* is the assertion that ordinary light is a composition of heterogeneous rays, each of which has its own distinct properties. Until Newton's time only one of these properties had been observed, the rays' capacity to excite given sensations of color. That was the rub. Sensations could never be reduced to quantitative treatment. Newton discovered two new properties of rays which were subject to quantitative treatment, and in his hands the color of a ray, that is, the sensation it excites, became merely a convenient label. Each ray is distinguished by its unique index of refraction and by a unique reflexibility measured by the thickness of the film that reflects it. As in the *Principia,* mathematical order was asserted as a scientific discovery. *Mutatis mutandis,* virtually the same argument took place over both books. Cartesian science could not recognize the force of a demonstration concluding in order. Newton referred to the "disposition" of rays to be refracted at a given angle; the word "disposition" smacked of occult qualities. Newton has told us, Huygens complained, that from their origin rays of light are different; he has not told us in what this difference consists. In a word, he has not told us the cause.

In this case, also, Newton had a hypothesis, and he could probably have speeded the acceptance of his work by stating it from the beginning. He held a corpuscular theory of light and believed that the particles of which red rays consist are larger than the particles of blue ones. Newton's theory of colors would have been more acceptable to his age with the hypothesis added, but here also he was reluctant to dilute a demonstration of order with speculations as to its cause. When we consider that his corpuscular theory was overthrown a century after his death, and that the wave theory has since been supplemented by a new corpuscular one, we must agree that he was right not to tie his theory of color to a speculative conception of light.

We can also use Newton's conception of mathematical order to illuminate his experimental work. His basic experiment on light was the projection of a spectrum from a prism onto a screen. A small round beam of white light was projected as an oblong image which displayed the colors of the rainbow in order. This experiment was not entirely new. Before Newton both the colors and the dispersion of the beam had been explained as modifications of the light produced by the prism. No one had bothered to measure the dispersion. Newton was convinced that they arose from the differential refraction of the individual rays. How was he to demonstrate his position? In what he labeled the *experimentum crucis,* the experiment where the road divides, he isolated individual rays emerging from the prism and refracted them through a second prism. In the second prism there was no further dispersion. The rays that were refracted more sharply in the first prism were refracted more sharply in the second. What is more important, each ray displayed a constant index of refraction at both prisms. The ultimate force of the argument lay in its demonstration of mathematical order.

One of the men who challenged Newton's work on colors was a Jesuit named Anthony Lucas. To Newton's experiments he replied with experiments of his own which seemed to point toward different conclusions. Newton refused to discuss them at first, but referred Lucas back to the *experimentum crucis.* It is not number of experiments but weight that counts, he wrote; and, where one will do, what need of many? Lucas was indignant with this reply. Newton had some experiments, he had others; by what criterion did Newton assert that his were the more weighty? Lucas' argument has a certain plausibility at first sight, but, as we examine it, the plausibility is seen to depend on the denial of order. Each experiment is unique. Its outcome may contradict that of another. Hence we collect as many experiments as possible and try to conclude apparently by counting up the two sides. If we insist on the logic of Lucas' position, it appears to me, we are led to the assertion of chaos. Indeed Lucas did conclude that the colors of the spectrum are caused by accident. Newton's experimentation, on the other hand, instead of accumulating instances, followed by a logical process of development, with the outcome of one experiment helping to frame the next. Since nature is orderly, two experiments on the same problem cannot contradict one another. A contradiction can only be apparent, and one or the other must be mistaken. Hence the assertion that one experiment can suffice. When he chose to do so, he easily pointed out the defects in Lucas' experiments.

Newton the experimenter can be contrasted with Descartes. In the *Discourse* Descartes advised the natural philosopher to concentrate on ordinary phenomena. Extraordinary ones were more apt to confuse than to enlighten. Newton's work implicitly denied this. Already as an undergraduate he observed a number of special phenomena that seemed of critical importance to him—phenomena concerned with capillary action, the surface tension of fluids, and the expansion of gases to mention some of them. One can follow Newton's speculations on nature over a period of nearly fifty years and find him continuing to cite the same phenomena as evidence. Implicitly he was affirming that no phenomena can happen by chance. All are the inevitable result of necessary principles, and the extraordinary may reveal the principles at work more clearly than the common. Experiments may produce phenomena that are extraordinary in the full sense of the word—phenomena that transcend the ordinary, phenomena that nature unmolested does not display. Experimentation is a process of putting questions to nature; order in nature constrains her to reply. Intelligent experimentation consists in defining the questions so precisely that the answer is free of ambiguity. Thus Newton's experiments on light produced some very extraordinary phenomena indeed, phenomena with no resemblance whatever to natural phenomena. Their very artificiality was the measure of Newton's success in exploiting the order of nature to answer his questions.

Both in the *Principia* and in the *Opticks* the goal of Newtonian science was the description of mathematical order in nature. More than a little of the role he has played in the history of science derives from the demonstration contained in each work of what physics can achieve when it explicitly accepts mathematical order at the term of investigation.

JOHN C. GREENE

The Concept of Order
in Darwinism

The question of the Darwinian concept of order is one which
Darwin himself never posed. Disclaiming competence as a philosopher, he confined himself pretty much to scientific problems. His
concept of order was implicit rather than explicit. The same cannot
be said of Herbert Spencer and Thomas Henry Huxley, the other
two members of the great triumvirate of English Darwinism.
Spencer devoted his mature years to working out a philosophical
synthesis based on evolutionary concepts, and Huxley, though
trained as a biologist, became the chief exponent of Darwinism in
England. Their writings, taken in conjunction with Darwin's own
work, provide a basis for investigating the Darwinian concept of
order.

The starting point of the Darwinian approach to nature was the
mechanical philosophy of the seventeenth-century, the idea of nature as a law-bound system of matter in motion. Herbert Spencer's
sole purpose in philosophy, he explained to his American disciple
John Fiske, was "the interpretation of all concrete phenomena in

JOHN C. GREENE has been professor of history at the University of Kansas and has
now taken a permanent position at the University of Connecticut. His specialty
is the genesis of evolutionary conceptions in natural science and in social thought,
including the conflict between science and religion in Western thought. He is
known for his books, *Death of Adam* and *Darwin and the Modern World View*,
both of which have appeared in paperback.

terms of the redistribution of matter and motion." Likewise, Huxley declared it to be "the fundamental proposition of Evolution" that "the whole world, living and not living, is the result of the mutual interaction, according to definite laws, of the forces possessed by the molecules of which the primitive nebulosity of the universe was composed." [1] This view, Huxley added, was undoubtedly held in its essentials by René Descartes, the spirit of whose *Principles of Philosophy* had been revived in the "profound and vigourous writings of Mr. Spencer."

From a certain point of view Huxley was right in linking Spencer and Darwinism with Descartes. It was Descartes who said, "Give me extension and movement and I will remake the world," and who, accordingly, proposed the first mechanical theory of the origin and development of the stars, solar system, and earth from a primitive even distribution of matter throughout space. Newton was horrified at the suggestion that the present state of nature could be derived from a previous one by "feigning hypotheses to explain all things mechanically." Science, he declared, was not concerned with the origins of the structures of nature, but with

. . . these and such like Questions. . . . Whence is it that Nature doth nothing in vain; and whence arises all that Order and Beauty which we see in the World? To what end are Comets, and whence is it Planets move all one and the same way in Orbs concentrick, while Comets move all manner of ways in Orbs very excentrick. . . . How came the Bodies of Animals to be contrived with so much Art, and for what ends were their several Parts? [2]

Newton's concept of nature was an unstable compound of two different views: (1) The idea of nature as a law-bound system of matter in motion, and (2) the idea of nature as a framework of rationally contrived structures fitted as a stage for the activities of intelligent beings. The first component came to him from the seventeenth-century revolution in physics and cosmology that began with Galileo and Descartes and found consummate expression in his own *Principia*. The second component was derived from Christian natural theology, from the static version of the doctrine of creation in the special form this doctrine assumed in the late seventeenth

---

[1] Thomas Henry Huxley, "Evolution in Biology," *Darwiniana: Essays* (New York: D. Appleton and Co., 1908), p. 206. Essay first published in 1878 in *Encyclopaedia Britannica*, 9th ed., Vol. VIII.

[2] Isaac Newton, *Opticks: Or a Treatise of the Reflections, Refractions, Inflections and Colours of Light* (4th ed.; London, 1730), p. 343.

century. In the long run, however, the two views of nature which Newton and his English colleagues attempted to fuse into a single view proved incompatible. If nature was really a system of particles of matter in motion such that every state of the system was predictable by mathematical rule from previous states, it was hard to see how any particular state of the system could be regarded as initial or final, or why any particular result of the functioning of the system should be regarded as especially designed to be as it was. Indeed, the mechanical view of nature presented an irresistible temptation to speculative minds to explain the origin of the present structures of nature by imagining a previous state of the system of matter in motion from which they must inevitably have been produced by the operation of the laws of nature. In astronomy, this kind of speculation led from Descartes to Immanuel Kant, Pierre Simon de Laplace, Sir William Herschel, and the nebular hypothesis. In geology it produced the thoroughgoing uniformitarianism of James Hutton and Sir Charles Lyell. In biology, it led to Darwin through George Louis Leclerc de Buffon, Erasmus Darwin, Jean de Lamarck, and others. From this point of view, Darwin's theory of evolution by natural selection was the logical outcome of the Cartesian concept of nature as a law-bound system of matter in motion.

But was the Darwinian view of nature nothing more than Descartes' mechanical philosophy? Was Darwin simply a latter-day Descartes? Obviously not, but what was the new element that had altered the general view of nature in the two hundred years intervening between Descartes and Darwin? It was not the notion of universal change, not the idea of deriving the present state of nature from previous states. It was rather the idea of progress, the idea that the operations of the system of matter in motion could produce not merely new configurations of matter but also new levels of being, the sentient emerging from the purely physical, the rational from the merely sentient. For Descartes, matter and mind were two radically different things; matter was extended substance, mind thinking substance. That the motions of matter should produce thinking beings was inconceivable. It was equally inconceivable to those who, like Newton, subscribed to a static version of the doctrine of creation. From their point of view, matter existed to provide a stage for the activities of intelligent, moral beings. The material structures of nature were wisely designed to subserve this end. But, as evidences of mutability in the seemingly permanent structures of nature accumulated and as the implication of universal mutability latent in the mechanical view of nature was gradually drawn out, it slowly became apparent that the inorganic environment was subject to constant slow change. From this it was but a step to recognizing that, if the inorganic environment was constantly changing, organic beings must change too or perish through lack of adaptation. Mutability must be as universal in the organic world as in the inorganic.

Yet another step remained to be taken. Universal change is one thing, evolution quite another. The concept of evolution involves the idea of directional change, of the gradual emergence of new levels of organization. It was Lamarck who took this step, who conceived the system of matter in motion as capable of producing rudimentary forms of life which then underwent gradual transformation and complication until the whole existing array of plant and animal forms, including man, had been produced. Cartesian dualism was explicitly rejected. For Lamarck, mind was simply an aspect of the functioning of living organisms produced in the long course of time by the operations of the material system.

Darwin, then, did not invent the concept of evolution. He had no need to, for it had already been promulgated. With Lamarck's general concept of a gradual evolution of living beings from nonliving matter and of higher from lower forms of life through the operations of a material system during vast eons of time, Darwin was in substantial agreement. But, being more cautious and less philosophic than Lamarck, he declined to push his generalizations beyond what the evidence would support. Since it did not yet fully support the descent of all animals, much less of all animals and plants, from a single set of ancestors, Darwin did not affirm this. Nor did he think the time had come to attack the problem of the origins of life. But he clearly believed that it was only a matter of time until these problems would be resolved in accordance with a general evolutionism.

It was with respect to the mechanism, or general process, by which organic change was effected that Darwin disagreed fundamentally with Lamarck, and this disagreement was to have profound implications for the philosophy of nature. Lamarck assumed a natural tendency toward complication of organization. At times he spoke vaguely of "the cause that tends toward complication." More specifically, he assumed that organisms were endowed by nature with a capacity to undergo organic change in response to the demands of a changing environment. Through use and disuse, organs developed or atrophied, and these acquired characters, Lamarck thought, were transmitted to succeeding generations. In unusual situations, entirely new organs developed in response to the "felt needs" of the organisms involved. For Lamarck, progress was built into organic nature. It proceeded through the mechanisms of organic response to the changing demands of the environment. Animals did not become extinct; they simply changed. And the long-run direction of change was toward ever higher, ever more complex forms of organization.

Darwin conceived the process of organic change rather differently. He agreed that organs and instincts were modified through use and disuse and that these modifications were inherited, at least in some cases. But he placed his main reliance on congenital variations, slight differences at birth resulting from the mysterious functioning of the mechanism of heredity. If these variations happened to be such as to afford the organism possessing them some advantage in the struggle for food, living space, a mate, and so forth, that organism would be more likely to survive and reproduce its kind. In due course the organisms possessing the advantageous character would outnumber and perhaps completely supplant other organisms. Thus, by a process of random variation, struggle for existence, and natural selection, populations would undergo slow modification in directions dictated by the requirements for survival. This theory of natural selection, supported by mountains of evidence Darwin had piled up in the course of twenty years of research, converted the scientific community and the educated world at large to belief in organic evolution and thus paved the way for the acceptance in many quarters of a general evolutionism—cosmic, biological, and social. At the same time it gave that general evolutionism a definite character and structure, differentiating it from other evolutionary philosophies.

But, although it was Darwin who converted the scientific community to belief in organic evolution, it was Herbert Spencer who first set forth the general view of reality that was to acquire the sanction of Darwin's name. Two years before Darwin published his *Origin of Species,* Spencer had outlined an evolutionary philosophy embracing the universe and man. As bold and speculative as Darwin was cautious and empirical, Spencer early accepted the nebular hypothesis in astronomy and Lamarck's developmental hypothesis in biology. To these he added his own kind of social evolutionism, based on concepts of population pressure, struggle for existence, and survival of the fittest. By 1857 he had arrived at a grand synthesis of human knowledge in terms of the idea of progressive development. In every branch of science, he declared in his essay "Progress: Its Law and Cause," there was evidence of a gradual and necessary progression from homogeneity to heterogeneity, from lower and simpler states of organization to higher and more complex ones. Progress was "not an accident, not a thing within human control, but a beneficent necessity."

After the publication of Darwin's *Origin of Species,* Spencer was in a position to subsume both biological and social evolution under the concept of natural selection. In the light of Darwin's theory, progress could no longer be regarded as synonymous with change (since natural selection might in some cases maintain the status quo or produce retrogression to simpler levels of organization), but the progressive tendency of the struggle for existence in the long run seemed beyond doubt. In his *First Principles* Spencer substituted the term "evolution" for his earlier term "progress," as being less anthropocentric and teleological in connotation, and promulgated a new and improved version of the law governing the realms of nature and history: "Evolution," he wrote, "is an integration of matter and concomitant dissipation of motion; during which the matter passes from an indefinite, incoherent homogeneity to a definite, coherent heterogeneity; and during which the retained motion undergoes a parallel transformation."

With respect to physical phenomena, Spencer drew on the idea of the conservation of energy (or "force," as he called it) and leaned heavily on the nebular hypothesis. Biology and sociology were unified by the theory of natural selection.

As with organic evolution, [he wrote,] so with super-organic evolution. Though, taking the entire assemblage of societies, evolution may be held inevitable as an ultimate effect of the co-operating factors, intrinsic and extrinsic, acting on them all through indefinite periods of time; yet it cannot be held inevitable in each particular society, or even probable. A social organism, like an individual organism, undergoes modifications until it comes into equilibrium with environing conditions; and thereupon continues without further change of structure. When the conditions are changed meteorologically, or geologically, or by alterations in the Flora and Fauna, or by migration consequent on pressure of population, or by flight before usurping races, some change of social structure is entailed. But this change does not necessarily imply advance. Often it is towards neither a higher nor a lower structure. Where the habitat entails modes of life that are inferior, some degradation results. Only occasionally is the new combination of factors such as to cause a change constituting a step in social evolution, and initiating a social type which spreads and supplants inferior social types. For with these super-organic aggregates, as with the organic aggregates, progression in some produces retrogression in others: the more-evolved societies drive the less-evolved societies into unfavorable habitats; and so entail on them decrease of size, or decay of structure.[3]

It appears, then, that Darwinism (or at least English Darwinism) might better be called Spencerianism.

Darwin himself eschewed philosophical speculation, but his general ideas, so far as we can infer them from his writings and correspondence, seem to have been in harmony with Spencer's. Nature was a law-bound system of matter in motion. Progress, though not inevitable in any particular case, was the necessary long-run outcome of natural selection in both nature and history. In *The Descent of Man,* Darwin out-Spencers Spencer in proclaiming the beneficent effects of natural selection:

Man, like every other animal, has no doubt advanced to his present high condition through a struggle for existence consequent on his rapid multiplication; and if he is to advance still higher, it is to be feared that he must remain subject to a severe struggle. Otherwise he would sink into indolence, and the more gifted men would not be more successful in the battle of life than the less gifted. Hence our natural rate of increase, though leading to many and obvious evils, must not be greatly diminished by any means. There should be open competition for all men; and the most able should not be prevented by laws or customs from succeeding best and rearing the largest number of offspring.[4]

Huxley took sharp exception to Spencer's attempt to derive ethics from the concepts of evolutionary biology, but in other respects he shared the Spencerian point of view:

Harmonious order governing eternally continuous progress—the web and woof of matter and force interweaving by slow degrees, without a broken thread, that veil which lies between us and the Infinite—that universe which alone we know or can know; such is the picture which science draws of the world, and in proportion as any part of that picture is in unison with the rest, so may we feel sure that it is rightly painted.[5]

[3] Herbert Spencer, *The Principles of Sociology* (New York: D. Appleton and Co., 1877), I, 106–8.

[4] Charles Darwin, *The Descent of Man, and Selection in Relation to Sex* (2nd ed.; New York: 1886), p. 618.

[5] Thomas Henry Huxley, "The Origin of Species," *Darwiniana: Essays*, p. 58. Essay first published in the *Westminster Review*, April, 1860.

Except for their literary quality, these words might as well have been penned by Spencer as by Huxley.

From the point of view of the Darwinians themselves, Darwinism was simply the familiar mechanical view of nature extended to account not only for the origin of stars, solar system, and earth but also of vegetative, sentient, and rational life. This extension seemed natural and inevitable, but it was to have revolutionary consequences little dreamed of by those who inaugurated it. By making mind derivative from matter, and upsetting the hierarchy of levels of being, it destroyed the very basis upon which confidence in the order of nature had rested. In the Cartesian and Newtonian cosmologies, order was imposed on nature by the fiat of the Creator, who created matter with certain properties and endowed it with motion. To Newton it seemed probable that "God in the Beginning form'd Matter in solid, massy, hard, impenetrable, moveable Particles of such Sizes and Figures, and with such other Properties, and such Proportion to Space, as most conduced to the End for which he form'd them," [6] and that the same God set these particles in order so as to produce from the beginning the harmonious universe that appears before our eyes. Descartes, and after him Kant, preferred to let God create matter in an unorganized state, endowing it with properties that would insure the evolution of an orderly universe by the operation of natural laws. In either case, the order visible in the universe was proof of God's existence, and God was the cause of that order. Matter, said Kant, was

. . . bound to certain laws, and when it is freely abandoned to these laws it must necessarily bring forth beautiful combinations. It has no freedom to deviate from this perfect plan. Since it is thus subject to a supremely wise purpose, it must necessarily have been put into such harmonious relationships by a First Cause ruling over it; and *there is a God, just because nature even in chaos cannot proceed otherwise than regularly and according to order.*[7]

Strong overtones of a similar Christian providentialism and mechanized natural theology are to be found in the writings of the Darwinians a century later. "Every increment of knowledge," Spencer declared, "goes to show that constancy is an essential attri-

---

[6] Newton, *Opticks,* p. 376.
[7] Immanuel Kant, *Universal Natural History and Theory of the Heavens* . . . , in William Hastie (ed. and trans.) , *Kant's Cosmogony* . . . (Glasgow, 1900) , p. 26 [italics added].

bute of the Divine rule. . . . And for the end of these unbending ordinances of nature—we find it to be the universal good." Or again: "Almost all men of enlightened views agree that man is essentially a progressive being—that he was intended to be so by the Creator—and that there are implanted in him desires for improvement, and aspirations after perfection, ultimately tending to produce a higher moral and intellectual condition of the world." [8] In like vein, Darwin conceived the process of natural selection as the means whereby a wise Creator had brought about adaptation and improvement in the organic world: "And as natural selection works solely by and for the good of each being, all corporeal and mental endowments will tend to progress toward perfection." [9] Huxley, too, joined the chorus. "Harmonious order governing eternally continuous progress," "the providential order established in the world of life"—these phrases reveal the influence of Christian providentialism and nineteenth-century optimism on Darwinian thought.

But, whereas Newton and Kant had argued confidently from the order visible in nature to the Creator God responsible for that order, the Darwinians found themselves increasingly unable and unwilling to do so. Newton's argument had been based on the design of the structures of nature, as, for example, the rotation and revolution of the planets and their satellites in the same direction in approximately the same plane. But this kind of physico-theology, immortalized in the nineteenth century in William Paley's *Natural Theology* (1802), fell to the ground when Buffon, Kant, Laplace, and others showed that the uniformities observed in the solar system could be derived from a previous state of the system of matter in motion through the operation of natural laws, and Darwin showed that natural selection could account for the adaptations in the organic world on which Paley had relied so heavily.

There still remained Kant's idea that the orderly effects produced by the functioning of the world machine proved that the machine with its laws, elements, and forces had been made in wisdom and foreordained to produce good and beautiful results. But here, too, the Darwinians began to have misgivings. True, there was progress

[8] Herbert Spencer, *Social Statics: Or, the Conditions Essential to Human Happiness Specified, and the First of Them Developed* (London, 1850) , p. 53. The second quotation is from an article by Spencer in *The Nonconformist*, II (1842) , 700.

[9] Charles Darwin, *The Origin of Species: A Variorum Text,* ed. Morse Peckham (Philadelphia: University of Pennsylvania Press, 1959) , p. 758.

in nature, but it seemed to be achieved in a wasteful, blundering, and cruel way. Huxley replied to those who accused Darwin of undermining teleology that there was a wider teleology which viewed the whole sequence of events since the primitive nebulosity of the universe as a development preordained in the properties of the molecules comprising that primeval cosmic vapor. But he felt compelled to add that this assumption could be neither proved nor disproved and that, even if it were true, it would still be impossible to say whether any particular result of the operation of the mechanical system was more than an unessential incident of its functioning, like the ticking of a clock. To this question, he observed, "there seems to be no reply . . . any more than to the further, not irrational question, why trouble one's self about matters which are out of reach, when the working of the mechanism itself, which is of infinite practical importance, affords scope for all our energies." [10]

Thus, the order of nature, conceived originally as founded on the wise ordinances of God the Creator, became for the Darwinians a kind of brute fact. Science could testify to the existence of laws of nature but could say nothing of their origin or significance. It could study the mechanisms of the world machine and learn to use them for human purposes, but nature had ceased to be a ladder by which man might ascend "through nature to nature's God." It had become, instead, a curtain separating man from the Unknowable—"that veil which lies between us and the Infinite—that universe which alone we know or can know." It was no accident that Huxley coined the word "agnostic."

The Darwinian faith in an iron-clad order of nature is all the more curious in view of the fact that the so-called law of natural selection was a law in a quite different sense from that in which the Darwinians conceived a law of nature. To them and their contemporaries a law of nature meant an invariant relationship between events, an unbroken chain of cause and effect. It had ceased to be conceivable, said Huxley, that chance should have any place in the universe: "None but parsons believe in chance." True, Darwin spoke of chance variations, but this simply meant that variations arose from unknown causes and without reference to the requirements for survival. In reality, however, the notion of chance went much deeper than this in Darwin's theory. The law of natural

[10] Thomas Henry Huxley, "The Genealogy of Animals," *Darwiniana: Essays*, p. 113. Essay first published in 1869.

selection was not a law analogous to Boyle's law or Hooke's law. It was a law of differential reproduction, presupposing a statistical concept of order. It was, protested Sir John Herschel, "a law of higglety-pigglety."

The American philosopher Charles S. Peirce was more perceptive. What had seemed to Herschel an outrageous intrusion of chance into an orderly universe seemed to Peirce a convincing refutation of mechanical determinism and the concept of natural law associated with it.

In biology, [wrote Peirce,] that tremendous upheaval caused in 1860 by Darwin's theory of fortuitous variations was but the consequence of a theorem in probabilities, namely the theorem that if very many similar things are subject to many slight fortuitous variations, as much in one direction as in the opposite direction, which when they aggregate a sufficient effect upon any one of those things in one direction must eliminate it from nature, while there is no corresponding effect of an aggregate of variations in other directions, the result must, in the long run, be to produce a change of the average character of the class of things in the latter direction.[11]

Peirce then went on to substitute an evolutionary conception of natural law for the old notion of natural laws as rigid patterns of behavior imposed on matter by the Creator. In Peirce's evolutionary philosophy the laws of nature are themselves evolved as the universe moves from a chaotic spontaneity toward perfect order.

Since Peirce's time the deterministic view of nature has ceased to be taken for granted, largely because of certain developments in physics but also because of the application of genetical theory to evolutionary biology. Sir Ronald Fisher, one of the founders of population genetics, explains the matter thus:

The positive evidence for determinism provided by scientific experimentation on a molar scale is seen to be inconclusive as soon as it is recognised that the predictability of the behavior of large masses is a necessary statistical consequence of the large number of independent particles of which they are composed, and would be manifested whatever were the nature of the ultimate reality. . . . The study of atoms, and sub-atomic particles and processes, can, it now appears, only be carried on by recognising indeterminism as inherent in their nature. It is particularly important, in this respect, that there is not a vague or uncertain degree of indeterminism, but a specific amount, calculable from one of the fundamental

[11] Charles S. Peirce, quoted in Philip P. Wiener, *Evolution and the Founders of Pragmatism* (Cambridge, Mass.: Harvard University Press, 1949) , p. 81.

constants of physics. No appeal to subjectivity, or to human limitations, can explain it away.[12]

In keeping with this point of view, modern genetical theory stresses the unpredictability and creativity of evolutionary development. Evolution is creative, says Fisher, "because it has a casual aspect."

These are the back and the front of the same quality. Looking back at the cause we can recognize it as creative; it has brought about something which could not have been predicted—something which cannot be referred back to antecedent events. Looking forward to it as a future event, there is in it something which we can recognize as casual. It is viewed thus like the result of a game of chance; we can imagine ourselves able to foresee all its possible forms, and to state in advance the probability that each will occur. We can no longer imagine ourselves capable of foreseeing just which of them will occur.[13]

Fisher's reference to the creativity of evolution takes us back to the second main article of faith in the Darwinian credo, namely, that the order of nature is progressive. Here, too, the Darwinians encountered difficulties as soon as the supporting influence of Christian providentialism and nineteenth-century optimism began to wane. The second law of thermodynamics gave little basis for cosmic optimism, and Herbert Spencer was forced to concede that there were limits to the process of aggregation. In 1868 he still believed that Evolution (spelled with a capital *E*) "can end only in the establishment of the greatest perfection and the most complete happiness," but after that, he noted, must come a disaggregation of matter followed by new evolutions and dissolutions *ad infinitum*.

In biology the concept of progress was beset by two difficulties: (1) the difficulty of defining the criteria of progress, and (2) the difficulty of explaining why random variation and natural selection should produce not merely changes in the average characters of populations but something worthy of being called progress. On the whole, the nineteenth-century Darwinians, though vaguely aware of these difficulties, did not discuss them systematically. They were content to assume that man was the highest form of life on earth and to argue that, since every organ or system of organs was capable of indefinite improvement with respect to the performance of its

[12] Ronald A. Fisher, *Creative Aspects of Natural Law* (Cambridge, Eng.: Cambridge University Press, 1950) , p. 3.
[13] *Ibid.*, p. 4.

function, it must eventually undergo that improvement in the course of millions of years of variation and natural selection.

In all this there was really no concept of order. The existence of organisms as functioning systems was taken for granted. Variations were regarded as arising unpredictably from unknown causes without reference to their possible utility or disutility to the organisms in which they arose. Selection itself was a process of elimination involving no intelligent choice. True, the fittest survived, but the concept of fitness was highly ambiguous. At times the Darwinians recognized that the term "fittest" carried no implication of "best" or "highest," since what was well adapted to one environment might be poorly adapted to another. But, on the whole, they could not help believing that the winners in the various competitions going on in nature were superior in some absolute sense to the losers, just as the races that had produced Western civilization were, in their opinion, superior to those they had bested. Thus nature, though it yielded no evidence of a designing intelligence capable of giving direction to organic change, yet moved, however slowly and haphazardly, toward higher and higher levels of order in what Huxley called "nature's grand progression from blind force to conscious will and intellect."

These contradictions and ambiguities became even more apparent when the Darwinian-Spencerian concepts were applied to human society and history. Here again one looks in vain for a concept of order. Spencer wrote a book called *Social Statics,* but it proved to be largely concerned with the laws of social progress. In Spencer's view, society was a collection of individuals capable of being maintained in a social state either by force and fear or by voluntary agreement. Social progress resulted from the gradual triumph of individuals, tribes, and races endowed with a hereditary capacity for voluntary cooperation over those less well endowed in this respect. In the end, said Spencer, government would be unnecessary because every individual would possess by nature an instinctual regard for the rights of others. One encounters a similar optimism in some of Darwin's writings.

I suppose that you do not doubt, [he wrote Lyell in 1859], that the intellectual powers are as important for the welfare of each being as corporeal structures; if so, I can see no difficulty in the most intellectual individuals of a species being continually selected; and the intellect of the new species thus improved, aided probably by effects of inherited mental exercise. I look at this process as now going on with the races of man; the less intellectual races being exterminated.[14]

That progress of the intellect would be accompanied by moral progress Darwin had little doubt. "Looking to future generations," he prophesied in *The Descent of Man,* "there is no cause to fear that the social instinct will grow weaker, and we may expect that virtuous habits will grow stronger, becoming perhaps fixed by inheritance. In this case the struggle between our higher and lower impulses will be less severe, and virtue will be triumphant." [15]

For both Darwin and Spencer, social order depended primarily on the intellectual and instinctual endowment of the individuals comprising society, and this endowment was viewed as undergoing progressive improvement through a process of natural selection. The possibility that an increase in intellectual capacity might aggravate rather than ameliorate the problem of social order seems not to have occurred to them. Spencer lived long enough to feel misgivings about the beneficent tendency of racial and national conflict, however. History, instead of moving smoothly along the path from social order based on force and fear to social order based on voluntary agreement, produced a resurgence of militarism in the late nineteenth century. The clock of progress seemed to be running backward. Faced with this development, Spencer called for a halt to national conflict. The integration of simple groups into compound and doubly compound ones by military conquest had been carried "as far as seems either practicable or desirable," he cautioned. Progress in the future should result from "the quiet pressure of a spreading industrial civilization on a barbarism which slowly dwindles." But barbarism refused to dwindle. Erupting with savage violence in the twentieth century, it attacked the very foundations of the free society Spencer had championed, claiming as its sanction Spencer's own doctrine of the survival of the fittest.

In view of what has been said, it might seem that Darwinism as a world view was so thoroughly permeated with nineteenth-century attitudes and assumptions that it could not possibly survive in the altered intellectual environment of the twentieth century. But such

[14] Charles Darwin to Charles Lyell, October 11, 1859, in *The Life and Letters of Charles Darwin . . .* , ed. Francis Darwin (New York, 1898) , II, 7.

[15] Charles Darwin, *The Descent of Man,* p. 125.

is not the case. Darwinism is still very much with us, modified in some respects but remarkably similar in general outline to its nineteenth-century pattern. In the writings of Julian Huxley, for example, the Spencerian ideal of an all-embracing evolutionary science shines forth in all its pristine splendor. One finds the same linking of cosmic, biological, and cultural evolution in a single continuum of progressive development, the same naturalism in the concept of man, the same search for analogies between biological and social evolution, the same confidence in science and its power to create an ever new and better future for the human race. There are differences, too, but these relate chiefly to the Spencerian-Darwinian emphasis on competition and conflict as engines of social progress. Huxley and his disciples look instead to science and human planning to maintain the upward trend of cultural evolution.

So far as the concept of order is concerned, it is as equivocal in modern Darwinism as it was in the nineteenth-century variety. The universe is still represented as moving toward ever higher levels of order and harmony without any ordering principle other than human intelligence. Social order is now attributed more to human planning than to social instincts, and the improvement of the human stock is left to eugenicists rather than to natural selection. But the question who is to plan the planners remains unanswered. Progress, not order, was and is the leit-motif of Darwinism.

PETER CAWS

Order and Value in the Sciences

The three preceding papers have been about the concept of order, and they have also been about Aristotle, Newton, and Darwin. A good deal of what has been said about Aristotle, Newton, and Darwin, however, has had very little to do with the concept of order. This is no doubt inevitable in matters of scholarship—one has to get the historical setting right, draw the proper distinctions, and so on. But I am unfitted for scholarship, if that is what it means; I have great difficulty in remembering who said what, I am always getting chronologies inverted, and so forth. The important thing seems to me never whether x said y, but what reasons anybody might have had—or might still have—for saying y, and what might be meant by it. That is partly a historical problem, to the solution of which historical scholarship is indispensable, but it is partly a philosophical one which can be tackled on its own ground. I shall therefore raise a comparatively simple-minded question about the

PETER J. CAWS was educated as both physicist (in England) and philosopher (in the United States). His interest in order comprehends a general study of scientific theory, measurement, inductive logic, and theory of value. He has served as chairman of the Department of Philosophy, University of Kansas, and executive associate of Carnegie Corporation of New York. He is now professor of philosophy in Hunter College of the City University of New York. He is the author of *The Philosophy of Science: A Systematic Account* (1965) and *Science and the Theory of Value* (1967).

concept of order as such, rather than in any particular historical connection.

It will be convenient to start, nevertheless, with a remark of Professor Greene's in his lecture on Darwin, to the effect that the concern of the Darwinians was with progress rather than order, that in fact they had no very clear concept of order at all. The relative dispositions of species, taken as mere fact, were for them a starting point for other considerations and displayed no particular orderliness in themselves. This is a remarkable illustration of something I believe to be of fundamental importance, namely, that no state of affairs can be said to be ordered merely on account of its being the way it is, however regular its internal structure. My question, then, is, Why does order appear to us as order, and why is it preferable to disorder?

Every state of affairs, even the most chaotic, is ordered in the sense that every element of it occupies a definite place with respect to every other element. To paraphrase Butler, things are as they are and not another way. It is sometimes thought to be a mark of a special kind of order if a mathematical function can be written that specifies the relations between the elements, but again a function can be written for any set of relations, simply because every set of relations *is* a function, of one sort or another. The concepts of order and of mathematical function are exhibited—vacuously, it is true— by every state of affairs whatever. The more usual use of the concepts arises if there is a *repetition* of some set of relations. Repetitions lead to expectations, and expectations lead to discomfort if they are not fulfilled. And it is this disturbance at *dis*order which leads to the explicit specification of an order. Not every repetition counts, of course. It might be that a number of people had sat at a table in a certain arrangement on a number of occasions, but it might then not be noticed if on a new occasion two of them changed places. It might not matter. But if the change resulted in the separation of two of them who counted on always sitting together it would be noticed and it would matter, and then the change would be seen as introducing, at least for the two people in question, an element of disorder.

This kind of example could be multiplied. The arrangement of clothes in a closet rarely matters, it does not count as an order, nobody would care if they were moved about (although vacuously, as we have seen, they always happen to be in some order or other) ;

the arrangement of books on shelves often matters, it does therefore count as an order (an alphabetical order, perhaps), and the librarian would care if they were moved about. An order is an arrangement with respect to which *it would matter if it were otherwise.* And this holds for order in science, in art, in civil life, wherever in fact the concept applies. Even in the vacuous case, once the random arrangement had been recorded, it would matter that it should have been as recorded and not otherwise, since that would be the condition of the accuracy and usefulness of the record.

On the most primitive level, the order of nature—the succession of night and day and of the seasons, for example—is just the character of our environment which if changed would affect us most profoundly. A number of nights together, followed by a day or two, and then more nights—or a long series of winters, one following another—would produce a great deal of consternation; it is just the nonoccurrence of such anomalies which makes nature, from our point of view, orderly. (Hurricanes, volcanic eruptions, tidal waves, and so forth are just as much part of the order of nature, objectively regarded, but it is safe to say that the ordinary man does not look at them in this light.) The concept of order as what matters in this negative way has applications now which are quite remote from such pressing concerns, and extends to its mattering, for example, if somebody uses the wrong fork at dinner. The mattering can be either instinctive or learned, but it is always immediate, or is derived from some immediate concern. If somebody says, "It doesn't matter to me whether they're in order or not," he is using the term "order" in a conventional sense, but this use would be impossible if there had not been people to whom such things did matter.

The question about order, then, is not why things should be disposed in a certain way, but why it should matter that they are disposed in this way. And that transforms the question into a question about value. To say that something is ordered is to say that it embodies a value; to say that it would matter if it were otherwise is to say that it ought to be as it is. (And to say that order is preferable to disorder is tautological.) Values also come to light principally by contrast with the negative case; I realize the value of something most when I am in danger of losing it, or when I have not yet attained it. If something embodies value we do not wish to see it changed—it is properly ordered; an artist's work is finished at the point where he or some other observer realizes that any further alteration would spoil it. (Learning when *not* to make changes is one of the most difficult aesthetic lessons.) Similarly, if something fails to embody a value we feel it ought to embody, if, for example, a situation of social injustice exists, we have an impression of disorder and seek to introduce changes until the situation is corrected.

Art and morals are not, of course, the only things that matter to us. Truth matters, and so does understanding, and it is because of this that the scientific concept of order is every bit as involved with value as the moral and aesthetic concepts. If we ask *why* these things matter, expecting their mattering to be explained in terms of something factual, I think we make a serious mistake—not that no light can be thrown on the question, but that in the end what matters is phenomenologically given just as surely as what appears is phenomenologically given. Until recently, however—and often still—the fact that orders embody values, if recognized at all, was taken as an indication that the value in question came from something else, either metaphysical or religious. Aristotle certainly took this view; the whole teleological attitude consigns the value involved to a distant goal, wholly separated from the present order. And for Newton the mathematical order of nature spoke not of man's concern but of God's power. In Newton's case, however, we can see more clearly how getting knowledge of the world matters, how a situation in which the intellect is not at rest finally gives way to understanding, to an ordered explanation, so that for the time being the quest for truth is at an end. (The analysis of this process is the strongest feature of the pragmatist theory of inquiry, although it would certainly be going too far to suggest, as that theory does, that truth *consists* in the intellect's being at rest.)

It is with Darwin, however, that the relation between order and value falls into perspective, largely because, as remarked earlier, the Darwinians said very little about either. The one lesson of Darwinism was that to look for the value of some element of nature (and hence for an explanation of its place in the order of nature) in its origins or its destiny was to commit the genetic fallacy—or its inverse, which might be called the eschatological fallacy. Man's place in nature, to use Huxley's phrase, does not locate man with respect to nature, it locates nature with respect to man. (Huxley might not have liked this way of putting it—I cover such remarks with my initial disclaimer of scholarly intent.) The point is that it is man's involvement with his world which leads him to find order in it, and this applies in all branches of science. It is therefore of no essential importance if this order arises at random out of chaos, or if, to take an example from modern physics, gross regularities are only a smoothing over of submicroscopic uncertainties. It is an order because we know it as such, and that is how it comes to be one. It comes to be as it factually *is* through some sequence of physical causes, whether or not determinable by us, but that sequence is ordered only vacuously—any other sequence would have done as well if it had led to the same outcome.

There is, it is true, a distinction to be drawn between orders which our involvement with the world leads us to recognize as such, which we *discover* in the world when natural configurations of objects or events matter to us, and orders which we bring about in the world, which we *create*. The most obvious example of created order is a work of art. But I conclude these fragmentary remarks with the observation that, while the order with which science deals is discovered, scientific theory as an ordered system is created. Theories have been created not only because the control of nature matters, as indeed it does, but also because the understanding of it matters. The values science embodies, seen in this light, are not so far from those embodied in art. Art and science are both human enterprises, products of the creative imagination, and each represents order in one of its highest forms. But as far as that goes no human enterprise is without its value, if only to the human being who undertakes it, so that the concept of order can be expected to pervade all humanistic inquiries, among which science must certainly be counted.

These remarks have been rewritten from the notes used at Grinnell, with the help of a transcript of the tape recording made at the time. They belong in the context of the papers read by Messrs. Greene, McMullin, and Westfall.

Order in the Sciences

RICHARD COLE

The Logical Order and the Causal Order

Hume's problem with the concept of cause amounts to this: cause is a relation linking two observable events, one prior to the other in time; yet a complete description of the prior event is consistent with contradictories of propositions which describe the subsequent event. The prior event is prior in time, but not in logic; the subsequent event follows in time, but its description does not follow from the description of the prior event as a conclusion follows from premises in deductive argument. Nevertheless, Hume insisted, attributing a causal connection between the events, we understand and suppose this connection to be necessary. Where, asked Hume, do we get this notion of necessary connection between two events? Given only the description of the prior event, it is logically possible that the subsequent event not occur. A paradoxical proportion is set up: cause is to effect as premise is to conclusion; yet in valid deductive argument, given true premises, the conclusion cannot be otherwise than true. For Hume, the conceivability of a state of affairs other than

RICHARD COLE was educated at Texas in mathematics and at Chicago in philosophy. He has worked in industry as a mathematician, but since 1959 has taught at various schools, including Grinnell College, 1962–65, and since then at the University of Kansas. His papers show a great concern with the modalities of logic, especially possibility, the history of science, questions of meaning and truth, and metaphysics. His current research is on *The Concept of Complexity: Techniques of Mechanical Inductive Reasoning*.

that which did in fact ensue undercuts the claim that the cause necessitates the effect. We can imagine a cue ball hurtling toward an eight ball, striking it—and then the eight ball just sits there. Or the eight ball disappears. Or the eight ball diminishes or expands.

The association of the notion of cause with deductive discourse has a long history. For the Greeks, inquiries into cause were reasonings; the Greek word is "syllogism." Aristotle used the term "cause" in the sense of "reason why," and the four Aristotelian kinds of "reasons why" showed up as middle terms of demonstrative syllogisms. For both Plato and Aristotle an inquiry into cause involved a search for a reasoning in which the effect to be explained was embedded as the conclusion of that reasoning. The point of the inquiry was not to find the conclusion, for the conclusion was already given as true, but to find the reasoning itself.

Descartes, Hobbes, and Leibniz, like the Greeks, essentially related an inquiry into cause to demonstrative argument. For these modern philosophers, if one wanted to know the cause of some given x, one analyzed how x involved its cause. The result of such analysis was to uncover a sufficent condition for x. Immanuel Kant proposed that the necessary connection which Hume found present in the concept "cause" is provided by a superaddition to causal judgments of an a priori concept provided by reason itself. This a priori superaddition Kant calls the category of cause, and this category is itself derived from the logical notion of consequent following from antecedent. The parallelism of cause to effect as antecedent to consequent is no accident. Kant explains the parallel between the causal order and the logical order by saying that the first is a synthesis of the temporal order in the latter.

Modern skeptics also pay heed to this parallel. In modern skeptical philosophies the notion of cause tends to disappear altogether, and the skeptic, in making the concept of cause disappear, tacitly recognizes just this point. It is because "cause," in its hardest sense, requires a logically necessary link between event and event that the modern skeptical philosopher like Hume is suspicious of it. Interestingly, the notion of hypothetical explanation is often substituted for the more traditional concept of cause, and the logical structure of such hypothetical explanations is similar to the logic of a causal explanation.

There is, then, an impressive body of historical data linking the order of reasoning with the causal order, whether or not such causal order is supposed to exist. But it can hardly be said that the term "cause" has been used in the same sense by all philosophers. As a matter of fact, nowadays, the term "cause" is used in a way (even when the term is made to dissipate) that does not appear to have a counterpart in ancient or even recent modern philosophy before Newton. Though Aristotle's famous four causes are indeed a part of our modern conceptual apparatus, the usual modern understanding of this term is not equivalent to any of Aristotle's causes. Indeed, that this is the case has often confused modern students of Aristotle, for the word "cause" is rarely if ever used in any of Aristotle's senses. It is true that the modern notion of cause is something like Aristotle's notion of efficient cause, yet there is this difference: the Aristotelian efficient cause was an agent, or source, of that which is to be explained; the modern notion of cause is that it is a relation linking events.

Aristotle's four causes and the modern notion constitute a family of concepts. A name for this family could appropriately be "reasons why." All members of this family exhibit a logical similarity; they are all in one way or another associated with deductive discourse. To see the way in which the modern notion differs from Aristotle's four causes, and to see how all five causes function in modern discourse, consider the following deductive arguments.

1. The heart pumps faster when a man is running because his metabolic rate increases, the rate at which waste products in his body are formed increases, the body has to remove these waste products by means of increased circulation, the heart—the function of which is to pump blood—must pump faster to increase the flow of blood.

This argument employs Aristotle's notion of final cause. Nowadays we call such explanatory arguments functional explanations.

2. The piston attached to a wheel, as in a steam locomotive, moves back and forth when the wheel turns because of the way it is attached to the wheel.

This argument employs the Aristotelian notion of formal cause.

3. Concrete hardens because it contains cement.

Here is an example of Aristotle's material cause.

4. The eight ball moved because it was struck by the cue ball. The cue ball's motion was the cause of the motion of the eight ball.

This is an example of Aristotle's efficient cause. Hume's doubts about the necessary connection between cause and effect turn on this sense of cause. Compare this to the Newtonian explanation for the motion of the eight ball. The eight ball moves, according to Newton, because a force acted on it for a certain length of time. For Hume we had two things under consideration: the motion of the cue ball and the motion of the eight ball. For Newton we have at least three things to take into account in relating the motion of the cue ball to the motion of the eight ball: these two motions and the notion of force.

The logical structure of all of Aristotle's four kinds of causal explanations and causal explanation in a more modern sense are similar. That which is to be explained occurs as a conclusion in a deductive argument in all five types of explanation. But it is in connection with the modern notion of cause that Hume's puzzlement over the inclusion of a necessary connection between cause and effect is acute. In the other examples concern over necessity does in fact arise. But such concern can be isolated on the question as to whether or not the premises are in fact necessarily true. In the attempt to understand a causal relation linking two events, we encounter Hume's problem. We find ourselves able to imagine the prior event occurring and the subsequent event not occurring at all. Yet, in making a judgment of causality, we understand that the prior event somehow forces the subsequent event. This supposed bond of physical necessitation makes us wonder not only about the necessary truth of any premise of an argument but also about the necessity of using such arguments at all. We are tempted to give it up, being satisfied instead with statistical generalizations about what usually follows what.

A causal explanation has this logical form: you have given a description of the prior set of events and of a subsequent event; you are asked to show that the latter follows from the former. As a matter of fact, Hume was quite right in observing that if this is all you have, there is no link of logic connecting them, only succession in time. But what is involved in, for example, a causal explanation of the Newtonian variety is not simply these two sets of descriptions —one set occurring as premises and the other as conclusion—but also the addition to the argument of certain principles or laws of nature, such that, given the description of the prior events and the propositions expressing the laws of nature, we can then show that the description of a subsequent event follows *deductively* from the conjunction of these two sets of premises.

Consider, for example, the Newtonian view of the physics of collision of billiard balls. For Hume, the cause would be identified with the motion of the cue ball and its striking the eight ball. The effect would be identified with the subsequent motion of the eight ball. The cause, then, of the eight ball's motion would be the cue ball's motion and its striking the eight ball. But this is not an accurate description of a Newtonian causal explanation. For Newton, the cause of the motion of the eight ball, or rather of its coming into motion, is that a certain force acted on the eight ball. Now "force" is a theoretical term that is explicated in quite theoretical and general ways in Newton's laws. What is missing in Hume, and what is included in Newton, is the introduction of theoretical principles and terms such that, though it is not possible to derive the necessary occurrence of the effect from a description of what Hume would have called its cause, it is possible by strict deduction to conclude that given the propositions describing the prior event, and given propositions expressing the Newtonian laws, it then follows of logical necessity that the second ball will move as it did.

For Newton the cause is no observable event. Rather it is the referent of a theoretical term embedded in scientific theory, which theory mediates the prior and subsequent events. The role that the necessity of logical inference plays in such a Newtonian causal explanation becomes clear. It is not that we can deduce one event from another, but that we can deduce one event from another using laws of nature.

Recognizing that a theoretical explanation involves the interposition of a theoretical middle changes but does not dispel Hume's criticism. Hume invites us to try to understand that some prior event is linked to some subsequent event by a necessary bond, yet Hume does not allow the interposition of such theoretical middles as are involved in, for example, Newtonian physics. Newtonian laws of nature, or any that may be substituted for them, would, from Hume's point of view, be themselves subject to a skeptical doubt. For Hume there is experiential but no theoretical certainty. And yet there is some gain in seeing that the interposition of theoretical laws of nature is somehow involved in causal explanations. If Hume's point about the nondeducibility of the description of the presumed effect from the presumed cause is compared with this point (making the effect deducible from the antecedent conditions by means of the superaddition of theoretical laws), then it can be seen that without the theoretical middle in a causal explanation Hume is right—there is no justifiable ground for necessarily linking cause and effect; or, if we accept causal explanations, then we are committed to everything that is involved in accepting a theoretical mediation.

The logic of causal explanation requires that the theory have a generality that goes far beyond immediate experience. In addition and more significantly, because the theory must make sense, and because theory involves the use of theoretical terms like "force," we are required, if we are to keep causal explanations, to accept a notion of an objective world that goes beyond and behind sense experience. In the early days of Newton's mechanical philosophy, Newton's concept of gravitational force was called occult by Cartesians. It is precisely this kind of thing that is required if we are to have causal explanations. We might dispense with "force" as a theoretical middle, but then we must substitute other theoretical terms. The logic of causal explanation requires the superaddition of an objective world that we know but do not see to the things that we see. This price may be too high for a good many modern scientists and philosophers to pay, yet the rational demand for causal explanation is so pervasive that the world we learn about through science consists of unobservable fields, particles too small in principle ever to be observed, and the like. Even quantum physicists, encouraged by their statistical methods to be radical empiricists, often, if not usually, objectify their abstract mathematical notions and talk about "wave packets" or the like, making theoretical sense of the mathematical connection between initial and final condition, and, in the bargain, achieving the satisfaction of a causal explanation.

The price of causal explanation, of course, has proved too high for a good many scientists and philosophers. Yet, when this classical characterization of the function of science is foresworn, the theoretical link between event and event is not also foresworn—what happens is the refusal to grant sense to this theoretical middle, though we find ourselves nevertheless appealing to it in teaching and learning. We talk about causal explanations as being heuristic devices, and we use the logic of causal explanation not so much to explain as to predict and control future events.

Setting aside for the moment the temptation to take sides, we must consider the difference between causal explanation and prediction. Logically, they are similar. In both a description of some event is conjoined with theory (meaningful or meaningless according to your philosophical opinion), and a description of a subsequent event is deduced. We have initial conditions, a certain amount of theory, and deduction of the result. The difference lies in this—that in causal explanation both the prior and subsequent events are past; in prediction the subsequent event has not yet occurred. In causal explanations, in other words, we do not bring into question the fact of the occurrence of that which is to be explained. In a prediction, we claim that the event will occur.

On the other hand, and this is an equally important point, it involves no logical inconsistency to assert that, even though Newton's laws when used in prediction always provide accurate and correct predictions, they are nevertheless all wrong, for other laws, not equivalent to Newton's, might produce the same result, and these may be the correct ones. On this account it would appear that Newton could be either altogether right or altogether wrong, and it would make no difference in prediction. And, when this view is pursued, the conclusion is that the theoretical machinery of Newtonian physics is to be judged, not according to its truth but according to its usefulness.

But, when this conclusion comes, the notion of physical necessity goes. And with it goes all causal explanation.

This is an unfortunate result for two reasons. First, to argue that causal explanations play no part, except as heuristic devices, in the mission of natural science, however fascinatingly neat the argument to this conclusion, does not accord with practice. It is necessary, for example, to say that Newton, in spite of what he thought he was doing, was in effect really constructing a useful instrument of prediction. We have to regard the bulk of education in science as only inessentially related to the proper job of science. Yet the working scientist, except occasionally, talks, thinks, and acts as though physical necessity, at least for some events, is a fact, and uses causal explanation both in communicating his results and in making them clear to himself.

But there may be a worse difficulty. The argument that makes the theoretical link between event and event a mere tool of prediction may rest upon a general distrust of theoretical language. It is reasonably prevalent to regard as significant only such discourse as is immediately descriptive of events, physical objects, or physical processes. Accepting this principle leads immediately to the destruction of causal explanations, though retaining theoretical elements for their utility in prediction. This mode of thought is well illustrated in the historical unease with the Newtonian forces. The criticism of this notion depends upon pointing out with no doubt consummate justice that "forces" are not observable. The presupposition of this criticism is, of course: "What is not observable is to be ruled out of scientific discourse, except for the sake of education and prediction."

But Newtonian causes *are* forces. The Newtonian explanation for the orbits of the planets, for example, rests upon the thesis that the sun's gravitation exerts a centripetal force on the planets. If this language is not significant, the only parts of this thesis that are salvageable are the descriptive, kinematic formulas giving positions of planets as a function of time. The notion of "force" is transmitted into the letter F in a formula, and this letter becomes eliminable in a calculation.

Whatever the merits of the criticism of "force" as an acceptable theoretical notion, if the argument leading to its rejection depends upon a principle that rejects theoretical notions generally, a vicious contradiction ensues. There is no argument that employs a "because" in any of its senses that depends entirely upon nontheoretical premises. The argument that concludes with the rejection of causal explanations is itself an excellent example of an argument that uses a "because" which links the conclusion with the theoretical premise, "What is not observable is ruled out." Consequently the argument, along with ruling out causes, rules out "becauses" as well, yet it depends upon the use of such a "because." What such arguments do is rule out reasoning altogether in favor of calculation; yet they are themselves reasonings. They make use, so to speak, of that which they conclude should not be made use of.

If we want to make sense of causal explanation and prediction without committing this error and without doing violence to what is in fact common scientific practice, we must give the problem another and a closer view.

Now it is a fact that theoretical science is used both to explain an event already known to have occurred and also to predict events in the future. That is to say that the demand on theory is to explain the past and predict the future. If its only role were to explain the past, then the only test of its truth would be a logical one; that is to say, if it fulfilled its function for providing a deductive link between fact and fact, then it must be accepted as a candidate for true theory. If the only role of theory were in prediction, then the measure of its truth would be the measure of its success. The more successful a prophet the theory made us, the truer it would become. But the dual role of theory imposes upon it a complex and a somewhat rigid restriction. Those theories which make past events explicable must also make us successful prophets, and those theories which make us successful prophets must also make past events explicable.

We can imagine a deterministic Newtonian who would have a considerable success in explaining events he already knows have occurred, and yet would refuse to make any predictions at all on the ground that he does not know what forces will be acting on bodies in the future. We can also imagine, and this may be a good deal easier nowadays, a logical empiricist who when asked by his son, "Daddy, why does the apple fall to the ground?" will respond, "Don't ask me why, Son. Ask me when it's going to hit the ground." The son replies, "Daddy, it's already hit the ground." Daddy would respond, "Then I'm no longer interested in it."

If I might paraphrase a famous saying of Immanuel Kant, explicability without predictability is empty; predictability without explicability is blind.

The claim that there is real physical necessity operating in nature is equivalent to the claim that certain laws of nature are necessarily true. This claim is not equivalent to the claim that nature is deterministic, for it may be that the laws of nature are necessarily true and yet there may be some events not covered by them. Nevertheless, in certain thorough-going determinisms a kind of imitation necessity is achieved for the laws of nature which it is claimed hold universally. For example, consider classical Laplacian determinism. Laplace said that if the state of the universe at any given instant were known, then it would be possible to predict with accuracy every future state of the universe. If, in attempting to take advantage of this ability, we made a prediction that did not bear out, this would go down as not having acquired sufficient relevant data as to the state of the universe. A deterministic system always has a kind of "fudge" factor that enables it to explain away on the basis of ignorance any prediction that fails. The ignorance that is supposed is not an ignorance of theory, but rather one of fact.

A thoroughgoing indeterminist, on the other hand, is never surprised at being surprised that his predictions fail, for this is what he comes to expect. On the other hand, he never has the satisfaction of being in a position to explain any given event. We could say that he is frequently disgruntled and never surprised, whereas the determinist is frequently surprised and never disgruntled.

If we combine the determinist's desire that every event be explicable with his desire that every event be predictable, the dogmatic determinist's fudge factor will not work, for he is not only required to explain away his failure to predict by positing some unknown force or something similar, or by saying, "If we only knew, then we could have predicted"; he must also explain the event which he failed to predict. It is, of course, open to a man to explain an unexpected result by looking for relevant facts that had not previously been taken into consideration, but it is also appropriate for him to look to a revision of theory in such circumstances. The fact of the matter is that, as science advances, we not only gain more knowledge of fact, but we also accumulate more theoretical sophistication. This means that the past becomes progressively more explicable and the future progressively more predictable—and both in virtue of theoretical advance.

We have here a sequence of good, better, and still better, and when we have such sequences we can frame the notion of the best, that is to say, of the ideal. What would an ideal science be? It would be one in which no event is inexplicable, and in which prediction is perfect. The restriction on theory would be that all theoretical propositions be necessarily true. The ideal science, then, would be one in which the notion of physical necessity and that of logical necessity come together. Every event, whether explained or predicted, must be seen to follow of logical necessity from the description of some prior events, and from these necessarily true laws of nature.

The way in which the determinist can be dogmatic is in supposing that we already have in our possession such an ideal theoretical science. The way in which the indeterminist is unnecessarily modest, that is to say, skeptical, is in refusing to admit that we have any part of the ideal science.

In imperfect science, Hume's worry about necessary connection between events is resolved by saying that the notion of physical necessity is an imitation of the notion of logical necessity; the causal order is a kind of second-rate logical order. My argument suggests that if the physical necessity which belongs to cause is borrowed from the notion of logical necessity, it is a kind of borrowing on account against the day, perhaps never to come, when science will be completed. Physical necessity is a kind of yearning after logical **necessity.**

CECIL J. SCHNEER

Science and History

I. INTRODUCTION

Although idealist historiographic views have been popular among academic historians in recent years, there has been little attention given to the relationship of this shift in historical emphasis to the perennial problem of history and science. In this paper I wish to examine the division between history and science from the point of view of a historical science, geology, which shares aims and methods with both. The division between history and science is one further aspect of a general division in our culture. It is the purpose of this paper to suggest one point of view from which the division disappears. History and science may be regarded as parallel in their common concern with the imposition of order upon the world of phenomena.

The leading idealist historiographer of recent time, Benedetto Croce, by his dismissal from the concern of history of everything

CECIL J. SCHNEER was trained at Harvard and Cornell as a geologist, and has worked in South America as a mining geologist. Since 1954 he has been at the University of New Hampshire where in 1967 he directed the New Hampshire Interdisciplinary Conference on the History of Geology. Professor Schneer is known not only for his work in crystallography but also for his book, *The Search for Order*, published in 1960 and reissued as a paperback under the title *The Evolution of Physical Science*.

except the history of thought (and written thought at that), appears to accept an essentially positivistic view of science. Similarly, R. G. Collingwood, in his insistence that the historian is not simply the passive recorder of events external to himself, implies that the theologian and the scientist are no more than observers, nonparticipants in the subject matter of their fields. In this view, the phenomena God and Nature lie outside of man. The reception of the one is theology; of the other, science. History and art, by contrast are free creations of the human spirit according to Collingwood. They are in fact the essence of that spirit. Yet Einstein has characterized science as a free creation of the human mind, and whether the idealist characterization of theology in such fundamentalist terms is sufficient or not I shall leave to the theologian.

We have to deal first with history, and for this paper let us accept the idealist view of history, quarreling not with Croce as historiographer but only with Croce as scientist or philosopher of science. His ideal characterization of history does not justify his positive characterization of science. Not the body of his thought, but the constraints which he has seen fit to place upon it, will be my concern. We also have to deal with science at the opposite end of our field of investigation. Here, rather than attempt a consistent philosophy of science, let us instead regard science as it exists now in the light of its history.

Between the poles of history and science there lies a vast and fertile field of ambiguity. As we extend our pseudopodia into this nutrient area, we encounter from the direction of history the history of science, or, in another direction, the science of history. Approaching this central ambiguity from the pole of science in the other direction, we encounter the historical sciences, which Croce terms *metastoria*—natural sciences (or histories) such as geology and cosmology. Going further, we find ourselves back at the science of history. In 1893 Henry Adams as president of the American Historical Association called on historians to "undertake the exploration necessary to formulate a 'science of history.' " [1] If there is in reality a valid science of history; if we may even in anticipation conceive of the temporal evolution of the human situation as governed by knowable, finite law, then with Collingwood I submit that historical

[1] W. H. Jordy, *Henry Adams: Scientific Historian* (New Haven, Conn.: Yale University Press, 1952).

knowledge is impossible; that history itself is reduced to a branch of science. We would have not two poles, but only a singularity of the field. As Morris R. Cohen wrote in 1947:

Those who insist that history is a science in the same way in which physics is a science often mean to assert that the subject matter of history is not the individual events but the laws or repeatable patterns of human behaviour. Those however who do so obviously confuse history with sociology. A science of sociology would be concerned with general laws and would leave to history the consideration of what actually happened in definite places at given times.[2]

The idealist historiographer will not accept the limitation of his role to mere chronicler any more readily than to scientist. There are valid laws or repeatable patterns of human behavior, historical, sociological, or psychological. What follows if these are sufficient in the sense that the mechanics of Book I of Newton's *Principia* is sufficient?[3] By "sufficient" we mean that, applied to the data, the chronicled sequence of events in time and place, as Newton's mechanics is applied to the observation of the planets and their waves, these laws yield new laws in accordance with the subsequent sequence of events. Just so Newton's laws of gravitation emerged from a covering of Kepler's empirical laws by the mechanics of Book I and in turn explained the tides, the motions of the moon, the flattening of the earth at the poles. If all these conditions are met, then indeed a *science* of history is possible. The activities of modern historians would be to the activities of the future historical scientists in possession of the laws, as the activities of the alchemists were to the activities of the radiochemist discoverers of Curium, Fermium, and Einsteinium. In 1789, Condorcet wrote:

If man can predict with almost total assurance the phenomena of which he understands the laws; if by the same token even when the laws are unknown to him, he can from the experience of the past foresee with a strong probability the events of the future; why should one regard as a chimaeric enterprise that of tracing with some verisimilitude the tableau of the future destiny of the human species from the results of its history? The sole foundation of belief in the natural sciences is the idea that the general laws, known or unknown, which regulate the phenomena of the universe are necessary and constant; and for what reason would this principle be

---

[2] M. R. Cohen, *The Meaning of Human History* (La Salle, Ill.: Open Court Publishing Co., 1947), quoted in D. B. Kitts, "Historical Explanation in Geology," *Journal of Geology*, Vol. III (1963).

[3] If they are not sufficient, we need not concern ourselves with them.

less true for the development of the faculties than for the other operations of nature? [4]

In principle, these laws would be reducible to the Laplacian minimum—to the aggregation of particles and their motions which to a suitably armed intelligence would yield the whole of the past and the whole of the future. "The human mind," Laplace asserted, ". . . in the perfection which it has been able to give to astronomy, [is] a modest example of such an intelligence." If he had foreseen the modern high-speed computer he would have considered the task as finished.

The ordinary historian proceeds oblivious of the fact that everything he may accomplish is ultimately to be derived by future sociologists and psychologists. These sociologists and psychologists in their turn ignore the fact that their efforts if successful will ultimately and finally yield the three laws of motion which Newton placed at the beginning of the *Principia,* and which he had in part obtained from Galileo and others. But we cannot accept the too easy and too simple premises from which these assertions are derived. As we do not aim at a chronicle of events, a sequence in time and space, we do not accept the hypothetical mechanical achievement of such a chronicle as invalidating our sense of history. We do not conceive of the historian as the passive observer, recorder of events external to himself. His function is the creation of the past in the mind of the historian—the bringing to life, the rebirth of the spirit, which Croce characterizes as true history. This cannot be relegated to Laplacian mechanism. The machine at best frees the human mind and frees the human spirit. It does not substitute for them.

We shall also have little concern with the history of science, not because we cannot grant it validity, as with scientific history, but rather because it is too close to the mainstream of historical thought as the idealist conceives it.

Finally we come to *metastoria,* to archeology, geology, cosmology. Are these properly characterized as between the poles we have set up, or are they—as the idealist historiographers would have it—as close to the pole of science as the history of science and all intellectual history is to the pole of history? Has historiography itself any concern with *metastoria* other than to dismiss it? Has *metastoria*

---

[4] A. Caritat, Marquis de Condorcet, "Esquisse d'un tableau . . . ," in A. Laurent, ed., *Les Grands Ecrivains scientifiques* (Paris: Colin, 1902), p. 137.

anything to learn from historiography, or is it, as it has been so frequently characterized, simply the application of physics and chemistry to specific problems? And, finally, our concern is with order, which these two disparate subjects alike attempt to impose upon the raw phenomena with which they are separately concerned.

I have elsewhere described science as a search for order. J. Robert Oppenheimer, with more sophistication, has characterized the process of science as the *hope* of order. In *metastoria*, which, if it is not science, is certainly in part the application of science, we may catch glimpses of the kind of order for which we searched in the past and for which we hope in the present in the physical sciences. At least we may search and hope in *metastoria* too for these kinds of order. But then if metastoria is to be a kind of history—different in coordinates but part of the same extension, separated from the pole of history not by a discontinuity, a gulf, a wall, but passing imperceptibly by degrees, as the difference passes into the differential— may we not search for, hope for in history, too, those kinds of order for which we search and hope in *metastoria?* And to the extent that these continuities persist we may actually find in history those traces of order, those patterns, that meaning which we demand, without which we find insupportable the human condition.

II. THE ANALOGY BETWEEN HISTORY AND MUSIC

Since I have already ventured far from the safe and familiar ground of geological science, like the unwary geologist whose zeal to examine yet one more outcrop betrays him into the midst of a dangerous and shaky bog, so that in desperation he leaps from one sinking hummock to the dubious support of another, I presume to call in music, a subject remote from any in which I might claim education. Yet, allowing for the weakness of analogy, music and history are processes with at least a superficial similarity. They are both processes in time. Or, rather, the phenomena of both—the musical notes, the historical events—are processes in time which become, transformed by the human mind, respectively music and history.

For the amateur listening to music there is an aesthetic experience which is brought about during and following the performance. This experience exists not in the past or in the future but solely in the present. Yet the sensation of notes in the present is completely determined by the notes which have immediately preceded it, and our appreciation of these sensations is determined by our cultural conditioning—in other words, by the impress of our past experience or by the interaction of the immediate perception with our minds. The musical experience is a development, a process in time which is, triggered though it may be by waves, vibrations, pipes, numbers, nevertheless a purely subjective experience. If the musical development is trivial or overly simple, we reject it as banal—the nursery tune, the romantic popular song. Yet even the obvious may be rescued from triviality when it presses upon our beliefs and emotions, when it represents an extramusical body of experience which lends to the purely mechanical perception an extramusical dimension. I am thinking of the moving song of the civil rights movement or the harsh impact of such music as the "Horst Wessel Lied," the Nazi anthem.

Like music, history is experienced in the present. The past is gone, the future not yet. As in music, the impact of the momentary event is completely determined by the past. Our episode is meaningless without its background, its perspective, just as in music the note is of high or low pitch not in the absolute but according to whether the preceding notes were higher or lower. It is sharp or flat according to the key. It is harmonious or discordant according to its relationship to the experience which has gone to make the percipient mind. Let us say that our episode is the death of a man by violence. Our historical appraisal is completely determined by the context. Is he a soldier killed in battle? Is he a war criminal? Is he the legitimate heir to the throne? Is he an anonymous man of Hiroshima? For the positivist historian the concern is with "what actually happened in definite places at given times."[5] Yet "no event intrinsically points beyond itself."[6] The aim of the positivist historian is the construction of a sequence of events in time, ordered by their causal relationships (which, however, being the result of natural law, are already known and need not be stated). To reduce history to this one-dimensional frame is to reduce Bach to the trace on an oscilloscope. What actually happened? In the one case death by violence; in the other, vibrations in the air. Bach may be performed by a master; but it is none the less the fact of Bach, the phenomenal Bach, for being performed badly by an incompetent.

[5] Cohen, *Meaning of Human History.*
[6] A. J. Ayer, *The Problem of Knowledge* (London: Macmillan, 1958), quoted in Kitts, "Historical Explanation in Geology."

The data, the documents, the chronicle of history are comparable to the wood, the rosin, the catgut side of music. What is done with this becomes history or music—or else there is only the material gut and noise that existed in the beginning. I am not here drawing a contrast between music and science. Vibrations, wood, rosin, even oscilloscopes are of no more intrinsic interest to the physicist than to the musician. To find in these a pattern, to link them through mathematics to fundamentals, to impose upon them an order of his own devising, is the main concern of the physicist.

The rosin and the catgut are the chaos of existence. To convert them to aesthetic experience is the province of music. To convert them to a theory of sound is the province of a Helmholtz. The death of a man, the ink on a parchment, the chip on a stone must somehow be converted into living thought to enter into our minds and to interact with the experience of our past and to convert us subtly from the men we were into something different, more profound, more complex. To convert the raw material—the ledger, the arrowhead, the injunction from the Galileo file in the Papal Archives—into living thought is the province of history. The ledger may be false; the Galileo injunction never existed; the arrowhead is a Japanese import. They are none the less the starting point, but only the starting point, for history, for the complex of ideas that grows out of the interaction of the mind of the historian with his problem to create a new pattern, a new form, a new mind. These the historian communicates with us. He shares with us this new fulfillment, an enrichment of the spirit which is to broaden our depth of experience. As we change the patterns of thought, which we designate the mind, we grow and change ourselves as men.

The music that goes to make a superb performance of the work of a master is represented in part by the pattern of magnetization of an impregnated plastic tape. From this it is converted to a complex of vibrations in the air. Nothing in this had anything to do with order —except that within this obvious disorder there is the germ of the music that was and is to be. The germ of order past and future, but hardly present, is there. The chaos of catgut, of vibrations, of acrylic plastics and ferromagnetic colloids becomes significant order, human order, harmony when it is appropriately transformed. This transformation from the surd receptacle of Plato to order is music.

The human experience, the human condition, we transform to order in various ways and various aspects. In history we read order into our experience. We assemble our perceptions; and the nature of our minds, whether biologically or culturally determined, is such as to impose upon the raw material of our experience a pattern, an order. We cannot accept, we reject the ideas of "idealessness," disorder, or meaninglessness in events. No historiographer, positivist or idealist, accepts contingency as meaningful history. When we are faced with a historical event of first magnitude, for example, the assassination of our president, we instinctively reject the idea that this is an expression of the meaninglessness, the absence of design in the universe. From those who immediately saw a conspiracy of the right to those who spun elaborate fantasies of intrigue and treason in high places, the essential blind stupidity which is the official explanation, the only explanation in any accord with evidence, is desperately unsatisfactory. Murders are committed by madmen, but history does not recognize madness. The maniacal view of history, the view of the three blind crones weaving their tangled distraught webs, is the one branch of historiography without support. It would not be history; it would be the transformation of chaos into chaos, the identity transformation, which is no transformation at all and which is no history at all because it is without order. We take the isolated act as we take the isolated note in music. As our senses cannot attach meaning to one vibration of the air, but only to a frequency—to so many cycles per second—so our historical consciousness rejects the single isolated event and accepts it only in the sense of an orderly pattern. We impose the pattern on our perception of the past, we transform it through the medium of our minds, recreating not singular events or chronicles in time but notes, harmonies, patterns, the rise and fall of empires, the transformation of societies (which are for us a complex of ideas) by means of ideas.

III. SCIENCE AND HISTORICAL SCIENCE

In these pages I wish to sketch briefly the argument from the history of science against the view that science is principally concerned with the construction or derivation of general laws from observations of objective phenomena. If physical science is not so characterized, it is not from this parent that historical science, *metastoria,* acquires a positivist cast. And if we disallow this "scientism" in the physical sciences themselves, shall we grant it refuge in the study of history? The idealist historiographer, in order to prune history of all vestiges of realism, sets up a fundamental philosophic dichotomy between history and science and chooses to regard science as a kind of photograph or tape recording of the physical world from which a series of general laws may be derived.

It is true that science is concerned with general law and that scientists, as Keynes said of Newton, have thought of themselves as magicians, uncovering a scheme of order prepared by other hands, by Nature and Nature's God. But it is also true that it is not the laws per se, or even their formal elegance (to borrow from the mathematical vocabulary), which is the main concern of science. Newton's laws are not so useful as Sir William Hamilton's formulation, nor are they so close to describing our observations as Einstein's. They are not by this rendered "wrong," but simply less than sufficient. Designed by the seventeenth-century mind, they fail to meet the requirements of the twentieth century. Bodies still fall to the earth, and the planets proceed in their courses as before, oblivious to the repeal or amendment of the law of gravity. These laws, as opposed to the phenomena which they imperfectly represent, are free creations of the human mind. They are the attempts to impose an intellectual order upon the chaos of experience.

Turning to *metastoria,* to historical sciences such as geology and cosmology, we see that these, too, began in the manner taken for absolute by the nineteenth-century positivist. They emerge from objectivism in the sense of regarding science as outside of and apart from the human mind. The first geologists of the seventeenth and eighteenth centuries saw the aim of science as the establishment of natural laws, a framework to be induced from the phenomena of the present, including the results of other sciences, and from which the application of deduction yields not only a past consonant with the evidences surviving into the present, but a future, the evidences for which have yet to come into being. In this category we place all generalizations such as the now outmoded cyclical view of geological history or the current theory of stellar evolution.

In the seventeenth century Robert Hooke, defining the new science of the earth, wrote, "The doctrine aimed at is, the Cause and Reason of the present Figure, Shape, and Constitution of the Surface of this Body of the Earth. . . ." [7] Hooke, the greatest mechanic of all time, in this definition at any rate excluded history, and for the new science, proposed the same analysis of figure and number

[7] Robert Hooke, *The Posthumous Works of R. H.,* Edited by Richard Waller (London, 1705) , p. 334.

which the seventeenth century took as synonymous with the new philosophy. In a modern expression of this point of view, D. B. Kitts writes that for both history and geology "the basic concern is with deriving and testing of singular statements. . . . Geologists and historians are interested in determining the specific dates and the specific places at which events took place and in constructing a historical chronicle on the basis of these determinations." [8]

It is this view of the history of nature which Croce accepts and which causes him to dismiss so scornfully those who would link the atom with the thought, who "run on without meeting any obstacle, from the cell, indeed from the nebula, to the French Revolution, and even to the socialist movements of the nineteenth century." [9] Natural history, by which Croce understands that realism which has for its aim the construction of a "chronological arrangement of things spatially distinct," he designates, as we have seen, *metastoria*. For idealist historiographers this represents science, or a part of science which they view as taxonomic, descriptive, and archivist in its essence. As they have rejected the classification and categorization, the description per se, and archivism as such from legitimate history, this presence in *metastoria* is for them a proof that *metastoria* has nothing to do with history. Natural history in other than a realistic sense, the function of mind in science, the aesthetic and purely intellectual content of science, Croce would have dismissed as myth, referring in fact to the authors of universal histories as mythmakers.

As history ceases to be history out of contact with the living document, as science ceases to be science apart from its continual intercourse with experience, natural history, or *metastoria,* "does not sift gold out of the rubbish but regenerates the rubbish anew and makes it a living plant." The archives, the documents, the data for geological history are the rocks and fossils, their distributions, configurations, and compositions "the *present* Figure, Shape, and Constitution of the Surface of this Body of the Earth," as Hooke so clearly saw.

If in digging a Mine, or the like, an artificial Coin or Urne, or the like Substance be found, no one scruples to affirm it to be of this or that Metal or Earth he finds them by trial to be of: Nor that they are Roman, Saxon,

---

[8] Kitts, "Historical Explanation in Geology," pp. 298–99.
[9] B. Croce, *History, Its Theory and Practice,* trans. D. Ainslie (new ed.; New York: Russell and Russell, 1960) , p. 129.

Norman, or the like, according to the Relievo, Impression, Characters, or Form they find them of. Now these Shells and other Bodies are the Medals, Urnes, or Monuments of Nature much more plain and discoverable . . . to correct natural Chronology . . . nor will there be wanting Media or Criteria of Chronology. . . .[10]

The goal of objectivity, a necessary counterweight to the theological and teleological *metastoria* of the eighteenth and nineteenth centuries, has come to occupy an illusorily central position in science. In the geological sciences objectivity is equated with the strictest archivism, with a puritanical avoidance of conjecture and interpretation. In the geological mythos the *field,* signifying geological surveying and collecting, is, like the heroine in the Western movie, symbol of a clinical virtue. Like the analytic laboratory for the chemist, the field for the geologist, the archivist side of his historical study, overshadows all else. The worst that can be said of a geologist is that he is an armchair geologist—this from the strange alliance between the scientist-realist and the philosopher-idealist. They both share the conviction that there is in science not the least shred of intellectual content.

The history of science affords us an existential perspective. Perhaps (and I stress the reservation) we do find in modern science that objectivity, that realism, that hardness and clarity of mind which characterize the fictional scientist, the man in the white suit, the scientific realist. Jacques Barzun reminds us of Dickens' Professor Dingo, arrested for defacing buildings with his geological hammer, who told the officer that the only building he knew was the temple of science. But, historically, Western science has grown from the fertile ground of the human imagination, from the drive for order and meaning and purpose. Alfred North Whitehead puts it: from Greek rationality and Hebrew monotheism. The birth of modern science in the seventeenth century, of Newtonian mechanics and inductive philosophy, was triggered by the cosmological problem, by the Copernican system and the efforts of Kepler, Galileo, and Hooke in its behalf.

The Copernican system was not so much a revolution in thought as it is customarily portrayed, but rather a rearrangement of the medieval nests of concentric spheres about a point, the *universe* of the Greeks—so that, without labels, it becomes difficult to distinguish the quaint woodcuts of the Copernican from the later Ptole-

[10] Hooke, *Posthumous Works,* p. 335.

maic schemes. That these in turn stemmed from Greek geometry, and from that identification of the world with form and number—with circular form and the numbers 7 and 10—which for the Greeks meant ordering existence, is accepted historical doctrine. Plato's problem, the "saving of the appearances," the attempt to reduce the apparent chaos of experience to simple numerical and geometric relationships, from which Greek cosmological doctrine stemmed, was the classical version of the still more ancient Pythagorean vision of a preordained harmony (which is to say number) to Cosmos.

If anyone were to say that science has no origin in such vague stuff, but is concerned with techniques and the mechanic arts, let him reflect on the failure of Chinese civilization to produce a science. The Chinese, not the Europeans of the millennia between Pythagoras and Copernicus, were objective, were realists, were without religion in the Western sense. Yet it was the Chinese who had the inventive genius that led to the techniques of cast iron, the crossbow, printing, paper, inks, clockworks, gunpowder, the magnetic compass, to name only a few. The Confucian mandarins who tutored the emperors and administered the prosperous elegant cities and the broad tree-lined avenues, the canals, the irrigation works, the munitions factories, the foundries, were dedicated to a purely rationalist code, a moral and ethical code that was itself subordinated to good taste and common sense.[11] In the accurately written official records which run back almost without interruption to the first bronze age dynasty in North China, we trace the development of a highly sophisticated astronomy-chronography by which, for example, we are enabled to fix the date of the nova that gave birth to the Crab nebula. It was not here among these court astronomers, these rational, calm administrators and men of practical affairs, but in the border marches where Slav met German and where men burned each other alive for the dubious satisfaction of saving their souls, that the Copernican transposition of the sun for the earth at the center of an ancient diagram set in motion the train of idea-events which we call modern civilization.

Although we have attributed the origins of modern science to a drive for order in the sense of the analysis of experience in simple, human rational terms, science has changed in many ways since its Renaissance beginnings. After Newton, the emphasis shifted from

[11] H. G. Creel, *Chinese Thought* (Chicago, Ill.: University of Chicago Press, 1953).

the particular problem of the solar system to the general subject of mechanics. The structure science erected was based on the idea of a predetermined order, visualized as the ultimate reduction to a priori fundamentals such as the three axioms of mechanics which are the laws of Newton. With the progress of science, electricity and magnetism were shown to obey the essentially Newtonian laws of Coulomb. An atomistic chemistry appeared. Even the phenomenological science of thermodynamics, intellectually rigorous and free of all except the purest of assumptions (such as the law of conservation of energy), was shown to be a statistical averaging of Newtonian laws over large quantities, the individual mechanical parts of which were imperceptible to "beings who have not the fineness of perception to enable them to appreciate quantities of the order of magnitude of those which relate to single particles." [12]

It was with the introduction of statistics to mechanics that the first cracks in the mechanical edifice were made. For now one spoke of averages and of imperceptibles and even of probabilities in place of law and observation and certainty. Scientific determinism remains in statistical mechanics, but it is a statistical, a probabilistic determinism. It is sufficient, but it introduces the first possibility of error because in practice, although not in theory, we are limited to probabilities, and probabilities—though overwhelming—are not certainty. Between a thing which is finite and a thing which is infinite, there is all the difference.[13]

The insufficiencies of Newtonian mechanics were manifest in, and the transformation of classical physics was accomplished by, the theories of relativity. These theories preserved determinism and rigorous law, and therefore classical concepts of order in nature, but at the same time were not incompatible with more fundamentally disturbing developments in physical thought. Ironically, Einstein pushed mechanics from its pedestal with the theory of special relativity at the same time that he was confirming its basic importance with the theory of the Brownian movement. In his papers on the Brownian movement, he established the direct connection between the kinetics of the visible, ponderable, particles of Brown, and the imperceptible particles of Gibbs's coarse beings—the molecules and

[12] J. W. Gibbs, *Elementary Principles in Statistical Mechanics* (New Haven, Conn.: Yale University Press, 1902).

[13] C. Huygens, *Treatise on Light* (1693), trans. S. P. Thompson (New York: Dover Publications, 1962).

atoms themselves. And if this philosophical inconsistency were not enough, he published in the same Volume XVII of *Annalen der Physik* the ideas which were to establish the quantum theory of Planck by extending it to light phenomena, and later to elasticity. Out of these and similar papers grew the wave and quantum mechanics of today. Limitations appear now in the statistics which make the probabilistic interpretations of the earlier statistical mechanics not simply convenient and practical necessities, but theoretical limits to knowledge and to determinism. At the root of things we find not Laplace's particles and their motions but a fundamental and permanent uncertainty. Our laws are not invalidated; they are seen in a new light as stemming from the observations of Gibbsian beings whose coarseness or fineness of perception is irrelevant. The laws are simply the laws of chance, which is to say the laws of not law or law outside of law. They are fundamentally, and not merely as a matter of convenience, statistical. Sir Arthur Eddington says that at the end of our long search for order in the universe we encounter a mirror: "We have found a strange footprint on the shores of the unknown. We have devised profound theories, one after another, to account for its origin. At last, we have succeeded in reconstructing the creature that made the footprint. And lo! it is our own." [14]

I have suggested that perhaps at the end of the long corridor we have been following we shall find only chaos, the formless nonbeing out of which the gods fashioned existence by ordering. In the end we recognize that our laws are of our own devising; that our science has fashioned finally a map of the human mind.

IV. TOWARD A PHILOSOPHY OF METASTORIA

Metastoria is not a system of laws or repetitive patterns of natural events in time. The simplest kind of law we might anticipate in a science of the history of nature would be one that was a direct parallel to laws as they are conceived in physics and chemistry. For example, the proportionate distribution of radioactive elements and their daughter elements may be related to the time of crystallization of an igneous rock. Yet, on examination, this relationship is seen to be an application of physics and chemistry to the solution of a

[14] Sir Arthur Eddington, *Space, Time, and Gravitation* (Cambridge, Eng.: Cambridge University Press, 1929), quoted by E. Wind in *Philosophy and History* (Oxford: Clarendon Press, 1936).

geological problem, in much the same way as the X-ray applied to an old canvas may establish its authenticity. We cannot allow that the application of scientific law is a sufficient warranty of the results of the application. A horoscope cast with the assistance of impeccable trigonometric determinations of planetary configuration is not thereby transformed from astrology to astronomy. The trigonometry so meanly employed loses none of its mathematical purity. Its mere employment does not lend it an astrological character. Physics is not by its employment rendered into history, nor is geology, by this borrowing, reduced to physics.

The fundamental principles of geology, such as uniformitarianism or superposition, are not at all parallel to laws as they are conceived in physical science. The principle of uniformitarianism states that the same processes at work molding the earth's surface at the present time were operative in the past, and that they have produced the present configuration of the surface by continuous action over long periods of time. The law of superposition states that the uppermost in the sequence of sedimentary layers is the most recently deposited. The first principle is simply a slight revision of James Clerk Maxwell's statement of the general maxim of physical science: "The difference between one event and another does not depend on the mere difference of the times or the places at which they occur, but only on differences in the nature, configuration or motion of the bodies concerned."

The second can be derived from the definition of the process of sedimentation. Neither principle is uniquely geological. Both are unhistorical, outside of time.

Other attempts have been made to fit geology with a set of laws, but these have been descriptive and appropriate laws.[15] If in these examples we see that *metastoria* makes use of physical and chemical law, that we are concerned with nature and nature remains governed by natural law, it does not imply that *metastoria* is therefore merely the application of physical and chemical law. This would put *metastoria* in the same relationship to physics as Cohen implied for the relationship of history to sociology and psychology. No autonomous history of nature would be possible. But we have already rejected this rigid realism in physics and chemistry in favor of a Platonic drive toward order. How much more ought we to deny

[15] W. H. Bucher, *Deformation of the Earth's Crust* (Princeton, N.J.: Princeton University Press, 1933).

the applicability of a rule of a priori law for the history of nature? If the idealist historiographer, unconcerned for science, sees the whole study of nature as a gathering in of that which is there, which exists outside of and apart from the minds of men, great scientists do not concur. Science, too, we insist with Einstein, is a free creation of the human mind. Is the order for which we seek there in nature, or do we not rather impose it upon nature, selecting those aspects of nature which fit our requirements of regularity, discarding or at least relegating to future study those aspects which do not?

For the phlogiston chemist the conversion of a shiny metal by heat into an earthy calx meant the loss of the fiery element—phlogiston. Phlogiston plus calx was the compound—metal. Antoine Laurent Lavoisier renamed the phlogiston "oxygen" and placed it in the air instead of in the metal. He explained the same formation of the calx from metal by making the calx the compound containing the phlogiston (oxygen) element. The experiment, the observations, the raw material of the idea of combustion were known for half a million years. Lavoisier's idea is neater in some ways than that of the phlogistonite, but deficient in others. For example, he misnamed his fiery element "oxygen," meaning "acid-former," which it is not; and he thought of it as a combination of light and a base. We could multiply examples endlessly. By science, we cannot mean the mere experiment, the operations, the description. We must mean the complex of ideas, the elaborate superstructure which we have erected on the Greco-Hebraic foundations of our culture by way of the seventeenth-century European Renaissance.

The metastorian, like the historian, is continually refreshed by contact with sources; like the scientist, he returns again and again to the fertile field of experience. Yet the sources of their descriptions do not make historical science. It is the imaginative reconstruction with full richness of detail of the physical past in time which makes *metastoria*. Geology exists in the minds of the geologists. Outside of this intellectual endeavor, there are stones and bones.

Is there a spiritual or moral content to *metastoria*, or shall we dismiss this as the vain posturings of scientists swollen with power? Has it really made no difference in our understanding of the human condition, whether the earth is at the center of the universe or the sun? Whether the black man is of our species or a lesser breed without the law? Whether we subscribe to myth or truth? Are we so far from the seventeenth-century founders of our science, from

Newton who saw it as God's glory to conceal and man's to reveal the secrets of the universe? Would we be so dull as to reject the lavish drama of mating and extermination that is the theory of evolution? If our science is indeed a free creation of the human mind, if the order which we find in nature is indeed the order on which we ourselves have insisted, then the kind of science or history which we write reflects our society, our culture, and our mind.

The dullard, the dryasdust, the pedant, the pure archivist offend the spirit by rendering lifeless document and fossil into dust, and through the spirit they wound the intellect. History would begin with writing as if this were the only means of communication, as if even in the seventeenth century Hooke had not pointed out the almost infinite variety of the kinds of "writing" that come to us from the past: the faunal assemblages, the stellar spectra, the phase assemblages, the isotopic ratios. The pretense of objectivity, the restriction to total documentation, the exclusion of human values are equally the reflections of mind and in no wise an imposition of nature. José Clemente Orozco's Dartmouth mural, skeletons in academic garb are the doctors presiding at the birth of an infant skeleton, swaddled in the cap and gown of lifeless pedantry.

Although there are physical and chemical limitations to *metastoria,* one cannot speak of a hierarchy of evidences, or let physical law take precedence over historical inference. The famous blunder of Lord Kelvin is a case in point. Kelvin found in the two laws of thermodynamics, the conservation of energy and the irreversibility of process, that absolute certainty which his generation had seen illusory in science after science. From the thermodynamics of the sun he concluded that the duration of life on earth was relatively brief, and that the vast times demanded by geological evidences and the theory of evolution were impossible. He could not conceive of the future science of nuclear physics and radioactivity, which was to make his assumptions irrelevant, because he could not admit of constraints to be placed on the universality of the first and second laws. If there is a moral to be drawn from this, it is that *metastoria* must indeed unfold within the framework of nature, but natural law is an ideal construction imposed upon nature. Natural law is the product of the human mind acting in and upon nature—not capable of indefinite extension. The realm of history may be approached from the ordinary laboratory only with extreme caution.

The geological field itself, the evidence existing in the present, the rubbish of lifeless "facts" from which we hope with Goethe to generate the living plant of history are not in themselves that history, nor do they contain their history within themselves as the conclusion is contained within the premises. The thermodynamicist, when he has specified the state of a system, the values of its coordinates, its temperature, pressure, chemical composition, regards his analysis as complete and the system taken into total comprehension. But the properties of interest could be completely specified and the history of the system still unknown.

If we apply a magnetic field to a piece of iron, gradually increasing the strength of the field, the intensity of magnetization of the iron in the direction of the field increases to a maximum or saturation value. Turning off the field reduces the intensity of magnetization of the iron, but it does not remove it. To cancel the magnetization, a field in the reverse direction must be applied. It is not possible to state that the application of a field of such and such a strength will produce a certain magnetization of the iron. This depends upon the previous state of magnetization of the iron, or in other words on the history of the specimen. Conversely, knowing the state of the specimen and the field does not uniquely prescribe its history. It might have reached its state from a state of greater intensity while the field was being reduced, or it might have reached its state from a state of lesser intensity while the field was being increased. Or, since it responds disproportionately according to whether the field is increasing or decreasing, it might have kept a constant intensity of magnetization through a series of fluctuations of the field. On a graph showing field strength plotted against induced magnetism, the locus of points representing possible states of the field-magnet system is a characteristically bounded S-shaped area called a hysteresis loop. The changing states of a specimen would be represented by points making up a curve within the loop —a kind of life path of the specimen. Any curve within the loop is a possible life path for the specimen, and through any point representing a specimen at a given instant of time, an infinite number of curves can be passed. Given the fact, the magnet, we cannot specify its history closer than to the confines of the hysteresis loop although rigorous and accurate laws of magnetization are understood.

The phenomenon of hysteresis is not confined to ferromagnetism but is widely applicable. If I specify precisely the temperature (32°F.) and the composition (H_2O) of a system, I cannot derive from this the proportions of ice to water, and conversely, knowing this and the proportions, I cannot specify the pathway, the immediate past, let alone the history, of this simple system. If I find a body of rock with the characteristic granite texture of interlocking grains, I cannot know whether this was crystallized from a melt or formed as a sediment and subjected to stresses within the earth's crust. The same characteristic texture produced in the casting of metals may also be produced by cold rolling, analogous to the mountain-building stresses of geologic science, followed by annealing. In any polar process, that is, in any process which is directional such as the penetration of a fish hook, there is a hysteresis. What goes up comes down, but not in the same place. Our evidences of history, our documents, urns, fossils, portraits, journals, letters exist now, here, in the present; they are points, each in its hysteresis loop; they cannot themselves contain their histories, any more than the magnet, the granite, or the finished bronze can by its state contain its life path. Even in such restricted cases as that of the magnet, governed by well-defined scientific law, history cannot be specified more closely than the boundaries of the hysteresis loop.

The second law of thermodynamics tells us that the universe tends toward a state of complete disorder; that mountains shall be cut away and basins filled in until the totality of things is a vast conformity. As it predicts the future, so it is a guide to the past. It tells us that time runs in one direction, and therefore history and *metastoria* can never be reduced to applications of physical and chemical law. The equations of mechanics can be reversed with no loss of meaning. Hydrogen and oxygen go to make water—or water goes to make hydrogen and oxygen. The direction of the reaction requires the second law. For the geologist, as for the historian, the direction is all-important. The geologist's processes under the second law must all run down; order must give way to disorder, mountains and valleys to plains. But since mountains and valleys appear, since metals are concentrated in veins, obviously another class of geologic processes exists. The interplay of the two kinds of processes—those for which in accord with the second law of thermodynamics entropy and disorder are increasing, and those for which order is increasing and entropy is (locally) decreasing—this interplay is the dialectic of *metastoria*. Evolution is ordinarily considered as a positivistic and mechanistic theory, but this is superficial. We have accepted uncritically the evaluation of the great evolutionists

T. H. Huxley, Charles Darwin, Alfred Russel Wallace, and their opponents. The first Renaissance scientists failed to distinguish between their efforts at natural philosophy and the mother subject, the love of learning and scholarship within which it grew. This rejection of narrow categorization was itself a measure of their strength. The naturalists of the nineteenth century in the same spirit saw themselves as Newtons and Lavoisiers. Because the concept of the descent of man raised up a storm of clerical and philosophical objections; because the method of selection of evolution was environmental and natural, rather than supernatural, the theory itself was condemned as an intolerable extension of rigid physico-chemical mechanism. But actually evolution arose in opposition to the hard-core mechanism of men like Georges Cuvier and Louis Agassiz and was bitterly attacked by them.

"Instead of facts we are treated with marvelous bear, cuckoo, and other stories," Agassiz wrote scornfully; while Cuvier, who did not live to Darwin's time, characterized the speculative Joseph Priestley, as one who *"arrive dans la lice avec des opinions conçues d'avance, cherche à les faire valoir plus qu'à les examiner, et se jette, pour les soutenir, dans les hypothèses les plus contradictoires."* [16]

They prided themselves on making of zoology and geology a *"science tout précise et tout aussi méthodique que l'astronomie."* Cuvier's generation had no use for Erasmus Darwin, the soft-nosed grandfather of Charles, who cast his theory of evolution in the form of a poem to be read for Joseph Priestley and James Watt at the meetings of the Lunar Society of Birmingham; Agassiz' generation ridiculed Ebenezer Emmons and his Taconic rocks.

But, if evolution was not the operation of blind mechanistic chance, neither was it teleological. Contingency implies an impartiality or indifference of the chances. If a coin comes up heads three times in a row, there is still a 50 per cent chance that it will come up heads in the next throw. If these are genes which are to turn up, however, the chances are affected by heredity. Unlike the game of pinchpenny, the chances of the future are affected by the present, both genetically and environmentally. Natural selection is an environmental influence. Teleology does not enter into it.

Clearly organisms evolve, and society, visualized as global culture, is also an evolving organism. The student of history must regard the

[16] Georges Cuvier, *Receuil des Eloges Historiques* (Paris: Levrault, 1819), p. 191.

societies of the past in a given time stratum as closer to each other than to their successor societies of the present. Was it sheer coincidence that the Buddha, Confucius, the Hebrew prophets, and Zoroaster all date from the middle of the first millennium B.C.? The human race had been in existence for 100,000 years. The Academy of the Gate of Chhi was founded in 318 B.C., and the Porch of the Stoics dates from 300 B.C., a century and a half before the opening of the Silk Road and any obvious contacts between East and West. Yet the doctrine of the elements—spirit, earth, water—of Genesis, of Greece, of India, of China, was so different in concept, according to Joseph Needham, that as between East Asia and the West, at any rate, simultaneous independent invention is the only explanation.[17]

We reject the categorization of evolution as physical and chemical science applied to the organic world because evolution remains an ex post facto study. We must distinguish between evolution and genetics. Not only the process of evolution but the science of evolution remain autonomous studies, and both the process and our study of the process are independent of the advance or lack of advance of genetics, in the same way that geologic history must remain independent of the confidence of a William T. Kelvin in the laws of thermodynamics. Geology, too, remains an ex post facto study. Formerly, we regarded geologic history as cyclic, an unconscious modern plagiarism of ancient Greek thought, but we can no longer retreat to the simplicities of the alternation between geosyncline and anticlinorium and the rhythmic advance and retreat of the continental seas precipitating their academic sediments over the minds of generations of collegians.

At any stage of history, physico-chemical law governs. But what governs the passage from stage to stage? This may be only a matter of the probabilities and even of probabilities which mature, but such probabilities are not unintelligible. Plato saw that our sense impressions are illusory, but he insisted that they were all we have. We have no reason to abandon the attempt to distill from nature that which is intelligible—the order in nature. Unlike physics with its Maxwellian laws independent of time or place, *metastoria* is determined by the past in its evolution to the present. But, given the influence of the past, what then determines the probabilities?

[17] Joseph Needham, *Science and Civilization in China* (4 vols.; Cambridge, Eng.: Cambridge University Press, 1954–59), I, 154.

The physicist confronted with different sets of situations devises appropriate statistics for each. For classical physics, there is the Maxwell-Boltzmann statistics, while electrons obey the Fermi-Dirac statistics, and photons the Einstein-Bose statistics. But what is the statistics that governs organic evolution? cultural evolution? geomorphic evolution? stellar evolution?

If I shoot a single photon of light at two closely spaced holes, it will go through either one or the other but not both. If many photons go through, one after the other, a photographic plate behind tells me that the probabilities are calculable by mathematical equations of waves—as if my photons, interfering with each other in the manner of waves, were somehow aware of the presence or absence of the other hole. These waves are probability waves.

I find a set of equations by which I may predict the intensity of light at a given position, which is to say the proportionate number of photons scattered to this position. This number is related to the probability of finding a given photon at this position. The set of equations is of the same mathematical form as the equations for the diffraction of waves. In addition to the geometric description of the experiment, certain constants and variables appear in these equations—λ, v, c, and so forth—which I may identify with wave length, frequency, the velocity of light, but which I may also choose to regard as physical parameters, unspecified, with which I may fully describe past experiments of this sort and predict accurately the results of future experiments.

The view we receive of modern physics is essentially one of a statistical science in which the simplest cases are those which are the most disorderly, such as an ideal gas which lends itself admirably to the elementary treatment of kinetic-molecular theory and the classical statistics of Maxwell and Boltzmann. The introduction of varying degrees of departure from the postulated total disorder of the classical gas complicates our statistics immensely. A simple example is the breakdown of the concept of molecular motion as proportional to temperature. The quantum theory proposes a zero point energy, and the validity of this minimal energy concept is confirmed experimentally. It is a direct consequence of the quantization of energy.

At this point I should like to sketch a parallel approach to one specific problem in *metastoria*. The late Paul Niggli of Zurich with his students compiled statistical studies of the frequency of occurrence of particular forms of crystals of particular species.[18] These data were plotted in various ways and used by Professor Niggli as the standard against which to test ideas accounting for the form of crystals. The same data were similarly the observations against which all more recent ideas measure themselves. These data actually represent a small, but let us assume statistically valid, summary of the results of a large-scale experiment in the growth of crystals— all those which were grown in the past, all those which are being grown today, and all those which will be grown in the future, under natural conditions and also under the special case of natural conditions which is the experimental laboratory. Restricting our attention to one particular species, we observe great variety in appearance, in geographic and geologic provenance, which at first appears to rule out any sensible comments on crystal form. But crystallographers are aware that the twin laws of Hooke-Steno and Haüy guarantee a rigid and precise order within this confusion. Every plane bounding-face on every individual crystal of this species may be referred to one of a small group of nearby points of a three-dimensional lattice.

If our statistics show many plane bounding-faces associated with one point and few with another, the probability of occurrence of the first is proportionately greater than the probability of occurrence of the second. But this system of the weighted points of a three-dimensional lattice is already familiar to the student of crystallography. It is the datum of the X-ray diffraction experiment performed on a crystal of the same species adjusting the scale of the lattice. With a different adjustment of the scale of the same lattice, it becomes the datum of the experimental diffraction of electrons, or neutrons, or even molecular beams by a crystal of the same species. For the diffraction experiments the statistical weights of each lattice point are the respective probabilities of the scattering in a given direction of X-ray photons, or electrons, or neutrons, or molecular beams. These weights, or intensities, or energies are in turn calculated with the equations of wave diffraction. We introduce λ, v, c, and so forth, the symbols of the parameters of wave diffraction. We ascribe to these the physical significance of wave length, frequency, velocity, even in the case of beams of molecules or electrons. Would we not

[18] Paul Niggli, *Lehrbuch der Mineralogie und Kristallchemie* (Berlin: Borntraeger, 1941).

better exclaim with Newton, *"Hypotheses non fingo"* and leave the physical significance of these parameters out of consideration? "It is enough" says Newton, "that gravity does really exist, and act according to the laws which we have explained, and abundantly serves to account for all the motions of the celestial bodies, and of our sea." [19]

The statistical study of the forms of crystals obtained for Niggli's data is an averaging over geographic and geologic conditions through geologic time. Since we have assumed that Niggli's sample is large enough and widespread enough for statistical validity, we have of necessity assumed that it represents a measure of thermodynamic equilibrium. The relative weights of the lattice points are inversely proportional to the growth rates of the plane bounding-faces of the crystal represented by the points, and inversely proportional to the surface energies of the faces. Presumably, since our data are of the same mathematical form (although less rich in detail) as the data of diffraction, equations of the same mathematical form may be constructed. They have in fact been constructed. They are wave equations; they contain the same λ, ν, c, and so forth, performing the same mathematical functions as in the equations of wave diffraction. They are probability waves, but with them definite predictions are possible. It is not possible to predict with certainty the exact form of a particular crystal—but then it is not possible to predict with certainty through which of two close holes an approaching photon will pass. But it should be possible to predict the statistical distribution of forms from specific atomic structures, just as it is possible to predict the statistical distribution of the X-ray photons scattered in the diffraction experiment from these atomic structures. In the same way as such structures are obtained from the observed X-ray patterns, they should also be obtainable from the observed morphologies.

This procedure, as outlined, represents a projection of geologic information on a single plane of time—or, perhaps more accurately, on a single plane out of time. It is in this sense, unhistorical. It is also, in the sense of making prediction possible, closer to the physical sciences than to history; it is not scientific history in that it is not the construction of historical concepts from historical laws, but rather the use of historical or metastorical data to obtain a physical law.

[19] Isaac Newton, *Mathematical Principles of Natural Philosophy* (1729), trans. A. Motte (Berkeley: University of California Press, 1934), p. 547.

We are by no means dealing with total disorder as in the case of the classical gas. The distribution of the energies in the completely orderly system of the crystal must also be quantized. Is it then possible to look at other geologic systems and, if nothing else, at least appraise them as to the degree of their orderliness and therefore as to the degree of applicability of this statistical procedure? Do we find in *metastoria* not the laws of history but the laws of physics and chemistry?

It is well known that Henry Adams, misled by his friend, the geologist Clarence King, and under the influence of Kelvin's dogmatic adherence to the first and second laws of thermodynamics, attempted to apply the second law to historiography. The second law appears in the light of statistical mechanical analysis as a statement of the ultimate triumph of disorder. To use a homely analogy, if fresh water is added to the sea, we anticipate that the random stirring effect of all natural process will soon mix it so thoroughly with salt water as to render it indetectable. We do not anticipate that these same stirrings, currents, winds, waves, and so forth will even momentarily bring about a local fractionation of the sea water into fresh water and salt. The simple act of mixing involves a tying up, or binding, of energy—a loss of its availability for work, described as "entropy." The inevitability of this degradation, this irretrievable loss, this uncompensated mixing, is the second law of thermodynamics. Yet if Adams was naïve in using the second law to predict the immediate collapse of society, is it in reality no guide at all to the future? to the problem of race for example? The second law of thermodynamics tells us that the *apartheid* of the South African and the Alabaman alike are not more than temporary interruptions to the pace of human evolution, now enormously accelerated by the technology that places the remotest corners of the earth within hours of urban centers of civilization.

V. SUMMARY AND CONCLUSIONS

If we may speak of order in the physical sciences, then to the same extent we may speak of order in *metastoria,* in the historical sciences such as geology and cosmology. It is clear that the world in which geological history unfolds is the space-time continuum subject to the physical and chemical constraints which constitute natural law. These constraints are in essence scientific history. But, as we have seen, they govern not the construction of the *history* (which is that ideal creation of the spirit), but the transmission of the lifeless matter, the dust, the rocks, the documents, the arrowheads, around which we spin our web of history. As in one sense we may regard our laws of nature as negative expressions or statements of impossibility (for example, matter may neither be created nor destroyed; it is impossible to detect a difference in the velocity of light as between a moving and a stationary source; and so forth), so in the same sense we emerge with negative laws—statements of what we do not and cannot mean in *metastoria*. For example, we have a kind of law implied in the phenomenon of hysteresis: the ensemble of material evidences which make up the present are not susceptible of unique interpretation. A second law which I hesitate to reduce to any kind of simple statement is the summary of our discussion of the meaning of the concept of entropy in history. Essentially, we conclude that history is an irreversible process. We have taken an unconscionably lengthy and roundabout way of arriving at the conclusion of the nursery rhyme—that Humpty Dumpty cannot be put back together again. Finally, we also obtain from the sciences confirmation, if that were required, of the impossibility of the Laplacian mechanical reconstruction. It is impossible in theory, and not simply in practice, to tell us which of the two holes a photon has passed through after it has landed on the other side. As Laplace's reconstruction rested finally on the exact determination of the coordinates and momenta of the particles of the universe, and as these are forever indeterminate, so the total reconstruction must remain indeterminate. The exactitude, the determinism, the rule of law which we have renounced for the hard-core sciences, we shall not easily impose upon the study of history.

If the rigid, mechanical kind of order which we commonly or naïvely expect in the physical sciences is not to be extended through *metastoria* to the opposite pole of history, does the route perhaps run in the opposite direction? Does the study of history have lessons for the student of *metastoria* and of science? It is in history first that we have freed ourselves from the concepts which Karl Popper calls "historicism," from the imposition of a predetermined order—theological, "scientific," political. The study of history has passed slowly, painfully, through the stages of myth and of theological history and now is in the throes of ridding itself of the most potent of all fixations, the stage of "scientific history," of a mechanical, deterministic overriding pattern. The sciences, too, or rather what I have termed the "hard-core" sciences of physics and chemistry, have in the twentieth century abandoned the mechanical determinism of a previous era. The last vestiges of this determinism are to be found in the historical sciences. It is now time for these, too, to abandon the naïve realism of the eighteenth century.

If we accept the idealist view of history as a thing of man and mind, rather than the recovery of "what actually happened in a particular place at a particular time"; if we can grant that history is something incomparably greater than its parts, its documents, as music is something other than vibrations or traces on oscilloscopes; then, far from separating us from the physical sciences, such views bring us a deeper insight into the nature of historical science and even the possibility of a rapprochement, an end of the division in our culture and our society. For the history of physical science teaches us that this, too, must be something more than its material parts, than oscilloscopes and cometary paths and the flicker of a needle on a dial which by long and ingenious chains of reasoning is taken as the passage of something called an electron. We will not accept the nineteenth-century view of science as a search for general laws of nature, external to the mind of the scientist, but see it rather as an imposition of the human mind on the chaos of experience. "We must either give up talking of God and Nature," says Gentile, "or open our eyes and confess that we can mean nothing but our ideas of God and Nature. . . . Then Nature, as science gradually becomes aware of its own logical procedure and of the source and meaning of its problem, will reveal itself as a product of developing human thought." [20]

In this view the order that we find in history is the order that we read into it. We put it there, as the order that we find in nature is the order that we have ourselves made. Nature has not turned out to give those evidences of a predetermined order: those circles, those numbers 7 and 10, of which the Pythagoreans insisted the world was made; nor even the particles, their coordinates and momenta, of the mathematical physicists from Newton through Hamilton. We find instead, as our thought turns inward and deeper, order of an ever increasing complexity and of a growing richness of detail. The thought of man, the collective mind which is our society and our

[20] G. Gentile, "The Transcending of Time in History," in *Philosophy and History*, p. 93.

culture in the best sense, is an ordering through comprehension of our world. As the Greek proto-gods drew the world out of primeval chaos, we find ourselves creating the order which is the mind of man, of which the science of nature is a part. It is none the less order for being free of those simplicities of the Pythagorean mystique.

The order that we draw from history is in its turn the order that we put into it, but transformed by the process of history; a growth out of the minds of men before, out of Thucydides and Herodotus who, in putting in the order which they thought they were extracting, made meaningful those processes, those events which they described and, in selecting, made life immortal.

Order in Literature and the Arts

RUDOLF ARNHEIM

Order and Complexity in Landscape Design

Order may be defined as the degree and kind of lawfulness governing the relations among the parts of an entity. Such lawfulness, or
obedience to controlling principles, derives from the over-all theme
or structure, to which the behavior of all parts must conform. It also
applies to the make-up of each part within itself. Without order the
organs of the human body would work at loggerheads with each
other, and the various functions and strivings of the mind would
fight each other in confusion. Without order our senses could not
function: the visible shape of an object must be clearly organized if
we are to recognize, remember, compare it. Furthermore, if there
were no order in nature we could not profit from experience since
what we have learned in the past serves us only if like things persist
in looking alike and if similar consequences follow from similar
causes. If the world were not orderly and the mind unable to

RUDOLF ARNHEIM became known in the thirties for his book on film, called *Film
as Art* in its American edition (1957). In his teaching at Sarah Lawrence College
and the New School for Social Research he continued the tradition of Gestalt
psychology which he had learned in his native Germany. He has been appointed
professor of the psychology of art at the Carpenter Center for the Visual Arts,
Harvard University. He is noted for *Art and Visual Perception: A Psychology of
the Creative Eye* (1954) and *Toward a Psychology of Art* (Berkeley: University of
California Press, 1966) in which this essay also appears. He is a past president
of the American Society for Aesthetics.

perceive and create order man could not survive. Therefore man strives for order.

Complexity is the multiplicity of the relationships among the parts of an entity. By multiplicity I do not mean quantity. A pattern may consist of many parts connected by many relations and yet be quite simple, as, for example, that of a formal rosegarden. And the relations between few parts may add up to a most complex whole, as in an artfully trained and trimmed Japanese pine.

Order and complexity are antagonistic, in that order tends to reduce complexity while complexity tends to reduce order. To create order requires not only rearrangement but in most cases also the elimination of what does not fit the principles determining the order. On the other hand, when one increases the complexity of an object order will be harder to achieve.

Order and complexity, however, cannot do without each other. Complexity without order is chaos; order without complexity is boredom. Although order is needed to cope with the inner and the outer world, man cannot reduce his experience to a network of neatly predictable connections without losing the stimulating riches and surprises of life. Being complexly designed, man must function complexly if he is to be fully himself; and to this end the setting in which he operates must be complex also. It has long been recognized that the great works of man combine high order with high complexity.

Different states of mind require different degrees of order and complexity and, in consequence, suggest different interpretations of nature. If the mind is in need of measure and limpid harmony, it will either conceive of nature as an orderly cosmos—the way the Pythagoreans or Neoplatonists did—or abhor it as the savage foe of reason and safety, as exemplified by Western man's attitude toward mountainous wilderness through the Middle Ages until fairly recently. If, on the contrary, the mind longs for inexhaustible and unpredictable abundance and rejects order as artificial it will either seek refuge in the unfathomable variety of nature or condemn its lawfulness as mechanical. The historian is accustomed to distinguishing these attitudes as the classic and the romantic.

It is because of nature's own inherent ambiguity that such contradictory views can be held concerning its order. Science suggests that in the last analysis everything in nature is regulated by a few basic laws. In this sense nature has high order, which manifests itself visibly in the planetary system or in the starshape of the petals of a daisy. In the solar system as well as in the daisy a simple constellation of forces determines the entire structure, practically without disturbance; hence their orderly look. However, when we scrutinize an uncultivated setting of trees and shrubbery we notice no such undisturbed order. The potentially regular shape of each tree is diverted from its symmetry by the influence of wind and sun and crippled by the presence of other trees. In the natural landscape we tend to observe order in the large and in the small but less so in the intermediate range. Looking from a distance we see perhaps a forest or a town fitting itself smoothly to the simply shaped slope of a mountain; and the mountain, together with other mountains, may form a fairly orderly massif because the forces that shape forests and mountainscapes have something of the same simplicity that creates the symmetry of the flower. But, when we consider the natural objects of more nearly our own size, we find a different situation. Here also, it is true, we discover approximations of harmony, due to such over-all conditions as the lay of the land and the proportionate distribution of space resulting from the struggle for light and water; but at the same time there is equally evident a lack of coordination. The branches of each tree move along complicated paths, and there is little visible relationship between this bush and that fallen stump, this rock and that patch of wildflowers. Even here the forester and the botanist discern an orderly interplay of supply and demand, but the form-seeking eye notices disorder.

What is *disorder?* It is not the absence of all order but rather the clash of uncoordinated orders. An accumulation of pieces assumes the quality of disorder only when within each piece, or group of pieces, there appears a clearly discernible order, which, however, is neither continued nor contradicted by the neighboring order, but rather ignored, denied, distorted, made incomprehensible. The relationship between partners is disorderly when there is no clear-cut way of telling whether they conform or contrast, whether they are coordinated or subordinated. The term "disorder," as I use it here, describes a structural condition. It also implies a condemnation in the sense that disorder interferes with optimal human functioning. Nevertheless, given certain needs, disorder may be attractive and desirable. For example, it provides a crude, anarchic form of freedom, and as such it offers relief to the victims of regimentation.

Man's attitude toward nature is, in part, his reaction to the order or disorder he observes in it. This reaction, we may safely say, reflects his feelings about the kind of order he experiences in his own mind as well as in the community of his family, social group, or nation. For example, the heated controversy in the eighteenth century between the defenders of the formalized French garden and the partisans of the looser English style must surely be considered one aspect of the fight of liberalism against the rigid autocracies of the past.

When it comes to landscaping and gardening, that is, to man's shaping of nature, we must refer to another basic attitude, namely the varying notions about the *origin of order* as far as the relations between man and nature are concerned. It has been asserted that in Christianity the evaluation of nature depends largely on whether nature is viewed as the creation of God or as the product of the defection from God. In the first case, nature appears as the incarnation of the divine order, and man, a child of nature, creates order when he acts as an executor of natural order. In accordance with this point of view, desirable order is what looks natural, and the geometrical forms introduced by man appear as a dangerous impoverishment of the true order. Thus the battle for the "English" garden was fought in the name of nature, and care was taken to keep the formal order of the man-made landscape immanent rather than explicit. Man enters the garden gate not as the master of nature but as its prodigal son, humbly returning and graciously readmitted to the benefits of the order from which he strayed. This attitude appears most clearly in the pantheistic conceptions of our Western culture and—with due allowance for basic differences—in Chinese Taoism and its later modifications expressed in the Japanese Zen gardens of the fifteenth century. The design of the ancient Japanese gardens is, of course, most carefully controlled—with the intention, however, of hiding the formative contribution of man.

When, on the other hand, man alone is privileged to be eligible for salvation; when he is believed to be endowed with the spirit and is thereby distinguished in principle from beast and plant; when, to put it in secular language, he alone has reason, measure, and proportion, then he is considered the master of nature and assumes the right and the mission of imposing order—human order—upon the disorderly raw material of the physical world. The consequence is a style of gardening in which man is not enveloped and absorbed by nature but canopied and framed by subservient natural objects, which line the paths he treads like guards of honor and adopt the patently man-made shapes of rectangle and cube, sphere and cone, wall and arch. The garden becomes a vegetable extension of the architecture; in the words of Bartolomeo Ammanati, one of the designers of the Boboli gardens in Florence: *"Le cose che si murano debbono essere guida e superiori a quelle che si piantano"* ("What is built must serve as guide and be superior to what is planted") .

Even the most radical topiary art, however, cannot—and indeed does not wish to—suppress the natural properties of plants to the extent to which, for instance, stone will assume the shape imposed upon it by the mason. Even the accommodating boxwood reveals a natural structure totally incongruous with the geometrical envelope applied by the "fantastic admirers of symmetry" (Walpole) . Therefore complaints about the violation of nature are easily aroused. Nowadays we are inclined to consider landscaping as one of the many arts whose products are half artifact, half nature, and which should display rather than hide their twofold character. Foremost among these arts are the dance and the theater, which have experimented occasionally with the extreme formalization of the live human figure (classical ballet, expressionistic robots) . Photography and the motion picture also have tried to stylize natural objects and movement by various means. Experience seems to indicate, however, that such hybrid media achieve their happiest results when they frankly admit the contribution of the natural raw material by keeping the imposed order loose, open, partial.

Another way of making the point of the foregoing discussion is to say that the order of man-made landscapes varies as to the degree of their *definition*. By definition I mean the extent to which order is carried through in a setting or an individual object. In André Le Nôtre's gardens, definition is at a maximum. In the English style, which developed during the late eighteenth century, order is sometimes reduced to a loose spacing and grouping of plants, rocks, and water, which are otherwise left to their own devices. Note here, however, that the defining is done not only by man but by nature as well. In some trees and shrubs, such as the perfect Christmas tree, the willow, or the fern, all shapes seem to fit neatly into an over-all pattern; and a piece of granite offers more definition to the eye than does volcanic rock. A gardener who wishes to interfere with nature as little as possible may introduce a modicum of order by selecting plants of high natural definition. It is obvious that, on the other hand, nature actively interferes with definition. Plants grow and die; the seasons produce and remove foliage, change colors, play with moisture and snow; the movement of the sun, the moon, and the clouds constantly modifies the distribution of light. The visual definitions worked out by man are subject to endless incursions, and the shapes created by nature itself are always being destroyed.

Definition should not be confused with another dimension of order, which I shall call *rationality*. The classical French garden and the classical Japanese garden are both of particularly high definition. In the Zen gardens the shape of each tree, each rock, the outline of each pond is as completely controlled as are the symmetries and geometric contours of Versailles. And yet there is a profound difference, which we may describe by saying that the French preferred rational patterns whereas the Japanese were committed to irrational ones. I call a shape or relation visually rational when the eye can understand it as being formed according to some simple principle, such as straightness, symmetry, constant curvature, and so forth, and thus can use it as one of the models by which the mind codifies nature. The square is a rational shape for every person with an unimpaired brain, whereas the rectangle of the golden section cannot be recognized or reproduced with certainty by most persons. The most rational patterns are those which can be reduced to the relationship of equality; and it is possible, though open to verification, that only ratios reducible to equality can be identified by the eye.

Irrational shapes need not be disorderly. On the contrary, the rectangle of the golden section conveys to most observers the satisfying impression of being "just right," balanced and harmonious—as was demonstrated by the experiments of G. Th. Fechner in the nineteenth century. However, the observers cannot tell with precision why this is so, whereas they can be made to see that the distances between any corresponding points on parallel lines meet the condition of equality. In architecture, many shapes and relationships are rational while in painting rationality is an exception. The designers of the Japanese gardens avoid straight lines and parallels. Neither the units they employ in the shaping of natural objects nor the distances between these objects are multiples of each other. Shapes are not geometrically regular. And yet we receive the impression of complete control, complete lawfulness. Nothing, we feel, could be changed without disturbing the balance of the whole.

Everything is committed to its shape and rooted to its place by the necessity of the total order.

We noted that the low-definition landscape offers an escape from all-encompassing order. It diminishes subservience and presents instead the anarchic freedom of the spontaneous, the unrequired, the independent. The highly defined irrationality of the Japanese garden, on the other hand, presents a supreme universal order, into which man can fit himself by sensing it and letting it emanate from himself. But this experience of order is not based on the intuitive recognition of measurable relations. Rules and classifications are applicable, but they deal only with balance, structural similarities, and so forth, not with exact measurement. It is important to remember, nevertheless, that this irrational order works up to highspots of frank rationality, such as the stone lantern, the bridge, and the building. These clearly manmade objects do not express the mastery of man over nature. They do not appear as opposed to nature or as imposing their character upon it. Rather, rationality is presented as the ultimate outgrowth of the intangible order, a manifest confirmation of what the eye senses everywhere without being able to prove it. These tokens of rationality reassure man but do not tell him that he is in charge as does the French garden. The highly rational garden pattern in the French tradition proclaims man's triumph over nature, upon which he has imposed his own kind of order, subjecting nature to quantitative rules and classifications. We can sum up the character of these three archetypes of garden by comparing their different attitudes toward human dwellings: the low-definition garden hides the house; the highly defined, irrational garden leads up to the house; and the rational garden is dominated by it.

Having surveyed some over-all qualities of order we shall now analyze four particular types, namely, (1) homogeneity, (2) coordination, (3) hierarchy, and (4) accident. At the level of minimum complexity we find *homogeneity*. This simplest kind of order is obtained by applying some common quality to the entire pattern. A lawn, for example, derives order merely from its over-all plane shape, green color, and leafy texture. An expanse of water or a gravel road also has order by homogeneity. Texture, however, does not require straight evenness. A meadow sprinkled with wildflowers or a border of randomly mixed colors can be said to have the character of a texture, because we speak of *texture* when we do not perceive the particular relations among individual parts but see only the over-all similarity of the whole surface. With increasing distance from the observer, almost any landscape tends to assume the character of a texture, e.g., a mountainscape or a stretch of cultivated fields viewed from an airplane. Texture results when the elements of the pattern appear quite similar, or when their shapes and interrelations vary so irregularly that they cancel each other out instead of adding up to a distinct design. Uncultivated natural growth tends to assume this quality, and indeed almost any landscape or garden in its over-all aspect possesses the texture of vegetation, which distinguishes it from the different texture of man-made architecture. Depending on the taste of the times, the architect and designer will emphasize this difference of textures by giving the buildings shapes and colors contrasting with those of nature; or play down the difference, either by adapting the buildings to the texture of nature (ivy-covered walls; artificial ruins) or, vice versa, by applying architectural geometry to the garden.

Texture is not disorderly since disorder is the observed clash of uncoordinated orders. Rather, texture is orderless, as far as the internal relations of the pattern are concerned. So low is the level of this sort of homogeneous structure that it assigns no individual differences to its constituent parts. Since one place is like another, the visitor is not invited to identify or discern any part, nor is his own location or motion defined by the pattern. Therefore, a homogeneous order induces an unspecific mood rather than an articulate response, a drifting rather than an oriented aiming. Its boundlessness affords the elation of a primitive sense of freedom, the sense of "open spaces."

Such undefined roaming did not fit the spirit of the Japanese gardens and therefore we find homogeneous expanses used as "ground" rather than as "figure." Lakes are cut into by jagging tongues of land and punctured by islands and isolated rocks, and the raked gravel areas of the Zen gardens are either beset with distinctly patterned groups of stones or serve as the base for agglomerations of shrubs and trees. Thus the inarticulate surfaces assume the function of "negative" space.

At a somewhat higher level of complexity we find a type of order which I will call *coordination*. In a coordinated pattern all the parts constituting the whole are of similar importance and carry similar weight. The most elementary form of coordination is rather like what I just described as homogeneity. In an orchard, for example, the trees are so much alike as to add up to a homogeneous assembly. Often, however, the units of a coordinated pattern are quite different from each other. On a small scale this sort of order may provide for the pleasant combination of a piece of lawn, a group of shrubs, a pond, a few trees, and so forth, each holding its bit of ground and displaying its difference from the neighbors. On a larger scale we find the subdivision of a piece of property into orchard, herb garden, pleasure garden, and so forth, or—to use a gigantic example —the collection of Greek and Egyptian landscapes and buildings reproduced in Hadrian's Villa in Tivoli, near Rome. The demand that, in an orderly whole, everything should be in its proper place is fulfilled to the extent that a place is assigned to each kind and function. However, such a plan may show no order in the relations between the parts. To avoid such disorderly coordination the gardener will see to it that various units are sufficiently distinguished from one another by contrast, yet made to harmonize.

But even the judicious observance of contrast, variety, and harmony keeps the pattern at a relatively low level, at which order is defined only by the piecemeal relations between neighbors. Thus C. C. Hirschfeld, illustrating the need of variety, demands that "the open shall alternate with the closed, the light with the dark, the charming with the melancholy, the wild and romantic with the graceful. . . ." [1] Neighbors can be distinguished from each other clearly enough, but no over-all organization of the pattern defines the particular place to which a given element is assigned or the particular function it is to fulfill.

In calling this sort of order low, I merely describe its place on the scale of complexity. In no way am I implying that it should be considered inferior for the purpose of landscape design. On the contrary, this level of coordinated structure suits a broad range of needs by striking a balance between too little order and too much. It replaces the diffuse mood and the aimless roaming induced by homogeneous expanses with stimulating alternations and oppositions, and it defines the visitor's position and progression locally, thereby supplying him with partial orientation in space. At the same time, it leaves him with some of the freedom of being nowhere, instead of pinning him down at a spot completely determined by

[1] Christian Cay Laurenz Hirschfeld, *Theorie der Gartenkunst* (Leipzig: M. G. Weidmann, 1779) , p. 162.

the garden's total design. The virtues of such a structure are especially evident when it provides a succession of surprises as it does in the Japanese stroll-gardens of the sixteenth century by "stringing miniature scenic gems with garden-paths leading to ceremonial tea-houses." [2]

The organization of a coordinated structure need not be limited to piecemeal local relations among neighbors. It can attain a very tight order, in which each unit is determined in its individual place and appearance by a completely defined over-all network. An example is the famous stone garden of the Ryoanji temple in Kyoto. There, five small groups of rocks are placed on a rectangular court of white raked gravel in such a manner that nothing could be changed without destroying the delicate balance of the whole.

The high degree of definition in such a pattern naturally raises the level of complexity since more traits are called into play. Even so, the fact that the five units are coordinated, that is, have the same importance in the whole, limits the pattern to statements about homologues. There is no way of presenting the differences between what is dominant and what is dependent, what is central and what is peripheral. Given this structural limitation of the arrangement as a whole, it is significant that within each of the five groups at Ryoanji the stones tend to form a kind of pyramid, thus introducing secondarily the higher structural order of hierarchy.

A *hierarchy* is an order of some complexity, in which the elements are distributed along a gradient of importance. The dominant structural element may be a central point, as in a circular arrangement, or an axis, as in axial symmetry. The traditional European garden often combined both of these forms. It was laid out in relation to a "head" and a "spine," that is, to the central spot of the castle or mansion and the axis of the central avenue. In a pyramid or cone, two hierarchic dimensions, namely height and size, act as "co-variants": with increasing height the horizontal sections get smaller, so that the greatest height is also distinguished by being limited to one point, which adds the qualities of rarity, uniqueness, and centrality to that of top position. The dominant structural element is the "theme," simple or complex, to which the rest of the pattern is subordinated.

In a highly defined hierarchic pattern each part is determined by

[2] Matsunosuke Tatsui, *Japanese Gardens* (Tokyo: Japanese Travel Bureau, 1959), p. 9.

its relation to the central theme. Whereas in a coordinated structure all parts are homologous with each other, a hierarchy generally contains many groups of homologues, each with its own particular relation to the dominant center. In a symmetrical set-up, for example, "each alley has a brother, and half the garden just reflects the other." [3] Since the function of any one part can be understood only in its relation to the whole, an organized pattern such as a hierarchy must perforce be surveyable in order to make sense; that is, the view must be sufficiently unobstructed and the pattern must be either so small that it can be encompassed with a glance or so simple that a guiding image of the whole can be acquired and retained.

In the most radical version of hierarchy the whole pattern depends directly on one center. Mostly, however, the over-all structure consists of a group of subordinate hierarchies, from which in turn further and still smaller hierarchies may derive. Such a setup loosens the coercive centralization by giving the subordinate structures a modicum of autonomy. At the same time, every local hierarchy, in repeating the structure of the whole on a smaller scale, strengthens the consistency of the total pattern.

Since hierarchies are made up mostly of groups of homologues, we may say that they tend to be graded arrangements of coordinated structures, with the coordination serving as a stabilizing and simplifying counterbalance of the effect created by the whole. Inversely, coordinated structures become more complex, more dynamic when each of their constituents in itself represents a small hierarchy—as in the Ryoanji stone garden.

Evidently, hierarchic order is keyed to a state of mind that welcomes a centralized organization or upon which the power and glory of such centralization is to be impressed. Coordination, on the other hand, stands for a sort of federal set-up, in which each subject is at the same time an associate member of the government, that is, in which the governed are also the governors—a most dignified blend of freedom and constraint.

In addition to the types of order already mentioned, there exists another one, particularly congenial to the spirit of our own times, namely, the order of *accident*. Accident would seem to be the opposite of order, and that it is indeed when events actually take place without reference to each other. Such clashes are identical

---

[3] Alexander Pope, quoted in Horace Walpole, *On Modern Gardening* (New York: Young Books, 1931) , p. 16.

with what I earlier defined as disorder. For the purpose of the present paper I am referring to accident not as a method of producing a landscape but as an effect to be obtained through planning. Disorder, although created by means of accident, is no valid representation of accident. Disorder defines no relationships whatever, whereas accident is a well-defined structural condition, namely, the relationship of independence, which can be brought about only by disciplined organization. The order of accident can be highly defined and is, of course, always irrational. Among the styles of landscaping in the past it is most nearly represented by that of the Zen gardens, which probably arouse so much attention nowadays for this very reason. In these patterns, order is not achieved by an explicit principle—such as the principle of similarity or equality in the simpler kinds of coordinated pattern or that of gradation in the hierarchies. Instead, the order is implicit. It is due to nothing but the individual configuration of the individual parts constituting it. This structural pattern, demonstrating the kind of order attainable in, and appropriate to, a decentralized community, has been prevalent in much modern art and music and can be expected to exert its influence on modern landscaping as well.

Up to this point, order has been described as a matter of various kinds of grouping—a rather static affair. If the order of a landscape offered nothing but spatial distributions, it could hardly contribute to conveying that sense of life which we cherish so greatly. But, fortunately, all perception is dynamic, and therefore order, being an aspect of perception, is dynamic also. Each of the aspects or elements of which visual patterns are composed is perceived as a pattern of forces, and these forces radiate in various directions and create a gradient of decreasing intensities around each center. This means that, quite apart from its actual shape, every visual object— be it a tree, a stone lantern, or a spot of bright color—is perceived as the center of a hierarchy, with "directed tensions" descending from the center and rising toward it. Depending on the structure of the whole plan, these elementary hierarchies will fit into a more comprehensive pattern of a similar dynamic character or they will compensate each other in the framework of what I have called a coordinated structure. Thus a hierarchy has an inherent direction or sequence whereas in a coordinated system the various tensions balance out to an animated standstill. In a state of disorder, the over-all effect tends to be static because the various irregularly directed forces add up to nothing better than a sort of visual "ground noise."

The perceptual dynamics of a tree can be seen as centering in the stem, from which forces issue through the branches, expanding from the center toward the periphery. This is an example of directed tensions being perceived as one-way tracks. Mostly, however, they point both ways, ambiguously. For example, the conic envelope of a fir tree leads upward to the top as well as downward from the top. Similarly, terraces and sloping steps are visually directed downward and upward.

The directions of the forces created by such visual dynamics contribute greatly to the physiognomy of the setting. There is an almost complacent stability in patterns spreading within the horizontal plane, whereas upward and downward movement implies a dramatic interaction with the force of gravity. In the abbot's garden of the Nanzenji temple in Kyoto there is a most impressive accumulation, raising the visitor's glance from rocks and spherical shrubs near the ground to treetops, rooftops, and finally the slope of a wooded hill behind the precinct.

In addition to dynamic shape, actual *movement* also helps to enliven the order. There are informal variations introduced by the motions of the plants in the wind. There is the movement of water. Again the Japanese gardens supply us with clear-cut examples. The picture gardens, composed to be viewed from one definite vantage point inside the house, derive their dynamics from asymmetrical placement and the kind of accumulation just described, thereby justifying Basho's *haiku* poem: "The mountain and the garden move entering the summer parlor." In addition, a stream of water often travels through the picture garden, issuing generally from a waterfall on the left, eastern corner and traversing the lake, which occupies the center of the sight. Thereby an order of sequence is superimposed upon the timeless order of the picture landscape, and the onlooker is induced to view the elements of the composition not only in their togetherness but also in succession.

In the stroll garden, on the other hand, the changing viewpoint of the walking visitor provides a succession of settings and a perspective shifting of relative positions within each setting. Given the infinite variety of arrangements deriving from the moving viewpoint, there is naturally no valid order to many of these aspects in itself. The sequences tend rather to be made up—like much music or film action—of rigorously composed high spots connected by transitional passages, which are ordered in time rather than in the simultaneity of space.

The time character of sequences is compelling only when the structure of the total pattern is not completely surveyable but instead reveals itself in a succession of small or large surprises. When we walk around a tree to view it from all sides, we experience not so much a succession of views as the gradual exploration of a given immobile spatial order. But a drive around a lake or mountain of complex shape may assume the character of an orderly or disorderly sequence. Thus, gardens meant to convey a sense of permanent solidity tend to be surveyable; whereas a conception of life as constant change expresses itself in gardens that shun vistas and lead us along the crooked path of wonder.[4]

[4] Cf. also Rudolf Arnheim, *Art and Visual Perception* (Berkeley: University of California Press, 1954).

KENNETH BURKE

Order, Action, and Victimage

The purpose of this paper is to discuss certain terministic principles that are necessary for an adequate account of human motives. The writer builds his statement by reference to some other articles that partly agree and partly disagree with it. His aim is not to summarize these articles in their entirety, but to bring out certain essential aspects of them in a way that throws light on his own position. Above all, the writer holds that, in a discussion of peculiarly human motivation, stress should be explicitly and systematically placed upon a theory of "symbolic action," as viewed in the perspective of a "cycle of terms implicit in the idea of 'Order.'"

The attempt is to show the following. (1) Following Darwin,

KENNETH BURKE's work has combined literary criticism with a study of human relations. His specific concern is with symbols, for through symbols he is able to grasp the many-faceted reality of human experience in a kind of philosophic system. He is best known for his *Grammar of Motives* and *Rhetoric of Motives*, followed by *Rhetoric of Religion*, to be completed in *Symbolic of Motives*. He has been music critic, poet, translator, and has received many awards, among them a fellowship at the Center for Advanced Study of the Behavioral Sciences. His latest publications are *Language as Symbolic Action* and *Collected Poems*.

This essay is a sequel to the author's essay "On the First Three Chapters of Genesis" (pp. 37–64 of *Daedalus*, Summer, 1958, an issue devoted to *Symbolism in Religion and Literature*), which was also published in a revised form in *The Rhetoric of Religion* (Boston, Mass: Beacon Press, 1961), in which Burke extended the analysis to St. Augustine's *Confessions*.

Richard E. Carney places great stress upon man's "continuity with nature," and thereby does not give proper consideration to man's distinctive aptitude for symbol systems. (2) Isidor Chein wavers on this point, owing to an oversimplified dialectic of "active" and "passive." (3) Though the important motivational element with which Henry A. Murray deals provides a needed corrective to both Carney and Chein, the specialized nature of his essay entails major omissions. (4) Whereas (with Carney's a poor third) all three of the criticized statements make partial contributions to a mature terminology of "action," none properly recognizes the motivational implications of "Order" (in a sociopolitical sense of the term). (5) The writer concludes with some observations designed to indicate how and why a systematic concern with "Order" would figure in an ideal terminology of specifically human motives.

I. ESSAYS ON "MAN" AND "SATAN"

While this paper will bear on matters I have discussed elsewhere (notably in *A Grammar of Motives, A Rhetoric of Motives,* and *The Rhetoric of Religion*), three recently published articles by other writers serve well to point up many of such problems in a somewhat different way. And I dare hope that, when I am stating my position by variously agreeing and disagreeing with these articles, their great relevance to the subject of order will guarantee, if not the rightness, at least the relevance, of my observations.

I call the position "Dramatistic" because it features the concept of "action" (secondarily involving a strategic distinction between "action" and "motion"). I call the position "Logological" because it lays primary stress upon the element of "symbolicity" in the motivating of human action, man's *reflexive* ability, as a symbol-wielding animal, to use symbols about symbols, or words about words. (Secondarily, "Logology" involves a systematic attempt to view "words about God" in ways that throw a heuristic light upon the purely empirical concern with "words about words.")

The Journal of Social Issues for October, 1962, comprised two exceptionally vigorous essays: "The Image of Man," by Isidor Chein, and "Personality and Career of Satan," by Henry A. Murray. The editors summed up the enterprise under the engagingly succinct title, "Man and Satan." On reading these suggestive pieces, I was struck by the fact that they neatly complemented each other. Chein's treatment of "Man" is primarily concerned with honorific connotations implicit in the idea of an "act" (notions of purpose, freedom, and the significant difference between an act and what I would call "sheer motion"). The companion essay, by Murray, in effect rounds out the grammar of benign action by a stress upon the principle of absolutely malign passion, as embodied in the image and idea of the Devil.

Though Chein is primarily concerned with a terminology that, in his opinion, would do adequately by "Man's essential dignity and worth" (p. 18), he is not unmindful of human failings in this regard. Basically, however, he would celebrate a terminology of "action" *in contrast with* terminologies that stress "the passive image concept" (p. 10 n). The passions of Murray's Satan are treated basically in terms that dramatism and logology would most certainly include under the head of "symbolic action." For Murray is programmatically concerned with certain "products of the imagination" that, in his view, are "major determinants of behavior" (p. 36). By and large, the two essays are related thus: the first is systematically concerned with the grammar of action, and slights the principle of victimage; the second is systematically concerned with the principle of victimage (the "sinful" connotations of action), and slights Chein's concern with the purely formal "grammar" of action. All told, though in the opening chapters of Genesis the idea of a Fall is implicit in the idea of Creation, the authors divide their labors, in that Chein secularly applied the myth of the Creation without reference to the corresponding myth of the Fall, while Murray is secularly concerned with the figure that, though he "managed, somehow, to keep his name out of Genesis" (p. 51), perfectly sums up the principle of the Fall in his role as "arch-tempter" and "arch-hater" (p. 42).

On considering the two essays together, I confess to feeling a bit exultant. I believe I can show that my "Dramatistic" and "Logological" treatment of the problems to do with Order, as stated "mythically" in the first three chapters of Genesis, naturally encompasses both of the facets which these two essays treat largely in isolation from each other. And for some time I have been planning to write a statement along these lines. In the meantime, the subject took another turn, when I saw a third piece, a flyleaf by Richard E. Carney, somewhat heatedly attacking Chein's article. And now the irony is that, whereas I had wanted to find fault with Chein's article, I must first join forces with him against Carney.

II. MAN AND THE "CONTINUITY OF NATURE"

As explained in *The Rhetoric of Religion,* a Logological approach to theological issues involves a methodic search for secular analogues between "words" and "The Word." Carney's article involves a similar tactic, though he employs it in a quite different way. Avowing that "the basic issue is, man or Man?" he will have nothing to do with Chein's capitalized term, "Man." He stoutly insists upon lower-case "man." In sum, "Any image of man which disengages him from the continuity of nature is . . . scientifically unacceptable." And he asserts: "Citations from the Bible, ancient rabbis, or common observation are sufficient in themselves for philosophy or poetry. For science, such material forms the crudest sort of raw data and is suspect on several counts (there is a difference between science and logic, you know!) ." [1]

Before airing my differences with Chein, I'd like to discuss Carney's insistence upon "the continuity of nature." I happen to have reviewed recently (in *The New Leader,* November 11, 1963) *Darwin for Today: The Essence of His Works,* a selection of passages that the editor, Stanley Edgar Hyman, considered fittest for survival in a one-volume condensation of Darwin's three million words. Darwin, of course, subscribed to the view upheld by Carney. He expressly objected to "placing man in a distinct kingdom" (p. 248) . He aimed to show "that the mental faculties of man and the lower animals do not differ in kind, although immensely in degree." He quotes with approval T. H. Huxley's proposition that there "is no justification for placing man in a distinct order" (p. 251) . And I for one would not haggle with him when he says, "If man had not been his own classifier, he would never have thought of founding a separate order for his own reception" (p. 251) .

However, a logological emphasis upon the special motivating force of "symbolicity" (as with the statement we have already quoted from Murray on "products of the imagination" as "major determinants of behavior") leads one to be struck by the fact that Darwin devotes surprisingly little space to man's special prowess with symbol systems. (Unless I have overlooked some, there are not many more than a dozen pages on the subject in all *Origin of*

---

[1] I do not give page references for Carney's statements because they are on a single flyleaf inserted in a later issue of *The Journal of Social Issues.* Although I give page references to the other articles, this paper is meant to provide in itself sufficient presentation of the matters discussed.

Species and *Descent of Man*.) And he does not concern himself with the kind of Hegelian evolutionism that stresses "self-consciousness" (as with Aristotle's similarly patterned expression, "thought of thought"), a *reflexive* faculty characteristic of human language, with its special "second-level" aptitude for talk-about-talk.

Accordingly, in my review of the Darwin collection, I offered an ironic "defense" of "Man," as distinct from mere "man" and other animals, along these lines:

One might reasonably hold that, regardless of man's biologic origins, his specific aptitude for [reflexive] symbol-systems marks the passing of a critical point (as with the steps that divide water from ice or steam). At least, in all decency, and lest we dishonor the many nonhuman species that are trying to eke out an honest living, we should categorically distinguish between all those other poor devils and the kind of symbol-wielding animal that can produce Isms, Madison Avenue, Wall Street, yellow journals, a Hitler, a Birchite, an occasional soft-spoken, cross-burning southerner, and exalted calls to wage thermo-nuclear, chemical, and bacteriological war in the name of progress and freedom. Mr. Darwin, it was not nice of you to play down the fact that we are something special, endowed with the ability to be the unkindest kind of all.

In brief, I would uphold the proposition that the *reflexive* symbolicity characteristic of peculiarly human speculation can be properly treated as *different in kind* from the realm of motives characteristic of other animals. And in this sense, a principle of *discontinuity* would be in order. All animals, we may assume, take other animals' *behavior* into account. But man (or Man!) is the kind of animal whose special quirks of symbolicity enable him to formulate the *theory* of behavior*ism*.

Murray's entertaining article on the metamorphoses of Satan and Satanism is in itself ample evidence of important elements we are justified in considering as a motivational realm not characteristic of other animals (unless one would impute to animals a kind of symbolicity for which we have no empirical evidence, even in the societies of bees and ants, with their apparent codes of "information"). And until Carney shows that other animals can put out a flyleaf like his, strenuously agitated about theoretic matters, we may feel justified in insisting upon a principle of *discontinuity*, a qualitative distinction between other animals and our peculiar cantankerous species, "Ism-directed" Man. (On page 7, Chein deals with the same point when he says: "The class Man includes the psychologist who adopts the image of Man as an impotent being;

and this psychologist, like everyone else, cannot live by this image. He may try to apply it to everyone else, but he cannot apply it to himself as a basis of action." And surely in his section entitled "Motivation: Entropy or Commitment?" Chein is celebrating, as peculiarly typical of the human realm, the kind of thinking that attains a culmination in "Ismic" terminologies, in keeping with the Old Testament viewed as a book of Juda*ism,* later adopted and adapted to the ends of "Christianism.")

In brief, a logological stress upon reflexive symbolicity as a special realm of motives suggests thoroughly secular grounds for questioning whether the principle of continuity is adequate for defining man's place in a scale with other animals.

III. A PROBLEM OF "AUTHORITY"

Carney touches upon another point which, at first glance, might seem but peripheral, yet on closer inspection is found to be central. I refer to his statement that it is "scientifically unethical to appeal to authority, revelation," and so forth. First, I must confess, I see no reason why we should not ascribe a certain "authority" and "revelation" to ancient myths, if they are properly "discounted" for secular purposes, as with much of Murray's inquiry into "The Personality and Career of Satan." I was concerned with such "authority" and "revelation" in my study of the relation between the "Cycle of Terms Implicit in the Idea of 'Order' " and their analogue in the myth of the Creation and the Fall as narrated in the first three chapters of Genesis. (The issue is discussed at length in *The Rhetoric of Religion,* so I shall here mention only the minimum considerations necessary for present purposes.)

On the other hand, can empirical science distrust authority even remotely as much in practice as in theory? There is an ironic situation that seems to plague all scientific surveys, for instance. Science owes its rise largely to a distrust of established authority. Yet, by the very nature of the case, all surveys are so unwieldy that most readers must simply take their findings on trust. And, where a great many individual interviews were involved, the reader almost never has enough specific material on individual cases to let him decide for himself whether the cases were properly evaluated.

If a critic makes judgments about the nature and quality of a poem, or about the cogency of an argument, we can see for ourselves whether we agree with him. But if a researcher gives us the summarized "factual" results of many interviews, we must largely take his statements on faith, even though "in principle" we may retain the *right* to doubt. But it is usually a mere *formal* "right"—and in practice we judge the report according to whether or not the institution that guarantees the reliability of its fact strikes us as sufficiently "authoritative" to be relied on.

The irony of the situation is that, by their very (and wholly justified!) stress upon the all-importance of *factual* data, scientific investigators inevitably involve us in the need to view the "facts" as "authoritative"; and the men who present them are accepted as "authorities" in their field. Carney himself seems to take as much for granted, when he writes, "The cardinal sin is to use one's status as a scientist to gain authority in healing, religion, politics, art, or any other worthwhile human endeavor." By his reference to "one's status as a scientist" he must certainly include, in practice, a man's established reputation in his field.

I think of a news story, for instance, in the *New York Times,* November 11, 1963. The "MIDWEST," we are told in the headlines, "LOBBIES FOR ATOM PROJECT." The story concerns a plan that "Is Embroiled in Rivalries of Scientists and Politicians." And the report begins: "A proposal to build an atom smasher for a group of Midwestern universities has turned scientists into politicians and politicians into lobbyists for scientists."

How else can the problem be handled? Necessarily, the politicians and other laymen must accept the authority of the scientists on faith. Even to an extent the scientists must accept one another's authority on faith, for the very nature of specialization requires such a working attitude. And, to the extent of their persuasive ability, the experts will presumably use their authority to help affect a political decision. Indeed, every time politicians consult an expert with regard to new legislation affecting the allocation of funds for projects, they are necessarily asking the expert to use his authority in helping to shape a political decision.

On one occasion, in connection with a "factual" survey by a skilled researcher in whose report I had complete confidence, I pointed out how much of his findings I had to take on faith (unless the verbatim account of every interview in every detail could have been presented for me to examine personally as a basis for my judgment) . I requested that, if he ever found a convenient solution for this almost inevitable sort of "scientific authoritarianism," he let me know. That was some time back, but he has not yet sent me any glad tidings.

On the other hand, one could properly plead for the notion that Chein was quite justified in quoting, for purely secular and empirical purposes, the Biblical assurance that man was made "in God's image." Both psychology and anthropology have taught us: often some ancient or primitive text contains vital principles lost in many current motivational theories that were slapped together after a few rudimentary laboratory experiments. The only proper questioning of Chein's appeal to the "authority" or "revelation" of myth would involve his oversimplified way of interpreting such "evidence." [2]

IV. THREE DRAMATISTIC AXIOMS

A third point. When Carney writes, "In the mature organism the processes which lead to choice and commitment are assumed (and relatively well proven) to be historically but not directly related to some primary physiological function," that would be a good place for us to consider the three basic Dramatistic axioms regarding the relation between action and motion: (1) there can be no action without motion; (2) there can be motion without action; (3) action cannot be reduced to motion.

An instance of the first axiom would be the assumption that, so far as the empirical realm is concerned, we cannot carry on the activity of "thought" without reliance upon some corresponding set of what Chein (p. 8) would call "neuromuscular adjustments." An instance of the second axiom would be the sheer motions of the earth, winds, and tides, which could go about their business were there not a single symbol-using animal present to treat of them in

---

[2] Recently, in a kind of enrapt (or enwrapped?) horror, I lay awake until six o'clock in the morning, listening to my radio through an earphone, while I followed speeches citing an endless motley array of "authorities" in orations for or against the fluoridation of New York City's water supply. Few indeed were the arguments that were not countered, somewhere along the line, by a reference to some purely "factual" survey made by such-and-such authoritative organization (each speaker seeking by assertion to establish the scientific standing of his sources). Clearly, it was impossible to decide this issue without reliance on authority, along with personal prejudice in the choice of "authorities" (and, on the part of some public figures in the controversy, considerations of likely private risk or gain not stated by them, though sometimes hinted by their opponents). At times my study of rhetorical devices led me to suspect that the astute proponents of fluoridation had hired stooges to discredit the opposition by attacking fluoridation lamely.

symbol systems. For an instance of the third, consider this case: the *rules* of football involve the realm of action. They were formulated by a kind of animal capable of reflexive symbolicity (the "Ismic" species). And any particular game played by persons in accordance with those rules involves "activity" on the part of the players, referees, spectators, and so forth. But though such acts are impossible without a highly complex set of sheerly physical *motions* (as the ball and the players' bodies are variously moved about the field), a merely physicalist description of a game would not be an adequate substitute for the rule book, as regards questions of motivation.

Until the whole issue is thrashed out through discussion, I cannot be sure to what extent Carney and Chein would go along with these three Dramatistic axioms. Perhaps I am blinded by my own formulas here. But both writers seem to me implicitly working along these lines, despite Carney's strong sense of opposition to Chein, and despite my differences with both of them. Thus, while holding that all "choice and commitment" bear an indirect relation "to some primary physiological function," Carney repudiates "the supposed picture of a biology or a psychology dominated by socially indifferent, narrowly behavioral, passive respondentists." Here, it seems to me, there are rudiments of the third Dramatist principle, that "action" is not reducible to "motion." And while admonishing against "naïve reductionists" who make too much of such sheerly "biological" incentives as "thirst and hunger" where "human motives" are concerned, Chein also admonishes: "Do not misunderstand me. I do not reject physiological psychology as a legitimate field of scientific inquiry. I deem it a fine thing that there are scientists who concern themselves with the body" (p. 21). This would seem in tune with the first Dramatistic principle, "no action without motion," as regards the realm of the empirical.

Yet, by out-and-out Dramatistic tests, "action" in the full sense of the term is possible only to human animals ("persons") typically prone to a complicated kind of motivation that, while being built atop the sheerly physiological realm as the minimum ground of their empirical existence, requires exceptional aptitude for reflexive symbolicity (the "self-conscious" realm of principles, rules, theories, "isms"). And, though Murray's engaging essay on the wiles of Satan meets to perfection this criterion of "action" (as revealed in its corresponding "passion"), Carney's statement in its present brevity certainly does not.

V. "ACTION" IN MAN AND OTHER ANIMALS

At first glance, Chein might seem to be even more concerned with such a view of action than is Murray. Indeed, in "turning to the Bible" for his "basic references on the image of Man" (p. 35), by implication he is clearly voting for such a position in principle. But in the course of working out his thesis he gets involved in a theory of action which, while subtle and ingenious, by his own explicit testimony adds up to this:

> I think that such a hierarchy, or *nest,* of motives is not beyond a rat—so that, even in the case of a rat, not all of its motives are wholly constitution-ally-environmentally determined. Man can, of course, carry out such hier-archical processes to a degree that presumably cannot be matched by a rat. He can, for instance, enter into activities with extremely long-range goals. . . . When we get to deal with motives that are rooted in motives, we have come a long way indeed from actions like reflexes which are fully deter-mined by the interplay of constitution and environment [p. 15].

Here his expression, "motives that are rooted in motives," bears some resemblance to the particular kind of reflexivity (in contrast with sheer "reflexes") that is found in human "Isms." And, to that extent, he is on the right track. But insofar as it is a kind of pattern that also motivates (though to a lesser degree) the behavior of rats, has not Chein despite himself slipped away from capital-letter "Man," and *inadvertently joined forces with Carney's principle of continuity,* enshrined in lowercase "man"? A "hierarchy, or *nest,* of motives," as defined by Chein, is not necessarily of the reflexive sort that culminates in the peculiarly human aptitude for the "Ismic."

Similarly, while Chein parallels *in his way* the logological propo-sition that implicit in the idea of action are the ideas of freedom and purpose (succinctly summed up by the formula, italics his, in the footnote on pages 12–13: "I define behavior as *spontaneous directed activity*"), on page 14 you will find him discussing the "degrees of freedom" in the behavior of an animal. Similarly (p. 15 n), when talking of human freedom, he observes: "No serious writer that I can think of has ever confused *freedom* with *unlimited freedom.*" The point is well taken, but if it also applies to the "behavior" (equals "activity") of a rat, then rats and persons are "free" in the same way!

Several further paradoxes seem implied: if both rats and persons can "act," then to that extent rats are persons; and, if persons are "morally responsible" (as according to the view of "Man" in Genesis), then by the same token rats are "morally responsible" in the sense indicated by the myth in Genesis. The situation gets still more paradoxical (as regards a plea for "Man" against "man") when we are told (in a footnote, pp. 25–26) that "behavior is taken to be basically rational." If we stop at that point, and recall that Chein has already equated "behavior" with "action," it would seem to follow that not only is "cognition" basically rational, and man's behavior basically rational, but also the behavior of a rat is basically rational. In brief, "rationality" is here situated not in the motives of *symbolicity*, but in the realm of sheerly *natural behavior*. Where should we stop? A normal heartbeat is basically rational? The growth of a tree is basically rational? Nature is basically rational? If you dislodge a stone, its plunge downhill is basically rational?

Or are we being unfair to Chein, in thus driving toward so awkwardly pre-Humean a position? For we should make clear exactly how Chein's next sentence qualifies the one already quoted:

If irrationality appears, this is not because the individual does not act rationally in terms of the data that he takes into account, but because of a failure in *scope*—i.e., a failure to take into account all of the relevant environmental data that are available and/or a failure to act in terms of the total environmental system.

By this test, there is a sense in which the stone's fall would presumably be the most "rational" act of all; for, necessarily, it falls exactly as it "should," in response to whatever *total* conditions are relevant to the nature of its fall. It simply cannot fall otherwise than "just right." If it violates our "rational" rules for its behavior, we know that, to be "rational" animals, we had better revise our rules until its behavior does fit the rules.

As regards our action-motion pair, the stone's behavior would be in the realm of sheer motion (in keeping with the second Dramatistic axiom, that there can be motion without action). And in his discussion of "scope," Chein is obviously dealing with the motivational problem that we dealt with Dramatistically in terms of action. (See, in *A Grammar of Motives,* the section on "Scope and Reduction.") Indeed, if you will go back now and re-examine his words on "scope" which I have quoted, you will note that he speaks of rationality as involving action *in terms of* a total motivational system. I submit that there is a crucial ambiguity in this expression, "in terms of." It is one thing to speak of a rat as acting "in terms of" a maze that enables it, by "rational" conduct, to manipulate the planned unnaturalness of the maze and get the food it naturally needs. It is another thing to speak of a man acting rationally "in terms of" a total motivational system. For, in this second case, one would be involved in much the sort of "rational behavior" that flowers in Spinoza's view of action *sub specie aeternitatis*. And, though it may *transcend* symbolicity, such transcendence is necessarily sought *through* symbolicity, since action in the full human sense of the term (as distinct from sheer animal "behavior") involves man's prowess as a symbol-wielding agent.

Yes, to use the expression "in terms of" in the fullest literal sense involves such considerations of "action" and "passion" as one confronts in Spinoza's *Ethics*. It involves ways of equating "freedom" with "adequate ideas" and "bondage" with "inadequate ideas." In brief, we are in the realm of "Isms," the realm of action and passion in the peculiarly human sense. The kind of *animal* that can worry about problems of motivational *scope* is the kind of animal that is motivationally distinguished by a particular kind of symbolicity. And in that special sense we must empirically proceed on the assumption (until proved false) that action, freedom, purpose are possible only to the human animal, and that other animals are to be described wholly behavioristically, in terms of *sheer motion*. At least, this is a Dramatistic imperative, unless one is to round things out by ascribing to animals, trees, and even stones the properties of personality, "rationality," and "moral responsibility" (that is, the "ability to answer," an ability "natural" to symbolicity, which can say yes or no).

VI. GRAMMAR AND "THE TRUTH"

Chein says (p. 13 n), "Grammar is, of course, indifferent to truth." As author of a book entitled *A Grammar of Motives*, however, I must point out a sense in which, as I use the term, the "grammar of action" does have an important bearing on our building of a "true" terminology. Above all, I contend, systematic talk of action vows one to be similarly systematic in one's treatment of "passion" and the "reflexive." And on precisely this score I would question whether Chein's use of this grammar is adequate to the problem. For instance:

On page 2 he says, "We must choose between two images. The first is that of Man as an *active, responsible agent*, not simply a *helpless, powerless reagent."* That is, in his dialectic, the passive is explicitly assigned to the "image" of man he is opposing, a "model" (p. 3) that "leaves Man a passive victim of the interplay between constitution and environment no less than do the non-purposive S-R models." On page 5, he says that theories of conditioning "presuppose a passive image of Man," and thus there is a "passive-being image implicit in conditioning theory." On page 7 he admonishes that "no man can act in terms of the image of himself as a totally impotent being." Chein's own position, on the other hand, hinges largely about a theory of "activity in progress" (p. 8).

I submit that the grammar of action, as so aligned, does not allow for the proper attitude toward human motivation. And the treatment of such a grammar in Spinoza indicates where Chein's weakness lies. For Spinoza by no means relegates passiveness solely to an image of man as conceived by rival theorists. Rather, his nomenclature stresses first of all *man's own intrinsic proneness to passivity.* Man is not to be rescued categorically by an honorific image celebrating his powers as a free, purposive agent. Rather, by definition, man is *in bondage* except to the extent that he exercises his ability to form "adequate ideas" about the necessities by which he is beset. He must see things "in terms of" such "de-termination."

Thus, if you take *literally* Chein's reference to the rationality of action *in terms of* a total motivational system, you promptly realize what is formally missing in his concern with " a hierarchy, or *nest,* of motives" (p. 15) that characterizes the "free" and "rational" action of both rat (lower case) and Man (capitalized). His account of "behavior as a motive" (pp. 9–11) cries out for an explicit grounding in a concern with the powers of symbolicity.

The kind of animal that can say, "Let us build a fire," can approach the task with a power of abstraction that wholly transcends the kind of motivational sequences Chein calls "succeeding interactions" (chains characterized merely by the fact that one thing leads to another, as with current information theory on the possible nature of biologic growth). Chein rightly distinguishes "purposive" action from such sheer succession. But his discussion of a contrasted kind of "molar activity" needs grounding in an explicit concern with this primary abstract aspect of attention, made possible by symbolicity, a kind of attention that may not always see things in terms of *names,* but does always see things in terms of the *namable.* Otherwise, as Chein himself has noted, his theory of action applies

to both Man and rat. What happened to the making of Man in
God's image? On the other hand, from the Logological point of
view, what kind of "Man" would be "in God's image"? God was the
sort of person who *said* "Let there be"—and there was. God *acted*
by the *creative word*. And man, with the "creativity" of his symbol
systems, is formed in that image. Chein brings out the element of
creativity, but neglects both the principle of *verbal fiat* here, and the
principle of *divisiveness* (considerations which are central to a
"Logological" interpretation of the Creation myth, particularly
since the principle of *divisiveness* proclaimed in God's successive
days of Creation implicitly contains the conditions necessary for a
Fall).

If, on the other hand, one *fully* applies the grammar of action *and
passion* in charting the motives of the symbol-wielding animal,
instead of categorically rejecting the "passive image concept" by
ascribing it exclusively to the erroneous views of a psychology that
one would reject, the situation looks quite different. While rejecting
all reductionist schemes when judged as rounded statements about
the essence of human motivation, one welcomes them as scientific or
quasi-scientific *caricatures,* somewhat like Aesop's fables, that take
off human failings by discussing them in terms of animal behavior.
All such schemes (including those that Chein excoriates under the
caption, "Man or Robot?") are valued by Logology for their help-
fulness as moral tracts, helping us in many ways to realize how
readily man can fall into the grooves of passiveness and automatism.
(I grant, however, the scientists themselves might resent their projects being admired for such sheerly homiletic reasons. Maybe they
would rather be hated than admired on such "unscientifically"
ironic grounds.)

Besides any such insights into human frailties that may be suggested by what Chein would call "a strictly physiological inquiry"
(p. 21), one must keep reminded of the ways whereby even the
"Ismic" prowess of "Man" can be made to function as a mere
Stimulus to elicit an automatic Response (for instance, when the
demagogic spellbinder exploits a terminology by rhetorical devices
to which audiences respond as with a behaviorist's "conditioned
reflex"). Man's instincts having become confused by the great technological "progress" which can also tremendously reinforce his errors, at every turn his powers make him prone to vast new areas of
such "passivity" (suffering and goading) unless he can save himself

by the action of still greater symbolic prowess in the "rational" formulation and spread of "adequate ideas." In brief, though models building up a "passive image" of man (p. 10 n) would not be adequate to a full definition of human essence, they do throw light upon respects in which man's essence makes him naturally prone to the servitude of "inadequate ideas."

VII. ANIMALITY, SYMBOLICITY, AND THEIR OVERLAP

Given man's nature as a symbol-using animal, some of his motivations should derive from his animality (his rudimentary biologic needs and "drives"), some from his symbolicity, and some from various combinations of the two. Man being the kind of animal that lives by locomotion, certain rudiments of "freedom" as a "value" would be implicit in the sheerly physical need for freedom of movement. Needs for food, sleep, shelter, and sex would also be rooted in purely biologic kinds of "purpose," the sheer physiology of motion (though hard to isolate in this form, since all such "drives" are so greatly modified by custom). Psychogenic illness would be a clear instance of overlap between animality and symbolicity.

When Chein gets to what he calls the "imbrication of motives" (as with his statement on page 17: "Because being admired may enhance a person's power and because power may evoke admiration, admiration-seeking and power-seeking become reciprocally motivating—and both may motivate and be motivated by striving for achievement," and so forth), he is dealing with motivational complexes that, whatever their grounding in physiological instincts, are mainly to be explained in terms of symbolicity, in its relation to institutions themselves largely dependent upon symbolicity for their development.

The rules for the *programing* of the motions in a computer are guided wholly by principles of symbolicity. The sheer *motions* of the computer "scientifically burlesque" the grammar of action, passion, and reflexive in terms of effectors, receptor, and feedback, respectively.

On pages 22–25, Chein is concerned with the question of whether the personality is "something integumented . . . residing within the skin," a view which Allport contrasts with Eastern philosophy. Logology would agree with Chein's questioning of the need for "an integumented view of the personality." But, in doing so, it would explicitly introduce the action-motion pair thus: in the realm of sheer motion, there is the centrality of the nervous system, a material "principle of individuation" whereby my toothache is peculiarly mine and not yours. However, beyond such individuation by centrality of the nervous system, there is the physiological fact that even conditions "inside the skin" merge with conditions "outside the skin," and could exist only insofar as they are part of this larger *universal matrix*. (Here is where "Eastern philosophy" would have a point.) And there is the further fact that, as with "identity" and "role-taking," the "personality" involves complex social relationships not wholly reducible to terms of the individual, possible to persons only as parts of a social collectivity, marked at every stage by the complexities of symbolic action (so that personal name and reputation merge into social expectations, obligations, property rights, individual identification by the collective nature of language and traditions generally) . Thus, the rudimentary sense of oneself as an individual (as attested by a *proper* name) may be greatly modified in the direction of self-sacrifice and self-effacement (a trend indicated somewhat by a *family* name) . Every mature statement of the case will, in its way, introduce all such considerations. I would merely want to express the belief that an explicit use of the action-motion pair offers a fairly direct way of stating the situation.

VIII. THE BASIC POINT OF DIFFERENCE

Many other points should be considered, if it were our task here simply to write a complex analysis and critique of Chein's essay. But actually our purpose is of a quite different sort; and many of these comments are offered primarily through recognition of the fact that this discussion could not be conducted properly as a "debate." For not only do our positions often coincide; Chein may introduce at one point a qualification which he had omitted at another.

For instance, though his theory of behavior as motive is stated without any explicit concern with the critical importance of symbolicity, beyond question his idea of the human "self" (p. 24) *implies* the peculiarly human aptitude for "rationality" in this narrower sense of the term, a sense which would not quite fit with his remark (pp. 25–26 n) : "Another aspect of my image of Man (and, for that matter, of animals) that is relevant here is that behavior is to be taken as basically rational) ." For, in effect, he is here defining all creatures as "rational" animals. Yet, in the interests of fairness, I must note important spots where the explicit omission of some qualification or reservation does not indicate its absolute absence; it may be there ambiguously, implicitly, as when we discover that, in his reference to the "rational" behavior of animals and/or "Man," he nonetheless implicitly attributes to Man great "imbrication of motives" (p. 32 n) and necessary considerations of "scope" when acting "in terms of" a "total motivational system" (p. 26 n). Surely, a distinctive aspect of specifically *human* "rationality," as so described, places essential reliance upon the resources of symbolicity.

But our main point regarding Chein's article does involve the rejection of his essay at its very core, as on pages 18–19, where he expressly states his intention to proclaim "Man's essential dignity and worth," Man's "majesty," and asserts:

Whether you take the Bible text as divine revelation or as a humanly inspired allegory which nevertheless expresses one of mankind's greatest and most influential aspirations, the point of my little bit of Biblical exegesis has been to show that a central theme of the coupling of the image of Man with the image of God is the role assigned to Man with respect to his own creation . . . any psychological science that does not face up to the aspects of the image that I have tried to develop . . . can certainly justify no commitment of psychologists to a belief in the dignity and worth of the individual human being.

My point is: Chein would get his "humanly inspired allegory" for his model of Man by referring only to the *first* chapter of Genesis. I am *necessarily* scandalized at this, since I wrote a book based on the thesis that any rounded use of this myth for secular purposes involved the first *three* chapters of Genesis. And instead of stopping, like Chein, with "a simple commandment" involving God's creative fiat, I went on *to view the Creation and Fall in integrally related principles.*

Accordingly I laid equal emphasis upon *another* commandment (in 2:17) : "But of the tree of the knowledge of good and evil, thou shalt not eat of it." And I included Chapter 3, since it tells of the "temptation" which this commandment made possible (by introducing a proscription) , and of the turn from the "Edenic Covenant" to the "Adamic Covenant" that attended the "first man's" fall. (Had only *Eve* fallen, according to orthodox theology the human race would not have "inherited original sin.")

Though Murray's article on Satan has no direct systematic concern with the grammar of action that Chein has dealt with at length (in contrast, we would say, with terminologies of motion), it does well indeed by the principle of temptation, in focusing attention on the very prince of temptation. Yet, surprisingly enough, Murray's view of religion (as summarized on page 39) is nearly as far from the secular insights to be derived from a stress upon *covenants* as is Chein's project for Man's terminological glorification.

His "credo," he says, is a "belief" in "the evidence set forth by anthropologists and psychoanalysts, particularly by Frazer and by Freud, in favor of the proposition that religions are products of human imaginations revised by rationality." Religion answers the question: "science for what? philosophy for what? and art for what? but not religion for what? because it is the function of religion to provide the best conceivable answers to all those 'whats.'" To this end, its "propositions and stories" should be "as true as they can be at any given time, that is, as congruent with the deepest realities of human nature." They should be "as comprehensive and as self-consistent" as possible. And they "should comfort the distressed, and, by presenting visions of a realizable better future, engender hope, and encourage efforts to achieve this." And they should be "susceptible to correction and reconstruction."

It may seem ungenerous to find fault with so appealing a statement. Yet, our primary concern with the subject of *Order* almost inevitably reminds us what is missing from Murray's definition, and was missing from Chein's. Surely the opening chapters of Genesis *have to do with the founding of an Order, and with the establishing of the most radical sanctions conceivable for the laws by which that Order is to be upheld.*

This is no place for me to write over again my "Logological" analysis of such "Covenant Theology," an analysis based above all on the fact that the negative does not exist in nonsymbolic nature but is a device peculiar to our symbol systems. However, a few major points should be mentioned.

IX. A "LOGOLOGICAL" INTERPRETATION OF "COVENANT THEOLOGY"

The thou-shalt-not's of law by which Order is upheld are found to be specifically ingrained in the genius of Man, the typically symbol-using animal. The myth of the Creation and the Fall tells us as much by telling us that God is the ultimate grounding of human personality (since we are "made in his image"), and that he imposed upon us the principle of negativity, in pronouncing the "first" thou-shalt-not. My analysis in *The Rhetoric of Religion* is designed to show how this *mythic* "first" stands for an essential "first." That is, the *temporally* prior stands for the *logically* prior, the logical priority residing in the fact that, *implicit* in the principle of the Law's thou-shalt-not's, there is the formal possibility of rounding out the pattern by saying "No" to the thou-shalt-not (the possibility of "negating the negation," if we were to apply the Hegelian formula).

The negativity of Dante's Hell and of Goethe's Mephistopheles, along with the *non serviam* that Joyce uses to such good effect (in *The Portrait of the Artist as a Young Man*) to establish the "Satanic" quality of Stephen's aestheticism, all help us to realize the negativistic role that the Devil plays *to perfection* in connection with the principles of temptation and punishment that are also implicit in the idea of Order. In Genesis, Satan's functions were performed by a combination of the serpent's wiles and Eve's guile and the Lord God's disgruntlement. Viewed logologically, Satan is the "perfection" of the moralistic negative, in the sense that he becomes both the "perfect" tempter and the "perfect" overseer of the punishments visited upon those who yield to temptation.

The clearest statements I can offer on the subject of "perfection" as so conceived are in my *Permanence and Change* (Hermes edition, pp. 292–94), and my "Definition of Man" (*Hudson Review* [Winter 1963–64] pp. 491–514). Suffice it here to note that, though logology does not attempt, along Aristotelian lines, to discover the perfectionist principle of the "entelechy" in physics (the realm of sheer motion), logology does hold that an "entelechial" or "perfectionist" impulse is intrinsic to the action of symbol systems. And it would view in such a light these statements by Murray: "Religious thought tends, or should tend, toward the ideal" (p. 48); "absolute evil cannot be derived from a mild form of pride, but only from the most extreme form, which I shall call *absolute malignant pride*" (*ibid.*); and "all forms of wickedness became crystallized into a single fiendish Satan who, like a proliferating cancer, invaded the susceptible collective minds of men" (p. 50). Logologically viewed, in a scheme concerned with the radical grounding for the thou-shalt-not's of Law and Order, "rational" imaginings to do with the "personality and career" of Satan would strive "naturally" toward the image of a figure that *perfectly* combined the temptations and punishments of Order (and even the *sanctions* of Order, in the sense that, as Lord of Hell, his powers of punishment, though dependent upon the Power whose Fiats set up the Order, are said absolutely to be there for exercise against those who radically violate the Order) . The depth and range that Murray rightly associates with religious thought could also be treated as an aspect of the "perfectionist" principle we find in symbolicity, representing as it does an attempt to be as thoroughgoing or ultimate as possible in questions of human motivation.

The Devil is a charmer—and so is Murray's article on him. It makes for resonant reading. But, as judged by Logological tests, even Murray does not do right by the theology of *Covenants*. Ironically enough, the Old Testament is skimpy indeed as regards Satan (except that his *office* as tempter was perfectly performed by the serpent in the garden) ; but he gets a much better deal in the New Testament, which one might otherwise tend to think of as stressing the *promissory* aspect of religion. In any case, viewing religion *in its role as a sanction for Order,* Logology is led to recognize that promises are not so unambiguously comforting as they might seem to be on their face. By the promise of aid, for instance, one country can subject another to its policies, in threatening to withhold that aid. Hence, even if one chose to accept, for the sake of the argument, Murray's proposition that religion has its roots in devices to "engender hope" and "comfort the distressed," there would still be reason to note that, when a religion becomes *institutionalized,* much of its strength and structure will derive *from its use as a sanction for Order (either traditional or new)* . Murray's article assembles many "rational" images of Satan that could contribute, in one way or another, to such a function. I would merely want to round matters out by having the whole subject placed technically or formally in terms of the relation between the "grammar of action" and a "cycle of terms implicit in the idea of 'Order.' " (This is the job I tried to do in *The Rhetoric of Religion.*)

X. HOW ADAM AND SATAN "FREELY" YET "NECESSARILY" SINNED

Consider, for instance, this statement by Murray on page 47:

If (by definition) God is omniscient and capable of fore-knowledge, he must have *known* that he was not giving Lucifer (or Adam later) enough steadfastness for them to persevere in perpetual obedience. . . . That they would therefore disobey eventually, and . . . that he would punish each of them for this, despite the fact that he himself had planted the bent toward disobedience (the id tendency) and failed to imbed sufficient power to inhibit it (ego tendency).

From the strictly Logological point of view, such observations would be rephrased as follows. First, rounding out the terminology as given, we assume that there is no explicit reference to the superego here because God himself implicitly stands for that role. Next, in keeping with our systematic attempts to translate "words about God" into "words about words," we would ask: what would be the Logological equivalent for the statement that God "had planted the bent toward disobedience (the id tendency) and failed to imbed sufficient power to inhibit it (the ego tendency)"?

In answer, we would begin by trying to eliminate the story form of statement here. Thus, the *narrative* sequence involving *temporal* steps from Creation to Fall would be replaced by a set of *nontemporal implications*. Whereas *narratively* we read of a God who first created an Order including creatures endowed with the power (which would eventually be used) to disobey that Order, we would begin *Logologically* with the observation that implicit in the idea of Order is the idea of disobedience. An Order is protected formally by the thou-shalt-not's of Law. And *formally*, the negative contains the possibility of its negation (the possibility of saying "No" to any thou-shalt-not). If a command cannot be disobeyed, there is no point to giving it. One commands or requests *people* to do things. One does not "give orders" to *things* (except in primitive magic, which treated *things* as capable of "responding" like *persons*). Otherwise put: a command makes disobedience possible, in the sense that, according to Saint Paul, the Law "made sin." Without a "thou shalt not," there can be no disobedience. But, since Order implies the negativity of Law, the idea of Order *necessarily* implies the idea of *possible* disobedience.

The negative is terministically involved in another way (along the line of Spinoza's formula, *omnis determinatio est negatio*). Any principle of classification (as with the six "classes" of things enumerated *narratively* in terms of God's six creative "days") involves negation (this is *not* that), Yes and No thus being the two most "perfect" distinctions as regards the morality of choice. But such division, with the principle of negativity implicit in it, sets up the conditions for *divisiveness,* which is technically a "Fall" from a state of "perfect" unity. Thus whereas, Logologically, the idea of Order "leads to" the idea of disobedience (or, otherwise put, the idea of disobedience is implicit in the idea of Order), such a terministic relationship would be stated in the narrative terms of myth (or "story") as a temporal sequence in which *first* came the Creation *and then* the Fall.

Thus, from the strictly Logological point of view, theology's quasi-narrative concern with God's "foreknowledge" on the Fall that would follow the Creation is translated into a sheerly nontemporal terministic relationship: the idea of a Fall is implicit in the idea of a Creation; and the negativity of such Order is perfectly embodied in the moral negativity of a thou-shalt-not that is explicit in the case of God's instructions to our "first parents," but implicit in the case of Lucifer's original subordination to God (a state that Lucifer's own "career" proved to be based on the implication, "thou shalt not say *non serviam*").

But, in saying that the idea of *possible* disobedience *necessarily* inheres in the idea of Order (such Order as the Book presents in terms of a *verbal* fiat), we might seem to have left ourselves an easy way out. So we shall try to be Logologically more exacting. As regards our two key terms, "Order" and "Action," one might state the case thus: the idea of Order *necessarily* implies (among other implications) the idea of *disobedience* to that Order; but the idea of Action *necessarily* implies the *possibility* of *either* obeying or disobeying the Order.

As regards the perfect formality of responsibility, Adam and Lucifer could answer either "Yes" or "No" to any explicit or implied injunction. This possibility of choice *formally* inheres in the nature of a negative command, and would constitute the Logological equivalent of what, in theology, is called "grace." Formally, "grace," as so defined, also endows the typically symbol-using creature with the "responsibility" of "freedom," since formally implicit in the idea of a thou-shalt-not is the possibility of saying either "Yes" or "No" (with corresponding "responsibility"). And, by the same token, formally implicit in the idea of a thou-shalt-not there is the possibility of "persevering," that is, of continuing to "respond" by saying "Yes" to the thou-shalt-not. Every moral choice formally presents such alternatives, though certainly not always with the "perfection" of our Yes-No answers to a researcher's questionnaire that only allows us to check one or the other of just these two.

Up to this point, then, *Logology* would necessarily agree with the orthodox *theological* notion that, however badly things turned out, both Lucifer and Adam were formally endowed with the "grace" to resist temptation, if they had but chosen to say "Yes" to the thou-shalt-not.

But Logology is not yet through with this problem. Both Satan (in his rebellion) and Adam (in his fall) have a particular role to play. Their role is to *represent the principle of disobedience implicit in the idea of Order.* In this role, they *necessarily* fail to persevere in virtue. *For how otherwise could they properly represent the principle of disobedience?* Is not their disobedience a narrative requirement of their role?

Similarly, one might say that a soldier, if drafted for war, is still free to disobey orders, in case he is commanded to kill. But if such a soldier is put in a story that casts him in the role of one-who-voluntarily-kills-when-commanded-to-kill, he obviously *must* kill.

In this sense, both Lucifer and Adam *necessarily* disobeyed. For if they had not, what would have happened to their story? And how could theology have shown, in "mythic" terms (of quasi-prehistory) how *essential* the possible act of "disobedience" is to an animal that is primarily characterized by its powers of symbolicity, powers that in turn critically involve the principle of negativity?

XI. IN CONCLUSION

In sum, I am contending that, though these two articles are both quite admirable, and though they contribute much to the correcting of each other's insufficiencies, both still leave much to be desired, as regards a specifically "Logological" statement of their case. Neither author has been systematic enough in secularizing his theology, a kind of translation that requires, first, a *formally* Dramatistic "grammar of action" and, next, a formally Logological concern with a "cycle of terms implicit in the idea of Order."

It is quite likely that neither author is any more interested in passing such "Logological" tests than Darwin or Carney would be. No, that is not quite accurate. Both Chein and Murray are *much* closer to such concerns. But I do believe: if I can but help my readers to get the feel of what I am after, they will agree with me that, after we have gone beyond Carney, this is the only *thorough* way to proceed, when methodically secularizing thoughts on the Creation and the Fall. And I dare feel that a study of "Order" such as this provides the best place of all in which to put forth such a claim.

MONROE C. BEARDSLEY

Order and Disorder in Art

Several of the contributions to the present series discuss metaphysical and epistemological aspects of the concept of order. My contribution belongs among those concerned with normative problems—with the relations of order to value. Not that order is itself a value concept, but that in some contexts order is taken to be a ground of goodness: something desirable for itself or for its consequences, something that can legitimately be cited as a reason in support of affirmative value judgments.

Nowhere, I think (except perhaps by the most rigorously totalitarian political theorists), has the connection between order and value been made so intimate as in aesthetics. The earliest systematic thinkers about art were strongly impressed by this affinity. Plato, in his *Philebus* (64e), argued that "beauty and excellence" are constituted by measure (*metron*) and proportion (*symmetron*) (cf. *Timaeus* 87cd, *Politicus* 284a, *Sophist* 228b). Plotinus rejected the

MONROE C. BEARDSLEY, long associated with Swarthmore College, became known early in his career for his essays (with W. K. Wimsatt) on the intentional fallacy and the affective fallacy. His *Aesthetics: Problems in the Philosophy of Criticism*, which appeared in 1958, is the comprehensive contemporary work in the field; his *Aesthetics from Classical Greece to the Present: A Short History* appeared in 1966. With Elizabeth Lane Beardsley he has edited the *Foundations of Philosophy* series. Professor Beardsley is president of the American Society for Aesthetics.

Stoic identification of beauty with symmetry because it entailed that simple things cannot be beautiful (for example, single colors). But when he came to discuss the participation in "Ideal Form" by which physical things become beautiful, his emphasis was on order. Ideal Form "has grouped and co-ordinated what from a diversity of parts was to become a unity; it has rallied confusion into cooperation" (*Enneads* I.vi.2). On the other hand, "an ugly thing is something that has not been entirely mastered by pattern, that is by Reason" (V.viii.1). St. Augustine, to cite one more thinker, conceived order in terms of number. "Everything is beautiful that is in due order," he said (*De vera religione* xli.77). "Ask what delights you in dancing, and number will reply: 'Lo, here am I.' Examine the beauty of bodily form, and you will find that everything is in its place by number" (*De libero arbitrio* II.xvi.42).

I introduce these citations only as reminders. The tradition they represent is the oldest aesthetic tradition in the West. It maintained its dominance for nearly two thousand years and is still vital. The essential principles are (1) that what makes a work of art good or excellent is its beauty, and (2) that what distinguishes beautiful things from other things is a high degree of some kind of order. Such a position, of course, raises a great many questions, which the philosophers in this tradition wrestled with. One we might keep in mind is this: under the heading of order we find (a) the concept of organization, as opposed to confusion; (b) the concept of unity, as opposed to disunity; and (c) the concept of proportion, or good proportion—are there three kinds of order, then, or do some of these reduce to others?

The classical tradition was first sharply challenged toward the end of the seventeenth century, when a combination of circumstances (new literary forces, a shift of taste for nature, the rediscovery of "Longinus") opened up a radically different line of thought that was ultimately to reach its highest point in some twentieth-century art. I need not recount this whole movement, but shall only recall a few of its key ideas. Lord Shaftesbury shows the point of division very well; as a Platonist, he thought of beauty in terms of "truth, proportion, order and symmetry," [1] but at the same time he was drawn to the contemplation of nature in its wild state; its vast deserts and seas, jungles and mighty rocks and chasms "want not

---

[1] Anthony Ashley Cooper Shaftesbury, *Characteristics of Men, Manners, Opinions, Times* (1711), I, 296.

their peculiar beauties." [2] It was these "peculiar beauties," opposed as they are to everything calm, cool, and rational, that became the eighteenth-century sublime, which, as Kant said, exceeds the capacities of the understanding. The eighteenth-century aestheticians devoted much effort, with considerable success, to the analysis of this concept, as distinct from beauty (and they suggested other categories, such as the picturesque) . In Romantic theory, when creation of art became no longer the construction of pattern, but the "spontaneous overflow of powerful feeling," one might almost say that an opposite aesthetic was attained. For what was valued and enjoyed in art seems, on this view, to be precisely disorder: the unrestrained, the unpremeditated, the unorganized.

I suppose it is easy enough to work up large confrontations in any subject, if we oversimplify history. And I do not want to lay too much stress on this short survey. The purpose is to point up a genuine problem, about the connection between order and aesthetic value. For the historical ambivalence is still strongly present. And, indeed, two developments in comparatively recent years have raised this old problem again in an especially challenging way, so that the present seems like a good time to reconsider it with some care. I propose to discuss each of these two developments, to try to assess their significance, and then to offer some general observations by way of conclusion.

I

One striking and puzzling feature of the revolution in the arts that has occurred over the past half-century or so is the increasing use of chance, or accident, in the creation of art. In recent years this development has become most obvious, self-conscious, and even fashionable. If there is, as I suppose, an intimate connection between randomness and disorder, we may say that never has the revolt against order been carried further than it has in recent years. And so never has the problem about the relation between artistic value and order been so sharply pressed. Tychistic art, if we may so name the art produced by accident, seems, in its practical aim as in its theoretical underpinnings, to be a challenge to the entire past, whether Classic or Romantic.

It is worth remembering, to keep the contrast in perspective, that

[2] *Ibid.,* II, 122.

artists have always been in some degree prepared to take advantage of their occasional strokes of luck. And some celebrated examples of chance have been cherished—mainly as curiosities. Thus Leonardo, in his *Treatise on Painting,* recommended that the painter try to see images in damp-stained walls and stones of varying color. He remarks that Botticelli told him that you can throw a sponge full of paint at a wall, and in its casual blot make out the vague patterns of a landscape. The sponge was borrowed from Pliny, who tells (in his *Natural History*) of a painter who found the flying sponge the best way to depict the foam at the mouth of a mad dog. But these instances never gave rise to a theory, or a school, of fine art.

The current compositional procedures (if so they may be called) are by now quite widely known, but examples may still be in order. The informal methods of painting (where "painting" means only "the application of paint to a surface") used most brilliantly by the late Jackson Pollock have been widely imitated, and indeed have stimulated even more thoroughly unplanned activity—throwing and sloshing paint, like Georges Mathieu, applying it by means of boxing gloves, dancing feet, and even the tires of a moving Volkswagen. Yves Klein has produced "draggings"—the chosen instrument being a nude model smeared with pigment, who is pulled across heavy paper.[3]

These energetic goings-on seem inspired by a fanatical desire to let nature take its course in the production of visual designs. But the courting of accident has been present to some degree in all abstract expressionism, even in what may be called its classical period—a brief hour of glory. Abstract expressionism used to be called "action painting" to emphasize its spontaneity (and also its sincerity; it flourished during the Eisenhower period, as Frank Getlein has pointed out) . Part of the point of not looking ahead, of not designing before beginning, was to leave plenty of room for chance.

Since nothing is left to the vagaries of fate more utterly than what man casts away on the refuse heap, it is not surprising that the fascination with accident should have aroused a lively interest in trash. I saw an exhibit called "The Junk Object" at the Ohio State University in October, 1963. The catalogue stated that "Contemplating the junk-object we rediscover the validity of the formative

[3] For further examples, see Lester D. Longman, "Have We Been Had? Yes," *Oberlin Alumni Magazine,* X, 12–14; Leonard B. Meyer, "Art by Accident," *Horizon,* III, No. 1 (September, 1960) , 31–32, 121–24.

act, lest we reappear in the wilderness naked. But there is nothing in the junk-object that compels or even recommends one act rather than another. The imperative to act in an unspecified direction is the ground of freedom." This theory of freedom disguises it so successfully that it would hardly be recognized by its greatest admirers, such as Kant and Mill. The air of casualness so prized in the objects themselves (a battered root-beer dispenser, rusted mufflers, smashed headlights, and so forth) contrasted somewhat paradoxically with the evident care used in selecting them, and the elegant manner in which they were mounted. But there could be no doubt that the condition in which they appeared was not the result of any intention.

It must be conceded, I think, that the art of painting has led the way in the tychistic movement. But composers (to give them the courtesy title) have not lagged far behind. Outstanding among the active workers is, of course, Karlheinz Stockhausen, who has discovered ways of preventing deliberate intention from playing too large a role in the composition and performance of some of his works. Following the earlier example of Henry Cowell, some of his scores give fragments, arranged at random on the page, which the performer is instructed to play in any order that happens to strike his fancy, and to continue until one of the fragments happens to have been played three times. Morton Feldman prescribes no definite notes at all. Earle Brown has used tables of random numbers to decide pitches; John Cage favors Chinese dice, or transparent pages that can be juggled to get new juxtapositions; or he lets the notes be determined by imperfections of the paper on which he happens to be writing. He praises "indeterminacy," which he defines as "identifying with no matter what eventuality"; and he claims to conduct musical "experiments," which he defines as "simply an action the outcome of which is not foreseen." These handy, though startling, definitions are given in his recent book, *Silence,* a collection of his various writings and speakings.[4]

In the field of literature, similar signs are to be observed. The use of chance methods of selecting words for poems has been tried, but it cannot be said to have caught on—except in the case of a few

---

[4] John Cage, *Silence* (Middletown, Conn.: Wesleyan University Press, 1961). For further examples, see Hubert Lamb, "Music in the Age of Zak," *Harpers Magazine,* XXVI (May, 1963), 76–85; Meyer, "Art by Accident," pp. 31–32, 121–24.

celebrated hoaxes, the point of which was to show that some critics will fall for anything. It is not clear that the drama has ever surpassed the surrealist movies of Luis Buñuel, *Un Chien Andalou* (1928) and *L'Âge d'Or* (1930). Several French novelists in recent years have been trying to break down, in their works, the rational connections that traditionally make a novel coherent—causality, motivation, self-identity, spatial and temporal relations, and so forth. In a kind of antibook named *Mobile* (subtitled "A Study for a Representation of the United States"), Michel Butor recently produced fifty chapters in which a mixture of whimsical typography and jumbled fragments of disconnected information give an impression of rather total disorder. But the accidental novel has now come into its own, commercially, with the publication of Marc Saporta's *Composition No. 1*. This work, available for $3.95, comes in unbound pages which "the reader is requested to shuffle like a deck of cards." Of course each shuffling produces a different work, so it is a bargain. But it does not matter which you read. The hero X may wind up well or ill; "The life of X is in your hands."

The explanations and justifications of these developments, given by either the artists or their skeptical observers, have been extraordinarily profound. According to one view, only chance art is an appropriate response to the chaos of modern life on the part of an artist who values his integrity. Others say that the art of "indeterminacy" is needed because we now know that microphysical events are subject to Werner Heisenberg's uncertainty principle. Worse still, because the second law of thermodynamics promises an inexorable downhill march to a statistical heat-death, what else can a conscientious artist do but play along with nature by maximizing the entropy of his works? Still others have found in Zen the true philosophy of accidental art—no pressure or push, no fuss or fret. The Zen art of "controlling accident," as Alan Watts has said, turns into "goofing off."

One of the most challenging theses about this movement is that of Leonard B. Meyer, who says that we *may* be at the end of an era—a point when "teleological art" (that is, painting with structure, literature with plot and character, music that is goal-directed) is giving way to antiteleological art. "For these radical empiricists, *the Renaissance is over*."[5] His argument for this thesis is most interest-

[5] Leonard B. Meyer, "The End of the Renaissance?" *The Hudson Review*, XVI (1963), 186.

ing and suggestive, but I think it is mistaken. When you put all these different practices together, as he does in his article, you get an illusory sense of a common pattern of movement. But further analysis reveals that chance does not, in fact, mean the same in all the arts since the results are not the same. Despite superficial resemblances, what happens in accidental painting has a very different relationship to the past from what happens in accidental music.

Consider the physical aspects of a painting, in the broad sense of applying paint, by whatever means. The physical properties of paint, and the corresponding laws of gravity, viscosity, friction, surface tension, and so forth, are always at work. Leaving paint to chance means leaving it to the operation of these laws. But they are likely to introduce, quite mechanically, certain kinds of order. So cracks in sidewalks and windshields, not to mention spiral nebulae and snow crystals, will often present coherent and interesting patterns. And when paint that is dripped or dribbled is subjected to the kind of artful control that Pollock came to exercise, for all his spontaneity, it is not surprising that fresh and intense qualities are occasionally achieved. I remember seeing a television program that dealt, rather unkindly, with some avant-garde Parisian artists. The chosen medium of one man is the double bass. He buys an old one, carts it home, lays out a large piece of plywood, holds the double bass by the neck, swings it over his shoulder as hard as possible, and smashes it to pieces on the plywood board. Then he nails the pieces down as they lie, and that is his masterpiece, a large collage. Now this is not so silly as it seems, if we look at the matter rationally. The double-bass pieces are, of course, subject to simple physical laws, and it is not surprising that they fall into a kind of explosive, but somewhat coherent, pattern. And if some of them slide off the board or do not skid out far enough, you can always shove them into a better position with your foot (which this artist did).

When the painting is an action painting, the natural swing of the arm or movements of the feet may well give it a form that is to some degree satisfactory—though this is not guaranteed. I have seen one of the paintings done by the late Betsy, a chimpanzee at the Baltimore Zoo. When various colors were placed on the paper, and she was put to work, her movements were, in one sense, random, for they were not governed by any master plan. But the curving motions of her arms, and the rhythms introduced by fingers and toes, produced a pattern that was by no means dull. (In a paper presented at the American Society for Aesthetics in October, 1963, Professor Donald R. Meyer, of Ohio State University, produced experimental evidence that chimpanzees prefer symmetrical patterns to random ones, just as human beings do; but Betsy was more of an action painter.)

In short, accidental visual art is, in large part, not really tychistic but stochastic—governed by probabilities imposed by physical conditions. And so, even in its greatest extremities (except for leaving the canvas blank, perhaps), contemporary painting is essentially not a revolt against the past at all. It is a renunciation, in the sense that it explores what can be got out of much more limited means than Rembrandt or Rubens or Poussin commanded. But its resources, that is, what it actually presents to us, are those that have always been used by the visual designer. And what else could they be? For whether the shapes are patterns of pigment, rusty mufflers, or pieces of a double bass, they are still shapes and have to be enjoyed, if they permit it, as shapes.

The situation in music is radically different. For here the continuity of the musical process, the sense of going somewhere and of hearing something unfold, is not just a feature of past Western music, but something essential to its nature. A mere sequence of sounds is not (in my view) music at all, and cannot provide that sort of enjoyment which is peculiar to music, though a collection of spots made by dripping paints can be a visual pattern and, in some degree, can be relished as such. The true analogue of tychistic music is the painting made by filling in squares according to a table of random numbers—and such a work is indeed uninteresting. When pitches are chosen by casting dice or shuffling transparencies, or when the parts of the composition are ordered by random glances, there is nothing at work comparable to the natural laws that can impart some order to paint even when it is left largely to its own devices. And the results, when melody, harmony, rhythm, and larger structural relationships are all carefully avoided, are not worthy of serious consideration. The one thing that can be said on their behalf is what, according to John Cage, cannot unfortunately be said for the classic composers: they have not lost their power to irritate.

There is no opportunity here to discuss literature; my argument, if I could develop it, would be that chance means something still different here. The nature of language is such that when two words, say an adjective and a noun, are combined in random fashion, the odds are that some meaning, however meager, can be found in the combination. When many words are combined at random, the odds against their having any meaning as a whole increase rapidly. But perceptive and charitable readers will frequently find some vague, elusive sense, so long as there is syntactical order. When we combine dramatic scenes, as in movie shots or pages of a novel, the mind will make every effort to find connections and will often do so, even though they were not foreseen. Any two conjoined human gestures or movements, for example, will convey some notion of a possible human situation. This is one of the things that the surrealists discovered a long time back, and some of the best-known contemporary cinema directors are making the most of it.

At his best, it seems to me, the chance-artist is exploiting methods that might present fresh possibilities, novel combinations and qualities—and his success depends, as it always has, on his alertness to recognize aesthetic value when it turns up, on his keenness of perception, on his critical discrimination. So long as he does not renounce these faculties, leaving everything to chance, he differs only in degree from his predecessors. And his work raises no fundamentally new problems for aesthetics. Its most important theoretical lesson, I believe, is that aesthetic enjoyment can range over a wide gamut of perceptual qualities, and find (or partially create) a measure of perceptual order even when the senses give it only hints and suggestions.

II

The brief quotations I gave earlier from Plato and Augustine show that those early aestheticians who made the concept of order central to art also thought it susceptible of mathematical analysis, either as "measure" or as "number." And we know how the mathematical dreams of the ancients have haunted the arts and the aesthetics of the West. The theory of proportions, which began humbly among the Egyptians as a method of enlarging pictures, became a canon of perfection. With the revival of Neoplatonism, the theorists of the Italian and of the northern Renaissance (Alberti and Dürer, for example) searched assiduously for mathematical ratios that would hold up in theory and in practice. And down to our own day, and the famous Modular of Le Corbusier, the hope has kept alive among artists. Meanwhile, theorists of the "golden number," of "dynamic symmetry," and of "aesthetic measure" have sought for mathematical functions to describe those conditions under which beauty or aesthetic value will appear at its most intense.[6]

But the most significant attempt to provide a precise description of order in art is that which has been made only in the past decade with the help of Information Theory. In certain aspects this enterprise is still in its infancy, but enough has been accomplished to indicate some of the possibilities and some of the difficulties, and it deserves a central place in any discussion of artistic order. Since the most interesting and convincing applications have been to music, I will confine myself largely to this art; but later I will say a little about the special problems of visual design.

The fundamental concepts of Information Theory are widely known, but it may be helpful to remind ourselves of them here. We start with a series of signals, constituting (in a technical sense) a *message*—where the individual signals belong to a limited variety of types, say dots and dashes, or letters of the alphabet. If the signals occur in a random order, each is completely unpredictable on the basis of what has gone before. In that case, each signal is said to have maximum *entropy,* or to give maximum *information.* Information, in this technical sense, of course, has nothing to do with facts or truths; it is merely what the receiver learns, or acquires, by receiving the signal. If he has no reason to expect a dot, and then he hears a dot, he has learned something new. If, on the other hand, the preceding signals consist only of a long string of dots, so that he is almost certain that the nth signal will be a dot, then the nth signal will give him practically no information at all. It is largely redundant, again in a technical sense, since most of the information it gives has already been given by the preceding signals, $1 \ldots n-1$. Redundancy is, then, the inverse of information; the more information a signal contains, the less redundancy, and vice versa.

For our present purposes, it is not necessary to review the mathematical treatment of information (or redundancy); it will be enough to recall the general principles. How is amount of information to be measured? The first principle applies when the signals are equiprobable. Let us say, for example, that every signal is selected from a set of M different types; then the probability of getting a

[6] See, for example, Rudolf Wittkower, "The Changing Concept of Proportion," *Daedalus,* Winter, 1960, pp. 199–215.

signal of a particular type is 1/M. And the information is measured as a logarithm of M to the base 2: $\log_2 M$. The unit of information derives from the simplest case, when $M = 2$ (for example, when every signal is either a dot or a dash). In that case, every signal, having a probability of 1/2, is said to give 1 *bit* of information. As the number of signal types increases, the odds against each type increase, and so the amount of information given by each signal also increases. If the signals are all selected from the 5 regular solids, for example, then (still assuming equiprobability) the information given by each signal is $\log_2 5 = 2.32$ bits.

The second principle applies where the available signal-types are not equiprobable, where the message is *stochastic,* rather than purely *tychistic.* This would be the case, for example, if the regular solids were used, but the sending apparatus (using this term in a broad sense) was programed so that the frequency of occurrence of each regular solid was inversely proportional to the number of its sides—the tetrahedron occurring five times as often, say, as the icosahedron. For in this situation the receiver of the message could reasonably form the expectation, or prediction, that the nth signal is more likely to be a tetrahedron than an icosahedron. And therefore, if it does turn out to be a tetrahedron, this is not very surprising and gives a comparatively small amount of information; while if it turns out to be an icosahedron, this is much more surprising and gives a comparatively large amount of information. And so the information value of a signal with a given probability P is $\log_2 \dfrac{1}{p}$. Out of 100 signals, about 8.2 would be icosahedra; i.e., the probability of an icosahedral signal would be .082. Thus (approximately) the information value of an icosahedron would be

$$\log_2 \frac{1}{.082} = \log_2 12.2 = 3.6 \text{ bits}$$

But the information value of a tetrahedral signal would be less than 1.5 bits.

Now these mathematical abstractions seem at first glance to have little to do with art; it was, indeed, a brilliant insight to see that they could be extended in an interesting way to music. The simplest and most direct application is to melody. For a melody can be regarded as a message consisting of a series of discrete and distinguishable signals. Those who have applied Information Theory to music have generally prefaced their work by saying that music is, after all, a system of communication. But this remark can be misleading; it has nothing to do with anything communicated *by* music; it merely means that a melody is something that can be regarded as *sent* from one person to another, from the xylophone player, say, who taps out a dozen tones, to his auditors. The particular tonal and scale systems to which the melody belongs can be regarded as conditions that limit the variety of types from which each signal is selected. Thus, if the melody is diatonic (so-called white-note music) and we treat octaves as identical, we can say that every signal in the melody belongs to one of eight types, where silence is considered one of the signals. (If the melody is completely chromatic, there will then be thirteen types.)

Now, if a series of notes selected from the eight diatonic tones (including the silent o-tone, or rest) is tapped out at random to make a message, each tone will give $\log_2 8 = 3$ bits of information. Call this method A. Of course this may not produce a melody, or not much of a melody. But suppose we impose certain restrictions on the process by which the message is generated. For example, we might limit our messages to sixteen signals and allow a message to start on any white key, but make the following rule: the next signal after any given signal must be within one tone of the preceding one. Thus, if A is struck, the next note must be either G, A, B, or a silence. Call this method B. Immediately we find that the messages generated according to this rule tend to be much more melodious, have more musical coherence, than the purely random ones. But, at the same time, we have achieved this goal by reducing the amount of information given by each note. For now every signal (after the first) must be chosen from four possibilities, rather than eight, and so its information value is $\log_2 4 = 2$ bits.

This sort of consideration leads to the hypothesis that there is some fundamental connection between musical coherence and information value. When we went from method A to method B, we decreased the information given by each note; that is to say, we increased redundancy. At the same time we made the melody more coherent; that is, in one sense, we introduced a greater *order* into the melodic process. Is order in music, then, nothing but redundancy? If so, we would have, for the first time, a clear and exact measure of the amount of order embodied in any given melody, whether by Dufay, Monteverdi, Haydn, or Alban Berg. All we need to know are the limits of the set from which the notes of the melody

are selected, and the particular "stylistic" rules limiting their relationships with each other (whether, for example, single or successive leaps of a major seventh or a tritone are prohibited) . Of course,
we should also have to apply the same analysis to harmony and
rhythm, to make the account complete.

But an even more exciting prospect opens up. Consider that in
moving from method *A* to method *B* we increased redundancy, and
at the same time (I assume it will be agreed) we effected an
improvement. Or at least we increased the probability that the
melody we obtain will be a better one. A poor melody can be
constructed following method *B,* but if we construct a hundred by
method *A* and a hundred by method *B,* more of the latter will be
musically enjoyable. Put it another way: the first clause of Beethoven's setting of the "Ode to Joy" in the *D minor Symphony* could
have been obtained by using either method. But the odds against
getting that melody by method *A* are enormous; they are very much
less with method *B*. This suggests a positive correlation between
musical value (aesthetic value in music) and redundancy, or order.
But, on the other hand, if we were to impose further rules, decreasing the information content of each note, it does not follow that we
could continue to increase the musical value. For example, we
might rule that no note may be played twice in a row. Call this
method *C*. That would limit the choice of each signal to three, and
it would eliminate Beethoven's melody. Indeed, it is very difficult, if
not impossible, to think of any well-known melody that would
follow the rules of method *C* for more than eight or ten notes.

What all this suggests, then, is that the best melodies lie somewhere between *A* and *C,* between complete randomness and a very
tight control. Not a maximal or a minimal, but an optimal, amount
of order would then measure the highest degree of aesthetic value
attainable within the general conditions available—that, for example, we use a chromatic, or diatonic, or pentatonic scale. If this
conclusion can be established, and generalized to more complex
musical processes, we will at last have realized the age-old ambition
to provide a mathematical criterion for aesthetic value.

A number of those who have studied Information Theory and
music have touched on this problem, but as far as I can make out
there have only been two very sustained attempts to formulate such
a criterion.

The first of these is that of Leonard B. Meyer, who in this as in other areas has been a pioneer inquirer into musical aesthetics. After a careful study of "deviations" in musical processes—that is, the ways in which a melody, though tending toward a goal, may postpone its arrival—he concludes that "what creates or increases the information contained in a piece of music increases its value." [7] But Meyer makes clear that this generalization rests on a very important presupposition. If, as we have seen, the notes were given out at random, information would be at its maximum; in Meyer's terminology, "uncertainty" would be complete—but this would be "undesirable uncertainty." [8] However, if a musical process is stochastic, that is, governed by an "ordered probability system," then any uncertainty is set against the background of this system. So long as the underlying system is not disturbed, a particular melody may introduce "uncertainty" in various degrees, by shying away from the tonic just when the tonic is expected, for example. The more probable it is (given preceding notes) that the nth note will be the tonic, the more information is introduced by letting the nth note be something else—as for example in (b) or (c) instead of (a) :

There are two terms here that may be confusing and deserve some clarification; indeed, one of them leads into a fundamental problem. To speak of the little ornament in (b) as "increasing uncertainty" may suggest that it makes the occurrence of the final G less likely; but this is not so. The melody, we will assume (it may be the movement of a Mozart sonata), is squarely in the key of G, and the final phrases clearly tend toward the tonic chord. The ornament does not make us any less sure that G will be coming along; it only gives us something else instead of what we strongly expected; thus it increases the total information content of the melody. Meyer shows, in an acute analysis of two fugue subjects, how one is a much better melody because it takes opportunities to increase information on the way to its goal.[9]

[7] Leonard B. Meyer, "Some Remarks on Value and Greatness in Music," *Journal of Aesthetics and Art Criticism*, XVII (June, 1959), 490.
[8] *Ibid.*, p. 491.
[9] *Ibid.*, pp. 488–93.

To speak of a "system of probabilities" in connection with a melody introduces another puzzle. The essential fact to which the term points can be easily illustrated. Suppose we have heard enough of a melody to place it in the key of C. Now consider a particular note, say F. When we hear this note, we hear it as having potential relationships to other notes. It has a strong pull downward toward E, for example; a weaker pull downward toward D; a still weaker pull upward to G; a very weak one toward B. It is hard to talk about these relationships; the words "pull" and "thrust" are only roughly descriptive. I suggest the term "anticipatory tendency." And I take it to be something we hear in the musical process itself. It is in terms of such tendencies that we find ourselves moved by the music. The melody may float along fulfilling its strongest tendencies or turn away into the weaker ones, relaxing and building tensions as it goes. The strength of each tendency will be a function of the preceding musical context. How strong is the tendency toward the tonic, say, at a given time, will depend on whether the preceding notes move in its general direction or away from it.

Now, we can describe these tendencies in phenomenally subjective terms, as "expectation" and "surprise." We can say that the ornament in (b) surprises us more than the tonic tone would because we were expecting the tonic tone quite strongly. But if we talk about expectations and surprises in this context, we must recognize that these terms have a rather unusual sense. For after I have heard the sonata several times, and know a lot of it by heart, the final ornamental cadence no longer surprises me, in one sense; I completely expect it. But its *musical* surprisingness (its contrariety to *musical* expectation) has not changed; the melody, so to speak, still "wants to go" to the tonic, and it is that want that is frustrated, not my subjective wish or hope. That is why "prediction" must be used with caution here, too. We might say that at a certain point in the melody the tonic is more predictable than the fourth. But when I know the melody by heart, then, in one sense, every note becomes predictable; and yet the differences in tendency strength remain.

We can also try, as Meyer does, to describe anticipatory tendency in terms of probabilities. Thus we might say that, given the F, it is more probable that the next note will be an E than that it will be a G. This does not rule out its being a G, of course. But, whatever the melody actually does, its effect depends on the probability system it belongs to (or the network of anticipatory tendencies). It is only because E is more probable than G that the actual rise to G increases tension and power.

Now these anticipatory tendencies are not strictly probabilities. Suppose we are given a chromatic melody, constructed according to a preset twelve-tone row. So-called "total serial music" is like this: every feature of it is determined by antecedently chosen rules. Since, once we know the rules, all probabilities reach certainty, the information value reduces to zero. But such music sounds very much like random music; anticipatory tendency is at a minimum.

Suppose, however, we interpret probability here in terms of frequency. In total serial music, every pitch occurs as frequently as any other, and in that sense every pitch can be said to be equally likely. That would explain why the general effect is very much as though a computer had generated the notes according to a table of random numbers.

Now, compare Beethoven's "Ode to Joy"—not just the first clause of it. Can we account for the strength of the various anticipatory tendencies here in terms of transitional frequencies? That is, given a particular tone, can we say that its pull toward other tones is determined by the frequency with which it is followed by them in this melody? The tone E, for example, occurs in this melody fifteen times (in the key of D major) ; it is followed once by itself, once by A, six times by D, and seven times by F♯.[10] Does it follow that the E tends more strongly toward F♯ than toward the tonic D? Certainly not.

But this analysis would leave out a vital factor in the situation. For when we come to the hearing of the melody we have already heard countless diatonic melodies, and we hear this melody in terms of all that previous experience. Again, Leonard Meyer has probably done the most to explore the consequences of this fact. And clearly he is right that, if we define the probability system in terms of frequencies, it is not the frequencies of the particular melody, but those of a whole set of melodies belonging to some general category (say all diatonic major melodies) , that we will have to consider. If we conceive of a melody as a series of simple musical events, consisting of one note following another—and also transpose them all to the key of C—then we can calculate frequencies of this sort. Now

[10] See the discussion of this point by Victor Zuckerkandl, *Sound and Symbol: Music and the External World* (New York: Pantheon Books, 1956) , p. 45; cf. chaps. i and iv.

suppose we discovered certain fairly constant frequencies: that the fourth moves to the third more often than to the fifth, or (to introduce higher-order relationships) that the sequence F,E,D is followed by C much more often than by A. Then we could easily apply Information Theory to music. For a melody, so analyzed, would constitute what is called a "Markov chain," that is, a sequence in which the probability of a given signal depends on the signal or signals immediately preceding it.

To the extent that strength of anticipatory tendency is measured by actual frequency of the melodic movements (or transitions), the basic movement of music can be described in Information Theory terms. And hope may be held out for a function that will define optimal order. Experiments with computer music have certainly shown that there is a rough correspondence, at least for simple melodies. If the frequencies of sequences in a set of folk songs, for example, are fed into a computer, and the computer is asked to observe these frequencies in composing its own melodies, it will come up with melodies (among others) that sound like folk songs.[11] The best ones, it may be hypothesized, will be those that, on the average, deviate a certain amount from the existing probabilities, i.e., contain a certain amount of information. I do not see how Meyer could be right in his hypothesis that they would contain the maximum possible information, given the antecedent probabilities; that would be true of a melody that always moved to the least probable next note (say the tritone or seventh). But Meyer would presumably formulate his presupposition more strictly. A melody to some degree sets its own probability system as it develops. Once it shows us that it belongs to the general group of diatonic major melodies, and that it subscribes roughly to the prevailing probability system, then it should deviate as much as possible without destroying that general commitment. For example, in the first clause of the Beethoven melody the tonic D appears only once, and then but briefly, but the harmonic system implied by the first few notes already suggests its presence, and even if it were completely avoided it could still be the implicit goal of the entire melody. (Kurt Weill's "Mack the Knife," from *The Threepenny Opera,* is a good example of this.)

[11] Cf. the stochastic composition of nursery tones by Richard C. Pinkerton, "Information Theory and Melody," *Scientific American,* CXCIV (February, 1956), 77–86.

It remains a question, though, whether prevailing frequencies will serve as an adequate measure of anticipatory tendency. Meyer himself has noted that "not all the probabilities embodied in a musical composition are determined by frequencies." Some depend on "ways of thinking." [12] And of course Gestalt psychologists would contend that given a set of tones, in a scale relation, certain internal characteristics of the set may emerge. These relationships may affect very powerfully the actual strength of the anticipatory tendencies. For example, if we prohibited the playing of most melodies in which the seventh or leading tone was followed by the tonic, so that this event hardly ever occurred, it might nevertheless be the case that, when the seventh did occur, its pull toward the tonic would still be very strong. I do not plan to enter into this thorny and unsettled question. But if Gestalt factors affect anticipatory tendency over and above what frequency would determine, it will not be possible to assign exact numerical measurements, based on frequency alone, to the "probability system" of a musical process.

One other related problem might be mentioned here. When Markov-chain music is composed by a computer—as in the *Illiac Suite* programed by Lejaren A. Hiller, Jr., and Leonard M. Isaacson [13]—it is likely to be describable in the way J. R. Pierce describes the *Illiac Suite:* it "has a good deal of local structure but is weak and wandering as a whole." [14] In my terminology, it has style, or texture, but not large-scale form, or structure. As Pierce adds, it would be feasible to program the computer to repeat some passages, or some melodic sequences, according to a prior arrangement, to give the composition something of the character of a rondo or concerto grosso. But it seems to me that only fairly small-scale music can be approximately treated as a Markov chain; in larger compositions, the points of especially great or especially minimal information (or redundancy) may be determined not so much by what has immediately preceded them as by what has occurred at a parallel point much earlier in the composition. For example, the *lack* of a modulation in the middle of the recapitulation of a Mozart sonata allegro movement gives little information if we consider only that at

[12] Leonard B. Meyer, "Meaning in Music and Information Theory," *Journal of Aesthetics and Art Criticism*, XV (June, 1957) , 422.

[13] Lejaren A. Hiller, Jr., and Leonard M. Isaacson, *Experimental Music: Composition with an Electronic Computer* (New York: McGraw-Hill, 1959) .

[14] J. R. Pierce, *Symbols, Signals, and Noise: The Nature and Process of Communication* (New York: Harper & Row, 1961) , p. 259.

that point we are in fact expecting the key to continue, but it gives much information when we keep in mind that at the same point in the exposition there *was* a modulation.

A somewhat different approach to the problem of musical value is that made by David Kraehenbuehl and Edgar Coons, in two articles a few years ago. Their aim is to provide, so to speak, a more internalized criterion of optimal order. For this purpose, they redefine "information" as "a measure of the degree to which a single prediction or an array of predictions is 'nonconfirmed' by the present event." [15] When a particular melody conforms to an antecedently known probability system, in Meyer's sense, then their definition of information will correspond to the usual one. But it permits tentative estimates of information value to be developed on the basis of the melody itself. In other words, the melody, as it develops, establishes its own probability system. Their proposal, then, is that musical value is to be measured by "degree of information reduction." [16] The important musical fact consists in the building up of a comparatively high state of entropy, or information, and then reducing it sharply. This can go on at different musical levels, from single notes to large structural sections. Kraehenbuehl and Coons provide a mathematical measure of information increase and information reduction, and they define two "indexes" of musical value: (1) an "index of articulateness," that is, the average information flux, including both increases and reductions; and (2) an "index of hierarchy," that is, the average of information reductions.[17] In terms of the second index, for instance, if we consider a series of four musical events, it turns out that the sequence A A B A ranks highest. A A A A does not build up a state of high information, according to their calculations, since once we hear A we expect it to continue; A A A B, on the other hand, achieves a state of high information value with B, since it is not prepared for, but does not reduce this state. But A A B A does both; it gives us a rise in information value with the B, and then reduces it sharply with the

[15] Edgar Coons and David Kraehenbuehl, "Information as a Measure of Structure in Music," *Journal of Music Theory*, II (1958), 129; cf. Kraehenbuehl and Coons, "Information as a Measure of the Experience of Music," *Journal of Aesthetics and Art Criticism*, XVII (June, 1959), 511.

[16] Kraehenbuehl and Coons, "Information as a Measure of the Experience of Music," p. 516.

[17] Coons and Kraehenbuehl, "Information as a Measure of Structure in Music," pp. 148–50.

return to A. Hence the frequency of this structure, the authors suggest, in popular songs.

It is interesting to note that this internal measure helps to correct one limitation of the external one. For Kraehenbuehl and Coons use the optimal information value of the A A B A form to explain its popularity, and their measure of the information value of the bridge passage B is not affected by the fact that the frequency of the structure would enable us to predict a change at that point, even at first hearing. The nature and significance of the shift from A to B as a musical event is the same in their system, no matter how often it may occur, and presumably its musical value remains constant— though, of course, if we become surfeited with events of this kind, we may no longer be in a condition to extract that value from them. I think this is a good feature of their method, especially when applied to large-scale musical events.

But when we consider small-scale musical events, such as the moment-to-moment movements of a melody, it does not seem to me that their method is nearly subtle enough. It does not take into account the kind of antecedent network of anticipatory tendencies such as Meyer emphasizes. They consider each musical event mainly in terms of whether it is similar to or different from something that has occurred before, and they seem to assume that we listen to music with a generalized and persistent expectation that what has been will continue to be. But this oversimplifies the hearer's state of mind very considerably. The moment we grasp a series of a few notes as part of a melody, rather than just as a series of notes, we are already hearing it as conforming to, or deviating in some degree from, some network of anticipatory tendencies, and that is long before the melody itself can have an opportunity to establish its own network.

The application of information theory to visual design has proved less successful so far.[18] Here the problem is to see how far the concept of redundancy can be used to analyze pattern, or Gestalt, and thus replace a somewhat vague and qualitative concept with a precise and measurable one. The problem can readily be solved for sets of visual designs, as they are used in some psychological experiments, but it is hard to say what constitutes redundancy in a single pattern. Thus, consider, for example, a 3 x 3 matrix of spaces, such as used in tick-tack-toe, and let every square contain either a nought

[18] The difficulties are discussed by Wendell R. Garner, *Uncertainty and Structure as Psychological Concepts* (New York: John Wiley & Sons, 1962), chap. vi.

or a cross. There are $2^9 = 512$ possible patterns of this type. And suppose sixteen of these possible patterns are used in an experiment in which the subject learns to recognize patterns, or learn names for them. Then redundancy can be measured as the difference between the total set of available patterns (512) and the subset actually used (16). But suppose we are merely comparing one of the tick-tack-toe patterns with another, say

X O X	X X O
O X O	X O X
X O X	O O O
(a)	(b)

Clearly *a* is better organized than *b;* and if redundancy is a measure of organization where is the redundancy to be found?

Certain possibilities are evident, and some exploration has been done. For example, if we consider repetition as the essential locus of redundancy—where the repeated element gives less information than its first occurrence—we might try measuring redundancy in terms of repetitions. One way might be to consider symmetries, or mirror reflections along an axis. In the tick-tack-toe figure there are four possible axes (vertical, horizontal, and two diagonal) along which the patterns could be folded into themselves. Figure *a* is symmetrical along every one of these axes; figure *b* is symmetrical along none of them. William R. Sickles and George W. Hartmann have analyzed order in terms of parallelisms.[19] Another method, suggested by Fred Attneave, is to convert the two-dimensional problem into a one-dimensional one, and look for serial order.[20] Thus, suppose each of the patterns was treated like a single series, reading each row across. Then *a* would be equivalent to X O X O X O X O X, and *b* would be equivalent to X X O X O X O O O. The last half of *a* is quite predictable, once we see the first half; hence it has a high redundancy. But only a few of the items in *b* would be predicted by many subjects, and so its redundancy would be minimal. It seems that something would be lost by this method. For example, suppose we have the pattern

[19] William R. Sickles and George W. Hartmann, "The Theory of Order," *Psychological Review,* XLIX (1942), 403–21; cf. Julian Hochberg and Edward McAlister, "A Quantitative Approach to Figural 'Goodness,' " *Journal of Experimental Psychology,* XLVI (1953), 361–64.

[20] Fred Attneave, "Some Informational Aspects of Visual Perception," *Psychological Review,* LXI (1954), 183–93.

O X O
X X X
O X O

c

This has a high redundancy by the symmetry criterion, and indeed this cross is clearly a very organized pattern. But in serial form *c* would be O X O X X X O X O, which has a lower redundancy than seems suitable. Of course, this difficulty could be remedied if a pattern were reduced not to a single series, but to a set of series, counting the units in different orders.

The proposal has also been made to reduce the measurement of single-pattern redundancy to that of sets of patterns.[21] Essentially, the idea would be this: consider each single pattern as one that has been selected not only from the whole possible set (512), but from some subset of the whole set. Then the redundancy of the individual pattern can be regarded as the redundancy of the relevant subset. For example, if we consider *a*—and also *c*—an example of a pattern that is four-ways symmetrical, then we can calculate how many of the 256 patterns have this property (8). Or, if the pattern in question has symmetry only along a horizontal axis, then it would belong to a subset of sixty-four patterns. But as yet we do not have a clearly justifiable criterion for deciding what subset to assign the pattern to, in order to measure its redundancy this way.

In the last analysis, it may seem too early to attempt a general judgment about the Information Theory of optimal aesthetic order. It has been extremely clarifying on several important points. But there are two limitations that seem to me inherent in it—that prevent it from telling the whole story about aesthetic value.

In the first place, the Information Theory approach to the concept of optimal order presupposes that it is to be found somewhere along a single continuum "between the two extremes of order and chaos. . . . Most musical compositions reflect a balance between the extremes of *order disorder*, and . . . stylistic differences depend to a considerable extent upon fluctuations relative to these two poles." [22] The same assumption is made by D. E. Berlyne.[23] Whether there is one continuum here or two is a very ancient question, though it

---

[21] See Garner, *Uncertainty and Structure as Psychological Concepts*, pp. 204–5.
[22] Hiller and Isaacson, *Experimental Music*, pp. 17, 167.
[23] D. E. Berlyne, *Conflict, Arousal, and Curiosity* (New York: McGraw-Hill, 1950), chaps. ii and ix.

does not seem to have been very explicitly formulated. "Unity and variety," for example, is most often understood as a double concept. While there is some inverse connection between the two, they are not assumed to be exact inverses, such that an increase in one automatically decreases the other. But this is not wholly clear, partly because the word "variety" seems in part opposed to unity, or at least to some of the terms (such as "harmony" and "symmetry") often associated with unity. That is one reason why I prefer the term "complexity," for all the dubiousness that has sometimes been attributed to it.

If we identify unity with order, and complexity with disorder, they become exact inverses, and the question of discovering the optimal point tends to get asked in some such way as this: How much unity do you want? Or how much disorder can you stand? Perhaps these questions have a use. But I believe that we cannot adequately define the relevant formal properties of works of art in terms of a single dimension. Complexity is not the same as disunity; unity is not the same as simplicity.

From the point of view of Information Theory, there must be a close connection, if not an identity, between disorder and complexity. Complexity is, of course, a very puzzling psychological concept, but some of the factors that fit into it can be analyzed in Information Theory terms. For example, the complexity of a melody (other things being equal) may be said to increase with the number of different pitches from which its notes are selected. As this number increases, so does the information value of each note. Or again, a melody may be said to be more complex if it involves longer skips—more sixths and sevenths, say, as compared with seconds and thirds. And again, in terms of a probability system, this melody would have a higher information value. But in these cases it seems to me I can imagine two melodies to be equally unified, even though one has longer intervals. Both may hang together in firm coherence, round off to a wholly satisfactory close. Here, it seems to me, what Information Theory measures is not so much unity/disunity as simplicity/complexity. I do not deny that they often correlate. For example, when complexities are introduced into a musical process the unity may be weakened, unless further internal relations are also introduced to bind the parts together. But when a theme is complicated, as in Meyer's comparison of the figure subjects from Bach and Geminiani, the resulting theme is not necessarily less unified if its over-all contour remains clear and its final goal as probable as ever.

These questions are not easy to deal with, when our intuitive sense of degrees of unity and simplicity is so imprecise. And of course it is one of the great values of Information Theory in this area that it provides some exact concepts that may be very important even if they do not yet replace our vaguer intuitive ones.

III

I promised two arguments against the attempt to make optimal redundancy the sole criterion of aesthetic value, either in music or elsewhere. The first one was against the identification of complexity and disorder. The second one leads out into more general issues, and so I will use it as an introduction to them.

Whether or not the unity/disunity continuum can be satisfactorily merged with the simplicity/complexity continuum, there will remain a third feature of art that can probably not be dealt with in Information Theory terms, and yet that cannot be ignored in aesthetic evaluation. Nearly all aestheticians, from the beginning, would agree, I think, that when we judge a work of art to be good it is relevant to support this judgment by pointing out (among other things) that the work is highly unified. And, again, I have argued that complexity is always a relevant ground of praise [24]—and in this I am glad to agree with the position so well defended by Leonard Meyer.[25] It is interesting to note, by the way, that if both of these contentions are correct then the two dimensions I have just discussed must indeed be distinct, or together these contentions would amount to a complete triviality, for any work would have to be praised no matter how unified (simple) or lacking in unity (complex) it might be. Now, I also believe that there is a third sort of reason that is relevant to the judgment of art: what I have called the intensity of its human regional qualities.[26] As I tried to indicate in my little historical sketch at the beginning of this paper, the classical aestheticians were very clear in their minds about the relevance and importance of the first and second reasons; it was only later that the third reason came to be made explicit and emphasized.

[24] Monroe C. Beardsley, *Aesthetics: Problems in the Philosophy of Criticism* (New York: Harcourt, Brace, and World, 1958), pp. 462–68.

[25] Meyer, "Some Remarks on Value and Greatness in Music," pp. 486–500.

[26] Beardsley, *Aesthetics*, p. 462.

There is no occasion here to enlarge upon the concept of human regional quality. Briefly, what I have in mind is that music, for example, may be solemn, serene, vivacious, dignified, dramatic, and so forth. I consider the possession of such qualities—and others that are too subtle to be described with any assurance and yet not too subtle to be heard—to be a notable and admirable feature of music. I can imagine, I think, two melodies turned out by the same computer, according to the same system of probabilities, not differing significantly in their total information value, that are nevertheless very different in their qualities as melodies—one weak, insipid, flaccid, and tame; the other with a lyrical poignancy that stamps it as fine and memorable. I do not deny, of course, that the nature and intensity of the quality is a function of the actual constituent notes and their intervallic and rhythmic relationships; I only doubt that it is a direct function of total information value, whether of the "index of articulateness," or the "index of hierarchy," or some other that might be constructed.

These considerations ought to remind us of the dual nature of art, that it somehow shows a special predilection for *both* form and quality. It is this duality that has made possible the enormous range of artistic creation and of aesthetic delight—a range that in modern times artists and thinkers have striven to widen. We can enjoy aesthetically works ranging from the coolest and most rigidly formal to the warmest (or hottest) and freest—that is, our enjoyment can remain aesthetic provided that formalistic art is rich enough to yield a pervasive beauty, through the sensuous appeal of its elements, and provided that informal art is controlled enough to provide some inward coherence and over-all self-sufficiency. It is this duality that has also posed deep problems for the philosopher and reflective critic. Plato, as I suggested earlier, no doubt under the influence of his metaphysics, tried to account for beauty in purely formal terms; in this view, order, or unity amid variety, is alone good. Other thinkers, convinced that this view is too limited, have tried to think of the best art as somehow adding a bit of disorder to an underlying order, flavoring form with the sort of thing that John Crowe Ransom once called a "local texture of irrelevance." But it turned out that the alleged irrelevance was, when it really worked, a more subtle kind of relevance after all. The aesthetic Information Theorists propose a happy medium, an ideal point along the scale of order and disorder. But that again, if my arguments are sound, will not do. Schiller came closer to the heart of the matter in his concept of the "living form" (*Lebensform*), the synthesis of two impulses. More simply, I say that intensity of quality and perfection of form are both involved, however paradoxically and conflictingly; each is an aim of art; good art achieves at least one to a high degree, without losing sight of the other; and great good art somehow manages to make much of both.

The artist, no doubt, is one who rearranges the world and makes us something more satisfactory. But we must not think of him as imposing a Platonic measure or a divine symmetry upon the things of this world; he is not only an orderer. For he is also a creator in a more passionate sense, a maker of objects with individuality, a character of their own, and the power to move us speakingly through that character. He is a man who lives (or works) distractingly with both wildness and discipline, to a higher degree than the rest of us. He must be capable of remarkable feats of destruction, breaking down old familiar Gestalts, associating and disassociating. But, at the same time, he must have extraordinary sensitivity to form, seeing form where others miss it, connecting the hitherto unconnectable, making relatedness where there was only association. In this way, his work becomes itself a paradigm of order and freedom.

> It was her voice that made
> The sky acutest at its vanishing.
> She measured to the hour its solitude.
> She was the single artificer of the world
> In which she sang. And when she sang, the sea,
> Whatever self it had, became the self
> That was her song, for she was the maker. Then we,
> As we beheld her striding there alone,
> Knew that there never was a world for her
> Except the one she sang and, singing, made.
> Wallace Stevens, "The Idea of Order at Key West"

So much, in general terms, I believe, is an important first approximation to the truth. But it also calls our attention to the aesthetic tasks that lie ahead of us, if we are to move on to closer approximations. We cannot get along, in discussing art, without certain formal concepts, and notably unity or its equivalents. Yet we are very far, still, from being able to speak with precision here, or even from having sorted out adequately the various possible strands of meaning that may be confused together in this concept. Here is something that needs to be worked on; and techniques like those provided by Information Theory are going to be extremely helpful.

By way of conclusion, I should like to suggest briefly some of the distinctions that seem to be needed and seem to need clarification. Along with others, they may enable us at some stage to give clear and unequivocal answers to questions about order and disorder in art, and their relations to aesthetic value. There are at least two levels of quality, as I have been assuming: the local qualities of the elements (the patches of color, the notes of the melody) that are the ultimate ingredients of art, and the regional qualities that emerge from complexes of them. Similarly, there are at least two levels of form: textural form, or comparatively small-scale interrelationships; and structural form, or large-scale interrelationships. Textural form depends on order in one quite clear and obvious sense, for everything that can be done, for aesthetic purposes, with color patches and tones depends on the serial orders that are essential to them. The fact that color patches can be serially ordered in terms of hue, saturation, intensity, for example, and that tones can be ordered in pitch and loudness, is the very foundation of their capacity to be built up into larger structures. And it is, presumably, because smells and tastes do not form such serial orders that they serve ill as elements for works of art. Order in this sense, though not itself constitutive of art, is presupposed by it.

We speak of larger entities, the major segments of a work, as being formally interrelated when they form parts of a dominant pattern of some kind—when one is related to the other as preparation to climax, or when one is in balance with the other. A musical composition that comes to a clearly defined and decisive climax, a novel that relates its subplot to its main plot in some parallelistic fashion, a painting that has a center of focus, may be said to be ordered, rather than disordered. This is evidently quite a different kind of order or, perhaps better, a different sense of the term. If the term "order" is extended to include unified structural form, then order becomes (in this sense) a feature of the work itself, one of its most important features.

The biologist, Paul Weiss, has summed up a "balanced view of nature" in a "formula which bears a close resemblance to—and in my opinion is the root of—an aesthetic code: order in the gross, and freedom, diversity, and uniqueness in the small, are not only compatible, but are conjugated." [27] He has in mind the pattern, say, of the white oak leaf, the snail's shell, or the dragonfly's wing, which remains invariant, in its dominant pattern, through endless variations in the smaller parts. This is a neoclassic view of art, I think, and my conclusion is somewhat opposite. Order enters art in the small, in the textural relations among the elements; and it enters in the structural relations among the larger segments. But freedom, diversity, and uniqueness mark the special emergent quality of the whole, what stamps the work with individuality. This is what makes it, like one of Mozart's piano concertos or Haydn's string quartets—and despite its belonging to a large family—something we can recognize and cherish and return to for its own special sake. No more than in civic society is artistic order an end in itself; its justification is the liberation it makes possible.

[27] Paul Weiss, "Organic Form: Scientific and Aesthetic Aspects," *Daedalus*, Winter, 1960, p. 180.

JOHN CROSSETT

Love in the Western Hierarchy

When Aeneas sees Helen in the ruins of Troy, he decides to kill her. For him, she is the cause of the war. His mother, Venus, preserves him from the fate of being remembered as the man who killed Helen. She persuades him that Helen is not the real cause of the war, but only a pretext—a distinction first made by Thucydides; the real cause, she claims, is the will of the gods. Venus' argument, though historically sophisticated, is disingenuous, for she herself is the real cause of the war, and she is, we must remember, the archetype of Helen. Yet we can scarcely expect her to admit this fact, especially in such circumstances. When she claims that the gods are responsible, she is making the connection between *moira* and the gods far more specific than it is ever made in Homer; throughout the *Aeneid,* and for Virgil and his contemporaries, who included Augustus, fate is the will of the gods; it is not some ambiguous system of allotted destinies which the gods must uphold.

With considerable psychological skill, Venus diverts the attention

JOHN M. CROSSETT, a member of the Department of Classical Languages at Grinnell College, returns each summer to Enosburg Falls, Vermont. There the Virgil Press publishes his poems (hand set by the author). His career at Columbia University, at Harvard University, and elsewhere has been marked by contributions to the study of English literature, Greek, and Latin. He is coeditor of *Liberal and Conservative: Issues for College Students.*

of Aeneas from Helen to his family, from destruction to creation. Here begins Virgil's moral rehabilitation of Venus; she is to compensate for her part in the destruction of Troy by aiding in the foundation of Rome. In thus rehabilitating Venus, Virgil was continuing the work of his poetic mentor, Lucretius; and, equally, was participating in a universal philosophic movement in the Western world: the transformation of Venus from an amoral power of lust to a cosmic symbol of order. Plato had begun this process in the speech of Pausanias, in the *Symposium;* there the Pandemian Venus is distinguished from the Uranian Venus, the love of body is distinguished from the love of mind. Now to Plato, the love of the mind, though of supreme value, was, for men, to be reflected in the political order. His two major works are both political: the *Republic* and the *Laws.* Love of the mind, of the divine order, was a historical as well as a philosophical aim, and men were seeking not only to construct a perfect *polis* intellectually, in Utopias, but also to construct them on earth, in Athens or Sparta. When the various *poleis* failed to achieve any harmony, either with each other or with Asia and the East, a new and larger organization came into being: the projected unification of Alexander the Great. This dream of a universal state, although abortive, was the archetype of the first successful universal state, Rome. The still larger extension of that ideal remains, as yet, unfulfilled: the League of Nations, the Nazi Third Reich, the *pax Americana,* and the United Nations are all imperfect copies.

Transformations like that of Venus exist elsewhere in the literature of the ancient world: perhaps the most perfect example occurs in Aeschylus' *Oresteia,* where the Erinyes are persuaded by the wise ministration of Athena to become the Eumenides. The metamorphosis, however, does not come about without a struggle; and we may expect also to see a struggle in the *Aeneid.* That struggle is dramatized in the love affair between Dido and Aeneas.

When Aeneas listens to Venus, and turns his attention from Helen to Creusa, from a symbol of love as lust and passion to a symbol of love as family and order, he makes a decision as vital to the action of the poem as that in Book I of the *Iliad,* when Achilles decides not to slay Agamemnon but to withdraw from battle. The implications of the decision, however, are of far greater consequence to the world than were those of Achilles' decision. Killing Helen would serve no purpose; it would merely symbolize the destruction of that Troy which Paris and his Pandemian Venus most truly represented. We prefer to think of Hector and Andromache as the truer representatives; but we must remember that Hector is fighting for Helen, that he always treated her with kindness and respect, and that he does not take sides in the debate, in Book VII, over whether the Trojans should return Helen. For Aeneas to save Creusa, his father, his son, and himself will serve a real purpose: it will preserve the continuity of Hector's way of life; it will maintain the generations of man, for all those elements are symbolized in the persons of Anchises, Ascanius, and Creusa. Venus conceals from Aeneas that Creusa is fated not to escape; that the plan of destiny requires a mingling of bloods and races; and that Aeneas must wed again, the daughter of the Latin race. Aeneas loves Creusa; no one who has read the mournful scene in which he strives vainly to embrace her evanescent and insubstantial shade can ever forget the anguish, the pathos, the heartbreak. Much of the sadness lies in the prophecy to which Creusa gives voice: it is her duty to tell Aeneas that he must found a new kingdom, and that a part of that task is to wed again.

For seven years Aeneas wanders the Mediterranean, harried by the implacable hatred of Juno, the goddess of marriage. All readers are reminded of the wanderings of Odysseus; but the differences must be remembered, too. Odysseus has a kingdom and a wife and a grown son waiting for him; Aeneas, when he gets to where he is going—and he is not sure of where that is, or how to get there, or when he will succeed in doing so—will have to start a kingdom from scratch, and will have to wed a stranger whom he does not love. No Penelope or faithful dog or old herdsman or father or grown son awaits him. Instead, a new war, with a new Achilles, and new heartbreak, and loss, and fatigue.

To prevent the founding of Rome, Juno has Aeneas wrecked on the coast of Africa, in the kingdom of Dido.[1] There, while dutifully exploring for the sake of his remnant crew, he meets Venus, disguised as a Spartan girl: she bears a bow, and her legs are bare.

---

[1] Just as Venus is transformed from an amoral force to a moral agent, Juno is transformed from a jealous and nagging wife to an implacable competitor for the control of destiny. To support this view Virgil could point to her hatred of Hercules, that hero who endured many labors and became a god, and who is a type of Aeneas, who in turn is a type of Augustus. See Hermann Fränkel, *Ovid* (Sather Classical Series, Vol. XVIII [Berkeley: University of California Press, 1956]), p. 212, n. 24.

Aeneas asks her whether she is the goddess Diana—the irony of that question is bittersweet and appealing. He also asks her where he is, for we must remember that this man with a mission, this fated creature, is lost. His whole life has been one of loss: first his city and country are taken away from him; then his wife; then his father; and now he is on the verge of losing his fleet, his friends, and even himself. To his question Venus gives more information than is needed, for she not only tells him that he is in the kingdom of Dido, but also recounts the history of that sad queen, whose fate is parallel to that of Aeneas. She, too, fled her homeland; she, too, seeks to found a new kingdom; she, too, lost a spouse whom she deeply loved. The scene is set for the sympathy that develops into love, a love that Aeneas' own mother fosters and shatters. Venus then asks Aeneas who he is.

Aeneas answers, after a deep sigh, in three words. Now it was no easy thing for an ancient hero to be asked who he was; when Diomedes asks Glaucus, in Book VI of the *Iliad,* who he is, the answer consumes several pages. In replying, Glaucus shows, at its fullest, the form the hero's answer was to take: a list of his illustrious ancestors, a summary of his educational ideals, and a mention of his own exploits. Aeneas, however, is cut off from this form: his ancestors have been ignominiously defeated; his way of life has been destroyed; and his own valor has ended in defeat. He has no claim, no *euchos,* that will sound like much, and he is not sure whether this girl has even heard of Troy—pathetically (and parenthetically) he asks her whether she has. In short, he is stripped and naked of distinction, of external signs of glory. Even his poor fleet has been wrecked, and he himself is hungry and lost. All that he has left is a consciousness of his own moral worth, a memory of his ideals. This he sums up in the word *pius:* "*Sum pius Aeneas*" (I, 378).[2] The statement sticks in the craw of many modern readers, who think that a man ought not to go around saying that he is a good man, for no matter how one translates the phrase, the epithet is self-imposed and honorific.

Critical efforts to defend Aeneas have, I think, been misplaced.

---

[2] The translators all have a difficult time with this passage; here are some samples: "the good Aeneas I am call'd" (Dryden); "Aeneas am I . . . famed above earth for acts of piety" (Wordsworth); "I am true-hearted Aeneas" (C. Day Lewis); "I am Aeneas, a good devoted man" (Humphries); "I, the devout Aeneas" (Guinagh).

They take two forms: one, Virgil is imitating Homer's stock epithets; two, he is seeking to praise the central Roman virtue. Such explanations, however, only show why Virgil used the term; they do not show why Aeneas used it. Homeric parallels are unconvincing: first, Homer's epithets refer to physical traits, e.g., "swift-footed Achilles" or "Hector tamer of horses"; second, Homeric heroes do not use these epithets of themselves. Even the parallel most often cited, that of Odysseus, when he identifies himself to King Alcinous, does not fit, for Odysseus, though admitting that he is world-famous, uses no epithet of himself. It is, of course, true that *pietas* is the central Roman virtue—or at least the Romans thought it was. Cicero says (*de Haruspicum Responso* 9.19):

> It was not by our numbers that we overcame the Spaniards, nor by our strength the Gauls, nor by our cunning the Carthaginians, nor by our arts the Greeks . . . but by *pietas* . . . our recognition that all things are ruled and directed by the will of the gods. This is how we have overcome all races and all peoples.

Still, even if we grant Virgil that *pietas* is the central Roman virtue, we cannot explain that Aeneas uses the word for this reason. After all, at this point he knows nothing of Rome; that knowledge comes only later, when he hears his father's prophecies in the underworld. What we need to find is some dramatic motive in the poem, one that squares with the conditions and the character of the man. If we are to take the *Aeneid* seriously, as a historical phenomenon, as an embodiment of the Augustan ideal, as an expression of *Romanitas,* and as a poem, we must find the meaning of *pius* in the poem, as well as in sources outside the poem. Only thus will the dramatic struggle of *pietas* and *amor,* of Aeneas and Dido, be entirely persuasive.

There are, I believe, a number of related dramatic explanations. First, Aeneas is obviously a gentleman; we have no evidence up to this point that he has ever wronged a woman. Hence, when he discovers this unprotected virgin in the woods, he hastens to assure her that she is safe. The word *pius* would clearly show her that his intentions were honorable. We must remember that, though disguised, she is still Venus, the goddess of love, who radiates an attractiveness, a sexual appeal, capable of appealing to any man, to say nothing of one who has been deprived of the joys of love for seven years. Venus' disguise is ironic: it is at once a tantalizing appeal and a reminder to duty, for she is arrayed as a Spartan maiden. Conversely, the word *pius* is intended to bolster Aeneas' own sense of morality. Confronted with the gorgeous and unprotected girl, and subject to all the virile desires of a male, he is trying to recall to himself his own sense of duty, devotion, and decency. Most important, however, is the problem posed by Venus' question: "Who are you?" she asks. And Aeneas answers by mentioning the one thing he has left: his own consciousness of his moral worth. It is all of his heroism that remains. The question is not so much to find out why he said what he did, but to see what else he could say.

We must also remind ourselves here that neither Virgil nor Aeneas knew anything of the Christian ideal of humility, that virtue of which Christians are so proud. Even John Milton, who must, I suppose, be called a Christian by anyone's standards, has the great angel Raphael tell Adam (*Paradise Lost,* VIII, 571–73):

> oftimes nothing profits more
> Than self-esteem, grounded on just and right
> Well managed.

What did Aeneas mean when he used the word *pius?* Although the word is used nineteen times of him in the poem, he uses it of himself only this once. Virgil uses it of him fifteen times; other characters thrice. A study of these uses reveals that there are eleven kinds of situations where the word is applied: (1) when Aeneas mourns over and buries the dead; (2) when he obeys the gods' order regardless of personal feelings; (3) when he yields to natural forces, such as a storm; (4) when he makes an orderly arrangement of ritual, as in the funeral games; (5) when he prays to avert the destruction of the Trojan fleet from the fire cast by the Trojan women; (6) when he shows due reverence to the gods by going to Apollo's shrine first, even before exploring or hunting for food; (7) when he is described as one who will give due payment for services rendered; (8) when he reminds a cocky opponent that his cockiness was improper; (9) when he grieves over a good fallen foeman, whose worth he appreciates and whose body he treats with respect; (10) when he is used as a standard of fitness, as when Evander says that Pallas' death was worthy of *pius* Aeneas; (11) when he observes international law: e.g., bareheaded and unarmed, he tries to persuade the Trojans to keep the truce terms even if the enemy have violated them.

Underlying all these is a sense of propriety, of fitness: that is, Aeneas has a hierarchy of values; he knows what is worth how much and in what order, and tries to give to each thing its due. Behind this notion, or emerging from it, is a sort of stoic view of the universe as being itself animate and hierarchical, a place of order. Now order can exist only where one has a multiplicity of different things; absolute uniformity, whether of one substance or like things, precludes order, though perhaps the second would at least allow the minimal order of substance and space. Once one has a multiplicity of things, one must recognize that everything is what it is and not another thing. I do not intend to say that existence is static: the word "thing" here might be a process or an action, but it still would be recognizable as being what it is and not something else. Then, after one has identified each item of the multiplicity, one must treat each thing in accordance with its definable nature and its relationship to other things. First things come first, and so on. That which comes first is whatever supports and maintains and animates the whole hierarchy.

In the poem that which animates and maintains the whole is the pantheon. For Aeneas, piety seems to consist of an anthropomorphic religion tinged with stoicism; Venus becomes an inclusive symbol for the blend, she who is creativity, attraction, and connection personified, and whose power develops the unity of being. So Love was this principle for Empedocles; so it was for Lucretius, in whom Venus becomes an august, beautiful, and powerful symbol of order. The Romans claimed to be descended from Mars and Venus, from Strife and Love, from the antithetical principles whose merging represents the harmony of the cosmos. Rome attempted to reflect that divine and mythic harmony in the political order—which included, we must always remember, all that we tend to distinguish: the social, economic, theological, psychological, aesthetic. Many critics and readers have felt that Virgil was merely imitating the machinery of the gods as a poetic device, suitable for an epic. He was, in truth, taking that machinery and seeking to invest it with a decorum both dramatic and philosophic. The Roman pantheon is a hierarchy and symbolizes the hierarchy of values. If the symbols also have a dramatic life and reality of their own, that is all to the good: those symbols are best which we take literally, as all good poets, critics, and readers know. Robinson Crusoe, for example, may be treated as a symbol for everyman; but when we read the book, we see a particular man facing particular problems, and it is only later that we elevate and theorize him into a symbol of some idea or principle. Allegorical writers fail most often at this very point, that is, they create symbols but not characters.

So it is with the gods of Aeneas. They are to be seen as real and dramatic personages in the action of the plot. Because Venus is his mother, Aeneas can and should feel *pietas* for her; and in so far as her actions are not the willful impulse of the Pandemian Venus, but the considered actions of the Uranian Venus, which contribute to the working out of destiny, that is, to the will of the gods and the transfer of their own hierarchical order into the world of men, his *pietas* extends itself upward to the other gods and to the idea of hierarchy itself. So, too, it extends itself downward to other men, both friends and foes. Aeneas' most dramatic and tense moral agonies will come precisely at those moments when he comes closest to forgetting and denying his *pietas,* his sense of propriety and obligation. His greatest moment of moral agony will come when he is caught in a conflict between two acts of *pietas.* Every one of the eleven classifications listed above has meaning only because the gods and the hierarchy exist. The gap between divine order and human attempts to reflect that order is shown in the pathetic scene in which Aeneas reaches out his arms to the departing figure of Venus, even as he had sought to embrace the ghost of Creusa—a scene in which we are reminded of the many ways in which Venus appeals to Aeneas: mother, goddess, love, wife, protectress. When, he cries out to her, will we be allowed to exchange true words (*veras voces*)? The word *veras* is one of those examples of diction which Tennyson described: "all the charm of all the Muses often flowering in a lonely word." It is not, I think, too fanciful to see here a foreshadowing of the soul's cry for divine love and union. In this act of loving *pietas,* Aeneas dramatizes the first great conflict he is about to enter, the conflict of *pietas* and *amor.* He who had begun by wishing to slay Helen is about to succumb to a type of Helen. When Venus forces her son, on that desolate African coast, to describe himself as *pius,* she is about to plunge him into a whirlpool of chaotic emotional problems in which his last claim to fame, his *pietas,* his last sense of identity and self, will be threatened and stained. Her disguise is a perfect symbol of his problem: Venus as a Spartan girl, Venus as Diana, goddess of chastity. Like the Spartan boy, Aeneas will have to eat his heart out for the sake of the state, a word which, in its largest sense, is equivalent to order, to hierarchy. Her sympathetic picture of Dido is calculated to touch Aeneas' deep sense of loneliness, for no one in ancient literature is more aware of the anguish and pity and loneliness that characterize life. As he says (I, 462), when he sees the great mural of Troy: "Life is full of tears; and man's mortality touches the heart."

This loneliness, reminiscent of Augustus and of Marcus Aurelius, with whom Aeneas shares many characteristics, derives directly from his *pietas;* for he who performs his duty is always alone. It is the nature of man to find fellow-feeling in what we call "only human," a word which has become for us a synonym for "weak." The stern voice of duty allows for no weakness, no "humanity" in this sense of the word. And when *pietas* confronts *amor,* it will be wracked both by its longing to be merely human and by its desire to remain what it is. When Aeneas says to Venus, *"Sum pius Aeneas,"* he is addressing the one deity to whom the virtue of piety means nothing. Cupid, his brother, will harass him no less than he does anyone else, for Love is blind. And in so far as Aeneas loves, he will become blind. When one falls in love, as Ortega says, the "attention [is] abnormally fastened upon another person." [3] Note the word "abnormally." Love upsets the hierarchy of values; in fact, it replaces it. All other things either become valueless or cease to exist. For Aeneas, the figure of Dido will assume those abnormal proportions; and contributing to that displacement will be his own mother, Venus, the goddess of love, and his arch-enemy, Juno, the goddess of marriage. Added to this is the irony that the figure of Dido does not exist outside a hierarchy, as Wallis Simpson existed outside the hierarchy of Edward VIII, but instead brings with her as a part of her setting and herself a political hierarchy that is almost a perfect substitute for the political hierarchy that Aeneas is to establish. All that is missing is the dirty work of starting a city from scratch and a lot of nasty wars with the local inhabitants.

Dido's generosity is overwhelming; clearly she loves Aeneas more than he loves her, and for him she is willing to give everything that she is and has: her love, her honor, her kingdom, and herself. Aeneas accepts them all. Then, at the merest whisper from heaven, he abandons her. To many he seems a heel and a cad. Traditionally the conflict has been seen as one between *amor* and *pietas,* between love and duty; and we, with our Romantic impulses, find difficulty in excusing Aeneas for preferring duty. Our intellects may accept

[3] José Ortega y Gasset, *On Love,* trans. Toby Talbot (New York: 1957), p. 52.

the arguments offered to show that he was right; but our hearts resent his conduct. What we fail to see is that the nature of the conflict changes, and we must see it now not as a conflict between love and duty, but as one between duty and duty. It is true that Aeneas loves Dido, but he also has a tremendous debt to her. In a sense, he owes her love. She has given up everything to and for him; and when someone does you a favor, you are indebted. The greater the favor, the greater the debt. Now, for a man with as strong a sense of obligation, of *pietas*, as Aeneas, for a man to whom the supreme value of life is the hierarchy of values, to be in debt means that he must pay. *Pietas* has the legalistic meaning of paying what is due, and what is due Dido is love. When the gods tell him to abandon Dido, he is prevented from paying his debt, a debt that he not only ought to pay but that he also wants to pay. Instead he must choose to forego both the payment and the pleasure.

I wish to emphasize the word "choose." Although it is Aeneas' "Fate" to found Rome, it is not a fate that will come about willy-nilly; only if he accepts his fate can it come to be. That acceptance is an act of will. Mercury brings him the warning of Zeus, but it is a warning couched in the form of argument, not simple command. So Athena had appealed to Achilles, in Book I of the *Iliad:* "I have come down to persuade you—if you will listen to me." Both Aeneas and Achilles have the choice of refusing, and, although refusal may result in pain, so will acceptance. To compare those pains requires, as does any comparison, that the two have something in common. Hence the traditional way of viewing the conflict as one between love and duty is, I think, faulty, for those categories are mutually exclusive. If, however, we see the conflict as one between duty and duty, with love as the sugar-coating on one of the pills, we then have a basis for comparison. Suppose, for example, that you owe two persons money and have enough only to pay one, and that the sum is indivisible, like a penny. Proportional payment is thus ruled out; one can only decide whom to pay by assessing whose need is greater. That need, in turn, must be decided not by intensity of personal feeling, but by disastrousness of consequences. Only by looking at the problem this way could a man of *pietas* make a decision in keeping with his character; to decide on the basis of *amor* would be to deny his character, and so to deny fate in a far more fundamental fashion than he would by obedience to the gods' behests.

What will nonpayment cause Dido? Intense pain, shame, loss of affection, and some very sleepless nights and anguished days. Rather than face these she commits suicide. *Amor,* which places the whole value of existence, of the hierarchy of things, on one object, one mortal, cannot itself exist when the object disappears. Dido's suicide seems dramatically proper and is ethically consistent with the nature of her being—or at least with that being which the gods force upon her. Hers is a tragedy of pathos, for the gods enter her body and soul and take away her free will. All that could save her from this fate, in the full sense of that word, is for Aeneas to violate his fate and his character. But *amor,* Venus, is not greater than *pietas,* the pantheon, or, perhaps better, Pandemian Venus is not so important as Uranian Venus; earth is less than heaven. We cannot, however, blame Dido's death on Aeneas, for it is not a necessary consequence of nonpayment. She could continue to live, to govern her city, and could even wed again if she chose. Her inability to do so foreshadows the destruction of her kingdom, which is to pit itself against the *pietas* of Rome, and is to lose.

What will nonpayment cause the gods? Some sense of pain, though not so keen as Dido's, at the loss of one who has, up to now, been a good and faithful servant. More important, however, is the loss to the hierarchy, not only to that of the gods, but to that of man as well. If Aeneas remains in Carthage, he will destroy divine efforts to make the world a place of *pietas,* a place that reflects the political and social order of the hierarchy of heaven. In its place will be put a world of *amor,* of Carthaginian culture, of material sensation. Rome would not exist, that empire that brought law, order, and culture to millions and that enabled the Western world to be, for a while, what it is still seeking to re-establish. To say that Aeneas should have paid Dido and not the gods is to reject all that we regard as best in the Western world. So we must compare the self-imposed loss of one life with the inflicted loss of millions of lives, including our own. As Agamemnon slew Iphigeneia at Aulis, so Aeneas leaves Dido—but with this difference: Agamemnon is embarked on a mission of destruction, Aeneas on a mission of creation. And Aeneas does not slay Dido; that she does to herself.

When Aeneas first sees Carthage, he sees a city being built—a type of Rome—and envies its inhabitants their magnificent *labor.* Yet within a few hours he will begin to corrupt that *labor* and to replace it with *otium,* with a deadly and enervating leisure. Before his arrival, Dido is leading a life of *pietas,* which is inextricably bound up with *labor,* the kind of life that Aeneas himself is destined to lead. Together they begin to use the city, a symbol of empire, not as an end in itself but as a means to *amor,* as a mere backdrop for passion. The figures of Antony and Cleopatra would loom large for Virgil's contemporaries here; they loom equally for us, who still find the story of those two fascinating. Such lives can end only in the sterile death of self-consumption, a fate for which Dido's funeral pyre is a beautiful symbol. In sailing away from Carthage, Aeneas is sailing away from death toward life, a life of practical creativity and corporate eternity: or so Virgil and Augustus believed and would have readers believe.[4]

As Aeneas looked back to the African coast, and saw the smoke of the flaming pyre, he may have believed that great Pandemian Venus was dead; but deities do not die so easily. Not only did the spirit of that Venus remain in those burning African sands, to arouse St. Augustine centuries later, but it also sailed with Aeneas. Although the rape of the Sabine women can be seen as an act of *pietas,* as a part of the *labor* of building Rome, the rape of Lucretia cannot; that was an act of *amor,* and it ended the kingdom Aeneas founded. When Augustus reconstituted that kingdom, he did so with full consciousness that he was also re-establishing a world of *pietas.* To do so required that the Romans renounce the world of *amor.* In the work of Virgil we see the course of this renunciation: it starts from the celebration of the life of *amor* in the *Eclogues,* where Gallus, the founder of the elegiac school of Latin love poets, is the hero, and ends with the celebration of the life of *pietas* in the *Aeneid,* with its new hero, Aeneas.[5] Between lie the *Georgics,* that symbolically named poem, where *labor* specifically replaces *amor.* In the tenth *Eclogue* Virgil sang his highest praise of Gallus, and asserted that Love conquers all *(omnia vincit amor)* ; in the *Georgics,* with their emphasis on farming, cultivation, order, tranquillity, and civilization, what conquers all is *labor (labor omnia vincit),* honestly called *improbus:* painful, monstrous, hard.

Not all Romans were willing to renounce the life of *amor,* and in a figure such as Catullus, who becomes the paradigm of this life, we

---

[4] It is in the reign of Augustus that Rome begins to be called *Urbs Aeterna,* for example, Tibullus ii.5.23. See Kirby Flower Smith's list of parallels in his note on this passage in his edition of *Tibullus: Elegies* (New York, 1931) .

[5] The *Eclogues* do, of course, touch on a variety of themes, from the amorous to the apocalyptic. Still, four of the ten deal almost exclusively with *amor,* and two others touch on the topic.

see the central problem of the Augustan peace made both dramatic and explicit. A perfect *pietas* required a life of *labor;* but that *labor* assumed a new form under Augustus—the job of building the empire began to be replaced by the job of managing it. No longer was the state wracked by either foreign or civil wars; Augustus slowed the process of conquest; and the *pax romana* began. Among its many blessings, the *pax romana* brought *otium,* leisure, which becomes the great value word of the age. As always, Virgil locates and dramatizes such terms for us: in the very first *Eclogue*—which conspicuously does not deal with *amor*—Tityrus sings that it was a god (i.e., Augustus) who gave him his *otium.* The vision of agricultural and rural tranquillity is sketched, in the *Eclogues,* in fragmentary and tangential fashion; in the *Georgics,* as we would expect, the vision is given full statement. Thus, at the end of the second *Georgic,* in his famous and lovely apostrophe to the fortunate farmers, Virgil conjoins the word *otium* with *secura quies* and *nescia fallere vita,* untroubled peace and innocence.

Virgil's pastoral conception of *otium* could have, of course, but scant meaning for urban Rome.[6] As Catullus (51) saw at once, *otium* allowed for a revival of the life of *amor,* with a related and resultant corruption:

> Otium, Catulle, tibi molestum est:
> Otio exsultas nimiumque gestis.
> Otium et reges prius et beatas
> Perdidit urbes.

> Leisure, Catullus, is burdensome to you;
> Too much do you exult and enjoy in leisure;
> Ere you leisure has destroyed kings and
> prosperous cities.

Ironically, the roots of this *otium* lay in the destruction of Carthage, which represented Rome's greatest *labor.* Roman historians and moralists—the two terms are almost interchangeable—saw the danger, as one can observe in Cato and Livy and Tacitus.[7] Catullus,

---

[6] See Fränkel, *Ovid,* p. 9, for an illuminating discussion of the relationship between *otium* and *negotium* (business).

[7] Tacitus' famous phrase, "the evils of a long peace," looks back over the period which Catullus and Virgil have in prospect. Horace, *Odes* ii.16, tries to define the inner nature of *otium.* Cicero in his work on *Duties* (iii.1) advises that one use *otium* to think about *negotium;* in his work on *Invention* (i.3) he associates it with cultural pursuits. Ovid makes the connection between *otium* and *amor* specific (*Remedium Amoris* 138): "Leisure is the cause of pleasure and

significantly, added his stanza to his translation of a poem by Sappho, in which Sappho asserts that one who is loved is equal to the gods. We are back, suddenly, to that scene in the *Odyssey*, in which Hermes says to Apollo, as they watch Aphrodite and Ares chained in bed by Hephaestus, that even to be caught in so embarrassing a fashion would be worth it.

In Propertius, Tibullus, and Ovid, who perfects the genre and the mode, we see how the life of *amor* takes the social and civic hierarchy, constructed by *pietas* in imitation of the divine hierarchy, and uses it as a backdrop for a life of material sensation. Augustus banished Ovid, but he could not banish the *Amores* or the *Ars Amatoria*, odes to the Pandemian Venus, which infected his own household; nor could he, even with the magnificent aid of Virgil, succeed completely in transforming her into a pure manifestation and symbol of *pietas*. The creative power of the political hierarchy had no goal other than the hierarchy itself; once that was established, and *otium* and *pax* gave men a chance to cease from *improbus labor*, they turned away from *pietas* to *amor*, even as Aeneas had done for a while at Carthage. Although the hierarchy was built well enough to endure this misuse for centuries, it eventually fell; nor were there wanting great minds to analyze the causes of that fall. Out of Dido's Africa came the greatest of those minds, that of St. Augustine, who meditated often on the story of Dido and Aeneas, and whose own life is parallel in a number of interesting symbolic ways to that story: "To Carthage I came, where there sang all around me in my ears a cauldron of unholy loves. I loved not yet, yet I loved to love, and out of a deep-seated want hated myself for wanting not."

The life of *amor*, which Augustine, like Aeneas, found in Carthage, he called, bluntly, *fornicatio*. Like Aeneas, he too sailed away from Carthage for Rome; yet Augustine could see that sailing away from *amor* was not necessarily sailing to *pietas*, at least not to a

---

the food of evil; If you take away leisure, Cupid's occupation is gone." In the *Metamorphoses* (v.372–76) , Venus, encouraging Cupid to strike Death with his arrows, argues that she is losing ground in her struggle with both Diana and Athena. The word appears, as we might expect, in the climactic moment of Aeneas' affair with Dido, when Mercury (*Aeneid* iv.372–76) asks the hero, "What do you hope for in wearing away your *otium* here in Africa?" In medieval times, one frequently sees references to the *sanctum otium* of the monastery; but the derivative *otiositas* comes to mean idleness, and is roundly denounced, as in the Rule of St. Benedict (chap. 48) , as the enemy of the soul.

pietas that would endure eternally. Behind him, on the African shore, he left not a burning Dido but his weeping mother Monica, not *amor* but *pietas*.[8] In the life of Monica, in her loving faith, Augustine could see that *amor* and *pietas* were not in necessary conflict. Yet what she could combine simply, naturally, he had to combine complexly, intellectually: in short, he had to fit *amor* into the hierarchy. Abandonment to it was, in a way, a truer mode of solving the problem than abandonment of it. Pushed and pulled by various loves, by lust, by philosophy, Augustine indulged in *fornicatio* and read Cicero and Plato. It was Plato who first sought to fit *eros* into the religion of ideas; but the Platonic solution was not ultimately adequate, for his god could not be loved. The *Magna Moralia* says, on precisely these grounds, "It would be absurd for a man to say that he loved god."[9] As those who broke the sound barrier by diving down rather than pulling up, so Augustine chose to plunge into love rather than sail away from it. As I am making but a hurried sketch of the idea, I cannot here describe the stages of this development: let it suffice that, for Augustine, the true philosopher was the lover of God (*verus philosophus amator Dei*).

Though he did not know it when he sailed for Rome, Augustine was, like a new Aeneas, destined to establish a new Rome, the *civitas Dei,* whose foundation was to be a *pietas* infused with *amor*. The history of the Western world since can be seen as a persistent attempt to give vitality to Augustine's initial effort. Many have sought to write the history of this *ab urbe condita,* but we have found as yet no Livy. The Aeneas who sought the way of *pietas* alone ended as Marcus Aurelius, writing his stoic meditations; the Christian Aeneas, Augustine, wrote not a meditation but a confession. His work as a founder suffered from later corruptions, just as

[8] Augustine does not, any more than other writers whom I shall mention in course, treat the conflict in the polar terms that Virgil uses: *pietas* and *amor*. For Augustine, *amor* was a general term denoting love of either good or evil; *dilectio* is love of the good. *Pietas* is the second rung on the Augustinian ladder to wisdom; see *De Doctrina Christiana* ii. 7.9, where it is given an extraordinary definition: not to differ with Holy Scripture. Augustine goes on to say that *pietas* is to believe what is written there as being better and truer than to think that we can attain truth by ourselves. Monica was a living manifestation of this *pietas*. Her son could find his way to such *pietas* only by passing through the vale of *amor*. In the *City of God* x.1, Augustine shows a full knowledge of the usual meanings of *pietas*.

[9] "Pseudo-Aristotle," *Magna Moralia* 1208b6, quoted by E. R. Dodds, *The Greeks and the Irrational* (Berkeley: University of California Press, 1951), p. 35.

Aeneas' work suffered from Tarquin; and when the Arabic influence led to the practice and tradition of courtly love, of *amor* in its old Pandemian sense, Augustine's great successor, Aquinas, sought to re-establish the primacy of *pietas,* of the hierarchical universe. That effort was too intellectual; hence Dante, although he took the Aquinian description of the hierarchy as the intellectual basis of his poem, turned equally to Virgil, who first dramatized the conflict of *amor* and *pietas;* and, in the figure of Beatrice, Dante sought to incorporate, one might almost say to incarnate, the figure of Uranian Venus, of *amor.* Recognition of this point makes clear Giuseppe Toffanin's remark, that "the originality of Dante is sufficiently proved by his attempt to infuse, into the accepted aristotelian science, the historical spiritualism of St. Augustine." [10] At the end of the *Paradiso,* the multiple images for Dante's experience and knowledge that *amor* is all include, as well as a rose and light, a book, one that gathered up all the leaves of the world. A book is both an image and an example of the *logos,* of the hierarchy that is *pietas.*[11]

Virgil, then, creates the kind of epic and epic theme that are to dominate the West; his greatest epic successors, Dante and Milton, both take the conflict of *amor* and *pietas* as central. Such lesser epics as *The Song of Roland* suffer precisely because they are too exclusively concerned with *pietas.* Were this the occasion, it would be pleasant to trace this idea in various major works of later authors: e.g., the Tristan myth, *Troilus and Criseyde, Faust, Don Juan,* and *Anna Karenina.* Denis de Rougemont, in his book *Love in the Western World,* has begun just such an analysis.

With the Renaissance the problem arises again, for the solutions offered by the great medievalists are no longer found to be suitable, however adequate they may be intellectually. Petrarch and Laura, though they continue the tradition of Dante and Beatrice, look to Abelard and Eloise as well; and from Petrarch issues the fountain which refreshes the conflict, in Provençal literature and then in the literature of the rest of Europe. Whatever definition of the Renaissance we may care to use, we shall agree that among its most

[10] Giuseppe Toffanin, *History of Humanism,* trans. Elio Gianturco (New York, 1954) , p. 59.

[11] What Alcidimas calls *eikon logou,* a verbal icon, in a sense quite different from that employed by William K. Wimsatt, Jr., in *The Verbal Icon;* Alcidimas, of course, is using the term contemptuously. See Alcidimas *About Sophists* 28, in *Antiphon,* ed. F. Blass (Leipzig, 1881) .

fertilizing influences is the revival of Plato and Augustine; and although a great deal of its intellectual activity concerns itself specifically with the question of free will—far more so than was ever true in antiquity—that concern is explicable as a manifestation of the old problem of *amor* and *pietas*. Virgil had begun the *Aeneid* by calling his hero *fato profugus;* and in the story of Dido and Aeneas the question of Aeneas' free will—as well as that of Dido—lurks in the background. In writers as diverse as Milton and Spinoza the question is asked directly and answered fully: in each man the answer is phrased in the language of *amor* and *pietas*. When Adam complains of the power *amor* has over him, Raphael answers, "Love hath his seat in Reason." This is a doctrine to which Spinoza gives geometrical substantiation; his conclusion is, thus far, the finest Western formula for combining our two elements: *amor intellectualis Dei*.

I do not expect that this article will result in a revival of Virgil, nor can I hope that my hurried historical sketch will be convincing, though I may hope that it will outline the form such demonstration will have to take. The conflict remains with us, as we can see in the work of Freud and in our general concern with the erotic as exemplified in the growth of pornography and of the servitude called "free love," in short, in the movement, especially on the part of the young, toward *fornicatio,* whether in literature or practice. At the risk of seeming fantastic or supersubtle, I might mention such recent public phenomena as the trend toward publicly sanctioned pornography, which started with the case of *Lady Chatterley's Lover,* moved on through, and down, Henry Miller's *Tropic of Capricorn,* and has now reached Cleland's *Memoirs of Fanny Hill;* or perhaps that example of what Wilde might term nature's imitating art, the love affair of the leading actors in the movie *Cleopatra;* or the perverse ingenuity of the teen-age starlet Eva Six, whose name is a symbolic blend of "Eve" and "Sex," and whose numerical surname falls one short of the Palladian number Seven. The problem in our day is, of course, only a part of the general tendency, since the Reformation, to elevate the sin of lust to a primary place in the hierarchy of sins. I recommend attention to Virgil not so much because I think he affords a palliative or panacea for the ill but because I believe that adequate awareness of the historical evolution of any problem helps first in understanding it and then, by means of that understanding, in solving it.

The popularity of Virgil has waxed and waned in accordance with those ages when either *pietas* or *amor* was in the ascendent: e.g., Boccaccio reports that, in Dante's youth, Virgil was distinctly out of favor; [12] in the Renaissance he was the cherished poet of such men as Sir Thomas More, Julius Caesar Scaliger, William Tyndale, and Francis Bacon. Modern taste has judged Homer to be superior, and, of the two Homeric poems, has preferred the *Iliad*. Homer does not, in the *Iliad*, confront the problem, for although Achilles withdraws from the war in a dispute over Briseis, it is not *amor* that moves him really, but his concern with his honor. The *Iliad* is the poem that most appeals to existentialists, a philosophic movement that, for the most part, has tried to deny the existence of the problem of *amor* and *pietas,* at least when put in those terms.[13] Yet in *The Plague*, by Camus, the journalist Rambert represents the conflict in exactly those terms, and elects, though without explanation, for *pietas*. One can respect, and even admire, Rambert's decision; but the mind wishes for an explanation, a justification. Until some artist, or philosopher, can give adequate expression to the problem, and its solution, we shall have to make shift with the historians. In the meantime, we might reread Virgil.

[12] Toffanin, *History of Humanism,* p. 10.

[13] In the *Odyssey,* Homer blends *pietas* and *amor* in too balanced a way to make the poem attractive to existentialists; to make Odysseus into a Christian humanist was too much even for Chapman's vigorous powers. Stanford in his note on *Odyssey* xxiv.537–38 argues persuasively that our final picture of Odysseus is not one of a husband, or a romantic adventurer, but of the "Iliadic hero of battle." See Homer's *Odyssey,* ed. W. B. Stanford (London, 1954), II, 430–31.

Order in Religion and Ethics

EDWARD CONZE

Dharma as a Spiritual, Social, and Cosmic Force

Buddhists do not normally speak of their own religion as "Buddh-ism," but usually refer to it as "the Dharma." The word "Dharma" is a Sanskrit term that comes from the root *dhr,* which means "to uphold," and to it also such words as *thronos, firmus,* and *fretus* are related. We read, for instance in the *Mahābhārata* (*Śāntiparvan* 109.11) : "They call it 'Dharma' because of its 'holding' (*dhāraṇād;* keeping things as they are) ; it is through Dharma that the people are severally held in their places (*vi-dhr-tāḥ*). That which is con-joined with holding (*dhāraṇa,* i.e., either 'upholding' or 'holding down') , that is determined as 'Dharma.' " In this basic meaning the term is still alive in India. Recently I looked into a copy of a pamphlet entitled *Sikh Mysticism,* by Dr. Mohan Singh Uberoi, and the first sentence my eyes lighted upon was "Dharma (Norm, Law),

EDWARD CONZE was born in London of German parents in 1904. He was educated in Germany, where he received his Ph.D. at Cologne. Between 1934 and 1965 he was with the Universities of London and Oxford, with a year as Distinguished Visiting Professor of Indian Studies at the University of Wisconsin. At present Dr. Conze is professor of Indic Studies at the University of Washington in Seattle. He is the author of eighteen books and several hundred articles on the subject of Buddhism; his widely read *Buddhism: Its Essence and Development* appeared originally in 1951, and *Buddhist Texts through the Ages* in 1954. *Buddhist Thought in India,* published in 1962, has recently appeared in paperback.

in its field, deals with the laws that sustain the universe," with a footnote to the effect that "Dharma operates as the support, duty-binding." [1] This is exactly how the Buddhists have always fundamentally understood the term. In Buddhist writings it has acquired a great, and to some extent even bewildering, variety of meanings. These I have sorted out from a philosophical point of view,[2] and long before me, in 1920, M. and W. Geiger collected all the relevant passages concerning Dhamma (Pali equivalent of the Sanskrit "Dharma") from the Pali Canon, distinguishing dozens of meanings and submeanings.[3]

I

In the present context we will ignore all these finer shades, and concentrate on that side of "Dharma" which makes it to some extent analogous to what we nowadays call "order." The *Pali-English Dictionary* speaks of "dhamma as the interpreted Order of the World," and says:

> That which the Buddha preached . . . was the order of law of the universe, immanent, eternal, uncreated, not as interpreted by him only, much less invented or decreed by him, but intelligible to a mind of his range and by him made so to mankind as bodhi: revelation, awakening. The Buddha is a discoverer of this order of the Dhamma, this universal logic, philosophy or righteousness ("Norm"), in which the rational and ethical elements are fused into one.[4]

Taken in and by itself, the Dharma is what we would call the "Absolute," one and single, without any duality or multiplicity in it; its inward unity and, if I may coin the term, its "unicity" preclude it from the very possibility of disorder. In its manifestations the Dharma pervades the universe and furnishes it with a certain number of fixed regularities, or fixed causal sequences—the final and indubitable facts of life which must be taken into account if we want to live fruitfully and serenely. Although it is the unconditioned One, it is not some barren remoteness, but infuses order

---

[1] Mohan Singh Uberoi, *Sikh Mysticism* (Amritsar, 1964), p. 12.

[2] Edward Conze, *Buddhist Thought in India* (London: George Allen and Unwin, 1962), pp. 92–106.

[3] M. and W. Geiger, *Pāli Dhamma vornehmlich in der kanonischen Literatur* (*Abhandlungen der bayrischen Academie der Wissenschaften Philosophische-Historische Klasse*, Vol. XXXI, No. 1, 1920).

[4] *Pali-English Dictionary*, ed. T. W. Rhys Davids and W. Stede (London: Pali Text Society, 1921), p. 171.

into the multiple appearances of the conditioned world, and conformity to it is the basis of the spiritual life. In Buddhism impermanence is a sign that there is something wrong with a thing, whereas the perfect Dharma and its irradiations abide for ever. To describe these dharmic laws would be to enumerate all the essential items of Buddhist doctrine, and I must be content with one single example, a verse from the *Dhammapada* (l. 5) which says: "Never can hatred be appeased by hatred; it will be appeased only by non-hatred. This is an everlasting (*sanantano*) dharma."

Special terms, like *dhamma-niyāmatā,* and so forth, denote the orderliness of dharmic processes, and we often hear that "whether Tathagatas do or do not appear, that state of Dharma, that established order of Dharma, that fixed sequence of Dharma is firmly established, i.e., that all compounded dharmas are impermanent, ill, not-self." [5] There is, however, nowhere an attempt to *prove* that either the Absolute or its workings in the world are orderly rather than chaotic or disorderly. One of the reasons may have been that the *a-dharma,* "that which is not Dharma," is manifestly so disorderly that one may infer that Dharma, its opposite, will represent Order. Those parts of the world which have escaped the control of Dharma are marked by strife (*raṇa*) and turmoil (*ḍamara*). On a more or less poetical and allegorical level this is often shown in the scriptures by contrasting the serenity, peace, and harmony of the world which is dominated by the Buddhas and Bodhisattvas (who are channels through which the transcendental Dharma reaches the world) with what is going on in the hells or among Mara's hosts. It is quite in keeping with Buddhist stylistic conventions that there are few, if any, attempts to give a positive definition of the glory of the order of Dharma. Instead one is content to infer it by copious descriptions of the disorders that result when one departs from the dharmic order. The spiritual realization (*sākṣātkriyā*) of this Dharma can be effected only by those who have left home and have become either monks or wandering ascetics. By a combination of "transic" meditation and gnosis they gain a direct intuition of the Dharma which "must be known by the wise, each one by and for himself (*paccatam veditabbo viññūhi*)." When they have done so, the fetters of this world drop off, and Nirvana, the ultimate goal of Buddhist endeavor, is achieved.

[5] See Conze, *Buddhist Thought in India,* p. 93.

II

From the Dharma of the monks we now move on to the Dharma of the kings. From at least the time of Asoka onward two kinds of Buddhism must be distinguished: that of the kings, at grips with the realities of the social world; and that of the monks, tranquilly renouncing the world and its agitations, provided the kings furnished them with the means to do so. It is well known that the inscriptions of Asoka make no reference to Nirvana, to the four holy truths, or to the other stock items of monastic Buddhism. But, when speaking of the distinguishing marks (*guṇa*) of Dharma, the great king tells his subjects that "it is commendable to abstain from slaughtering living beings," and that "it is also commendable not to spend or hoard too much." [6] It is impossible here to describe in detail the code of social conduct as laid down by Asoka. In any case, to observe Dharma brings happiness in this world and the next, whereas its disregard is bound to be punished at some time or other. In view of the predilection of Puritanism for condemning the sins of the flesh, it is noteworthy that when Asoka describes non-dharmic conduct, which he calls "evil" (*pāam*), he concentrates on sins of hate, i.e., fury, cruelty, anger, pride, and envy. [7]

The bilingual edict of Kandahār renders "Dharma" by *eusebeia* (piety), and this makes Asoka a kinsman of those ancient Romans who attributed their imperial successes to their *pietas*, to their scrupulous religious observances. " 'Tis by holding thyself the servant of the gods that thou dost rule; with them all things begin, to them ascribe the outcome," [8] wrote Horace, speaking poetically. At the same time the Stoic philosophers provided the Roman Empire with a philosophical ideology, which formulated certain precepts of "natural" as distinct from conventional law. This "natural law" is the closest parallel we have in Europe to the Dharma of Asoka and his successors.

What is the relation between the spiritual and the social side of Dharma? It seems to me obvious that the Buddhists could not have maintained themselves for so long in society if they had not contributed anything to its functioning. And also they may very well have

---

[6] R. K. Mookerji, *Asoka* (3rd ed.; Delhi: Motilal Banarsidass, 1962), p. 135.

[7] Mookerji, *Asoka*, pp. 71, 176.

[8] Horace *Odes* iii.6: "dis te minorem quod geris imperas: hinc omne principium; huc refer exitum."

had a doctrine about society, in spite of the fact that the canonical writings say so little about it. But that may be because the canonical writings concentrate on the problems concerning salvation from the world, and, just as the Gospels do, say almost nothing precise about the regulation of the world itself.

Where, then, have the Buddhists been able to practice their doctrine? That depended, of course, on their relative strength in relation to that of the secular ruler. One extreme would be Tibet, where during the last four hundred years there was in theory a pure theocracy, in which the spiritual head of the Samgha was also the ruler of the country, although in practice, of course, Chinese interference counted for a great deal. The other extreme would be the Japan of the Tokugawa period, where the monks were reduced to the position of tame pensioners of the state and deprived of nearly all social influence and initiative.

The normal pattern was a collaboration between the monks (Samgha) and an absolute and divine king. The monasteries were subject to the general control of government officials, and the kings themselves often had the last word in doctrinal disputes, deciding which was the orthodox sect and which was not. This kind of subordination of the church is known in Europe as Erastianism and has generally appeared quite normal and unobjectionable to Buddhists, who indeed find it hard to maintain monastic discipline on their own, as was shown in Ceylon and Burma. At the same time the government provides the Samgha with material necessities, and a varying proportion of the national income is drained away into the support of the monks, into the casting of images, into religious buildings, and so on. The Buddhists in their turn greatly influenced the general tone of government policy, although not so much its details. In Burma, for instance, "the monks, to whom even the king had to bow, are known, in history, to have intervened on the side of the oppressed and to have diverted royalty from feats of arms to feats of architecture, scholarship and husbandry." [9] The Buddhists also reinforced the belief that the king had divine sanction by associating him or his family with some member of the Buddhist pantheon. In this way the Manchu dynasty was somehow identified with the Bodhisattva Monju (Mañjuśrī), and so on.

At the same time, in Burma and elsewhere the kings showed their

[9] M. Mendelson, "Religion and Authority in Modern Burma," in *The World To-day* (London: Oxford University Press, 1960), p. 111.

fitness to rule by protecting and purifying the religion. This pattern began with the emperor Asoka, the "Beloved of the Gods," about 250 B.C. and for seventeen hundred years most of the great rulers of Asia have sought and won the collaboration of the Buddhist community. During the twentieth century this system has by now reached a condition of virtual extinction. Asoka inspired the ideal of a "universal ruler," or *cakravartin*, "who has conquered the earth from ocean to ocean, and rules it not by the rod or by the sword, but by Dharma." The *cakravartin* is a figure of cosmic significance, he has seven "treasures" which are his magical insignia, and he is to society what the Buddha is to the world of the spirit, his exact counterpart. This idea of a *cakravartin* has dominated Buddhist social thinking for seventeen hundred years, and each ruler who supported the Samgha was viewed as one. The pre-Asokan contractual theory of the origin of kingship is now replaced by the theory that the king holds his office by the authority of the gods, who have first ordained him, and is therefore entitled to be addressed as *deva* or *devaputra*. As Basham says, "this doctrine of divine appointment may be compared with that widely proclaimed in England during the Stuart period, and it is also closely akin to the Chinese doctrine of the 'Mandate of Heaven.' " [10] So what Buddhism seeks in the social sphere is a *dharma-rājā*, a king of Dharma. The same Dharma which rules the spiritual should, in other words, also dominate the social sphere.

The kind of society which Buddhists would regard as being in harmony with Dharma has at least four essential features.

1. First of all, Buddhism is obviously in favor of peace and against violence. Nonviolence (*ahimsā*) was what attracted Asoka to Buddhism, and it became the great inspiration of his reign. The scriptures naturally contain many admonitions in this direction. In the *Suvarṇaprabhāsa*, for instance, we hear:

Turn back the troops of their enemies and create in all the earthly kings of India a desire to avoid fighting, attacking, quarrelling, or disputing with their neighbours. These kings will gain their thrones by the due accumulation of the merit of former deeds; they will be satisfied with their own kingly state, and will not destroy one another, nor show their mettle by laying waste whole provinces.[11]

[10] A. L. Basham, "Jainism and Buddhism," in *Sources of Indian Tradition,* ed. William T. De Barry *et al.* (New York: Columbia University Press, 1958), pp. 132–36, 185.

[11] *Ibid.,* p. 184.

This is the precept, and some remarkable achievements may be recorded. In India, between 300 B.C. (the account of Megasthenes) and A.D. 400 (the report of Fa-hsien), there had been considerable progress in the direction of mildness and nonviolence. The death penalty, very frequently and cruelly inflicted in 300 B.C., had gone quite out of use. In Megasthenes' days all classes freely ate meat, while in the time of Fa-hsien only the outcasts did so. Buddhists abhor bloodshed of any kind. Among the Tibetans and Mongols they abolished animal sacrifices and made these fierce warriors quite pacific. A Buddhist society will therefore know no militarism, and the armed forces will be small and inefficient. Such things as vivisection are quite unthinkable, and also hunting and fishing will be left to the lowest of the low. In suppressing these misdemeanors, Buddhism relies not so much on repression as on convincing people that these are low-class ways of behaving and on confining them to the low-class people of whom there is a certain number in every society. Let there be butchers, but let them be ashamed of being butchers! Let there be hunters, fishers, and soldiers, but let them realize what a beastly crowd they are! In this way the whole tone of society will be raised. And, as a corollary, the rights of others should be respected, and Man should humbly coexist with others. We shall say more about that later.

2. Material prosperity is not altogether a bad thing, but frugality is desirable because greed is evil. One should not hoard because generosity is a great virtue, and material happiness is quite unimportant, "not worth one sixteenth part" of the spiritual happiness arising from a faultless and good life.

3. Buddhism clearly favors stable rather than "progressive" societies, and in the latter kind it is likely to die. From Asoka's edicts we see that everything which strengthens respect for tradition (*purāṇa*) seemed desirable to him, and among his "regulations of Dharma" (*dharma-niyama*) obedience to parents, elders, and teachers (guru) figures quite prominently.[12]

4. Buddhism also prefers a religious to a secular society. The latter would appear to be both undesirable and impossible. It is undesirable because it does not allow the centers of spiritual life to function, and because the surplus wealth is spent on armaments, dope, and feminine vanity rather than for religious purposes. It is

---

[12] Mookerji, *Asoka*, pp. 116, 169.

also impossible because, among other things, it must become so drab that it cannot last.

That is all, and someone who expects from the Buddhists a nice blueprint of a dharmic, or ideal, society must be disappointed. The reason is that all technical details depend on the concrete circumstances, whereas ultimately social prosperity is derived not from these but from spiritual and magical conditions.

In a time like ours, when society has become so thoroughly disordered that constant manipulation is needed to keep it going, it must seem most naïve and unsatisfactory to be told that one had only to honor the Dharma, and everything in the social world will be all right. Yet this is what we read in "The Sutra on Perfect Wisdom, explaining how Benevolent Kings may protect their countries," where the Buddha says (chap. V) :

Now I shall proclaim the Dharma which allows you to protect your countries. In all countries, when riots are imminent, calamities are descending, or robbers are coming to destroy (the houses and possessions of the inhabitants,) you, the kings, ought to receive, keep and read this Prajñāpāramitā, solemnly adorn the place of worship, to place (there) a hundred Buddha-images, a hundred images of Bodhisattvas, a hundred lion-seats, and to invite a hundred Dharma-masters that they may explain this Sutra. And before the seats you must light all kinds of lamps, burn all kinds of incense, spread all kinds of flowers. You must liberally offer clothes and bedding, food and medicine, houses, beds and seats, all offerings, and every day you must read this Sutra for two hours. If kings, great ministers, monks and nuns, male and female lay members of the community listen to it, receive and read it, and act according to the Dharma, the calamities shall be extinguished. Great kings, in the countries there are innumerable demons and spirits, each of them with innumerable followers; if they hear this Sutra, they shall protect your countries. If riots are imminent, the demons and spirits are uproarious beforehand; and it is for this reason that the people revolt; then robbery arises, and the people perish; the kings and the crown princes, the princes and the hundred magistrates mutually do right and wrong. If unnatural things happen in heaven and on the earth: the sun, the moon and the stars lose their times and their courses, and great fires, inundations and storms are prevalent, if all these calamities arise, all people must receive, keep and read this Prajñāpāramitā.

The ideas of causality implied here are certainly strange to our way of thinking. It was the belief of the Buddhists, shared by the Hindus and Chinese, that the welfare of the whole land, and even the regularity of the calendar and of heavenly phenomena generally, are dependent on the king, who is at the center of society, being attuned to the Dharma. When the king gets out of tune with the Dharma, then, to quote the *Suvarnaprabhāsa:*

> Then the land is afflicted with fierce and terrible crime,
> And it perishes and falls into the power of the enemy.
> Then property, families, and hoarded wealth all vanish,
> And with varied deeds of deceit men ruin one another.
> Whatever his reasons, if a king does not do his duty
> He ruins his kingdom, as a great elephant a bed of lotuses.
> Harsh winds blow, and rain falls out of season,
> Planets and stars are unpropitious, as are the moon and sun,
> Corn, flowers and fruit and seed do not ripen properly,
> And there is famine, when the king is negligent.
> From the wrath of the gods his kingdom will perish.
> All living beings will be ugly, having little vigour, very weak;
> They will eat much, but they will not be filled.
> They will have no strength, and no virility—
> All the beings in the land will be lacking in vigour.[13]

III

The third part of this paper concerns a topic so inherently incomprehensible to modern Americans that I fear very much that I will fail to make my meaning perfectly clear. I speak of the topic of magic. The whole functioning of Buddhism cannot be understood unless we realize that not only the monks and kings must be considered, but also a third class of people, who have been present in large numbers wherever Buddhism has struck root. These are the magicians. In present-day Burma, for instance, there are hundreds of groups or *gaings* who manipulate "various magical techniques associated with alchemy, *mantras,* medicine and cabbalistic signs." [14] By undergoing various rules of abstinence, they hope to gain a very long or even eternal life, and their highest aim is to see and hear the future Buddha Maitreya and to reach Nirvana by means of his sermons. The *gaings* are the successors of the Mahayana Tantrists, and they keep alive the longing for kingship. "The remarkable fact is that there are still, all over Burma, future kings and messiahs (these notions are very mixed up at the popular level) with courts of attendants waiting upon them daily until such time as they will mount the throne of the Land of Gold on earth or in heaven (this again is never too clear) and shower blessings and gifts on their

[13] Basham, "Jainism and Buddhism," pp. 186–87.
[14] Mendelson, "Religion and Authority in Modern Burma," p. 115.

devotees." [15] Mendelson calls this "messianic Buddhism," and it has a great importance in politics, since "the ideology of the *gaings* . . . permeates the life of all Burmese to some degree or other and countless soldiers, lawyers, civil servants, government officials and business men model their lives and decisions on the teachings of their *gaing* masters." With these magicians "involvement in the world and rejection of the world are two sides of one medal." [16] It is they who bridge the gulf between the worldliness of the layman and the unworldliness of the monk. And so it has always been.

To take another nearly contemporary example, the magical connotations of sovereignty have been particularly clear in Tibet. In a very fine essay Marco Pallis has recently defined the exact function of the Dalai Lama as an "activity of presence." [17] It is more a magical than a rational notion to believe that the Panchen and Dalai lamas are the great and precious "protectors" of Tibet not because of anything they actually do, but because their very presence assures the prosperity and happiness of all.

"Magical" in this sense is a term that covers those methods by which nomadic and agricultural populations all over the world have always regulated their lives, as contrasted with "scientific" methods, on which industrialized societies are based. The basic difference in their approach is that magic aims at producing harmony with the cosmos, whereas science increases our control over nature. For example, let us represent science by modern astronomy and magic by astrology. Astronomy became scientific only after it had discarded the ancient fables about "the harmony of the spheres" and the divinity of the stars; it then "discovered" that the celestial realm consists of nothing but a large number of pieces of matter, with a lot of space and all kinds of rays in between. Once it had accumulated sufficient knowledge it then proceeded to throw pieces of metal into that space, some of them even hitting the serene face of the moon. The Greeks would have been a bit doubtful about the wisdom of these activities, regarding them as a gross act of impiety which one day would surely provoke the thunderbolt of Zeus. A scientist can only shrug his shoulders at such childishness and will point out to you how much we have progressed since those days.

[15] *Ibid.*, p. 117.
[16] *Ibid.*, pp. 117, 118.
[17] Marco Pallis, *The Way and the Mountain* (London: Peter Owen, 1960), pp. 160–76.

Quite different is the attitude of astrology—and may I add at once that I wish only to illustrate its methods without attributing any validity to it. In astrology you rejoice to find that a gloomy person with a strong sense of duty is a Capricorn, that a "family man" is a Cancer, or that an overprecise, oversensitive, and overscrupulous person is a Virgo. You rejoice because this identification explains to you the behavior of these people and shows you to what you must adjust yourself. But it would not occur to you for a moment to try to make a Capricorn permanently cheerful, or in any other way to alter the characteristics of a person as indicated by his horoscope. The only result would be to make him into a bad and neurotic Capricorn, and so on. The central point is that astrology deals with an "ordered pattern," a "cosmos" that must be respected and that would merely be brought into disorder if it were interfered with. These categories do not apply to "nature" as understood by the natural sciences, which assume that nature has no such pattern, that it has no will of its own, and that it therefore behoves Man to control it for his own convenience. In terms of housebuilding, the symbol of magic would be the *Feng-shui,* that of science the bulldozer. We all know what a bulldozer is. The *Feng-shui,* Chinese for "Wind and Water," are the occult influences that determine the character of a locality and that must be preserved at all costs because, if they are obliterated, beauty and harmony will surely be crushed. In the *Feng-shui* system you make yourself quite small; in the bulldozer system you get bigger and more powerful all the time.

A little reflection will show that when you speak of achieving, or rather maintaining, harmony with the cosmos, you thereby imply two kinds of cosmos: yourself, who are the microcosm; and the universe around you, which is the macrocosm. Again in terms of astrology, the human body is a microcosm that corresponds to the zodiac, which is the macrocosm. In this way the head corresponds to Aries, the neck to Taurus, and so on until we come to Pisces, who must be content with the feet. If this correspondence were widely held to be true, it would have far-reaching consequences for medicine. But because magic and science are mutually incompatible there is no great likelihood that this lore will be admitted into the curriculum of our universities. It is interesting to note that in tantric Buddhism also an elaborate system was worked out which, based on the equivalence of events in macrocosm and microcosm, viewed the human body as a replica of the cosmos and treated it as an instrument of salvation and as the scene of the quest for enlightenment.

It was because Buddhism assured this harmony with the cosmos on which all social welfare depends that the laity was so eager to support the Order, house its members, and erect fine monuments in honor of their teachings. The world would not have put up for long with a community of monks who would turn their backs on those who fed them if they had not given something priceless to the world which it could not get in any other way. The visible manifestations of this concern for cosmic harmony are the magnificent stupas that adorn all parts of the Buddhist world and are the tangible focus of the religion. It was the business of the laity to build those stupas, though only the relics of the Lord Buddha could give them life. The stupas are as fundamental to Buddhism as the four holy truths, and it has been shown beyond doubt that they have a cosmic significance, that they are representative of the universe—not only the stupa at Borobudur, but also those at Sanchi, Barhut, and Shwe Dagon. This "cosmic architecture represents the world as a theatre for the working-out of the Dharma and for the awakening of all beings by its piercing rays." [18] Each stupa is an "imitation" of the life, or rather lives, of the Tathagata (an epithet of the Buddha), they allowed a whole society to unite in one common celebration, and thus had not only great moral, but also political consequences.

It was the French scholar Paul Mus who in his monumental work on Borobudur proved that the works of architecture, properly interpreted, show that the Buddhists felt responsible for the welfare of society as a whole, and that the Samgha, the community of monks, aimed at fostering and maintaining that cosmic harmony which is the source and basis of all social prosperity.[19] The great stupas of the Buddhists are the descendants of the Assyro-Babylonian ziggurats and the imperial cities of the Iranian kings, and they fulfill the same purpose. They were in fact mandalas, or magic circles, and it was Professor G. Tucci who first gave us a comprehensive survey of the often obscure metaphysical and psychological assumptions that activated the minds of those Buddhist thinkers who regarded mandalas

[18] Paul Mus, "Introduction," *Présence du Bouddhisme* (*France-Asie* [Saigon], Vol. XVI, 1959), pp. 187–200.

[19] Paul Mus, *Borobudur* (2 vols.; Hanoi, 1935).

as a means of salvation.[20] Some of these are archaic magical concepts that are found nearly everywhere in preindustrial cultures. There is, first, the universal magical practice of marking off a sacred, ritually pure spot by means of a circle. Then there is the idea of a diagram of the cosmos which, in its Buddhist form, is considered "as a vital process which develops from one essential Principle and rotates round one central axis, Mount Sumeru, the axis of the world." [21] This diagram was reproduced in ritual vases, royal palaces, stupas, temples, and mandalas. A vast complex of magical identifications, correspondences, transformations, and transfigurations was woven around these basic ideas. The Indians may have added the symbolism of the lotus and the evocation of deities by means of syllables which "constitute their occult principle." [22] The whole, taken together, makes it possible to express the basic cosmic and spiritual forces that govern our destiny "by means of symbols which, if they be wisely read by the initiate, will induce the liberating psychological experience." [23] What is assumed is that through symbols "one can give form to the infinite possibilities which lie in the depth of the unconscious, to unexpressed fears, to primordial impulses, and to age-old passions." [24]

It has been necessary to speak at such length about the magical side of Buddhism in order to present a balanced exposition of the Dharma for Dharma is a sort of tripod that needs all its three feet equally: the spiritual, the social, and the cosmic. I do not wish to conceal, however, a subsidiary reason, and that is to present the idea that these notions about "harmony with the cosmos" might be well worth re-examining at the present time. Recently I found myself in an airplane with a natural scientist, a colleague from the University of Wisconsin. When he learned that I am a professor of Buddhist studies, he wondered why anybody would wish to study a subject as useless as Buddhism. I gave him various reasons, one of them being that Buddhism might conceivably contain some kind of wisdom that would enable us to make a more intelligent use of the vast knowledge we have recently acquired. He really did not think much of

[20] G. Tucci, *The Theory and Practice of the Mandala* (London: Rider and Company, 1961).
[21] *Ibid.*, p. 23.
[22] *Ibid.*, pp. 30–37.
[23] *Ibid.*, p. 22.
[24] *Ibid.*

that one. For three quarters of an hour we circled over the thick fog that covered Chicago, and after a time we became slightly apprehensive. Suddenly my colleague turned to me and said, "Just think what we would feel if, while circling up here six thousand feet above Chicago, we were now told that there is no pilot on board. That exactly is the present situation of mankind"—and I had the chilling realization that this is precisely what has happened. The only thing a society based on Dharma can with absolute certainty claim in its favor is that it is bound to prevent such a situation as described by my friend from the department of oncology.

CHARLES HARTSHORNE

Order and Chaos

It is a good general principle to ask of each concept, what contrast does it express, or what does its positive application exclude? Of course some extremely general concepts scarcely exclude anything, for example the concept "reality." One does sometimes speak of unreal entities, but then one may, alternatively, regard such entities as a special class of realities. Fancied things are really fancied; as images or notions in someone's consciousness they have their place in the real world. But it remains correct that merely fancied things are in definite contrast to things that are also perceivable or could in some further sense be shown to exist. Only the latter are in the primary sense "real."

CHARLES HARTSHORNE became known as a young scholar for his editing, with Paul Weiss, of the *Collected Papers of Charles Sanders Peirce* (1931–35). He has taught at Harvard, Chicago, and Emory, and is now Ashbel Smith Professor at the University of Texas. He has long been engaged in redefining the nature of God, so as to do justice to the relations of God to the world and the concretely relative as well as abstractly absolute character of deity. He is the author of many books expounding an original metaphysical system. The most recent statement is *A Natural Theology for Our Time* (1967). Professor Hartshorne is also a noted authority on birdsong and has traveled widely to out-of-the-way places in search of rare examples of natural beauty. He has been president of the American Philosophical Association, Western Division, and was made an honorary doctor of humane letters by Haverford College in 1967.

What, I now ask, does the concept "order" exclude, or what contrast does it express? The adjective "orderly" is perhaps clearer than the substantive form. A related term is "regular." We have also the phrase, "a place for each thing, and each thing in its place." For the idea which contrasts with these, we have the words "disorderly," "irregular," "chaotic," and "random." The last word introduces what is at least less explicitly connoted by the others, the notion of chance. If there are three people filing through a narrow doorway, they might just happen to proceed "in the order of" their ages, or the order of their heights, or the alphabetical order of the first letter of their last names, or in any one of various other orders. But, if a hundred persons filed through the doorway, we should hardly expect to find a simple principle of their succession unless they had been instructed, or had agreed, to obey such a principle. And if the first four exhibited a simple order, say of ages, we could not know, without further information, that the other ninety-six would do so. Thus a "chance order" of events, if that is all it is, gives no information as to the future. And, as science has made man more than ever aware (though the seasons, the round of day and night, the moon's waxing and waning, and other phenomena long ago gave him the idea) it is the nonchance or predictable orders in events which are important for us. Chance regularities in the past are usually not even worth noticing if they furnish no guide to the future.

The remarkable thing about the Greeks is that, brilliant as they were, they penetrated only a little way beyond primitive man into the predictable orderliness of events. Aristotle did not even have the notion of inertia, though he had only to throw a stone, or run and attempt to stop suddenly, to experience illustrations. Instead of forming the notion, he attempted to explain away the phenomena that exhibited it. He similarly misinterpreted the visual manifestations of the earth's revolutions on its axis. Again, not only did he lack understanding of physiological inheritance, he adopted a theory that even raw common sense can do a fair job of refuting (the typically masculine theory that form comes only from the father). And he not only failed to guess the ultimate slow irregular regularity that consists in the gradual production of new species and the elimination of many old ones, he even adopted principles that forbade such a thing. He thought that there must be *eternal* regularity in the distribution of things into species (not, however, and here he was right, chemical species). We now know that the eternal regularities, if any, are much deeper hidden and very much more tolerant of partial irregularities and changes of form.

The relative failure of the Greeks to divine very much of the natural order had several causes. One was a kind of anthropomorphic naïveté. They (especially Aristotle) thought that the human individual was equipped, as a leisurely contemplator of nature, to derive insight into the "essences" of things merely by thinking carefully and cleverly about what he saw and handled in his environment. The human senses were counted on to exhibit things as they are, at least to an intelligent observer, who had only to abstract what was "essential," discarding the merely incidental features. That our senses are much too coarse to exhibit the basic structures of nature, that the human scale of appreciable magnitudes in time and space is adjusted to practical more than to theoretical needs, and that, consequently, to make much progress in the unraveling of nature's order, we must resort to extremely arduous, ingenious, roundabout methods and artificial aids, in some cases requiring a hundred generations and the cooperation of countless inquiries and technicians to work out—almost nothing of this seems to have been in Aristotle's mind. And Plato—who certainly sensed the difficulties more subtly—seems not to have been greatly interested in inspiring progress in natural science. Mathematics, metaphysics, philosophy of religion, politics, and ethics were his concern.

Early modern science made such startling discoveries of natural regularities that a great change in attitude was bound to occur (so far as this change was not already at work in the discoveries themselves). The change was not primarily that nature was now seen to be orderly, whereas the Greeks saw nature as a disorderly affair. On the contrary, the Greeks saw nature as highly orderly. Some of them even thought the regularity was absolute. Thus, the Stoics were mostly strict determinists. All things were in their places, as assigned to them by the eternal Reason, incarnate in the causal laws from which nothing was exempt. But the notion of order itself became much sharper in the Newtonian era. Quantities, mathematically predictable, were substituted for the vague qualities of Aristotelianism. The notion of strict determinism seemed both clearer and more credible, and the ideas of chance and disorder seemed to many to have been once for all overcome as a mere residuum of human ignorance or confused thinking. Over two hundred years of deterministic science and philosophy ensued. The suggestions of Aristotle and Plato (scholars differ as to their interpretation) that natural order, though everlasting, was perhaps subject to slight perturbations or exceptions due to the inability of "matter" to respond perfectly to the lure of forms, were largely dismissed, and all indeterminacy as to the outcome of situations was taken to be subjective only. Causality was absolute in all nature, chance was a mirage. Hume and Kant (apart from the latter's acceptance of freedom in the unknowable, nontemporal *noumenon*) agreed perfectly at this point, and Spinoza and Leibniz took essentially the same ground— for although Leibniz did not deny miracles, even these were for him part of the divine plan for the best possible world and were not disorderly in the sense of random or chaotic. In some sense or other, disorder was wholly relative to ignorance.

It is true that Descartes exempted the human will from the absolute natural order, and so did Locke. But on this point it was chiefly Spinoza, Hume, and Kant from whom the science and philosophy of the next two centuries took their cue, not from Descartes and Locke. With all Hume's skepticism he never hesitates to affirm the strictest determinism, and Kant says that the principles of Newtonian mechanics are perfectly true and will never need correction. If even Hegel departed appreciably and consistently from the deterministic view of nature, the fact has not reached the consciousness of this writer. Many of Hegel's followers have been explicit determinists. Also Schopenhauer is no different, at this point, from Spinoza or Kant. The law of causality was for him absolute and universal.

Of course there are always hardy souls who hold out against the fashion, or the *Zeitgeist*. Thus Christian Crusius, whom Kant respected, held that human freedom required one to relax the causal principle, or the principle of sufficient reason, and to give up the claim to its strict and universal validity. That all that happens has its reason "why it happens as it does and not otherwise" would mean that our choices were the only ones we could have made, and then they would not be genuine choices. So Crusius was a partial indeterminist. But his argument did not convince Kant. And the representative figures were determinists in their views of nature, including man as part of nature.

About a hundred years ago things began to change again. Unfortunately, the philosophers involved never achieved the renown of Hume or Kant. In Germany there was Gustav Fechner, known chiefly as a psychologist but with a rather original and profound cosmology; in France, Antoine Cournot, Jules Lequier, and Charles Renouvier, followed a little later by Emile Boutroux, and then Henri Bergson and others; also in Italy, Bernardino Varisco; and in the United States, William James, Charles S. Peirce, and John Dewey. Of these Fechner was the least radical in his departure from determinism. He even, for much of his career, called himself a determinist, but he gave the word a somewhat diluted meaning. Lequier and Boutroux were more radical, and so was James. A bit later Peirce arrived at his theory of Tychism, named from the Greek word for chance, whose reality Peirce not only affirmed but, with penetrating reasoning, accepted as a universal aspect of all nature. Since Peirce began his intellectual career as a scientific determinist, and since he was a practicing scientist much of his life and had done work in half a dozen of the more exact branches, he certainly was familiar with the reasons which Hume and Kant found so compelling for the deterministic position. Indeed, Peirce was a close student of Kant. These reasons are dealt with in his essay, "The Doctrine of Necessity Examined," [1] a most brilliant piece of argumentation.

Also about a century ago a very great physicist suggested that determinism was an unjustified inference from a historical fact, the fact that statistical laws were not, as such, discovered until much later than many apparently nonstatistical laws, such as those of Newton. Thus James Clerk Maxwell, like the genius that he was, foresaw one great intellectual issue of our century: are the basic laws statistical or nonstatistical? This question, which Maxwell saw so early, has scarcely occurred to some of our contemporaries even yet. But they are living in the past. The laws of gases, long before quantum mechanics, had already posed the problem. Maxwell and Peirce saw this immediately. Hans Reichenbach has shown that even in the Newtonian framework the postulate of nonstatistical determination of the individual particles of a gas is an idle gloss

[1] Charles Sanders Peirce, *Collected Papers,* ed. Charles Hartshorne and Paul Weiss (Cambridge, Mass.: Harvard University Press, 1935), Vol. VI, chap. ii; see also Appendix A.

upon the statistical interpretation, which alone is testable or applicable.[2]

Before quantum mechanics, and in addition to the law of gases, the following basic scientific principles, among others, suggested the same conclusion: Charles Darwin's theory of natural selection, Gregor Mendel's laws of inheritance, Josiah Willard Gibbs's phase law in chemistry. Darwin admitted with his usual candor that, *so far as used in his theory*, "chance" variations were exactly that, even though he personally believed there was no chance in nature. In neo-Darwinianism this attitude is rare, not because chance has been more definitely excluded, but for the opposite reason. Quantum uncertainty is relevant to genetic phenomena, hence a usable determinism seems out of the question. One may perhaps believe it, but it does no scientific work. Just this is what Hume and Kant failed utterly to foresee. That the supposedly absolute laws would more and more be displaced in working science by statistical ones is the opposite of what they anticipated, even though Kant did say that the physical micro-order of biological phenomena was too complex for man ever to unravel.

We seem now to be entering upon an essentially new intellectual phase, in which terms like "chance," "randomness," "probability," "possibility," are no longer to be dismissed, without fear of reproof, as but "words for our ignorance." This position may of course still be taken, but only as a personal attitude, not as a standard principle of science. In philosophical and scientific circles there is still some dispute about this, but at the very least strict determinism is on the defensive as it had not been for over two centuries, if ever.

It would be easy to show how fundamentally the philosophies of Hume and Kant depended for their credibility upon the view that determinism was obligatory. Their systems were thus not designed to deal with the situation in which we find ourselves today. This is particularly true of their philosophies of religion, in which they attempted the dismal task of making religious sense out of the Newtonian world machine. One consequence was that the problem of evil assumed its most hopelessly insoluble form. Today we must say that the deterministic version of this problem is wholly question-begging. If scientists cannot require us to accept determinism, there are excellent religious reasons against our doing so. For, if

2 Hans Reichenbach, *The Direction of Time* (Berkeley: University of California Press, 1956), p. 95.

there is an *absolute* natural order, then the only function for the Creator is to have determined everything whatever, good or bad. In a deterministic world, either God does everything, or he does nothing. There can be no third position. The intractability of the resulting problem of evil is scarcely even the worst of the consequences for religion. There is the, if possible, still worse problem: if God does everything, makes all decisions, then his creatures do nothing—it only appears that they act or decide. But, in that case, what conception can they form even of God's acting or deciding? Could mere puppets know that they were such?

True, theologians, like many others, have sometimes argued that it is perfectly possible for a decision to be voluntary or free, and yet completely determined by its causal conditions, and, if so, why could not God have fixed these conditions? The divine creative decree itself would, in fact, be the sufficient condition, and the seeming decision of creatures, though voluntary, would be the outcome infallibly produced. What is overlooked in this piece of theorizing is that the words "decision" and "action" are being used equivocally. God decides upon a world, and here decision has nothing behind it, is free in the sense that no conditions determine or even influence it in the least. For the world is contingent; its creation was not necessary, but radically free. We, however, "decide" or are "free" in an absolutely different sense, for with us the act is merely and precisely what the antecedent conditions determine it to be. Thus there are apparently two principles of freedom. The "problem" of evil presupposes an absolute dualism of conceptions under the one term "choice" (or "decision," "decree," "fiat").

The problem of evil in its acute form is a product of this equivocation. God was not in the least *caused* to make a partly bad world, he simply and arbitrarily did so; so man is *entirely* caused to perform his partly bad actions, but still the badness is not to be assigned to the world-maker, only to man. It is not merely the conception of responsibility that is here being misused, but equally so the conceptions of free action, decision, or choice. If freedom or choice is compatible with absolute causal determination in the one case, and with absolute causal indetermination in the other, what have the two in common but the word? And how can one justify such an absolute duality of simply caused and simply uncaused acts, and retain any validity for the postulate of causality? Also, if God's blessedness consists in his being absolutely uninfluenced in his acts by causes, why should he not be generous enough to grant the creatures an appropriately restricted and partial, but still genuine, form of this causal indeterminacy?

My belief is that theological determinism is one of man's greatest blunders. Early modern science seemed to encourage it, but no longer does science furnish excuse for this kind of bad theology. It now stands naked in its theological arbitrariness, unless philosophers no less arbitrarily come to its aid. I submit that this is a new opportunity to purify our religion and improve our philosophy.

Let us now look at the concept of chance or randomness in relation to purpose. We have inherited a most confused tradition, according to which chance and purpose are mutually exclusive. Thus the admission of real chance had to leap two hurdles, not just one: it seemed barred by the postulate of causality; but equally it seemed barred by the postulate of teleology, of nature as embodying purpose. *In reality, neither causality nor purpose is intelligible without chance.* I promise to give straightforward grounds for this double, perhaps surprising, declaration.

What is causality? It is that real possibility which is distinguished from pure, or merely logical, possibility. And "real" possibility is what *can* occur here and now, or there and then (that is, in given circumstances), whereas "pure" possibility is what *could* occur *somewhere* at *some time,* under some conceivable circumstances. Let us, then, consider a given situation and its "really possible" outcome. Either what can issue from a situation is simply what does issue from it, or this actual outcome is not the only one that was possible. Determinism identifies the actual outcome with what was really possible in the situation. But then the line between actuality and possibility is obliterated, and causality as real possibility is done away with. For the whole point of "possibility" is that it does *not* coincide with actuality, the latter being always an arbitrary selection among possibilities.

Determinism is a radical impoverishment, out of all recognition, of the causal concept, that is to say, the concept of real possibility. But then what is left? Answer: either sheer necessity, or the mere brute fact that events occur in regular ways. But in the latter case we have Hume's paradox: events have always in fact exhibited perfect regularities, but for all we know they are merely chance orders to be violated perhaps at any moment. On the other hand, the notion of becoming as the unwinding of absolute necessity is equally unintelligible. The reasonable view of causation is the intermediate one that causal conditions limit the then and there possible outcomes, but do not in advance completely define or determine a unique outcome. What, then, finally determines the outcome? Nothing is simpler: the outcome in a measure determines itself. This self-determination is freedom in the metaphysical or universal sense. In short, causality implies indeterminism! From the standpoint of the antecedent real possibilities, just which one is actualized is a matter of chance. For "chance," in one sense, just means not determined by the antecedent causes. But though the particular event is by chance, the laws or regularities in events are not. And it is these we need to know in advance, not the precise events themselves.

Let us now consider the relation of purpose to chance. If the realization of a single solitary purpose could constitute reality, then chance, in its other sense of what is "unintended," would be involved only in so far as the purpose itself did not result from any antecedent purpose and so would not be intended. But if purpose is essentially social, if it could not be merely solitary, but must always be one of a number of purposes by a number of purposive agents, then chance is in an additional sense inherent in purpose. For, suppose A intends x and B intends y, and both are successful; then what ensues is xy. Very well, who intended xy? Clearly no one, if the adoptions of the two intentions have been free acts. This formula will, I believe, withstand any amount of analysis which genuinely keeps track of its meanings. It was virtually stated by Aristotle, but its metaphysical import was largely missed for two millennia.

To summarize our argument for the reality of chance: causality requires chance because real possibility can be distinguished from mere actuality only thanks to an element of indeterminacy in each moment with respect to the future; and purpose requires chance because it is essentially social, and *a multiplicity of purposes must leave their conjoint outcomes unintended.*

In both cases ingenious escapes have repeatedly, and for millennia, been attempted. I believe they all fail. One may, for instance, suppose that A and B conspire to reach a common goal; and in some measure this does occur. But they could not possibly *limit* their decisions to merely common ones and still remain distinct agents; and thus the chance element is only reduced, not eliminated, by cooperation and conspiracy. Nor can the divine purpose eliminate chance, if it is to have really individual, that is, partly self-determined, creatures.

Since causality and purpose are as fundamental conceptions as we can easily form, and since they involve chance, the notion that chance is unreal can scarcely be sound. And it follows that the overcoming of the semblance of obligatory determinism in early modern science by the science of our day should give us an opportunity to arrive at a conception of reality superior to any which the Newtonian period knew.

Unfortunately there are still complexities by which many are misled. I shall try to clarify some of these. One is the apparent reduction to insignificance of quantum uncertainty in the higher organisms because of the huge numbers of particles involved. What is insufficiently noticed here is the question-begging assumption that *all* the creative freedom and consequent uncertainty or randomness of nature is confined to very small entities, and is exclusively of the kind now recognized in quantum mechanics—in other words the assumption that organic systems are merely very complicated groupings of particles which in themselves are just what they would be in inorganic systems. This gigantic extrapolation may be the "simplest" view of the situation, but this alone is close to proof that it is wrong. Simplicity is useful, but intellectual history suggests that it never proves absolutely correct in the end. One could give quantities of examples. And, besides, a human being is certainly not just a vast multitude of interrelated particles; it is, at a given moment, a single conscious person, and neither the concept of person nor that of consciousness is a category of quantum physics. The extrapolation in question (made by Albert Einstein and Erwin Schroedinger, for example) blandly assumes that it makes no difference to a particle that it is a member of an organic system—not to mention a conscious, personal one. The principle of causality, reasonably interpreted, forbids such "idle wheels" in nature. The real order must permit everything, including feeling and thought, to make a difference in what happens. But then quantum mechanics must be incomplete, and not the ultimate dynamics of natural happening. Some scientists (Werner Heisenberg, Eugene Wigner) have suggested as much, and in this they are more philosophical than many a philosopher. It is one thing to "limit" causality—as indeterminists do—by admitting a range of real possibilities in each case; it is another to suppose that certain whole classes of events, such as the occurrence of experiences and thoughts, contribute nothing to the locus and extent of these ranges, to the lawful regularities.

The most cogent of the defenses of determinism is the methodological one. The test and value of theories, it is said, is their predictive power; indeterminism, therefore, sets limits in advance to the future success of science, and so impedes progress. This much is true: we do test theories by deriving predictions from them and comparing these with what is observed. But there is another test of the success of science, which is the way it enlarges the range of options open to our choice. We sometimes speak of this as "control." What is commonly overlooked is that the more we control nature, the less do we predict her course. Eclipses, and the rising and setting of the sun and moon, are among the most precisely predictable of earthly events, and they are not controlled at all. Prediction in the absolute sense means an approximately or practically *zero* range of real possibilities, while great power of control, on the contrary, means a wide range. You cannot have it both ways. We control our conversation from moment to moment, but of course, and for that very reason, we do little to predict it. The exercise of control is a continuing thing; it cannot all be done in advance, for life itself is perpetual choice.

Conditional prediction, which alone is open to us where we do control events—"if this, then that"—sets up an ideal simplification of nature, and it abstracts not only from the complexity of real causal conditions but from future human decisions. Should we decide to do this, we may expect to encounter that—but then who is the "we"? All human beings in any way concerned? And what shall, or do, we in fact decide? This is a distinct question. Prediction is relative *in principle,* and the notion of simple absolute prediction is devoid of consistent meaning. So, therefore, is strict determinism. Man is not a mere spectator watching future events as one by one they become present; he is, in the last analysis, a creator, making events to be. The one thing he does not really want to do and could not do is to abdicate as creator in order to absolutize his spectatorial role. And in fact his science is increasing his creative (and, alas, destructive) power rather *more,* if anything, than it increases his foresight. Today this is becoming apparent to all. Scientists are not foretelling what this planet and its human residents will look like after ten, twenty, a hundred years of technological change—any more than, if as much as, Newton might have done.

It is also to be noted that statistical predictions can be tested, and in the more complex sciences and the sciences of living things they are about all that are tested. One speaks of "statistically insignificant" versus "statistically significant" correlations. Statistical determinism suffices. And, theoretically, even the absolute predictions of astronomy are probably to be interpreted as statistical. Thus the entire working content of science is in these terms. The rest is a sort of religion, the "deification of law"—in my view, a second-rate religion.

I knew an astronomer who admitted that he had no proof of determinism, but preferred it "on aesthetic grounds." My objection was that his aesthetics was unsound. Artists and enjoyers of art do not seek absolute order, order at all costs. Quite the contrary as Monroe Beardsley and others have told us, the open secret of art is in a judicious mingling of regularity and irregularity, of the foreseeable and the unforeseeable.[3] It is second-rate musicians who play in the most nearly predictable fashion; superb musicians continually deviate from the expected.[4] As the religion of absolute law is a false religion, so the aesthetics of absolute law is a false aesthetics. It is amusing to see how the writers on aesthetics in the deterministic ages tended to overstate the aspect of regularity in art. (Kant was surprisingly free from this defect.) They have learned to be more balanced in this respect.

A third cause of confusion is in the idea that "freedom" is a human prerogative. The other animals can, it was supposed, be left to the automatic sway of instinct and stimulation; only with man is there a problem of creativity, of genuine choice among possibilities. From this perspective, which is a typical anthropomorphic illusion, everything is bound to be seen wrongly. "Instinct" is only a word for the inborn conditions of behavior. Grant such conditions; still the multitudes of stimuli at a given moment in the life of an animal have to be reduced to the unity of a single over-all response. To predict this reduction of a multitude of inborn and environmental conditions to an integral momentary response (and no doubt unitary experience) in the animal, there is not even the sketchiest outline of a deterministic law. The nonhuman animal, too, has to be a creator in its humble little way.

[3] See Monroe C. Beardsley, "Order and Disorder in Art," in this volume.
[4] Leonard B. Meyer, *Emotion and Meaning in Music* (Chicago: University of Chicago Press, 1956), pp. 195–255.

The notion that admitting such animal freedom derogates from man's dignity is sheer lack of imagination. A dog's freedom of choice is between this little doggish action and that; a man's choices concern ideas, ideals, plans of action, designs for living, philosophies, scientific hypotheses, lines of poetry, bars of music. Anyone who cannot see that the mere notion of a range of possibilities *greater than zero* is quite compatible with indefinitely great differences in extent, and therefore in the importance or dignity of the freedom in question, is a person who may talk about the issue, but has not yet begun to think about it.

The fundamental philosophical question is not, Is man creative or metaphysically free? but, In what sense is such freedom a valid concept? And is it valid as a special case of causality—which in general or in principle does not involve freedom—or is it a universal aspect of causality itself? Anthropomorphic preoccupations obscure or distort the answers to these questions. Of course man's freedom is distinctive, but so was Shakespeare's among men, or Socrates', or Buddha's. Every case of a general conception has its special feature. But the distinctiveness need not be, and rarely is, the difference between zero and infinity! If man is simply free and other terrestrial animals simply not, what about the new-born infant whose "rationality" is much less provable in action than is that of an adult ape?

Freedom as a mere special case turns out to be unintelligible. It does not genuinely solve any problems. Its weakness has been a good part of the apparent strength of the deterministic position. But since there is a third way of viewing the matter, the strength is apparent only. Freedom may be the general case, an aspect of causality as such.

In pure anthropomorphism, only man chooses (among for him genuinely open possibilities); in pure theologism, only God chooses; in conventional religion, only God and man, or these plus the angels and devils. In rational metaphysics, either no individual chooses or all choose, among a range of possibilities—no matter how large or small (above zero). In one case (God) the range may be, in some sense, infinite. But the dilemma is rigorous: either admit the zero case as actual, and then the only escape from a blind dualism of two simply different kinds of causality is in the denial of freedom altogether; or reject the supposed zero case and take the notion of causality as that of a *range* of real possibilities.

If, however, this universalization of creative freedom is the only reasonable solution, then chance also must be universalized. For a range of truly open possibilities means that whichever one is actualized, the causal conditions failed to specify it as against its competitors, and the word "chance" just stands for something not antecedently specified, either as predestined or as intended. And, as we have seen, while A may intend his action and B his, the conjunction of the two actions can only be more or less unintended. Even though B is God, the logic still holds; his decision must conjoin with the other's in a manner not wholly intended even by him. The problem of evil receives herewith its sufficient solution. God does not "determine our acts," because this is nonsense—only A can give $A's$ act its final definiteness. To say that this implies "weakness" in God is to say that the inability to turn nonsense into reality is a weakness. And this saying is also nonsense. God is not weak in any intelligible sense just because he cannot do what intrinsically could not be done.

Let us take a last look at teleology. If *all* creatures have their little purposes, then in this sense teleology is universal. But so, we have seen, is an element of chance and partial "chaos," for these are inherent in the notion of multiple purpose. That chaos has narrow limits set to it is what all science seems to exhibit; the statistical laws express these limits. But how are the limits maintained? Surely not by virtue merely of innumerable little purposes in nature. The only explanation has to be in terms of a supreme purpose. This is the theistic account of order. But it destroys its own foundation if it ends by denying the reality of the little purposes it is to harmonize, or to whose discords it is to set limits. The old teleology, by implication, made the divine purpose the only efficacious one. This meant that the very idea of divine purpose had no human basis of meaning. Darwinism largely destroyed the hold of this teleology. But it never was a good or sensible doctrine. The new teleology must see providence in the beneficent framework of statistical law, thanks to which limits are set to the mutual frustrations of the various creatures, and a vast variety of forms of existence are enabled to coexist in essential harmony and beauty.

I have shown elsewhere how Darwin's inability to accept such a view of providence was due, *not* to his empirical facts or his theory of natural selection, but to his doctrinaire *denial of real chance*, a denial which, as he said himself, made no definite contribution to his theoretical structure.[5] It was chiefly a priori determinism, not empirical discoveries, that made Darwin a skeptic; and, as he rightly urged, theological determinism ought to have made the bishops skeptics all along, quite apart from natural selection, since this determinism turned not only the existence of evil but also the freedom of man into hopeless riddles. The great religious calamity was *not* the admission, but on the contrary the denial, of the pervasiveness of chance in nature. From this calamitous denial we still suffer. But at least the physicists are no longer very much to blame for it. Randomness is coming into its own in science; should not the idea of real freedom, creaturely and divine, now have its opportunity at last?

[5] Charles Hartshorne, *The Logic of Perfection* (La Salle, Ill.: Open Court Publishing Co., 1962), pp. 206–11.

JOSEPH M. KITAGAWA

Chaos, Order, and Freedom
in World Religions

Is it shame, so few should have climb'd from the dens in the level
   below,
Men, with a heart and a soul, no slaves of a four-footed will?
But if twenty million of summers are stored in the sunlight still,
We are far from the noon of man, there is time for the races to grow,
   Red of the Dawn!
Is it turning a fainter red? so be it, but when shall we lay
The ghost of the brute that is walking and haunting us yet, and be
   free?
                              —Tennyson

I. INTRODUCTION

Religion is a complex phenomenon, embodying within it diverse
elements and different dimensions of relationship between man and
the mysterious universe as well as relations among members of the
human community. Fortunately or unfortunately, no one has as yet
proposed a satisfactory definition of the term "religion" that is

JOSEPH M. KITAGAWA, born in Osaka, received his advanced training at Chicago
under Joachim Wach. There he has carried on intensive work in the history of
religions, particularly comparative work and an interpretation of many phases of
Japanese religion. Professor Kitagawa is editor of the *Journal of Religion* and
published *Religion in Japanese History* in 1966. This essay appears in a different
form in *History of Religions: Essays on the Problem of Understanding* (Chicago:
University of Chicago Press, 1967).

268

acceptable to everybody concerned, and obviously we are not going to solve this matter in the limited space at our disposal.[1] Nevertheless, before discussing the problem of "chaos, order, and freedom in world religions," we might mention some assumptions pertaining to religion that are generally accepted by students of *Religionswissenschaft* (History of Religions).

First, religion presupposes "religious experience," however this may be interpreted, on the part of *homo religiosus*. Call it the experience of the Holy (Rudolf Otto), or the Sacred (Mircea Eliade), or the Power (G. van der Leeuw), it is that something which underlies all religious phenomena.[2] For this reason, Eliade rightly reminds us that "to try to grasp the essence of such a phenomenon by means of physiology, psychology, sociology, economics, linguistics, art or any other study is false; it misses the one unique and irreducible element in it—the element of the sacred." [3]

Second, religion is more than a system of beliefs and doctrines. It is a way of life that aims at enlightenment, deliverance, or salvation. In other words, the central concern of religion is nothing less than soteriology. That is to say, what religion provides is not information about life and the world but the practical path of transformation of man.

Third, religions, generally, have three dimensions, to use Joachim Wach's schema, namely: (1) theoretical—beliefs and doctrines regarding the deity, the nature and destiny of man and of the world; (2) practical—rites of worship, sacramental acts, and forms of meditation; and (3) sociological—various types of religious groupings of leadership, and of relationships between religious groups and society.[4]

These descriptive statements, to be sure, are not meant to be used as definitions of religion. They might enable us, however, to differentiate religious phenomena from pseudo- or semireligious phenomena, such as communism and nationalism. On the other hand,

---

[1] Cf. Wilfred Cantwell Smith, *The Meaning and End of Religion* (New York: Macmillan Co., 1963).

[2] The most famous work on the subject of religious experience is Rudolf Otto, *The Idea of the Holy*, trans. John W. Harvey (London: Oxford University Press, 1923). For Eliade, see footnote 50; for van der Leeuw, footnote 7.

[3] Mircea Eliade, *Patterns in Comparative Religion*, trans. Rosemary Sheed (New York and London: Sheed & Ward, 1958), p. xi.

[4] See Joachim Wach, *The Comparative Study of Religions*, ed. J. M. Kitagawa (New York: Columbia University Press, 1958).

with these characteristics of religion in mind, we may include such systems as Confucianism, which is often regarded as a system of nonreligious ethical teaching, and Buddhism, which is considered by some to be essentially a system of philosophy, in the category of religion.

Another difficult question is how to classify diverse religious phenomena. On this question, we must frankly admit that there is no general agreement among scholars.[5] In the main, those who subscribe to evolutionist views tend to classify religions according to historical stages of religious development,[6] while those who try to understand religious phenomena structurally tend to classify them typologically by using phenomenological categories.[7] For our purposes, we may bypass the technical dimensions of this question and depict only three major types of religious experience that in some sense correspond to the historical development of religions. These three types of religious experience are (1) primitive religions, (2) classical religions, and (3) contemporary world religions. Our central focus is to examine how each type of religious experience copes with the problem, of "chaos, order, and freedom."

II. PRIMITIVE RELIGIONS

The emergence of man upon earth is a fascinating problem, which, however has no direct bearing upon our discussion. The discovery of *Zinjanthropus boisei* in northern Tanganyika places man's origins at a date at least over a million and a half years ago. The so-called "erect ape man" (*Pithecanthropus erectus*) and the "Chinese man of Peking" (*Sinanthropus pekinensis*) can be dated to the Middle Pleistocene epoch (around 400,000 years ago). Then there was the long age of the Neanderthal man (*Homo neanderthalensis*) before the appearance of *Homo sapiens* sometime in the late Paleolithic period, which is roughly 50,000 years ago. Although

[5] Cf. Duren J. H. Ward, *The Classification of Religions* (Chicago, Ill.: Open Court Publishing Co., 1909).

[6] For an articulate evolutionist view, see Robert N. Bellah, "Religious Revolution," hectograph (Cambridge, Mass.: Harvard University, no date).

[7] For a phenomenological and morphological approach to religious phenomena, see Eliade, *Patterns in Comparative Religion*, and G. van der Leeuw, *Religion in Essence and Manifestation*, trans. J. E. Turner (London: George Allen & Unwin, 1938).

starting with the chance discovery of the cave of Altamira in Spain in 1879, several other prehistoric sites, such as the grotto of La Mouthe, the caves of Les Combarelles and Font de Gaume, the cavern of Niaux, the grotto of Tuc d'Audoubert, and the caves of Trois Frères, Montespan, and Lascaux, have been found and studied by scholars, our knowledge of the religious life of the paleolithic hunter is still very scanty. It is conceivable, however, that the development of agriculture—called "the food-producing revolution" by V. Gordon Childe—must have brought about a major change in the religious outlook of prehistoric man.

The term "primitive religion" is often used to refer both to the archaic religion that was the religion of precivilized society, and the religion of the present-day primitive society.[8] Understandably, there are different kinds of religious beliefs and practices included in the broad category of "primitive religion." For example, the religion of food gatherers and hunters, characterized by belief in High Gods, the Lord of Animals, and totemism, shows a marked difference from the religion of primitive planters, epitomized by the symbolism of the Great Mother. Nevertheless, there are enough structural similarities among them so that we can lump them together with some justification. Unfortunately, the term "primitive religion" connotes different things to different people, depending on their preconceived notions of primitive man. In fact, one of the mysteries of our time is how our image of primitive man has changed from one extreme to the other. As E. E. Evans-Pritchard points out, "first he was little more than an animal who lived in poverty, violence, and fear; then he was a gentle person who lived in plenty, peace, and security. . . . First he was devoid of any religious feelings or belief; then he was entirely dominated by the sacred and immersed in ritual." [9] Likewise, some people tend to think of "primitive religion" as a qualitatively inferior religion of lawless savages, while

---

[8] E. E. Evans-Pritchard, *Social Anthropology* (Glencoe, Ill.: Free Press of Glencoe, 1951), p. 7: "The word 'primitive' in the sense in which it has become established in anthropological literature does not mean that the societies it qualifies are either earlier in time or inferior to other kinds of societies. As far as we know, primitive societies have just as long a history as our own, and while they are less developed than our society in some respects they are often more developed in others. This being so, the word was perhaps an unfortunate choice but it has now been too widely accepted as a technical term to be avoided."

[9] *Ibid.*, p. 65.

others consider it to be a pristine form of religion practiced by our innocent ancestors just outside the Garden of Eden. Obviously, both views miss the point.

As far as we are concerned, the term "primitive religion" does not imply a qualitative value judgment. Rather, it stands for a special kind of religious experience and apprehension indigenous to the archaic and primitive societies. In this connection, it is worth quoting Robert Redfield's statement that "the primitive and precivilized communities are held together essentially by common understanding as to the ultimate nature and purpose of life," for, in both cases, the society "exists not so much in the exchange of useful functions as in common understandings as to the ends given." [10] And it is our intention to suggest that the ultimate purpose of life was understood by the archaic and primitive men as participation in the act of creation of a "cosmos" out of "chaos" by imitating the celestial model, handed down in various kinds of myth.

The importance of myth and ritual in primitive religion cannot be exaggerated. Myths, it should be noted, are not tales concocted by the undisciplined imagination. "Myth," says Mircea Eliade, "narrates a sacred history; it relates an event that took place in primordial Time. . . . Myth tells how, through the deeds of Supernatural Beings, a reality came into existence. . . . Myth, then, is always an account of a 'creation'; it relates how something was produced, began to *be*." [11] In a similar vein, Charles H. Long states that myth, especially the creation myth, is an expression of man's cosmic orientation. "This orientation involves his apprehension of time and space, his participation in the world of animals and plants, his judgment concerning other men and the phenomena of the sky, the interrelationship of these dimensions, and finally the powers which have established and continue to maintain his being in the world." [12] In other words, the mythic mode, different from the rational and the scientific modes of apprehending reality, enables archaic and primitive men to grasp symbolically and simultaneously "man, society, and nature and past, present, and future" within a

[10] Robert Redfield, *The Primitive World and Its Transformations* (Ithaca, N.Y.: Cornell University Press, 1953), p. 12.

[11] Mircea Eliade, *Myth and Reality*, trans. W. R. Trask (New York: Harper & Row, 1963), pp. 5–6.

[12] Charles H. Long, *Alpha: The Myths of Creation* (New York: George Braziller, 1963), pp. 18–19.

unitary system.[13] This accounts for the fact that to them the mythical world and this world interpenetrate to the extent that human activities are explained and sanctioned in terms of what gods, ancestors, or heroes did in primordial Time.[14] To put it another way, by imitating the mythical accounts of supernatural beings, archaic and primitive men repeat and participate in the primordial act of creating cosmos out of chaos, and this implies establishing and maintaining norms and forms as well as order.[15]

The primitive mode of religious experience is dramatically expressed in rituals. The close interrelationship between myth and ritual has been suggested by many scholars. For example, according to Robertson Smith, myths are derived from ritual, whereas "every rite is originally based on a myth." [16] It is also significant to note that, just as in the case of myth, every ritual in the archaic and primitive societies has a divine model. As Eliade states, man repeats the act of the creation in ritual; "his religious calendar commemorates, in the space of a year, all the cosmogonic phases which took place *ab origine*. In fact, the sacred year ceaselessly repeats the Creation; man is contemporary with the cosmogony and with the anthropogony because ritual projects him into the mythical epoch of the beginning." [17] Thus, marriage rites are recognized as the repetition and continuation of the union of heaven and earth that took place in primordial Time. The New Year rites signify on the one hand the return to chaos and the creation of cosmos. In the initiation ceremonies, death signifies a temporary return to chaos; "hence it is the paradigmatic expression of the *end of a mode of*

[13] W. E. H. Stammer, "The Dreaming," in *Reader in Comparative Religion: An Anthropological Approach,* ed. William A. Lessa and Evon Z. Vogt (Evanston, Ill.: Row, Peterson & Co., 1958), p. 516.

[14] For examples of myths, see Long, *Alpha,* and Joseph Campbell, *The Masks of God: Primitive Mythology* (New York: Viking Press, 1959).

[15] Eliade suggests that settlement in a new territory, for example, is equivalent to an act of creation. When the Scandinavian colonists took possession of Iceland and cultivated it, "their enterprise was for them only the repetition of a primordial act: the transformation of chaos into cosmos by the divine act of Creation. By cultivating the desert soil, they in fact repeated the act of the gods, who organized chaos by giving it forms and norms." He also suggests that "in Vedic India the erection of an altar dedicated to Agni, which implied the microcosmic imitation of the Creation, constituted legal taking possession of a territory. Mircea Eliade, *The Myth of the Eternal Return,* trans. W. R. Trask (New York: Pantheon Books, 1954), pp. 10–11.

[16] Quoted in Joachim Wach, *Sociology of Religion* (Chicago, Ill.: University of Chicago Press, 1944), p. 26.

[17] Eliade, *Myth of the Eternal Return,* p. 22.

being—the model of ignorance and of the child's irresponsibility. Initiatory death provides the clean slate on which will be written the successive revelations whose end is the formation of a new man." [18]

There are two main characteristics of the rituals or cultus of the archaic and primitive societies. First, rituals are corporate acts of the whole tribe or the community; in a real sense, there is no distinction between performers and spectators. For example, a few years ago, the writer had an opportunity to participate in the Bear Festival of the Ainus in Hokkaido, Japan. We were impressed by the fact that man and animal, as well as invisible divine beings called *kamui*, played their respective roles in the great ritual. We then wrote:

> The *Iyomante* was a long ritual, and as it slowly moved from one stage to the next, there was a gradual heightening of religious feeling among those who took part. As the ritual approached its climax, one could not help being drawn into a drama, recapitulating a religious experience from the most remote past. The ecstatic expressions of those who participated in the singing, dancing, and praying gave one every reason to believe that for the Ainus, at any rate, the memorable experiences of their ancestors had become real again in the performance of *Iyomante*. [19]

Second, ritual is not isolated from other human activities as the only "religious" act in the archaic and primitive societies. Van der Leeuw reminds us that to primitive man every act is both ritual and work: "Song was prayer; drama was divine performance; dance was cult." [20] In this sense, the attitude of modern man toward life is grossly different from the attitude of the primitive man: "When we dance, we do not pray; when we pray, we do not dance. And when we work, we can neither dance nor pray. . . . The culture of primitive man is at the same time sport, dance, concert, and much more." [21] To be sure, there are apparent differences in human activities—farming, fishing, cooking, fighting, as well as art, witchcraft, oracles, and magic. But they are interdependent parts of a whole, or interpenetrating circles sharing a midpoint, which is the

[18] Mircea Eliade, *Birth and Rebirth: The Religious Meanings of Initiation in Human Culture*, trans. W. R. Trask (New York: Harper & Brothers, 1958), p. xiii.

[19] Joseph M. Kitagawa, "Ainu Bear Festival (Iyomante)," *History of Religions*, I, No. I (1961), 98.

[20] G. van der Leeuw, *Sacred and Profane Beauty: The Holy in Art*, trans. David E. Green (New York: Holt, Rinehart & Winston, 1963), p. 11.

[21] *Ibid.*, p. 34.

meaning and purpose of life, namely, participation in the divine act of creating and maintaining cosmos (order).

In this connection, W. E. H. Stammer convincingly argues that the social system of the Australian aborigines is self-protective and self-renewing, because the mode, ethos, and principle of aboriginal life are "variations on a single theme—continuity, constancy, balance, symmetry, regularity, system, or some such quality as these words convey." [22] In such a situation, what life *is* as well as what life *can be* is determined, so that life is basically a "one-possibility thing," to use his imaginative expression.[23] While the aborigines are endowed with intelligence, rationality, and creative drive, these faculties are directed primarily toward the maintenance of the "given order" of life, as apprehended by myths. In such a situation, if an accepted belief fails to correspond to a particular experience, "this merely shows that the experience was mistaken, or inadequate, or the contradiction is accounted for by secondary elaborations of belief which provide satisfactory explanations of the apparent inconsistency." [24] Essentially, primitive religion provides no real alternatives in life. There is no enlightenment, deliverance, or salvation in our sense of the term. The soteriology, if we may introduce such a term to the context of primitive religion, implies the primitive man's initiation into the ancestral orientation of his tribal or communal life that is expressed in the mythical apprehension of cosmos. It follows, then, that the *summum bonum* of primitive religion is continuity and preservation of this type of cosmic orientation which holds the inner unity of ritual, art, interhuman relationships, and all the rest. Understandably, there is no room for individual freedom in the archaic and primitive societies. However, the primitive people, as a people, have managed to attain an ontological freedom of a sort by defeating and overcoming what Eliade calls the "terror of history." [25]

III. CLASSICAL RELIGIONS

Inasmuch as it is impossible to discuss all the historical religions of the world individually, we have adopted the two arbitrary and ambiguous categories of "classical religions" and "contemporary

---

[22] Stammer, "The Dreaming," p. 522.

[23] *Ibid.*, p. 517.

[24] Evans-Pritchard, *Social Anthropology*, p. 99.

[25] Cf. Eliade, *Myth of the Eternal Return*, pp. 141–62; and Stammer, "The Dreaming," p. 521.

world religions" in order to portray, at least, certain differences in perspectives in their attitude toward the question of "chaos, order, and freedom." Under the category of "classical religions," we include religions of the ancient Near East, Iran, India, the Far East, and the Greco-Roman world, whereas more recent aspects of living religions are discussed under the heading of "contemporary world religions."

As far as archeological scholarship can ascertain, agriculture and stock breeding developed as early as the eighth millennium B.C. in the Iranian plateau. This marked the beginning of the so-called "food-producing revolution," which stimulated the rise of self-sustaining villages. The transition from the neolithic village pattern to a more advanced phase of the city and state was a long process. Around 3500 B.C., the first great civilization emerged in the Mesopotamian plain. Canals were dug for large-scale irrigation; writing, mathematics, and a systematic method of observing planetary movements were invented; monumental architecture, especially imposing temples, began to rise in the plain; and a new system of government emerged. Shortly afterward, other civilizations arose in Egypt, Crete, India, China, Mexico, Peru, and Palestine. All these civilizations were grounded in definite religious outlooks and orientations. Different though these religious traditions were, they shared these characteristics: (1) the emancipation of the *logos* from the *mythos*, (2) the devaluation of the phenomenal world and life coupled with recognition of another realm of reality, and (3) a high degree of sophistication and systemization of theoretical, practical, and sociological aspects of religion. In all these religious traditions, the existence of the cosmic order was taken for granted, variously known as Ma'at, Themis, Rta, Tao, and so forth, although their understanding of the nature of the cosmic order varied greatly. Closely related to the question of the cosmic order is man's understanding of his own nature and destiny, which determines to a great extent the differences of various religious traditions, not so much in philosophical speculation as in soteriological outlook.

1. One of the differences between the classical religions and the primitive religions is found in their attitudes toward myth. Earlier we pointed out that archaic and primitive men know only one mode of thinking, that is, the mythic, which enables them to grasp symbolically and simultaneously "man, society, and nature and past, pres-

ent, and future" within a unitary system. In such a unified system, everything in this world is endowed with life, so that every phenomenon appears to be a "Thou," in the sense in which Martin Buber uses this term. " 'Thou' is not contemplated with intellectual detachment; it is experienced as life confronts life, involving every faculty of man in a reciprocal relationship. Thoughts, no less than acts and feelings, are subordinated to this experience." [26] In observing certain movements of the planets, for example, the primitive mind "looks, not for the 'how,' but for the 'who,' when it looks for a cause . . . he does not expect to find an impersonal law regulating a process. He looks for a purposeful will committing an act." [27] Thus, in the primitive religions, everything is "Thou," and every event is a concrete act by a certain "Thou." There is no effort to stand outside the world of myth and reduce different experiences to certain universal principles.

The classical religions, on the other hand, recognize the distinction among "man, society, and nature" as well as among "past, present, and future," although their interrelations are explained in terms of myth. In Babylonia and elsewhere in the ancient world, the correct performance of the New Year ritual was considered essential to insure good harvest, but the importance of agricultural skill was also recognized. The great rivers—the Nile, the Tigris, the Euphrates, the Indus, the Yang Tze, and others—were no doubt believed to be living beings having their own will and temperament, worthy to receive gifts and sacrifices from the people. And yet, the regularity of their movements was observed in terms of mathematical calculations. Thus the classical religions retained the language of myth, but speculative inquiry into causal principles and universal laws was no longer inhibited and stultified completely by the mythic mode of thinking. In other words, there was a certain degree of emancipation of the *logos* and the *mythos*. For instance, the ancient Near Eastern man

. . . recognized the problem of origin and the problem of *telos,* of the aim and purpose of being. He recognized the invisible order of justice maintained by his customs, mores, institutions; and he connected this invisible

[26] H. and H. A. Frankfort, John Wilson, Thorkild Jacobsen, and William Irwin, *The Intellectual Adventure of Ancient Man* (Chicago, Ill.: University of Chicago Press, 1946) , p. 6.
[27] *Ibid.,* p. 15.

order with the visible order, with its succession of days and nights, seasons and years, obviously maintained by the sun. [He] even pondered the hierarchy of the different powers which he recognized in nature.[28]

2. Probably, the difference between the primitive religions and the classical religions is most conspicuously demonstrated in man's own view of himself. In the former, there is no recognition of man apart from nature. Or, to put it another way, man is a part of society which in turn is an integral part of nature and the cosmos. In the latter, however, man as something apart from society and the cosmos is recognized. Here again, various religious traditions developed different views of man.[29] Nevertheless, most of the classical religions accepted man as a psycho-physical-mental and spiritual being, a mortal endowed with memory, intelligence, and sexuality. There also developed speculations about the invisible inner self within man's physical being—*atman, spiritus, anima, Seele,* or *pneuma.* Undoubtedly the most sophisticated analysis of man was attempted by Greek thinkers,[30] although other religious traditions also provided theories and answers to the riddle of man and his destiny, too.

Most of the classical religions held a belief in the existence of some sort of cosmic order that provides ultimate meaning for human existence. However, the regulation of the relationships among the cosmic, social, and human realms was a difficult problem. Human beings, then and now, look for answers to the suffering, failure, and frustration of their existence. For example, according to Thorkild Jacobsen, man in ancient Mesopotamia

. . . no longer permitted his world to be essentially arbitrary; he demanded that it have a firm moral basis. Evil and illness, attacks by demons, are no longer considered mere happenings, accidents: the gods, by allowing them to happen, are ultimately responsible, for only when an offense has been committed should the personal god be angered and turn away. Thus

---

[28] *Ibid.,* p. 8.

[29] Cf. Joachim Wach, *Typen religiöser Anthropologie: Ein Vergleich der Lehre von Menschen im religionsphilosophischen Denken von Orient und Okzident* (*Philosophie und Geschichte,* Vol. XL [Tübingen: J. C. B. Mohr (P. Siebeck), 1932]); C. J. Bleeker (ed.), *Anthropologie Religieuse* (Leiden: E. J. Brill, 1955); and S. G. F. Brandon, *Man and His Destiny in the Great Religions* (Toronto, Ont.: University of Toronto Press, 1962).

[30] Joachim Wach, *Types of Religious Experience: Christian and Non-Christian* (Chicago, Ill.: University of Chicago Press, 1951), pp. 66–70; see also James Luther Adams, "The Changing Reputation of Human Nature," reprinted in a slightly revised form from *The Journal of Liberal Religion* (Autumn, 1942), Winter, 1943, pp. 7–10.

in human moral and ethical values man had found a yardstick with which he presumptuously proceeded to measure the gods and their deeds. A conflict was immediately apparent. Divine will and human ethics proved incommensurable.[31]

Caught by the discrepancy between human experience and the idea of a just cosmic order, various religions offered different explanations and solutions. Hinduism and the mystics of all religions are inclined to affirm the essential oneness of the human soul with God or the cosmic spirit, while Buddhism holds that problems of the human condition have no ontological reality. Ancient Greek and Babylonian religions, on the other hand, put the accent on the essential difference between the divine and human natures. Thus, the recognition and acceptance of human mortality was considered as the first order of wisdom. At any rate, these classical religions tended to devalue the phenomenal world and tried to locate the meaning of human existence in another realm of reality, however it was conceived.

In this connection, it is significant to note that some of the classical religions wrestled with the problem of time and history. One should recall that for the primitive religions the only time that was meaningful was the primordial Time, so that efforts were made to overcome and defeat the onslaught of empirical time and history. In a somewhat similar vein, a few of the classical religions adopted a cyclical view of time and taught men to live in an "eternal present." Some others like the ancient Egyptian and Chinese religions, on the other hand, stressed the normativeness of the golden past. It was the Persian religion of Zoroaster that interpreted the relation between the cosmic order and human experience in terms of a linear view of history. Accepting the cosmic dualism based on Ahura Mazdah and Angra Mainyu, representing Good and Evil, respectively, Zoroastrianism viewed history as a battleground in which the divine will, order, and purpose are threatened by Evil. This concept of history had a profound significance for man in the sense that the individual was compelled to make a moral decision to join either the side of Good or that of Evil in a struggle that takes place in the temporal historical process without any thought for oneself of "securing a good lot . . . in the *post-mortem* existence." [32] Zoroastrianism exerted a significant influence on Judaism, which stressed its God as

[31] Frankfort *et al., Intellectual Adventure of Ancient Man*, p. 213.
[32] Brandon, *Man and His Destiny*, p. 287.

the lord of the cosmic order who reveals his will through events in history. To the Jews, unlike the Egyptians and the Chinese, the locus of the meaning of history was to be found in its end (*eschaton*). No less important was the Christian view that amplified the Jewish notion of "history as the epiphany of God." [33]

3. As to the third characteristic of the classical religions, namely, sophistication and systematization of theoretical, practical, and sociological expressions of their religious experience, we can discuss them only superficially.[34] Here again a brief comparison with primitive religions may be pertinent. Earlier, we cited the view of Robert Redfield to the effect that the society of the archaic and primitive peoples—which he terms "folk society"—found its cohesiveness "in common understandings as to the ends given." It is significant to note that:

The ends are not stated as matters of doctrine, but are implied by the many acts which make up the living that goes on in the society. Therefore, the morale of a folk society—its power to act consistently over periods of time and to meet crises effectively—is not dependent upon discipline exerted by force or upon devotion to some single principle of action, but to the concurrence and consistency of many or all of the actions and conceptions which make up the whole round of life.[35]

In other words, according to the comprehensive world view of the primitive religions, not only is there no distinction between theory and practice, there is only one unified order that governs cosmic law, ritual law, and social law, so that the course of nature, of human life, and of society was seen as one harmonious whole. In the classical religions, however, the distinctiveness of three domains of religion—theoretical, practical, and sociological—was recognized, even though a high degree of correlation among these domains was maintained. In most religious traditions, theoretical development centered around theological, cosmological, and anthropological concerns that are expressed in terms of myth, doctrine, and dogma, although certain religions tended to be more theocentric, while others were more cosmocentric or anthropocentric.[36] In some cases,

[33] Cf. Eliade, *Myth of the Eternal Return*, p. 104.

[34] For Wach's explication of this three-fold scheme, see his *Comparative Study of Religions*.

[35] Robert Redfield, "The Folk Society," *American Journal of Sociology*, LII (January, 1947), 299.

[36] Wach, *Sociology of Religion*, p. 23: "The nature of God or gods, the origin and growth of deities (theogony), and their attributes, the relation of the deity

philosophy and ethics grew out of theology and religious doctrine. It was the Greek thinkers who developed the notion of *theoria,* and, as Wach points out, "we find in Aristotle's system a scheme for the organization of knowledge, evidencing the first beginnings of the pursuit of a theory for its own sake ('science') ." [37] At any rate, with the development of the theoretical aspects of religion oral traditions tend to be replaced by written traditions, and professional or semi-professional interpreters of doctrines come into existence.

Side by side with the theoretical development, we find the gradual articulation of practical or cultic expressions of religion, such as ritual, symbols (images) , sacraments, and various forms of sacrifices. In discussing the development of cults, it is well to remember that there is "the same continuous interplay between compulsion and tradition, on the one hand, and the constant drive for individual liberty-making for the emergence of new impulses and the creative activity of *homines religiosi,* on the other, which we observed in the development of thought patterns." [38] Equally important is the gradual stratification of religious groupings, leadership, and interhuman relations, based on the natural criteria of sex and age and/or on the religious criteria of charismata, skills, knowledge, healing power, and training. In this connection it is to be noted that in the classical religions the structure of religious groups as well as their relations to sociopolitical order were believed to be based on, and sanctioned by, the cosmic order, whether it was understood to exist above the gods as in Hinduism or under a divine being as in the Judeo-Christian tradition. Also, various institutions such as the sacred king in the ancient Near East, or the priestly caste in India, came into existence ostensibly for the purpose of safeguarding the cosmic order from the destructive power of chaos. Thus, while there was some room for freedom and spontaneity exemplified by prophetic and reform movements, most classical religions were primarily concerned with the preservation of order in the cosmic, human, and sociopolitical realms. Inevitably, man's soteriological yearning was subordinated to an overwhelming concern for the preservation of

---

to the world and its justification (theodicy) —all are delineated and expounded in theology. Cosmology is concerned with the origin, development, various phases and destiny of the world, while theological anthropology, including soteriology and eschatology, ponders over the origin, nature, and destiny of man."

[37] *Ibid.,* p. 24.

[38] *Ibid.,* p. 27.

order, so that salvation was sought either as the acceptance of order or the rejection of it. The dichotomy between "this worldly ethics" and "otherworldly spirituality" confronted all the classical religions.

IV. CONTEMPORARY WORLD RELIGIONS

The category of "contemporary world religions," as stated earlier, refers not to new forms of religion that have emerged in various parts of the world in recent decades but to the modern trends and ethos of historic religions that have been discussed in the previous section.[39] Unfortunately, the long and fascinating historical developments of the various classical religions cannot be discussed here. All we can do at this point is to remind ourselves that none of the historic religions has remained unchanged; each one has undergone numerous stages of transformation due to internal and external factors, even though some of the basic characteristics of each religion have been preserved.

Students of *Religionswissenschaft* today are greatly indebted to the work of Gerardus van der Leeuw, who among other things attempted to depict the main characteristics of historic religions in terms of typology. For example, Confucianism and eighteenth-century Deism are characterized by him as "Religions of Remoteness and of Flight"; Zoroastrianism as "the Religion of Struggle"; various forms of mysticism as "the Religion of Repose"; certain features of Judaism, Christianity, and Islam as "the Religion of Unrest"; a wide assortment of movements from polydemonism to polytheism as "Syncretism"; some phases of Greek religion as "the Religion of Strain and of Form"; Hinduism as "the Religion of Infinity and of Asceticism"; Buddhism as "the Religion of Nothingness and of Compassion"; Judaism as "the Religion of Will and of Obedience"; Islam as "the Religion of Majesty and of Humility"; and Christianity as "the Religion of Love." [40] Van der Leeuw also depicts three approaches of the religions to the world in respect to creative domination, theoretical domination, and obedience, and the three different goals sought by various religions as man, the world, and God.[41] In all fairness to van der Leeuw, we must bear in mind that his typological attempt, like similar efforts by other scholars, is not

[39] For discussion of individual religions, see Joseph M. Kitagawa (ed.) , *Modern Trends in World Religions* (La Salle, Ill.: Open Court Publishing Co., 1959) .

[40] Van der Leeuw, *Religion in Essence and Manifestation*, pp. 597–649.

[41] *Ibid.*, pp. 543–87.

meant to portray historic religions in a monolithic and one-dimensional manner. Each religion, at various stages of its historic development, often manifests contradictory features, as ably demonstrated by H. Richard Niebuhr in his discussion of the relation of Christ to culture, e.g., Christ against Culture, the Christ of Culture, Christ above Culture, Christ and Culture in Paradox, and Christ the Transformer of Culture.[42]

What is significant from our point of view is that the modern ethos and trends in all major religions share, to a greater or lesser extent, (1) preoccupation with the meaning of human existence, (2) this-worldly soteriology, and (3) the search for "freedom" rather than the preservation of "order." These three features are closely interrelated, of course. Needless to say, we are not advocating these as religious ideals for our time; we are simply depicting them as significant characteristics of "contemporary world religions."

1. Historically, the meaning of human existence (religious anthropology) has been one of the three main problems of many classical religions, the other two being the nature of Ultimate Reality or Deity (theology) and the origin, structure, and destiny of the universe (cosmology). In various religious traditions, different doctrines have been formulated regarding these three major topics. In this connection we agree with Paul Tillich that all these doctrinal statements were formulated essentially as answers to "questions." [43] And the fact is that the traditional balance of the triple doctrinal formula is no longer meaningful to modern man, because his existential "question" is primarily concerned with the meaning of human existence and is rather indifferent to the topics of deity and the universe. In other words, the discussion of deity and the universe are meaningful only when they are related to the problem of man. This shift in accent or emphasis has profound implications for the ethos of contemporary world religions in the sense that various religious traditions can no longer preserve the traditional doctrinal formulations and the symbol systems intact however meaningful

---

[42] H. Richard Niebuhr, *Christ and Culture* (New York: Harper & Brothers, 1951). See also Christopher Dawson, *Enquiries into Religion and Culture* (New York: Sheed & Ward, 1933); and S. Radhakrishnan, *Religion and Society* (London: George Allen & Unwin), 1947.

[43] Thus he proposes for Christian theology the method of correlation that "explains the contents of the Christian faith through existential questions and theological answers in mutual interdependence." Paul Tillich, *Systematic Theology* (Chicago, Ill.: University of Chicago Press, 1951), I, 60.

they may have been to premodern man. In this respect, the statement of Clement Webb is pertinent; that is, "the idolatry of today is often the true religion of yesterday, and the true religion of today the idolatry of tomorrow." [44] In today's world, all religions are compelled to wrestle with modern man's question as to how man can realize his highest possibilities in the midst of the brokenness and meaninglessness of our time.

This does not imply, however, that traditional doctrines of man have become completely obsolete in different religious traditions. Modern Hindus still accept the ancient belief that man's inner self is an aspect of Ultimate Reality. Contemporary Buddhists would subscribe, just as most Buddhists of all ages have done, to the notion that man is ever "becoming"; what appears as a self is therefore impermanent and basically unreal. And both Jews and Christians in our time still hold that man is "equipped with a reverence for the majesty of God who created him and endowed him with a sense of obligation as well as a longing for forgiveness. Man is a sinner not only in the sense of his finiteness but by an act of the will." [45] However, these doctrines are no longer accepted just because they have been sanctioned by religious traditions; they are meaningful to modern man only when these historic beliefs can be tested by experience and restated in a form of language that makes sense. Thus, Daniel Day Williams states the "question" behind the contemporary theological renaissance in the Christian world as follows: "What is there in the Christian faith which *gives us such an understanding of ourselves* that we must assert our loyalty to the Holy God above all the splendid and yet corruptible values of our civilization?" [46] Similar observations can be made in regard to the serious effort of contemporary Jews, Muslims, Hindus, and Buddhists to discover the foundations of their faiths. Indeed, in today's world the primary concern for religious men, no less than for their secular counterparts, is man and the meaning of his existence.

2. The second characteristic feature of contemporary world religions, namely, a "this-worldly soteriology," is closely related to the first. We might recall that all classical religions tended to devaluate

---

[44] Clement C. J. Webb, *God and Personality* (New York: Macmillan Co., 1918), p. 264.

[45] Wach, *Comparative Study of Religions*, p. 92.

[46] Daniel Day Williams, *What Present-Day Theologians Are Thinking* (New York: Harper & Brothers, 1952), p. 12. (My italics.)

phenomenal existence and recognized another realm of reality, however differently it was conceived in various religious systems. Religious iconography in many parts of the world dramatically portrays the stages and grades of the heavenly state as well as hell, purgatory, or the nether world. They were not invented merely to scare the ignorant masses as some skeptics and cynics think. To many adherents of the classical religions, the existence of other realms beside the phenomenal world order spoke with a compelling force. And man in his finitude was believed to be confined to this world, which is permeated by suffering, sinfulness, or imperfection. Thus, the religious outlook of the classical religions often had an overtone of "nostalgia for a lost paradise," to use Eliade's expression, or of longing for a heavenly reward in the afterworld. In this life, man was thought to be a sojourner or prisoner. Also, there was a conviction that all these different realms of existence were either regulated by the cosmic order or dominated by an omnipresent personal deity. Thus, for example, the Hebrew Psalmist said:

> If I ascend to heaven, thou art there!
> If I make my bed in Sheol, thou art there!
> If I take the wings of the morning
>   and dwell in the uttermost parts of the sea,
> Even there thy hand shall lead me,
>   and thy right hand shall hold me.[47]

It is important to note that a radical change has taken place in this respect in the thinking of modern people, so that they no longer take seriously the existence of another realm of reality. To be sure, they still use such expressions as Paradise, Pure Land, Nirvana, and the Kingdom of God. These terms have only symbolic meaning for the modern mentality. The colorful imagery of Dante, Milton, Bunyan, and their counterparts in the Jewish, Muslim, Hindu, and Buddhist traditions no longer convinces modern man that the present world is only a shadowy reflection of a more real world that exists somewhere else. To the modern man, this phenomenal world is the only real order of existence, and life here and now is the center of the world of meaning. The rejection of pluralistic realms of existence, however, coincided with the widening and broadening of the present world order and cosmos. The single cosmos of the modern man, despite its superficial resemblances, has very little in common with the undifferentiated cosmos of the primitive and

[47] Psalm 139:8–10 (R.S.V.) .

archaic man in that the modern cosmos is no longer a sacred reality for the experience of contemporary man. Increasingly the mystery of outer space has been diminished, and even the deities have been robbed of their heavenly thrones.

The loss of other realms of existence has compelled contemporary world religions to find the meaning of human destiny in this world —in culture, society, and human personality. Never has there been a period in the history of the human race when the relation of religion or faith to sociopolitical, economic, and cultural spheres has been taken so seriously as it is today. This does not mean that today we are witnessing another example of the phenomenon of the "ecclesiastification of culture," as in medieval Europe, or of the "secularization of religion," as in the days of rationalism. What we find now is an increasing realization on the part of contemporary world religions that, just as religious man must undergo the experience of personal transformation or *metanoia,* culture and society must be renewed and revitalized in order to fulfill their vocation in the midst of the ambiguities and upheavals of this world. Thus, even in Theravada Buddhism, which has been regarded by some as one of the most otherworldly of the religions, advocates of a soteriology centered on this world argue that Buddhist leaders must pursue "not a will-o'-the-wisp Nirvana secluded in the cells of their monasteries, but a Nirvana attained here and now by a life of self-forgetful activity . . . [so that] they would live in closer touch with humanity, would better understand and sympathize with human difficulties. . . ." [48] Likewise, leaders of contemporary Judaism, Christianity, Islam, and Hinduism are deeply involved in the building of new nations and in various spheres of social, educational, political, and cultural activities with the conviction that these areas of life are the very arena of salvation.

3. As has become apparent, the ethos and trends of contemporary world religions reflect the questions and existential contradictions of modern man, whose concern may be characterized as a pathological search for "freedom" rather than the preservation of "order." In today's idiom the term "freedom" has two different, but internally related, meanings. On the one hand, it refers to man's effort to be free from something, such as the established order of society, an outmoded standard of morality, or an archaic doctrinal system of

---

[48] *The Revolt in the Temple* (Colombo: Sinha Publications, 1953) , p. 586.

religion. On the other hand, freedom refers to the aspirations of man in discovering novelty and creativity in art, philosophy, religion, and in interhuman relations. Inevitably, modern man's search for "freedom" has resulted in the rejection of the foundation of the classical religions which believed that all aspects of the human, social, and natural orders were grounded in, and regulated by, the cosmic order. What was taken for granted by the classical religions was the notion of "order" or "law," not simply as a general descriptive formula depicting some specific complex of observable facts, but as a self-evident normative principle that governs all aspects of the universe. Thus, the effort was made by all the classical religions to preserve the "givenness" of the cosmic order as mirrored in the concrete structures of society and interhuman relationships. Such an understanding of cosmic order—its givenness and its normativeness —has been rejected by modern man, and to a great extent by the contemporary world religions as well. In today's world, "order" simply means either a general descriptive formula or something man must establish in order to avoid chaos and disharmony.

The glory of modern man is his faith in his own capacity to transcend the limitations which premodern man had accepted as the "givenness" of finitude. To the premodern man, the dignity of man was found in his finitude, precisely because finitude was the gift of the gods. Thus, the ancient Psalmist could say:

> When I look at thy heavens, the work of thy fingers,
>   the moon and the stars which thou hast established;
> What is man that thou art mindful of him,
>   and the son of man that thou dost care for him? [49]

But today finitude is regarded as a source of embarrassment for man. Life is believed to be an "infinite-possibility-thing," to use Robert N. Bellah's phrase, and man is determined to create freedom, overcoming the limitations of time and space. But the glory of the modern man is at the same time the cause of his tragedy, for he is caught in a new existential situation which he has created. In the words of Eliade:

He regards himself solely as the subject and agent of history, and he refuses all appeal to transcendence. In other words, he accepts no model for humanity outside the human condition as it can be seen in the various historical situations. Man *makes himself*, and he only makes himself completely in proportion as he desacralizes himself and the world. The

[49] Psalm 8:3–4 (R.S.V.) .

sacred is the prime obstacle to his freedom. He will become himself only when he is totally demysticized. He will not be truly free until he has killed the last god.[50]

Fortunately or unfortunately, the contemporary world religions are destined to address themselves to this tragic predicament of modern man, who is caught between his determination to gain freedom from the past with its transcendental sanctions, on the one hand, and his search for novelty, creativity, and freedom on the other. In this connection it must be noted that bold reinterpretations of traditional doctrines have already been attempted by some theologians and philosophers in the various religious traditions. For example, according to a contemporary Christian thinker, "the recognition that God requires freedom of the creatures for his own life is the best way to insure against a false conception of omnipotence as suppressing that freedom. Divine power is an ability to deal with free beings, not an ability to suppress or avoid their existence that they would not be free." [51] Similarly, a Buddhist Existentialist philosopher, echoing the Kierkegaardian formula of "either/or," advocates the formula of "neither/nor" to reinterpret man's freedom for the Absolute Nothingness.[52] But, for the most part, contemporary world religions have a long way to go before they can reinterpret their traditional doctrines in the light of modern man's existential situation.

The fact that the world religions are not adequately prepared to cope with the human situation today does not imply that the historic religions have become irrelevant or are dead. Undoubtedly, the challenge of the contemporary situation has released new energy that had hitherto been submerged in the tradition of the historic religions, as dramatically demonstrated by the passive resistance movement (*Satyagraha*) of Mahatma Gandhi in India and similar movements, on the part of Negroes in the American South and of the Buddhists in South Vietnam, to fight against injustice. This energy is also evident in the dedicated efforts of contemporary Jews, Muslims, and adherents of other religions to establish a new order

[50] Mircea Eliade, *The Sacred and the Profane,* trans. W. R. Trask (New York: Harcourt, Brace & Co., 1959) , p. 203.

[51] Charles Hartshorne and W. L. Reese, *Philosophers Speak of God* (Chicago, Ill.: University of Chicago Press, 1953) , p. 234.

[52] Cf. Yoshinori Takeuchi, "Buddhism and Existentialism," *Religion and Culture: Essays in Honor of Paul Tillich,* ed. Walter Leibrecht (New York: Harper & Brothers, 1959) , pp. 291–318.

of society. However, the greater and a far more difficult task that confronts the contemporary world religions is that of relating modern man's search for "freedom," which demands an awesome responsibility on the part of man, to the cosmic source of creativity, novelty, and freedom—the Sacred itself.

HERBERT SPIEGELBERG

Rules and Order: Toward a Phenomenology of Order

In this paper I propose to explore some aspects of what is meant by the term "order" as applied to certain normative phenomena. What do we mean when we say that things are "in order" or "out of order"? However, I shall not be satisfied with merely studying the meaning of words. What I want to find out is the structure of the phenomena behind the words.

But before approaching these phenomena directly we shall have to remove certain roadblocks in the way of such an approach. One such roadblock seems to me the present concept of rule as used in some contemporary philosophies. There was a time when the main obstacle to my approach was the concept of law, primarily in the form of moral law, which was considered the ultimate foundation of the field of ethics. This was true not only of the ethics of the Decalogue and other heteronomous systems, but even of the autonomous ethics of the Kantian moral law. In my Continental past I

HERBERT SPIEGELBERG, born in Strassburg (now France), did his doctorate at Munich under the phenomenologist Alexander Pfänder. Long professor of philosophy at Lawrence College, he is now at Washington University, St. Louis. There for three years he has conducted a workshop in phenomenology. Professor Spiegelberg is well known for *The Phenomenological Movement,* which went into its second edition in 1965. He is currently working on the impact of phenomenology on psychology and psychiatry. His *Gesetz und Sittengesetz* contains systematic and historic preparations for an ethics of moral order.

spent considerable time and ink in analyzing and criticizing this excessive emphasis on the concept of law, which I called at the time *Legismus*. Since then I have, at least to some extent, become happily naturalized to the Anglo-American way of doing moral philosophy. And my first impression was that, considering especially the way in which such ethical intuitionists as G. E. Moore and W. D. Ross and ethical naturalists such as John Dewey and Ralph B. Perry approached ethical and meta-ethical problems head-on without much if any reference to moral law, my previous road-clearing preoccupation was quite unnecessary and outdated. But now it seems to me that my relief was slightly premature and overoptimistic. Recent developments in the so-called linguistic philosophy emphasize prescriptions, rules, and principles as the final justification and support of all ethical decisions (e.g., Stephen Toulmin, P. H. Nowell-Smith, R. M. Hare, Marcus Singer) ; they do this to such a degree that one may well think they *are* the ultimate foundations of this new ethics. It may therefore again be in order to raise the question of the nature and proper place of these rules in moral philosophy. At least some remarks about this vast subject seem appropriate even in the present context, all the more since I believe that, properly understood, these very rules may lead us to the more basic phenomenon of order.

First, however, let me confess that I have grown increasingly suspicious of the role that the concept of rule has assumed in the pattern of recent philosophy as a whole. This begins with its alleged part in our experience of speech and language. It seems to be almost taken for granted that a language consists of rules for using symbols, and that in using one's language one conforms to the rules of the language "game"—a dubious analogy for something as serious and at times deadly serious as our ordinary communication. Is this even a faithful description of what we actually experience in using our language, except when we "play" with words? Who, especially in speaking his mother tongue, is even implicitly, let alone explicitly, aware of the rules of this language? Consider the often embarrassing experience for the native of any language when he has to explain to a foreign student why certain forms or combinations of words either will or won't do. All he can honestly say, if he is challenged to produce a rule, is: "I can't tell you why this is so. But I know it does (or doesn't) sound right." And then, in an attempt to rationalize his answer, he might try to improvise a rule that seems to him sound, but that more likely than not will not cover all the cases it should. Phenomenologically, we can build on a feeling of what does or does not go together concretely, but not on a general rule. Rules of language are at best the ex post facto discoveries of lexicographers and grammarians. But even lexicographers qua lexicographers do not set up any prescriptive rules. They merely report about actual practice, though about a more or less selected practice, e.g., of "educated people." Certainly a dictionary does not consist of prescriptive rules, not even in an abridged form, though its users may treat what the lexicographer reports as a guide for their future language behavior.[1] The only place where in English one may find reliable information about such matters is in H. W. Fowler's *Modern English Usage* or in its American counterpart, Marjorie Nicholson's *American-English Usage*. Yet even these works do not state imperative rules but mostly offer more or less tolerant advice, supported by examples of what the authors consider bad and good practice.

In view of this situation I take the whole emphasis on rules as the backbone of all language, especially of ordinary language, to be something of a myth, which it is time to challenge. This cult of rules is apt to impair our direct access to the phenomena, even in the case of such cultural phenomena as language.

Now this same thing is happening in ethics too. There is nothing wrong about the new interest in an intensive study of the language of morals, and I believe that even phenomenology has a lot to learn from this and can use it as a guide for a fuller study of the phenomena. But the question is whether in some of the present interpretations of ethical language the place of the rules has not been vastly exaggerated.

My first question with regard to this situation is: How important are rules in our actual moral experience and practice? It may well be true that whenever we try to justify our specific beliefs or actions we are apt to refer to general reasons. But usually this happens only in special situations when we are being challenged. Apart from them, I think that in our conduct we rarely, if ever, are explicitly or even implicitly aware of rules, and we could produce them only after considerable reflection. Even in moral verbalizing, social or merely in soliloquy, rules or prescriptions do not often figure. We

---

[1] For this and other problems, see, for example, C. Douglas McGee, "A Word for Dictionaries," *Mind*, LXIX (1960), 14–30.

might say: "This is mean." "That is admirable." "I must do so-and-so." But usually such phrases are related only in a very indirect fashion to rules. Hence I suspect that even in ethics we have become the victims of the rule myth, and that this myth is apt to distort the picture of our actual moral life.

However, a much more basic question has to be raised about this new rule-centered ethics: What are the logical structure and the status of these postulated moral rules? For not only are such terms as "rules" or "principles," as far as I can see, not sufficiently analyzed for their meaning and structure; in fact, they do not seem to be considered as in need of such analysis but taken as primitive concepts. In particular, I find myself wondering: Are these rules supposed to be regulations set up by a rulemaker and hence essentially dependent on his decision and enactment? Or are they considered to be norms which are not made but discovered by us in the process of ethical reflection, without any obvious relation to a rulemaker? I find in the major literature no clear and explicit answers to these questions.

To go one step further: rules and prescriptions are primarily logical structures, in that respect comparable to propositional statements. As statements refer to ontological states of affairs, or facts, which they claim to describe ("picture"), so rules refer to states of affairs which are to conform to these rules.[2] Now what is the status of these "ruled" states of affairs as outlined (or "depicted") in the rules? Do they depend on the rules, are they in this sense rule-made, or are they independent of these rules, autonomous and in that case antecedent to and independent of the rules which merely reflect them?

However, I do not intend to let myself be diverted into a full-

---

[2] The pattern underlying this analysis is actually none other than the one developed by Ludwig Wittgenstein in the *Tractatus*, International Library of Psychology, Philosophy, and Scientific Method (London, 1922), 2.01 ff., 3 ff., 3.1 ff., with its distinction of *Sachverhalt* (state of affairs or atomic fact) from *Gedanke* (thought), as expressed in the *Satz* (proposition). But it is based on the prior analyses of Edmund Husserl, especially in *Logische Untersuchungen* (Halle: Max Niemeyer, 1900), Vol. I, chap. xi, and Alexander Pfänder, *Logik, Jahrbuch für Philosophie und Phänomenologische Forschung*, Vol. IV (Halle: Max Niemeyer, 1921), and applied by Roman Ingarden to the literary work of art in *Das litterarische Kunstwerk* (Halle: Max Niemeyer, 1931; 2nd rev. ed, Tübingen, 1960), and to the normative field in my *Gesetz und Sittengesetz* (Zurich: Nierans, 1935). See also my *The Phenomenological Movement* (The Hague: Martinus Nijhoff, 1960; 2nd ed., 1965), pp. 95 ff.

fledged study of the logic of rules. I confess that I still consider the time excessive that I spent on the study of the logic of the laws, moral and nonmoral, in proportion to the need for the study of what is ruled or outlined by the law, i.e., the ontology of what corresponds to the rules or laws in the sense of the things ruled or ordered. So what I want to do here is to explore directly the phenomena to which the rules as their expressions refer and which I shall designate as the phenomena of normative order. I want to show first the difference between two basic types of normative order, artificial order or arrangement, and "natural," i.e., nonartificial, order. I shall then concentrate on the natural orders and try to show their essential structure by analyzing at least one basic type of such order. Finally, I shall try to offer at least an installment of a phenomenological justification of these ontological affirmations, if only to acknowledge an epistemological debt that will have to be paid much more thoroughly in the future.

Some remarks about the general nature of order may seem to be "in order" before discussing normative orders and their kinds in particular. But this might easily develop into a full-sized paper, if not into a book. So, in the present context I shall be content with giving a definition meant as a presupposition for the following discussion, but subject to subsequent re-examination. By "order" in general, then, I shall understand any pattern formed by a number of adjoining elements.

From now on my concern will be with the kind of pattern that I have called "normative or ideal order." A normative order, as I conceive of it, is one that is not merely self-contained, but that serves as a model for, and in this sense "appeals" to, empirical reality either by wanting it to conform or by permitting it to conform or *not* to conform. At this point we may leave the cases of permissive and prohibitive orders in abeyance. The outstanding cases are clearly those orders which constitute ideal models for reality. Hence, from now on I shall concentrate on normative or ought-orders, as I shall call them.

Among the normative orders I discern a fundamental difference according to the nature and ground of the ordering relationship within them. Perhaps the best way of approaching these two types is by utilizing a linguistic difference, if only to show that even the phenomenologist can learn from the linguistic approach. The difference I have in mind is actually peculiar to the English language. Nevertheless, to my knowledge no attention has been paid to it. I mean the difference between the use of the words "shall" and "ought," respectively. "Should" or "must" can usually be substituted for "ought," though there may be less urgency expressed in the case of the latter word.

Consider a rule such as, "All legislative power shall be invested in Congress." What difference would it make if we replaced "shall be" by "ought to be"? Contrariwise, consider a sentence such as, "Promises ought not to be given lightly." What change in meaning would occur if we substituted a "shall" for the "ought"?

I submit that the differences would be striking. But how are they to be described? As I see it, the fundamental difference is in the kind of order that these sentences project. The shall-sentence, characteristic of all statutory regulations,[3] sets forth an order in which the referents of the subject and predicate are put into a new relationship, not yet determined by their natures: it takes the "shall" to bring it about. It "fixes" it by bestowing on it a certain artificial stability. Of course there may be good reasons for putting them in such a relationship. But without such an establishment this relation does not exist. It is the special act of ordering that establishes such an order or arrangement.

It is quite different in the case of the ought- or should-sentences, which are conspicuous by their absence from statutory language. Here the relationship is one that the sentence merely expresses or reflects. In this sense I maintain that, in contrast to shall-sentences, ought-sentences are descriptive and make a claim to being true. Thus it is simply not true to say that promises may be given from

---

[3] It seems worth pointing out that the verb "shall" does not occur in ethics, except in the form of the ethical question "What shall I (or we) do?" but not in the answers to it, or in the second or third person form of the question, where "should" or "ought" are appropriate. This is true even of such authors as H. P. Nowell-Smith and R. M. Hare, who consider the question "What shall I do?" as fundamental for ethics. Nowell-Smith's distinction between "shall" and "ought" (*Ethics* [New York: Penguin Books, 1954], pp. 267–68) strikes me as not even in accord with ordinary English, where the "I shall" can be substituted for the "I ought" only when a prediction is justified or when "I am told." I feel much closer to the position of Wilfrid Sellars in "Imperatives, Intentions, and 'Ought'" (in *Morality and the Language of Conduct*, ed. H. N. Castañeda and G. Naknikian [Detroit, Mich.: Wayne State University Press, 1963]), who thinks that "shall" and its kindred express intentions of the speaker (p. 196) and "that the language of morals differs from the language which simply expresses the speaker's intentions" (p. 199).

mere politeness, without regard to our chances of fulfilling them. But what is here described? This is where the proper task of a phenomenology of "natural" order begins.

Now before turning from words to things let me point out that while other languages are not so fortunate as English in having such a clear difference between two normative terms, they have at least unambiguous equivalents for the descriptive "ought." Greek has two such auxiliary verbs (*dein* and *chren*), Latin has *oportere* and *debere,* French *devoir* and *falloir.* In German, *sollen* is typically ambiguous and occurs both in law and in ethics. But here, as in other languages, there are less ambiguous phrases equivalent to the English "it is proper, fitting, becoming, appropriate." Such sentences make claims to truth, which may very well be challenged and contested and, at least supposedly, supported and justified.

Let me also supply some direct illustrations of both arrangements and natural orders, independent of linguistic clues, before turning to a structural analysis of natural order. I shall try to present these as a gradated series.

We are becoming uncomfortably accustomed to certain strange arrangements of bits of flat objects such as pieces of newspaper, cloth, pressed flowers, and other artifacts under the name of collages, whose composite effect may or may not make sense to the unprepared observer, even if it does to the arranger. Perhaps most interesting are the elaborate "arrangements" which are set up by some children around the age of five, in which they line up their favorite possessions in patterns totally incomprehensible to an outsider, but all the more sacrosanct and jealously defended against playmates and elders who would try to upset this private world.

I submit that most of these configurations have a highly personal character. Apart from the wills of their designers they would be inconceivable, and without our knowledge of them often not even recognizable as arrangements. For there is here no intrinsic and intelligible link between one component and another, even if ex post facto a certain sense, e.g., an aesthetic sense, may be discovered. This would be definitely the case of the kind of "floral arrangements" developed by the Japanese. Even then it remains true that there can be no arrangement without an arranger who projects into it his personal election and "touch."

Now for some illustrations of natural order as contrasted with mere arrangements. Here I should like to introduce first a transitional case, again taken from the range of human affairs. Consider the patterns of objects on an orderly or a messy desk. These, too, are of course arrangements. However, some of them have the character of orderliness, others do not. Orderliness is most conspicuous when the piles of objects are neatly set apart. Such superficial order, however, which may delight the housewife but distress the working scholar, is not the only possible one. What may look like a perfect mess may be a very meaningful order because of the logical relation among books, papers, and letters pertaining to the same project. And such an arrangement, in spite of its messy appearance, may be preferable to one with all the looks of neatness. However, the important point is here that, as it now appears, not all arrangements are on the same level. Some of them display an intrinsic, natural order, recognizable as such even to the uninformed outsider, which others do not.

This kind of natural order is even more clearly displayed in nonhuman nature. Some of the indiscriminate enthusiasm for the order in nature may have little foundation in concrete experience. But even so the order in the configurations of a snow crystal, of the parts of a flower or fruit, or in the symmetry of an organism, must strike even the most skeptical observer as outstanding examples of nonartificial order.

Order in this sense can be perceived even before and without any thought of an orderer or arranger. For here the order is determined by the mutual relations of the components, as they fit together or at least add up to an overarching gestalt or configuration. Of course the realization of such an order in actual fact has its causes, which may well include a realizer of such order as distinguished from an order maker. But the ideal order itself admits no such order-making agent. At best he can confirm and support it. He cannot create it.

What I believe to have shown thus far is that not only in our language but in a direct approach to the phenomena we have evidence of two kinds of normative order, artificial and natural. I do not yet claim that I have established the actual existence of such orders, particularly of the natural order, whatever "actual existence" may mean in this case. It could still be that all this is merely phenomenal, especially since a purely phenomenological approach must leave this whole question of existence in suspense. But even the essential structure of these phenomena is still unexplored. As a matter of fact, we do not yet even know whether they have a structure that could be analyzed and possibly defined. Only too often in recent ethical theory it has been asserted and accepted that the "ought" as well as the "good" are indefinable and unanalyzable. The only valid test of such assertions would be the actual attempt at analysis. It is toward the testing of such assertions that the subsequent parts of this paper are meant to contribute.

However, in the present context I shall limit this undertaking to a particular kind of normative order, which is usually neglected in Anglo-American ethics—the ought-to-be. I consider this type not only simpler but more basic than what is usually given as the prototype of normative order, i.e., the ought-to-do or duty.

Actually, the existence of the ought-to-be as an independent element of ethics was first clearly stated by Henry Sidgwick. Subsequently, even such intuitionist philosophers as G. E. Moore, C. D. Broad, and W. D. Ross soon reduced it to a conditional ought-to-do or duty. It enjoyed increasing recognition in Continental ethics, not only in Max Scheler's and Nicolai Hartmann's phenomenological ethics, but also in Alexius Meinong's theory of objects. From this latter source it seems to have received new impetus in J. N. Findlay's emphasis on the importance of the wish and its ideal correlates.

Let us first survey this field by way of examples. Sidgwick introduces the following instance: "I sometimes judge that I 'ought' to know what a wiser man would know, or feel as a better man would feel, in my place, though I may know that I could not directly produce in myself such knowledge or feeling by any effort of will." [4] While this seems to me a very illuminating start, I see no good reason for restricting the ought-to-be to the range of human knowing or feeling. Thus I submit that, regardless of the poor chances of quick realization, there is a widespread conviction that there ought to be no unemployment or poverty, that a person ought to be free and in good health. Once one has gone so far, I see no reason to deny that even beings other than human may be the beneficiaries of such ought-to-be orders. Thus we may be convinced that living beings should not suffer needlessly, and perhaps even that some nonliving things ought to be preserved for their own sake. It may be more than pious wishing to believe that the universe should allow for meaning, that life should be worth living, and the like. There are after all not merely "fatuous" but "legitimate" wishes. In this

[4] Henry Sidgwick, *The Methods of Ethics* (7th ed., rev. by Constance Jones; Chicago, Ill.: University of Chicago Press, 1962), p. 33.

context one should also remember Kant's postulates of practical reason in the interest of a proper balance between virtue and happiness. Perhaps the ideal ought-to-be is one of the deepest and most valid motivations for the ontological proof of the existence of an all-perfect being, only that its advocates were too quick to infer from an *ought* to an *is,* something which one might feel tempted to call the supernaturalistic fallacy.

In thus expanding the range of the ought-to-be far beyond that of the moral ought-to-do, I do not mean to exclude the latter from the wider sphere. However, the ought-to-do adds to the ought-to-be a distinctive element, that of obligation or duty. But it does not do so in all cases of moral conduct. There is the range of ideal actions "beyond the call of duty," for which we can claim at best ideal oughtness matched by meritoriousness in the case of supererogatory efforts, not strict obligation.

If thus the range of ideal oughtness extends far beyond the merely moral ought-to-do, this does not imply that for a finite being such as man there is much point in speculating about oughtness on a cosmic scale, as long as he does not see at least a remote chance of doing something about it and taking responsibility. Cosmic fault-finding may be just as silly as cosmic adulation. Restraint in matters of deontological speculation about the ought-to-be on a cosmic scale may actually be the content of an ideal, if not an ethical, ought, and this not only because of man's limited insight. Preoccupation with such matters may interfere with man's proper self-development and mental and moral health; it may also make him look plain ridiculous.

Yet, no matter how far we stretch the range of the ideal ought-to-be, the main need in the present context is to understand its essential structure and to describe it, if only as a means to guide the reader to its verifying re-examination. The first thing to realize in this respect is that the ideal ought-to-be is by no means a simple, unstructured affair. Even a preliminary look at the examples above should make it plain that what is meant by such sentences as "man ought to be free" is not a homogeneous object, but a differentiated situation. Such sentences point to a pattern comparable to, if not symmetrical with, the one referred to by an is-statement. Hence the proper way for investigating the correlate of the ought-statement is to compare it with the factual state of affairs in its articulation of subject referent, predicate referent, and copula referent, which may be designated as "substratum," "attribute," and "ontic bond."

Seen in this light, the ideal ought-to-be, or oughtness for short, is at least a tripartite configuration. There is no ought by itself, but it is always the ought of something with regard to something else. More specifically, it is the oughtness of a certain attribute with regard to a certain substratum. What occurs in our consciousness is a complex of an ought-substratum, an ought-attribute, and the ought-connection between them, never an "ought" by itself. We might call this complex an ought-situation or a normative state of affairs. It obviously differs from a merely factual state of affairs. For in an ought-complex the attribute does not simply attach to, or inhere in, its substratum. Rather does it belong to it in a peculiar, nonfactual sense. Even if the attribute "free" does not actually attach to man, ideally it belongs to him. What does such belonging mean?

Let us first take a look at the other constituents of the ought-situation, the ought-substratum and the ought-attribute, which, ideally, belong to such a situation.

In their intrinsic structure these members of the ought-relation do not differ from the members of a factual state of affairs. It is only that in the ought-situation they assume new roles, the substratum the role of being material for an ought, the attribute the role of a form to be imposed on this material. There would be little gained by probing further into this change of roles. But it may be worth pointing out that in principle every type of being—not only persons, but also impersonal objects, properties, relations, and complexes—can be a substratum for an ought-to-be. It is even more important to realize that oughtness is not restricted to what is not yet real. It is true that oughtness is most obtrusive where reality does not, or does not yet, conform to it. But this must not mislead us into thinking that only things not yet in being can be substrata of oughtness. There is no contradiction in saying "Thus it is, and thus it ought to be." Hegel's bold thesis about the reasonableness of all there is does not by any means imply the dissolution of all oughtness. The only thing that may be safely asserted is that, wherever reality does not comply with oughtness, it undergoes a peculiar modification of oughtness, acquires a special "charge," for which Nicolai Hartmann coined the term "the actualized ought."

There is likewise no limitation in principle on ought-attributes as far as oughtness is concerned. Any attribute that is otherwise compatible with its substratum, whether simple, complex, or relational, can be the content of an ought-attribute.

Thus the decisive and distinctive element in an ought-situation is clearly located in the peculiar relation between ought-substratum and ought-attribute. This peculiar component might be called the ought-factor.

Now, this factor is not a structurally independent, self-contained entity. It is not a part, dependent or independent, of any being, nor a property comparable to a color or even a gestalt character. Specifically, it differs in structure from a value property, to be intuited or felt, such as nobleness or prettiness. Nor can it be a special mode of being or reality. It does not make sense to say that something "ought," as one can say that something is real or nonreal. "What is it that it ought to be?" would be the obvious retort to such an incomplete sentence.

Clearly, then, the ought-factor requires complementation. But what kind of complementation? It is not enough simply to add the ought-attribute. It would not do to assert "man ought free." We have to say "he ought *to be* free." And this is not merely a matter of linguistic convention. The ought-factor does not simply link up with a property. It is directed toward the being, or more precisely toward the existence, of this property in a given substratum. For in order that something can *be* such and such, it first has to *exist*. Existence is therefore the primary complement of the ought-factor. Each statement about oughtness is primarily one about an ought-to-exist.[5]

However, the fact that the ought-factor calls primarily for supplementation by the form of existence does not yet adequately describe its structure and its function. The ought-factor also calls for a special relation between the ought-substratum and the ought-attribute. In an ought-situation the two are not simply statically together as in a factual state of affairs. As I just pointed out, whether they are so in fact is irrelevant to the fundamental ought-situation. However, independent of this factual link, substratum and attribute are connected by a very different kind of bond, which I shall call an ought-bond.[6] It links the attribute to the substratum in such a way

[5] This point has already been made by Everett W. Hall, *What Is Value?* (London: Routledge and Kegan Paul, 1952), pp. 172–73.

[6] While the term "bond" clearly involves a metaphor, I submit that this metaphor has its foundation in the common element which such a situation has

that the two belong together, and require one another, more precisely that the attribute belongs to the substratum. Thus the ought-bond, in contrast to the static is-bond, has a dynamic character. Metaphorically, one might talk of attraction and even of elastic attraction, in view of the increased attraction in the case of a conflict with reality. In any case, the bond runs from the substratum to the attribute and ties it to the former, not vice versa. In this sense the relation is an asymmetric one.

This directedness of the dynamic ought-bond does not yet describe its complete function. True, the ought-situation does not depend on the factual state of affairs. But, as the linguistic evidence indicates, the ideal ought is not indifferent or neutral toward the existent world. On the contrary it is directed toward the realization of a state of affairs in which the ought-attribute would actually inhere in and not only ideally belong to the ought-substratum, a state of affairs in which men not only ought to be free, but actually *are* free. Metaphorically speaking, the ideal bond presses toward the real bond and refers to it by way of aiming or at least supporting. Less figuratively speaking, the ought-bond is directed toward the actual union of ought-substratum and ought-attribute in a factual state of affairs, where they are connected by an is-bond. This factual state of affairs is the target of the dynamic ought-bond, the directedness toward it, its essential characteristic.

But this characterization does not yet clear up the peculiar quality of the ought-bond, and especially not its peculiar dynamism. It is relatively easy to describe it by what it is not. It is certainly not a real bond with causal efficacy and power capable of actually bringing about the unification of substratum and attribute. Only by the intercession of a real agent, who would contribute his efforts toward the realization of the ideal ought, and to the fastening of the ideal bond, could it achieve this feat. Nor can the ought-factor prevent the occurrence of a state of affairs opposed to the ideal ought. However, such an opposition would not annihilate the ideal ought but might even intensify or actualize it. Thus the dynamics of the ought-bond is definitely not real. It is in a characteristic and specific sense "ideal."

The term "ideal" does, of course, little else but block out the

with a physical, e.g., a chemical bond. This nonphysical bond appears most clearly in the case of the moral ought, especially the ought-to-do of duty, where words such as "obligation" (from Latin *ligare*) contain the idea of a tie.

frame for this peculiar phenomenon. It says little more than that the ideal is not real. When it comes to describing it directly and positively, little can be done but to point to the experience in its concrete fullness, and to appeal for direct intuiting. In evoking vividly the situation when we experience the "pressure" of an ought, we might apprehend not only the *sui generis* character of this pressure, but also its peculiar demand character. There is no denying that here we have reached the limits of conceptual description. However, metaphorical expressions cautiously applied might help. So can analogies. Thus the kind of pressure which a proposition like "If *A* entails *B* and *B* entails *C*, then necessarily *A* entails *C*" exerts on our thinking may be compared with the ought-pressure to which I referred. Enough if this example can show that there are ideal phenomena other than those of ideal oughtness.

The ultimate unanalyzability and indefinability of the ideal bond does not imply that oughtness as a complex ought-situation cannot be analyzed and even defined in terms of this bond. Two essential features of the ought-to-be situation have now been identified: its polarization toward a factual state of affairs, i.e., toward the actual union of ought-substratum and ought-attribute in a real situation, and the ideal-dynamic character of this polarization. One could even define it as the complex of a substratum and a form held together by a peculiar bond that presses ideally toward their union in a factual state of affairs. But phenomenologically there would be little merit in such condensing definitions, whose communicative value, short of adequate guides to intuiting, would be doubtful indeed. Besides, ever so many features of the phenomenon will be squeezed out in as selective a device as a definition. And it is the full richness of the phenomenon in which phenomenology and phenomenological ontology are interested. The main point here was to show that such a philosophy does not have to capitulate before phenomena like oughtness because of their alleged unanalyzability and indefinability, as analytic moral philosophy and even moral intuitionism have so often done.

What, then, has been achieved in this sample analysis, sketchy as it has been? At least the structure of one normative ideal order has been explored, the ideal ought-to-be. But, apart from the need for further details, only the essence of this order has been discussed, not its existence. It may still be that what we mean by this order will ultimately turn out to be only a subjective figment. No premature claims in this sense are justified as yet, and there will have to be a careful study of the modes of being to which it may possibly lay claim. Also, nothing has as yet been done to show what the possible grounds of ideal oughtness are. This may turn out to be not so easy as seems to be usually assumed when, e.g., value is defined as what ought to be for its own sake. There may be values of such a delicate and exalted nature that their full realization would actually be a danger to them.

This is not the place to take up such unfinished business. Instead I would like to touch on one aspect of the theory of oughtness that may help a little in buttressing the preceding analyses. Many of these will appear not only unfamiliar—which might be all in their favor—but also highly artificial. In fact the charge of ontological, if not metaphysical, constructivism would not surprise me. To meet it fully, much more space and more time would be needed, especially time to reflect in order to test and verify the suggestions contained in my descriptive account.

Verification in this sense is indeed the crux of the matter. In order to facilitate it I should at least make a first effort to clear the approaches, and specifically to indicate in what manner one can become directly aware of ideal oughtness. This is one reason why I should like to outline here how phenomenology proper, in the sense of the description of the consciousness of normative orders and of their modes of givenness, can become an aid in the verification of ontological claims. For what I have offered thus far is in a sense only ontology, a description of *what* is given in the sense of the objective entities that we believe we see, without regard to the question of how they were given. We also have to pay attention to the ways of givenness, to watch and describe how these entities are perceived or otherwise given, how adequately or inadequately they are before us. This may also help us in looking for more adequate ways of approaching them. It will be of even greater importance in making a reasoned estimate of the certainty of our supposed knowledge, in other words, for epistemology.

In this spirit, then, I should like to give at least a few such suggestions for a phenomenology of normative order. Let us, for example, reflect on the kinds of acts in which we seem to become aware of such an ought situation as that man ought to be free.[7]

[7] I may add here that any other example of the type mentioned above, such as Sidgwick's, would do equally well. In fact since, as one of my students pointed

First, evoke the "picture" of man with all his potentialities of initiative, creativeness, and choice, or, more specifically, a child with all his playfulness and exuberance; also evoke the "picture" of freedom with all it involves by way of allowing its owner to make use of these potentialities, or, in the child's case, to romp and laugh. Now allow the two elements of the situation to "merge" and yield the "picture" of a freely functioning person. In so doing watch for their "reaction" to each other, notably whether at this point a certain mutual attraction, repulsion, or mere acceptance develops. Such watching has of course to be a watching for the peculiar kind of relation designated by oughtness, as distinguished from mere factual compatibility, necessity, or impossibility. "Requiredness," "fittingness," or "suitability" are other familiar words indicating the kind of phenomenon to which we must "tune in."

By way of imaginative counterexperiment, substitute now for freedom its opposite, unfreedom, with all its frustrations for its victim, say a galley slave or a member of a chain gang, or a child like Oliver Twist sent off to a workhouse. Then let it "interact" with the "picture" of man and watch for the "effect." It may be that such a counterexperiment in the imagination, if not in reality, as in concentration camps, will induce the best realization of oughtness.

Now the act in which this relation is found is certainly peculiar. It is neither a purely theoretical nor a purely emotional consciousness. Actually, it may have a certain similarity to the way in which, on a merely factual level, we perceive the fitting or not fitting of pieces in a puzzle, except that the kind of fitting here involved is nothing visual or tactual, but a special way of "sensing," to use a rather general but not inappropriate term. There are certainly all sorts of degrees of clarity and concreteness with which such a relation may be given. Its full presentation presupposes the full visualization of its ingredients. Taking account of the various modes of presentation and the various perspectives in which the phenomena can appear may even throw some light on the differences of opinion about normative order and suggest ways of reducing them.

Nevertheless, one may still feel puzzled about the strange kind of perception to which I am appealing. It certainly requires a much more penetrating investigation. Once the positivistic monopoly of

out to me, Dostoevski's Grand Inquisitor contested the ideal of freedom for reasons which do need weighing, even his implied antithesis (man ought to be under the control of the Church) could serve as an example.

sense perception has been broken, and such perceptions as those of time, relations, and values have been admitted, there is no good reason for rejecting the idea of a perception of normative order out of hand. Only critical self-observation can give the final answer.

What I would like to suggest, however, before leaving the matter in the lap of the reader, is that the kind of experience here suggested is by no means as unheard of as it may seem. I referred before to the distinction between various types of order (and disorder) as one with which we are familiar from everyday experience. How, then, are these phenomena given to our consciousness? Apparently we have some kind of awareness of how things do or do not belong together—even without, and independent of, previous experience. We immediately sense the order or disorder in concrete situations. Something in us is offended or gratified when we encounter such configurations. What is it? Is this the phenomenon behind what we commonly call our sense of order? Exploring this sense, which is anything but a merely emotional affair, may prove to be the key to even more important insights into the phenomenology of order.[8]

[8] The main argument of this paper is based on my unpublished book on the philosophical foundations of moral rights and duties, of which a German version is to appear at Martinus Nijhoff, The Hague, as a continuation of a book on law and moral law *(Gesetz und Sittengesetz: Vorstudien zu einer gesetzesfreien Ethik)* , which first appeared in Zurich in 1935.

For suggestions and criticisms I am particularly indebted to my colleague William Forthman, now at San Fernando Valley State College, who discussed this paper in a departmental colloquium, and to my friend Carl Wellmann of Lawrence University.

Order in Language, Learning, and Personality

W. DONALD OLIVER

Order and Personality

No pair of distinctions is more common, or more troublesome, in modern philosophy than the metaphysical between mind and matter and the epistemological between the subjective and the objective. Mind has been treated as if it were a place, a locus, a container, as space is the container for material things and physical events. It is a queer kind of locus, to be sure, for while it makes good sense to speak of a book as being in a room, or Chicago as in Illinois, the phrase, "in the mind" yields no clear picture of containedness to thoughtful analysis. Just *where* is a thought when it is in a mind? Or a fancy? Or a purpose or a plan? The anomalies generated by this application of a spatial metaphor to the "contents" of a mind have driven the behaviorists and positivists to suppress all references to mind, either as container or agent. What is, is what can be assigned definite spatial location; what cannot, is not. Refusal to talk about a puzzle is a way of suppressing, not of eliminating, it. The problem is there whether we care to admit its presence or not. The spatial connotation of "in" in "in the mind" may be unfortunate, but the distinction marked by the phrases "in the mind" and

W. DONALD OLIVER has long taught philosophy at the University of Missouri, but he is now enjoying life more without the chores of chairmanship. His specialty is theory of knowledge, and he has contributed notable papers on abstraction, and the relation of philosophy to psychology. Professor Oliver is best known for his *Theory of Order* (1951).

"in the world" is one that we cannot do without. The most unfortunate consequence of the elimination of mind, either as a container or as a concept meaningful in any of the senses that could be given it, is complete blockage of any attempt to deal with the person or the self as if it were a legitimate metaphysical entity. Indeed, as I shall try to show, a large part of the "content" of the self is precisely that which is traditionally located "in the mind." With this eliminated, there is no possibility of assembling the self from the remaining fragments.

A brief examination of the subjective-objective dichotomy will reveal its weaknesses. It may also suggest what might be done to strengthen it, or to replace it with other distinctions that will more adequately meet the needs it has been serving. "This is my opinion," I say, or, "This is a thought that just crossed my mind." Again, "I may only have imagined that he sneered when he said that," or, "I haven't made up my mind yet whether he is telling the truth or not." These expressions give clear warning that what is being reported is not to be taken as "objective fact," fact about the world at large, though they may be read as reporting facts about myself, about my internal mental states and indecisions. Here, in short, is a kind of content—thought, imagination, supposition—that is appropriately locatable within an individual but not within the world, except in the secondary, often problematic, sense that what is in an individual is also in the world. These expressions indicate the need for a distinction between something's being located in the world, in the flat sense of spatial inclusion, and its being located within a self as a thought, image, opinion, or, in general, a "mental event." Nor is the problem exclusively one of location. It is vastly complicated by the fact that often what is "within the self" is claimed to be also located in the world in that flat spatial sense. Consider, "I saw him sneer." This reports an "objective fact," the fact of the sneer as well as the fact that I observed it. Both the fact and I as observer of it are in the world. The "I saw it" merely records the fact that what happened in the world did not go unobserved. It accounts, in a sense, for the fact that the sneer is now on record and in no sense is to be taken as an explanation for the sneer, and, in the ordinary case, neither is it to be taken as evidence for the asserted fact that he did sneer. The professional doubter—the epistemologist—may transform it into evidence by advancing the claim that what was seen was not something in the world but something within the observer, a percept, image or "mental event," and that it was from this that he concluded that a sneer had occurred as an objective event. But it is not our intent when we report such a fact to offer "our percept" as evidence. We simply report, and, if what is reported is accepted as fact, that is the end of the matter.

Now compare "I saw him sneer" with "I thought I saw him sneer." The latter leaves the objective fact in doubt. That is, it leaves the question of the location of the fact, as one attaching to the world or to my inward experience, undecided. Of the inward experience I may be certain, but I am not prepared to vouch for the external fact. This uncertainty about what did happen in the world need not reflect primary doubt about the world. It is there all right, we are accustomed to say, and what happened in it did happen. What we doubt is that what we experienced is to be located in it rather than in ourselves. In expressing this uncertainty we are both registering awareness of the fact that we have something to do with locating an item in the world or in us, and confessing an inability to determine its proper locus.

Here I merely wish to point to the impasse in which the epistemologist finds himself the moment he attempts to generalize the situation I have been describing. Let the suspicion creep in that not only *this* bit of content, which I am admittedly unable to place in the world or in myself, but every other bit that finds its way into my experience has to be assigned a place by my dictum, and the very meaning of the inside and the outside of the self begins to drain off into nonsense. If whatever we experience as outside was put there by ourselves, then the outside, for each of us, actually exists on the inside, it being no more than a region of consciousness to which the conceptual label, "world" is applied. What is a member of the world is what I have decided is, and whatever is so abjectly dependent on the decision of a man must surely be a thing of his own creation!

It was for reasons such as these that William James suggested that we abandon the notion of things that *by their nature* belong in the world and others that belong in the mind.[1] He did not contest the distinction itself, but he reduced it to one of orders.[2] A mental

[1] William James, *Essays in Radical Empiricism* (New York: Longmans, Green and Co., 1912).

[2] "Order" is not the term James employed. He spoke simply of systems of relations. But my use of "order" appears to do no violence to his thought.

thing, he said, stands in different relations to other things from those of a physical thing. The one enters into a different order of phenomena from that of the other, though there is no reason why the same thing, as content of consciousness, cannot enter into both orders. What I see—a table, say—may be both a denizen of the physical world, because it is a member of the physical order of persistent, causally interrelated things, and of my mental world, because it persists as a memory and takes its place among the other events that stock my mind, behaving, as they do, in accordance with the laws of mental things. James did not live to develop this pregnant idea. Those who have taken it seriously—Bertrand Russell is chief among them—have scarcely turned it into something altogether creditable. I think there is a reason for the failure of James's theory to win general acceptance. In the *Essays in Radical Empiricism* he is too exclusively concerned with the issues that dominated philosophy at the turn of the century to envision the wealth of speculative ideas his use of orders was capable of spawning.[3] His radical empiricism was advanced, indeed, as a cure for a disease, as a way of avoiding the paradoxes that epistemology faced in his day. Certainly he was a man capable of looking behind and beyond any narrow purpose, but in this case he did not succeed in breaking the grip of the immediate problem. Probably because he was a scientifically trained psychologist, he saw the "law of mind" as unitary, fixed, and objective, just as he did not venture to suggest that there might be any ambiguity about the laws of physical nature. The mental was what fitted into the order of mental events, which order, apparently, could become altogether evident to the psychologist, and the physical was that which fitted, in similar unambiguous fashion, into the order of physical events. Thus there existed two orders, two sets of laws, with no problem of distinguishing between *them,* though there could occur ambiguous membership (objectively ambiguous, it should be noted) of an item of experience in both orders.

Now ambiguity of membership is not at all the same thing as

---

[3] James is no stranger to speculation. It could be asserted that in *The Varieties of Religious Experience* (New York: Longmans, Green and Co., 1935) and *A Pluralistic Universe* (New York: Longmans, Green and Co., 1909) he is exploring the opening offered by his radical empiricism. Still, he kept his "speculative" and his "positivistic" selves from public communication with one another. If his radical empiricism in any way stimulated his speculation, it seems to have been on the subconscious level of his mind.

ambiguity of orders. An item might behave partly as if it were a mental thing and partly as if it were physical, and then, if we were to insist on placing it in one category or the other and not in both, we would be in a quandary. But suppose that, instead of there being two distinct orders, the *orders* of the two realms were so intertwined as not to be unambiguously distinguishable. James attempted to solve the classical problem of interaction between mind and body by accepting items to common membership in the order of mind and that of body. In this way the orders themselves come to be related without ceasing each to be itself. The causality of the interaction had already vanished under the familiar Humean treatment, and it was probably because it had that James saw the possibility of separating the two "realms" by a distinction between principles of order as such a simple one. When he was in the phenomenological mood that characterizes *Essays in Radical Empiricism,* he saw all order as something given. It is simply there in the relations that items of experience take on as they occur.

Before I go on to say why I do not find the distinction between the order of the physical world and that of the mind to be an easy and simple one, I shall point out another respect in which James altered the status of the mental and the physical, this time, I think, for the better. He really leaves no occasion for further puzzlement over the problem with which I began this paper. There are two orders, not two realms. We do not have to conceive one set of entities as occupying space and another that strange medium called mind. Space and mind are not containing media, but are designative categories that merely tell us in what system of relations an item occurs. Hence there is no need to ask how a mind can be located in space by association with a body, while what it contains, as mental content, has no necessity of spatial relationship. The same comment applies to time. Memories can attach to bygone times, fancies to no world time at all; present percepts to a definite position in space (and time), fancies to no position in physical space, though they may have positions in a space and time of their own.

I return now to what I consider James's artificially sharp distinction between orders of mind and matter. If attention is not centered upon the general problem of reconciling a universal realm of matter with a universal realm of mind, without reducing either to the other, but, rather, is directed to specific problems faced by the individual as he seeks to disentangle the "objective" from the "subjective" within his experience, it will be found that more than the two categories, "mental" and "physical," are required. Within the scope of the philosopher's "mental," numerous distinctions have to be made. Chief among these are distinctions between modes—ways in which a given content is "held in mind." Some content occurs as idle fancy, some as contributory to a plan that has already been adopted, some as component in a plan that is under tentative consideration. These are not unimportant differences, though they are likely to be considered such when it is their status as mental content that is alone at issue. It is likely that what has obscured their importance is the practice of carrying into the mental realm the same habits that have been developed for dealing "objectively" with materials of the physical realm. Physical things are supposed to be uninfluenced by the attitudes men take toward them. To find out what is there, we must abstract from our attitudes, and so, too, it is supposed that certain objectively describable bits of mental content occur, and that to find out what they are we must abstract from attitudes. Thus James writes as if any given bit of experience were just what it is in itself, and it is the relations into which it falls with other bits of experience that fix its nature as mental or material. Yet it makes a great deal of difference to us whether what we are thinking about is part of an order of idle fancy or one of serious planning, though in neither instance would we necessarily wish to argue that the content is other than mental.

In brief, my negative thesis is that the two categories, "physical" and "mental," though certainly important, shed little light on the orders into which the experiences of an individual actually fall. Still less do they permit us to account for the role of the individual in the imposition of orders on the stuff of his experience. Indeed, though I can utilize James's insight into the use of order as a discriminator to displace that of metaphysical stuffs, I cannot follow him further than this. I must reintroduce what he has firmly excluded: causation, in the old-fashioned, pre-Humean sense of that term. In the statement of my positive thesis, I shall regard the person as a causal agent, capable of manipulating not only what is mental in his experience, but also some of the items that, by the Jamesian criterion, would be classified as physical. But in treating the individual as a causal agent, I shall not suppose that he is a metaphysical entity injected into nature from an "external" supernatural realm, nor that he is "beyond change," or in any absolute sense independent of the exigencies he must face within the physical world. Nor is my intent, as was James's in his radical empiricism, wholly descriptive. Since it is my conviction that what a man believes has an effect upon his behavior, I cannot claim that any theory I have to offer, if accepted, would leave man exactly as he was before. Since this is so, I would prefer that my theory be one that, when believed and acted on, would improve man's chances of bettering himself and enriching the fund of values available in his environment.

My positive thesis is, first, that there is no such thing as human nature. There are only individuals, persons, who may be more or less like one another, more or less different, but who may also become more like or more different. Second, while there is a sense in which all men live in the same world, there is another in which they do not. To a degree each individual inhabits his own world, which may overlap the worlds of other men and will inevitably overlap those of some of his fellows more than those of others. The worlds of individuals are restricted, sometimes by accident, sometimes by conscious acts, sometimes by acts not performed with the purpose of restricting. Indeed, they can be restricted in many ways. There is nothing inherently wrong with the restricted world. It is probably the only kind of world a man can live in with any degree of comfort and assurance. It is, however, not in worlds that I am here interested, but in the ways in which they can be restricted and the relations of the type of restriction placed upon them to personality. Third, personal worlds are not only restricted, but structured. Two worlds that share the same boundaries are not necessarily of the same structure. What is admitted into the one can be admitted into the other, but not necessarily to the same position in each. There are many ways in which position can be assigned. That is to say, there are many kinds of position, and the structure of a world is largely characterized by the kind or kinds that are dominant in it. The structure of a personal world is not "objective" in the sense of being independent of the person whose world it is. Abstracted from that person, it may fall into discrete "pieces" that, of themselves, make no sense and constitute no world. The person bestows structure upon his world, or, at the least, he accepts a structure that another person or persons have bestowed upon a world common to them and him. Men live in the same world to the extent that objects found in the world of one are also in those of the others, but, since these objects need not occupy the same position in all of these worlds, they do not of themselves define a personal world. Thus personal worlds can be "contained" within a common world that is the locus of all the objects to be found in any personal world. Whether or not such a common world has a structure in abstraction from the personal worlds it contains I shall not try to decide, interesting though this question is.

After this series of didactic statements, a few words of explanation and apology are due the reader. I have been preparing the ground for discussion of a concept of order that is loose enough in its requirements to fit a great variety of structures. The "laws" sought by physicists and other natural scientists, and by the more positivistic psychologists, determine too simple and rigid a structure to yield an understanding of personal worlds. The sort of order I have in mind is one to which purpose, aspiration, and value are not strangers. What is more, this order is not abstractable from persons and personalities. It is, in a sense, imposed upon a personal world by the person, though it is also true that that person's inheritance from parents and society, and the objects that wander into his world from the outside in whose creation he has had no part, do much toward determining its structure. The structure, however, radiates outward from the person, reflecting his reactions to objects and foreign influences rather than the nature of those objects and influences. It is appropriate, in trying to describe the structure of a personal world, to comment first upon the ineptness of any attempt to assign it literally spatial outer boundaries or inner divisions. Though one can speak of what is outside and inside the self, in a figurative manner, one cannot follow structural bonds without crossing and recrossing conventional boundaries that have been set up for the self, the mind, or the physical organism. To get a fruitful perspective of the self and its world, one must steel oneself to a disregard of these boundaries. One must also steel oneself against the common assumption that order, to be order, must be perfect, and that whatever is ordered is fixed, frozen. One of the more striking characteristics of order in personal worlds and in personality is the prevalence of areas of vagueness, of change, of instability. These are not necessarily imperfections. Instabilities of certain kinds may be genuine constituents of structure when the latter is properly conceived. Nor is unity of the person necessarily assured. When the "internal" structure of personality is not set sharply apart from the structure of the world in which that person lives by as definite a boundary as the physical skin, unity of a person is seen to depend upon the structure of the world as well as upon that of the so-called psychic and emotional components of the self. It is not only that unity of the self must be achieved within this world, but also that the self cannot be unified without bringing the world to a corresponding state of unity. That is to say, there are no hard and fast boundaries that would make it possible for the self to tidy up its internal order without concerning itself with the order of its environing world. Unity of self is therefore always precarious, something never achieved in the desired degree of perfection, and always in need of renewal and defense.

What, then, are the bonds and boundaries that determine the structure of the self and its world? There are many; only a selected few can here be introduced by way of examples. One important type of bond is intent. It can be conceived as a kind of tension that, as it is relaxed or tightened, fixes limits or boundaries. There are certain areas of internal consciousness that are private to the individual, but they are not ineluctably private. What transpires in them can be held, secretively, within the bounds of that individual consciousness, or can be revealed through the interpersonal medium of language or through direct action. The intent of the person, rather than the nature of the content, fixes the boundary between the private and the public. Furthermore, intent that issues in action can accomplish the transformation of what were "mental" entities, either private to the person or shared with others by verbal objectification, into physical ones. The environment of modern man is replete with objects that were once but "ideas" in the minds of inventors, theorists, and social planners. The intent to keep a thought to ourselves, to reveal it in words, or to permit it to enlist us in action thus plays a role in structuring not only the self, but also its world and, incidentally, the worlds of other selves.

Another bond, closely related to intent but more reflective in origin, is obligation. When obligation is recognized to be a compound of intent and an estimate of our abilities, it can be read as a sensitive indicator of the internal structure of a self as well as of its conceived relationships to its social and physical world. No doubt obligations are often forced upon a man; he inherits many from his society. But the manner in which he assumes them is a mark of his personality. Moral obligations are general in form. Their interpretation is largely up to the individual. The more specific obligations of a social role may be assumed by choice or by "necessity." In either case, the assumption reflects both the character of the individual and his conception of the relations in which he stands to his world. What he accepts as inevitable is what he conceives as issuing from circumstances beyond his control. What he freely assumes, because he thinks it is right that he should, or because he foresees a better world as issuing in consequence, reflects his conception of himself, of his power to modify the world, and his complex of values. Equally revealing of the structure of an individual and his world are his admissions and rejections of responsibility for acts already performed, including "acts of omission." These reflect not only his conception of his own power to control the course of "objective events," but also his conception of his ability to know and foresee the consequences of performing or not performing specific acts. Obligations tend to form complex structures of their own, but never in abstraction from a concrete world and a concrete self. The acceptance of one obligation may entail that of many others. The entailment, however, must be established through specific courses of action, specific deeds (specific even though only imagined) and their consequences within the world structure as it is conceived. Consequently, the obligations a man is willing to assume, and their converses, the responsibilities he admits, are signposts to the structure he has imposed upon himself and his world.

It remains to bring this very truncated discussion of bonds to bear on another essential "dimension" of order, that of boundaries or "barriers," as I called them in the last chapter of *Theory of Order*.[4] There must be limits to every act if it is to accomplish what is intended without "mushing out" into the universe in such a multitude of unforeseen consequences as to obscure its intended form. All action is selective in the means it adopts as well as the consequences it intends. In a similar though more diffuse way, a life is selective. It is, of course, limited by birth and death, and by spatial restrictions on the path the body can trace in a lifetime, and by the spatial scope of the influences it can exert and of the events it can encompass within its immediate experience. A personal world is the world of a self with such a limited life, and it is therefore a limited world. Yet its limits need not be related in any very significant way to those of the body associated with the self. I have already rejected the notion

[4] W. Donald Oliver, *Theory of Order* (Yellow Springs, Ohio: Antioch Press, 1952).

that experience is internal to the body. Experience, indeed, is more than just perceptual. A personal world, therefore, though it may be more or less limited by the spatial positions of the body through a lifetime, need not be. A far more significant factor in determination of limits of a personal world is the range of a person's interests. Another is the totality of channels which a person inherits through his social position or creates through his own efforts for influencing other men, purchasing their services, or securing their cooperation. Yet another is limitation on the skills that are available for manipulation of the immediate environment. But though these limits affect the *structure* of a world, none of them is necessarily absolute. What they do is restrict the scope of a man's intentual interaction with the world. A man encounters many things and situations that do not enlist his interest. He reacts by stepping over or around, pushing them out of his way, or otherwise treating them as things that are to be disposed of as quickly as possible without his becoming involved any more than is necessary. Just as we read the headlines in a newspaper, taking in something of the substance of each, but deciding that the announced topic is not worth following up, so we are aware of a "larger" world that cannot be said to be excluded from our personal world, but that lies on the periphery of the latter. Thus while there are no absolute limits, except birth and death, to a personal world, there are limits to what can be intense, personal, and fully meaningful within it.

To a degree a man is free to choose the world he lives in, and not only by choice of the neighborhood, the city, or the nation he will reside in. He chooses by arranging things and events, and other persons, in orders of importance to him. He chooses what he will and what he will not become involved in, responsible for. He can choose wisely or unwisely, of course. Some of his exclusions will prove to be unsuccessful, for there are environmental forces that cannot be ignored with impunity. Indeed, unless he imposes on himself the obligation to extend the range of his knowledge beyond that of his indigenous interests, to learn something about the world that is thrust upon him whether he likes it or not, he will not be likely to enjoy the freedom of choice I have been speaking of. Freedom is contingent on knowledge, but knowledge is the product of a very special kind of involvement, not at all the same as the involvement of action. By becoming involved in the world in the mode of knowledge, we win the freedom to choose what portions of it we shall permit to come into intimate contact with ourselves, or, as it could be put, what we shall take into ourselves and what we shall exclude. The choice in question, then, is not so much that of a world as one of structuring a world that is there, thrust upon us. The acts that issue in structure are ones of thrusting into the background and knitting into the central, intimate areas of a life. But this is not just building a world. It is, at the same time, and equally, creating a personality. That is the import of almost everything I have said. A personality is not something a man is born with, and it is not something that exfoliates from him as he matures, from the seed that brought him into biological existence. It results from his interaction with the world, social and natural. This, I suppose, would be readily admitted by many modern thinkers. If there is something bolder than this in my thesis, it is that the growth of a personality can and should be seen as the growth of a world. This, however, will be a shocking idea only to those who insist on thinking of a world as a container for all that is, whose limits, if any, are those of space and time. Once the concept of a world as characterized by an order, hence as distinguishable from other worlds by differences in order or types of order, is accepted, there is no difficulty in the notion of many worlds coexisting within *the* world.

The fact that a personal world is structured by beliefs, desires, and aspirations will condemn it in the eyes of those who have adopted the scientific ideal of knowledge as the only one worthy of philosophic consideration. Yet the world we react to, when we are reacting consciously and with intent, is the world as we believe it to be. Nor are our beliefs independent of our desires and aspirations. *What* we believe is there is real for what it portends, what it can be made to yield, what must be grappled with, what can be avoided. A being with no conception of a preferred future would not be interested in what is there, would have no need for beliefs, and would probably entertain none. The content of a personal world is not so much a selection of items from *the* world, as a structured selection of their potentialities. It is within the personal world that objects take on value for the contributions they can make to a meaningful life. It is there, then, that potentialities inherent in them are selected for actualization. The personal world is no unreal thing. It may contain illusions, to be sure, but it is not itself an illusion, unless, as does happen in certain pathological cases, a man abuses his power to exclude *the* world from his personal world and structures a world of fancy to withdraw into. We *prove* that our personal worlds are not illusory by the lives we live.

Whitehead wrote that the value of a proposition lies in it more often as a "lure for feeling" than as a statement of fact that must be true or false.[5] Within the context of Whitehead's philosophy this means many things that I am not prepared to endorse, but even to one who knows nothing of Whitehead it can suggest what I have been trying to say. The import of an experience, a bit of knowledge, an event, is revealed not by the position assigned it in the impersonal world of science, but by the way it is taken up into some personal world, the position assigned it there. Conversely, just so long as we persist in ignoring personal worlds we shall fail to understand man as a human being, rather than as an animal controlled by forces of hunger and greed and the physical complex that is called his body.

[5] A. N. Whitehead, *Process and Reality* (New York: Macmillan Co., 1929). Whitehead expresses the equivalent of this statement again and again; cf. especially pp. 281 and 416.

JOSHUA WHATMOUGH

Order in Language
and in Other Human Behavior

This subject is a tall order. The pun is easy and is apt to be considered cheap, perhaps even nasty. Order or "command" (that is, rule of law or authority) implies, as the merest tyro in etymology would see, stability or at least metastability. My topic, then, is language and other forms of human conduct as being orderly, but nevertheless always ready for change (metastable) unless or until overtaken by death, and hence characterized by ectropy, except when they die. For if they die, ectropy has yielded to entropy; for example, the case of Etruscan, but not of Greek.

JOSHUA WHATMOUGH, a linguist of international fame, was chairman of the Department of Linguistics at Harvard University from 1926 until his retirement in 1963. His efforts in applying mathematics to changes in language were not only to reconstruct ancient speech but to predict the future of speech. His fundamental conviction was that such changes were not random. Professor Whatmough died April 25, 1964. This lecture is therefore one of the latest in a long and fruitful career. *Studies Presented to Joshua Whatmough on his Sixtieth Birthday* appeared in 1957. Reviews written by Joshua Whatmough before his death have appeared posthumously in *Classical Philology*, the last review in April, 1967. His lecture "Continental Keltic" was included in the *Proceedings of the International Congress of Celtic Studies*, 1963, published by the University of Wales Press, Cardiff, 1966. In the fall of 1968, Harvard University Press is publishing Professor Whatmough's monumental *Dialectics of Ancient Gaul*, which heretofore has been available only in microfilm-xerox form. In the same year, an Italian edition of his work *Language—A Modern Synthesis* is scheduled for publication.

The topic evidently involves more than man and more than his unique capacity to talk. It is impossible to exclude any part of man's total environment, this planet upon which he lives, or the universe of which this planet is part. For these are what, among other things, he talks about, as well as the conditions in which he lives and behaves. That is why I call the subject a tall order.

But there is another reason for saying so, commonly forgotten, overlooked, or thrust aside. Then man and his world are treated as somehow separate and apart. The treatment is illogical. Man is part of the cosmos, by which I mean at most that which is accepted as known order (hence its name, cosmos or mundus). Why then does anyone treat them apart?

Perhaps for convenience of handling, since the human brain is but finite in its scope. (But let us not forget now at once to mention computers.) Another phase of this alleged convenience, actually this incapacity, is human conceit, man being, though frail as dust, yet lord of creation, or, as some would say, not merely human, but also divine. Hence man presumes to observe both himself and his world at one and the same time and falls inevitably either into solipsism or into confounding man with environment, the more so now that he has begun, through nuclear fission most conspicuously, to modify his environment more than ever before. This error is the serpent in the humanist's paradise: what humanists think, and, worse, what they teach in every church, school, college, and university in the land derives from and is formulated by *human* observers, since we no longer believe in revelation, any more than we believe in redemption, however much we may believe in original sin. Strictly we should *accept nothing* except that which can be separated from ourselves as agents and observers, not even about language, or about the rest of human behavior. Only an external observer could completely satisfy this requirement. I shall try to turn myself into just such an external observer, namely by measuring and counting, by computing, by practicing the *mathematike techne*.

What we can know of language (*le langage*) as well as of any language (*une langue*), as of chemistry, we know only by treating its events (epilegmata, utterances, *paroles*) as if man did not exist at all) except, alas, as the producer of the events). What we know of chemistry is accepted as known (knowledge, science, *scientia, mathema,* and sometimes *episteme*) through the grammar of chemistry, whether that grammar be spoken or written, that is symbolized by tokens (occurrences of words, epilegmata, etc., the classes of which are called types) in Japanese, German, Hottentot, Swahili, Shoshawnee, Paiute, Tagalog, or English, or what you will. This grammar of chemistry is a superstructure, over and above any one of those structures—Japanese and the rest. It has been found that such a superstructure is formulaic in character; it prefers formulas to words as its convention, in short mathematics, the best of all languages. Therefore, we treat language mathematically to find and establish its superstructure.

By "the best of all languages" I mean only the conventions, that is the grammar, of science, natural philosophy, not of the so-called "humanities" (as if science were not also the work of man—see, for example, the definition of humanities, in terms of current prejudice, in Webster's *Dictionary of Synonyms,* 1942, p. 514) —but of God or of the Devil, and as if science were not only the work of man but also concerned with the "life and activity of man." In contrast for instance with sociology, miscalled social science, God save the mark, only the grammar of science is world-wide and free from emotion. Religion, ethics, philosophy, to mention only the more obvious humanistic disciplines, are not world-wide—not yet, if ever, for diversity is not necessarily evil. Even biology in Russia is said to be no longer a Lysenko citadel, immune to and above all internal criticism. Truly scientific statements, then, are necessarily part of logical syntax, in George Boole's sense, and mathematical. This truism applies to **linguistics if linguistics** is, or is to be, scientific. As David Hilbert said, any subject, when it becomes truly scientific, is ripe to fall into the lap of mathematics. Metaphysics, psychology, and the like are partial and diverse, not unified or universal. We may admit the usefulness of diversity in unity, but we must deplore the authoritarian dogmatism which religion, sociology, and psychology tend to assume as a cloak of respectability in their restriction of individual freedom, riding us like a hag mounted upon a broomstick. A "free" society? Not at all. Even in this great republic you will be told by society in so many words, that society has the determination and its own ways of punishing individualists, and will exercise them: I have had this said to me, and I know I have been made to feel the force of this dogma. Literary critics, too, by their constant use of metaphor and meaningless abstraction, constantly evade honest investigation, for example by the assertion that Ovid *Amores* 1.6 is pervaded by an odor. That this statement is in fact without meaning is at once revealed by substituting the concrete term: does, then, the poem smell? As for the psychological and social dictates by which we are hag-ridden, being authoritarian, which science never is, no opposition is tolerated, not even free speech on these matters, not even in "the land of the free, and the home of the brave." Yet language is a sure means by which a man may remain *au courant* and on good terms, at all events in communication with, the society in which he lives and still preserve his own individuality.

In the *Proceedings of the Eighth International Congress of Linguists* held at Oslo in 1957 I have given an account of the attempts to gather, at first by mere arithmetical enumeration, crude—indeed quite simple—statistics of the relative frequency of occurrence of linguistic units in a number of different languages, to which I now refer the reader instead of repeating here what I have published there.[1] Descriptive grammar also has a long history, beginning (so far as our records go) with Chinese grammarians, who were also philologists, that, is they studied literature as well as language. Historical and comparative grammar, as now understood, is much more recent. All this was empirical, a pragmatic treatment of language, without the aid of strict statistical or of any sort of mathematical method, until late in the second decade of the present twentieth century of our epoch, regard being had to factual linguistic content, but little or no regard to finding a broad general exposition or to the formulation of a general theory of language or of any theoretical statement whatever. Certainly no attention was paid to the calculus of probabilities.

But one generalization might easily have been deduced, namely, the general regularity that pervades all language and languages, whether as a status historically, or statistically. Such regularity is in fact necessary and inevitable if language is to serve the need (purpose, if you will, though this only means feedback) of intelligibility and communication at all. Readers, I expect, will shudder and shrink at the word "purpose." I am not going to involve myself in teleological conflicts, but simply content myself with remarking that teleology or "purpose"[2] refers here to what is called, after the

[1] Joshua Whatmough, *Proceedings of the Eighth International Congress of Linguists* (Oslo: Oslo University Press, 1958) , pp. 62–80.
[2] Richard B. Braithwaite, *Scientific Explanation* (Cambridge, Eng.: Cambridge University Press, 1953) , p. 328.

example of modern mechanisms of control (for instance, an oil-burner thermostat) the negative feedback of cybernetics, but refers primarily to the feedback of the human brain of normal living and speaking human beings rather than of the machines for computing that they have built in our own day and generation.

Frequency counts, descriptive analysis, history and comparison of languages—all three converge in their conclusions upon this single overriding conclusion of order and regularity in language, all the way from phonemes, combinations of phonemes, morphemes and morphology, orders of arrangement and syntax, meanings and de-velopment of meanings: in a word description, history and compari-son, and probability. We are now in sight, for the first time, of a well-founded scientific and quite general theory of a genuine science of language, thanks to rigorous statistical and mathematical method, rigorously applied. This is my theory of Selective Variation in language, which gives a macroscopic account of language while providing for microscopic deviation, and says that selection rescues language from the ravages of unrestricted variation.

At this point I must, in private honor bound, mention one or two stages that mark the development of my views. First there is, in 1929, the first of the Harvard dissertations done under my direction, "Relative Frequency as a Determinant of Phonetic Change," [3] and subsequent work done by the same author. But soon this was damned in a bitter review by a disappointed man, without any reasons given, or at least reasons that appeared on the surface, one consequence of which was an attack by a powerful member of the Harvard faculty, who otherwise supported me through thick and thin. I advised the author to bide his time, assuring him that he would live to see justice done, and he did. The next step was the formulation of my theory of Selective Variation, which I was discuss-ing in my lecture room before 1941, as is shown by a question about it in an examination paper on General Linguistics at Harvard that year. I still refrained from publication until a proof was forthcom-ing. This proof came from Claude Shannon, a communications engineer, in *The Mathematical Theory of Communication*.[4] I now felt assured that I was right, and said so in the course of a lecture

---

[3] George Zipf, "Interlingual Communication in the Sciences," *Harvard Studies in Classical Philology*, XL (1929), 1–95.

[4] Claude E. Shannon and Warren Weaver, *The Mathematical Theory of Communication* (Urbana: University of Illinois Press, 1949).

given at Berkeley on July 13, 1951, the year in which I was president of the Linguistic Society of America, the salient points of which appeared in *Newsweek* [5] and in *Scientific American*.[6] Since then I have developed the theory in many publications; [7] in my Sather Lectures, *Poetic, Scientific, and Other Forms of Discourse;* [8] in lectures given in the course of a world-wide lecturing tour in 1958, see for example "The New Linguistics," [9] in my Lowell Institute Lectures, 1957, now being revised for publication; and in a Lowell Institute television broadcast, January 12, 1959. I do not apologize for recapitulating these steps. New views are not readily accepted by old dogs unable to learn new tricks, especially mathematical, which call for hard work from them; mathematical logic, which has, so far, less to say to them about linguistics, frightens them even more.

In passing let me remark that some distinguished sociologists (not many) have been known to admit that Grimm's Law (as it has come, not with complete justification, to be called), which deals with shifts in the consonant system of the Germanic languages, was the first clearly observed and undisputed instance of orderliness in any form of human conduct. It led, with the correction furnished by Grassman's and Verner's "laws," to the dogma of the German *"Jung-grammatiker"* that "phonetic 'laws' have no exceptions." This latter dogma has been long since abandoned in favor of the more temperate and fully justified statement that "phonematic substitution is regular." This sheet anchor to windward is scorned only by contemporary structuralists, usually ill trained in, when they are not totally ignorant of, this history and comparison of language and languages, not to mention statistics, probability theory, mathematics, and logic; many of them, though they parade what they take to be a grounding in linguistics, and much as they claim to know about language *tout court,* do not know any language but their mother tongue, and a knowledge of languages might surely be held to be the *sine qua non,* a prime requirement, of a would-be linguist: *hinc illae lacrimae.*

[5] *Newsweek,* July 30, 1951, p. 62.
[6] *Scientific American,* April, 1952, pp. 82–86.
[7] Joshua Whatmough, *Language* (New York: St. Martin's Press, 1956).
[8] Joshua Whatmough, *Poetic, Scientific and Other Forms of Discourse* (Berkeley: University of California Press, 1956).
[9] *Journal of the Society of English and American Literature* (Osaka), IV, No. 1 (October, 1959), 1–30; cf. *Journal of the Linguistic Society of Japan,* No. 34 (1958), pp. 63–76.

Something of the same sort is said about regularity and order in language in much more tenuous fashion, by A. J. Ayer [10] in his critique of the language of ethics and theology, but he writes within the field of philosophy, not of philology or linguistics. Unlike most linguists, however, I maintain that linguistics and philosophy have much to say to one another. For, to put the matter another way, this all-pervading regularity in language appears all along the road through the hierarchy of language, from everyday conversation and mere chitchat through law and religion, liturgy and homily, poetry, "literature," science and philosophy, to logic and mathematics; that is, from language at its simplest and least elaborate to language in its most highly refined forms. If the users of these several kinds of discourse do not realize the regularity, that is because, as the saying goes, it is "built in"; it needs little or no premeditation on the part of an ordinary, and none at all on the part of an accomplished, writer or speaker, who, in Juvenal's words, knows his language *"tamquam ungues digitosque suos,"* to embark upon a long sentence and come through safely to its end without an anacoluthon, even if he have a parenthesis, or indeed a parenthesis within a parenthesis, to entangle him in a barbed-wire obstacle. *Experto crede:* I know whereof I speak; people tell me I do it all the time and talk "like a little (or big) book."

To repeat, observe that I am now giving a macroscopic view of language; that microscopic deviations occur goes without saying— yet if these are deep-seated (James Joyce, Gerard Manley Hopkins, William Blake, Dylan Thomas), then they offend more than they enthrall by the rejection of order and intelligibility at one stroke. It is, to be sure, a matter of common observation that standards of usage vary—one does not address a bishop and a newsboy in the same manner. It is curious that in the United States especially educationists have persuaded school teachers of the wisdom (actually it is nonsense and wickedness, poisonous too) of allowing young children to talk and write as they will, without any standards at all —"leave your language alone" is their slogan—for it was Karl Marx, more than once in his *Deutsche Ideologie*,[11] who objected to standards of usage on the ground that they tend to perpetuate distinctions of class. We have a good deal of socialism in the United

[10] A. J. Ayer, *Language, Truth, and Logic* (New York: Dover Publications, 1952), pp. 20–22; cf. pp. 102–10.
[11] Karl Marx, *Die deutsche Ideologie* (Berlin: Dietz), 1953.

States, though it is not called that, and our society is no more classless than it is free.

It is important, therefore, to be quite clear that the study of language, like science, gains by escape from dogma and authority. The Linguistic Society of America has lent the whole weight of its authority to the dogma that only its brand of structural and descriptive analysis has any validity whatsoever. Anyone who objects—and I do object most strenuously—is condemned as a heretic and wrongheaded, if not wicked. It is unfortunate that its authority has captured the makers of the Third International (*absit omen*) Webster Dictionary of English, which otherwise has much to commend it; but many wise critics have regretted the admission of slang, obscenity, and profanity to its pages.

Linguistics, like science yet once more, is purified by mathematical theory; it is also made by the same means more accurate, more economical, and more elegant, capable of more applications of a practical nature, such as automatic translation and interlingual discourse. By contrast current descriptive and structural analysis is pseudo-scientific, like sociolinguistics, psycholinguistics, anthropolinguistics, and certain other tails that presume to claim to wag the linguistic dog. Moreover, mathematical linguistics is objective; all the others just named are not, notwithstanding all their claims, for they never escape the subjective taint that debases all subjects commonly called "humanistic," as pointed out at the beginning of this paper. Indeed, at times to many of its practitioners, descriptive analysis, it would appear, has become highly emotional if not psychopathic, and the greater the degree to which it yields in this way, the less scientific and the less significant it becomes, just as emotive language fails in semantic content, and it fails the more in direct ratio as it becomes more emotive.

After this long preamble, let us return to our muttons. Communication may take many forms, of which we are now directly concerned only with the linguistic; this also may take many forms, spoken or written, electric (telephonic and telegraphic), and now electronic (radio, television), and by a recent extension of these has acquired a new spatial dimension through the device of satellites, especially Syncom, Telstar II, and maser (microwave amplification by stimulated emission of radiation), which are most important for intercontinental, if not yet interstellar, but certainly for interlingual, communication by means of a superstructural code. This I foresaw as long ago as 1957, in a paper on "Mathematical Linguistics" published in the proceedings of the *International Conference on Scientific Information.*[12] For my pains I was called by some a visionary, but by one man, in the Research Laboratories of the Bell Telephone Company, a pioneer.

Languages employ as the most obvious units words, or what function as words (for example in Eskimo), for which I have proposed as a better term *epilegmata* (plural), that is, repetitive elements in more or less identical shape. I have read J. L. Austin's *How to Do Things with Words,*[13] but I find nothing in his philosophical hair-splitting that sheds any light on our present problem: even the word "word" is never defined. By *epilegma* I mean a longer or shorter recurrent event in the stream of speech, identified in the structure of the language in which it occurs, the recurrences being identical or different, if at all, only in respect of variations also identifiable in the structure of that same language: for example, the English *book, books, bookish, bookman, bookworm;* or *gentle, gentleman, gentlemanly, ungentlemanly.* Structure itself, an important interdisciplinary concept, has lately been the object of a UNESCO colloquium,[14] designed to prepare a definition for the projected *Dictionnaire Terminologique des Sciences Sociales,* from which it appears that even within the domain of linguistics there is considerable confusion and even wide difference of opinion and understanding of structure as operational (which I prefer) or as merely programmatic, which is that of most professional linguists, especially in cisatlantic regions.

Normal spoken language uses not signs but symbols to designate objects, events, and the relations between them. Symbols, as distinguished from signs, are open-ended: their value may vary from time to time and place to place, from person to person, even in the usage of one and the same person using one and the same language. "Written" language (including all its varieties of print, type, spelling, stenography, punched tape or cards, plastic disks, and all the rest) corresponds more or less accurately to the spoken language,

---

[12] Joshua Whatmough, "Mathematical Linguistics," *Proceedings of the International Conference on Scientific Information* (Washington, D.C., 1958), Area 5, pp. 201–20, a paper actually written the previous year.

[13] J. L. Austin, *How to Do Things with Words* (Cambridge, Mass.: Harvard University Press, 1962).

[14] UNESCO Colloquium, January 10–12, 1959. See the report edited by Bastide.

that is to speech. The essential difference between the "written" and the spoken is that the latter is tied to time and occasion, the former is not. Now the mathematical theory of communication has proved that in the stream of utterance or writing each successive unit in the linear sequence answers the question whether or not it occurs, "yes" or "no" (this is binary choice; "maybe" is excluded, and though the question is sometimes asked many times before the final choice is made, witness Byron's manuscripts, or Housman's notebooks, but not Blake's copperplates, the choice is still binary, just as in the game of Twenty Questions). More important, the same mathematical theory has proved that in the entire sequence the probability of the occurrence of any event (phoneme, cluster of phonemes, morpheme, morph, order of arrangement, syntactic feature, meaning) is determined by relative frequency, that is to say by the calculus of probability, thus confirming the empirical results both of structural analysis and of comparative and historical grammar.

Moreover, we find that the sequence is a controlled sequence, a stochastic process, in which each event depends on what went before; it is also ergodic, that is, a sufficiently large sample reveals all the features of the language, in accordance with the law of large numbers, and which is, after the opening gambit, predetermined (what is called a "Markov" process, from the name of the Russian scholar who established this fact). The fact of order had long been known before from descriptive grammar (for example the Sanskrit grammar of Pānini, ca. 300 B.C.) and from the observation of historians and comparativists like Edward Llwyd (*Archaeologia Britannica,* Oxford, 1707), Sir William Jones (1786), and their successors. Whether this linguistic order corresponds to cosmic order is a disputed question which Bertrand Russell and Rudolf Carnap argue in different ways, and about which they differ as to the extent that it does. There is also a grave problem, namely, how the human brain transforms quantities into qualities as undoubtedly it does: my guess is that it behaves like a digital and analogical computer combined, and that this may be an answer to A. J. Ayer's question. Quantities correspond to measurable physical properties; analogy makes the differences alike or partly alike. Thus we speak of a weak or strong profile, a sweet or foul smell, a straight line of architecture, but all these are fundamentally mathematical (harmonic equations, molecular combinations, and the curves of entasis, respectively). That order exists in language is not to be questioned, for without it intelligibility, the systematic symbolism of language, would be impossible.

Thus in English *e* is the most frequent phoneme; if *th-* (þ or ð) comes first, then in English *e, a,* or *r* may come next, but oddly enough not *l,* even though some would argue that to have *thr-* but not *thl-* leaves a hole in the pattern of the system. All this was foreshadowed in the Harvard dissertation of 1929 already mentioned. It was not well received, but the objections raised seemed to me unconvincing if not prejudiced. The mathematical proof of its fundamental correctness came twenty years later, stimulated by the exigencies of war.

The simplest equation $f.r = K$ (where f = frequency, r = rank, K = constant), a harmonic law, has been replaced by a complicated canonical law in order to furnish parameters necessary at extremely high or extremely low frequencies, at the two ends of a graph plotted on double log paper, from statistical counts, and the curve also requires smoothing. Here are some statistics based on a frequency count of words in James Joyce's *Ulysses,* a count made in the first place with the intention of disproving the law $f.r = K$, but which when made actually and in fact confirmed it:

Word		Frequency	Rank	Product
the		14,877	1	14,877
to		4,097	5	24,535
I		2,653	10	26,530
all		1,311	20	26,220
she		1,129	25	28,225
when		556	50	27,800
back		360	75	27,000
say		265	100	26,500
222	words	10	2,517	25,170
906	words	5	5,212	26,060
16,432	words	1	29,899	29,899

This corresponds neatly enough to the canonical curve that was obtained theoretically in the first place; the pragmatic result agrees, here and everywhere that it has been tested, in regard to all linguistic features—all the way from phonemes to meanings and syntax, even to over-all size of vocabulary in which actual authors and speakers differ enormously. Hence all linguistic symbolism is systematic and orderly; there is a repetitive pattern (rather like that in a roll of wallpaper as it is unfurled, but not so simple in design) ; the pattern (grammar) is homogeneous, coherent, consistent, and orderly in any given status, notwithstanding historic change and development. Since any pattern varies historically (compare old, middle, and modern English), it must also be selective. Selective Variation preserves the pattern from the chaos that would otherwise overtake it, and which some imagine is now overtaking English. Its population is indefinite and hypothetical, not infinite; but not finite either except in the case of a dead language like Sumerian—not Latin, for it lives on in Romance. In Sumerian or Hittite or Etruscan we have entropy, but in French or Italian we have ectropy, as in life itself. A living language, like life, feeds on its environment; it does not, however, reproduce itself, but its speakers do, and normally inherit the capacity to speak.

I am not familiar enough with all the relevant subject matter to be able to speak confidently or at length about order in other forms of human behavior. But I observe good order in the dance, particularly ballet; in music, particularly orchestrated; in athletic games, particularly teamwork; not in religion, law, or literary criticism; still less in advertising, politics, government; a little more in industry, trade, and business.

Everyone who accepts modern science as something that works, a going and growing concern, must, I think, also accept the presence and existence in it of the good order that science infers: there is no other way of accounting for experience save by an appeal to the supernatural. I maintain that there is no supernatural, that the entire concept was an invention of fools or knaves. We must, I suppose, respect the opinions of those who seek supernatural explanations; but we cannot agree with them or regard the teaching of that way out as other than regrettable and likely to lead to disaster.

In many respects, however, man as we know him seems to be unteachable, except by hard experience; but he might well learn from language, a very model of good order, if only he could be induced to use and not to misuse language and gain from its pro-presentative force and not seek private, instead of social, gain from its correlate, its other phase, misrepresentation. This other phase is inevitable from the nature of the case—without falsehood, error, and mistake we could not know truth. But we can recognize error, and exclude it. Perhaps the threat of radioactive fallout and of nuclear fission will bring man to his senses; possibly even the new environment, if life survives at all, may be accompanied by conditions of temperature and moisture not unlike those which prevailed when the earth was young and so induce a new evolutionary step, when communication, as superior to language as it is to the twittering of birds, may emerge.

This brings me to my suggestion of utilizing order in language in an interlingual and supralinguistic way. I have just received the most recent work done at the Harvard Computation Laboratory in which problems of syntax usually considered so hopelessly ambiguous as to be logically insoluble in a manner such as might serve interlingual communication have been brought many degrees nearer to definitive solution. From this it is clear that with the help of satellites already in orbit (Telstar II and Syncom) and further developments already in sight, together with the use of the device called maser, which amplifies weak signals as in speech without amplifying noise, and sends television pictures as well as accompanying voice (essentially a beam of ruby light that can handle simultaneously more messages than even coaxial cables, and can be beamed from any place in the world that has suitable transmitting apparatus, the dataphone, and received at any other place in the world that has suitable receiving apparatus, as Telstar goes round the world, or enough Syncom satellites in station so that it is not necessary to lose time by waiting for Telstar to arrive and stay long enough), the age is now ripe, in this international epoch, for the displacement of so-called "international" languages that really come to nothing more than creolized Romance (like Esperanto and Interlingua) or bastard English (like Basic and Pidgin) by a truly supralinguistic coded "language" (if I may be forgiven this seeming Irishism), a genuine means of interlingual communication. It is technically feasible, and the difficulties, which are purely linguistic, though great, are not insuperable. The messages will have to be coded on tape or disks, and both fed and received through a dataphone. Now all this is possible through, and only through, the essential good order that pervades language, as anyone may see from the simple fact that any and every language can be coded and that no intercepted message in code, no matter what the plain language, remains forever undeciphered. In many circumstances the accompanying television picture of the happenings described would be helpful, but it is no more essential or indispensable than the pictures that go with advertising or other letterpress, and often would be undesirable unless designed, not to uncover, but to mystify and disguise secrecy. Thus:

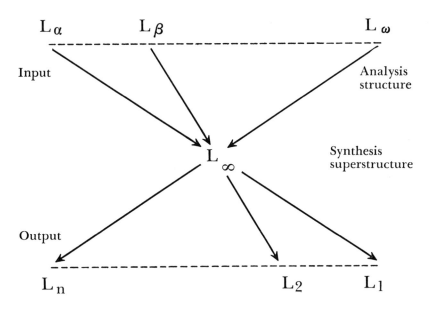

INPUT (in L=language)
STRUCTURE: Analysis
SUPERSTRUCTURE: Synthesis
OUTPUT (in L=language)

Here communication theory and linguistics march hand in hand. Messages in *L* would be flashed over land and sea for all twentieth-century men, whose crisis is precisely intercommunication and understanding. The crisis of man bound with the problem of language by ropes of steel is the problem of unity in diversity and diversity in unity, Orient and Occident, North and South. But when the problem is solved our modern Babel, in our plain of Shinar, will become, as it is by name, the Gate of God, the very building of which, in the old legend, came to a stop through the confusion of tongues. There is no need for conversation or wit to be diminished, as some think, by machines. Style will still come from those who command it. But keep the thing uncommercialized if it is not to be turned into a wasteland like the "shouties" of kinematograph, radio, and television.

When the Irish Free State treaty was being negotiated in 1921, Lloyd George and his private secretary conversed in Welsh to preserve secrecy; de Valera and his secretary retired to the adjoining room. Which was modern and which medieval? Not even the Irish could set the hands back on the clock. Nor in 1963 did President Kennedy converse in Erse.

Let us be quite sure, then, that thanks to its inherent order, communication on a global level is just around the corner; and (who knows?) may perhaps enhance good order in other forms of human activity to the gain and blessing of all the sons of men. Failing that we must await a utopia and uchronia, a never-never land at a never-never time.

Order in Human Society

CARL J. FRIEDRICH

The Dialectic of Political
Order and Freedom

I thought I might for this discussion of the dialectic of political
order and freedom start with a situation that has been a continuing
source of conflict in recent years. I am talking about Cyprus. Cyprus
is engaged in a desperate struggle involving, as I see it, political
order and freedom, and is in that sense quite characteristic for a
whole series of other situations which similarly involve either actually or potentially this kind of struggle. The civil strife that has
been raging is fought in the name of freedom. The Greek Cypriots
demand to be free to organize Cyprus in accordance with the
majority's wishes. Since they constitute the majority, this means the
freedom to suit themselves in ordering the community in accord-

CARL J. FRIEDRICH has taught in the Department of Government at Harvard
University since 1927, where he is Eaton Professor of the Science of Government.
Since 1956 he has also been professor at the University of Heidelberg and
director of the Institute of Political Science. Professionally he has helped bring
lawyers, social scientists, and philosophers together in the Society for Political
and Legal Philosophy. His studies in constitutional law and the theory of
federalism have important contemporary applications. Friedrich's *magnum opus*,
Man and His Government, appeared in 1963, and in the same year, as though to
mark a double career, appeared *Zur Theorie und Politik der Verfassung-
sordnung*. Grinnell College made him doctor of laws in 1952, the first of his
many honorary degrees except for that from his alma mater, Heidelberg.
This paper is in part based upon three chapters dealing with freedom and
order in the author's *Man and His Government* (New York: McGraw Hill,
1963).

ance with their own values, interests, and beliefs. The Turkish Cypriots counter with an insistence upon their freedom to live a life in accordance with their particular values, interests, and beliefs. Hence they want constitutionally and internationally guaranteed autonomy and/or participation in the government of Cyprus.

So one claim for freedom stands against the other claim for freedom—and order goes by the board. Since the two freedoms are incompatible, the order of the community is jeopardized by increasing violence. It is obvious to all except those involved in this situation that only a limitation upon the freedom of both groups can provide the basis for the order required to realize the freedom of both. I might put this in another way. To re-establish order, one would have to abolish democracy. This conclusion flows directly from what has just been said, and it is a conclusion that has been reached time and again though not necessarily in such extreme form. When the democratic forces got out of hand in France, the bringing in of De Gaulle and the establishment of the Fifth Republic meant, not the abolition of democracy in the case of France, but a very severe restriction upon democracy in France, a very large reduction in the freedom to which Frenchmen had been accustomed.

In all these situations we are confronted with the very core of the problem of political order and freedom which constitutes their dialectic. At this point I think I ought to pause and ask, What does dialectic mean?—because dialectic is a term with a hoary history of misunderstandings on the highest philosophical level. Dialectic is known to most people by the presumed methods of analysis employed in dialectic materialism, the sequence of thesis, antithesis, and synthesis in the historical succession of modes of production, their means of control, and the classes exercising this control. Marx had claimed that this was the key to the understanding of the truth of history. He had claimed that he had rectified the dialectic of Hegel, putting upside again what Hegel had put downside. That is to say, by making the material conditions the prime factor in human existence, rather than the idea and the spirit, he wanted to get rid of what he believed to be Hegel's idealizing distortion of the human situation. For Hegel's dialectic had been believed by its author to be descriptive, descriptive of the process of thought that one understands as he experiences it.

The great metaphysical idea of Hegel presumably was that we

thus understand the world, for our own thought and our own mind are part of the cosmos, and the cosmos is uniformly ordered. Therefore, if we understand the process of our mind correctly, we are justified in making the metaphysical assumption that we have grasped the order in the cosmos: the unexplained major premise being, as just stated, that the cosmos is throughout informed by the same principle that is to be discovered in the operations of our mind. Along with this notion of the descriptive quality of the dialectic, Hegel believed that he could discover, if he made the effort, the relativity of all contradictions. He thought that what he called the "vast power of negation" was ever at work, that anything that is said, any word that is used, posits its opposite. No synthesis, no matter how unique, can help eliciting its opposite, a contradiction. Interpreters have tried to make something very mystical and incomprehensible out of this view, but I think basically it is very simple. Here is the way Hegel begins his great logic: If you say being, you immediately, by saying being, imply nonbeing, imply its opposite. And, if you have said being and nonbeing, you face a contradiction. If you try to cope with contradiction, the fact that two givens that are mutually exclusive, you must search for something that transcends them both. This search leads you to the category of becoming. The argument is very simple basically: any term that you use implies its opposite, and by implying its opposite it creates a problem that can only be solved by seeking something that transcends them both, by synthesizing them.

The Hegelian way of putting the matter fascinated Marx. He asserted, however, that these contradictions were to be found in matter, in material conditions, in conditions of production. I am not going to use the word dialectic in this sense; I have merely sketched this approach to be sure to eliminate it. But, before proceeding, I must explore the meaning of the word dialectic in the classic tradition of Plato and Aristotle.

Plato did not think of the dialectic in ontological terms. For him dialectic was the effort of the mind by which it emerges from the cave of our ordinary existence and reaches to the higher sphere of light in which the ideas, and particularly *the* Idea, are held. That is the view Plato expounded in the *Republic*. Later he toned it down. He spoke of it more precisely in terms of analysis and synthesis, and this is the notion developed by Aristotle, who speaks of it as the usual method of philosophical discourse. He describes it at one point as the method by which the whole is divided into its parts. Analysis, dialectical analysis, takes things apart into their constituent elements.

Much later, Kant in his critical estimate of idealism (Kant is always labeled as an idealist, but he was an anti-idealist) called idealism the dialectic of appearance (*Schein*), to which no reality necessarily responds. I also do not wish to use dialectic in this sense, that is to say as a pattern of argument and analysis. I am using the notion of dialectic in the light of its history, taking both strands to some extent into account. Dialectic is to suggest an inherent contradiction between two closely and intricately related terms designating values. Freedom and order in politics constitute a special case of a recurrent political situation, namely, that of a conflict of values which are interdependent in that one cannot be realized without the other, and yet each, in its realization, contradicts and to some extent suspends the other. This is the most exciting and at the same time the most perplexing and depressing aspect of politics. Many people who condemn politics, thinking about such features of it as corruption, ambition, or secrecy, are actually confronted with the dialectic of politics, for you cannot operate politically without getting involved in every one of these phenomena. If you really want to get rid of them you have to get rid of politics, and if you get rid of politics you have to abandon the hope for the good life. In-built conflict means dialectic. One might say that in a sense values such as freedom and order are themselves engaged in a dialogue with each other. Since dialectic is derived from the Greek term *dialegesthai*, which means to converse, one might indeed say that these values themselves, as they exist and are there, continuously converse with each other, rather than those who experience them. To put it subjectively, one can say that man wants a free order and he wants an ordered freedom. Hence, he must accept disorder and he must accept unfreedom to a certain extent.

Disorder has a certain value. Alexander Pope, an aesthetic rationalist, once wrote:

> From vulgar bounds with brave disorder part
> And snatch a grace beyond the reach of art. . . .

This is the motto of what I have to say to you. The real master is shown in the skillful deviation from the rule, and this is as valuable in politics as it is in art. This seems to be contradicted by a famous saying of Goethe's, *"Erst in der Beschränkung zeigt sich der Meister,"* affirming that limitations are necessary for mastery. The master reveals himself only when working within the restrictions provided by the rules, and this is an insight, one of the deepest in connection with human achievement, which applies as much to the art of politics as to the art of poetry. But the point is the master's knowing when to disregard the rules, when to transcend them, when not to follow them. The value of disorder is thereby demonstrated. The superior administrator knows when to disregard the rules, as the superior judge who has situation sense knows when to follow precedent and when to disregard it. This runs counter to what a great many people think, who believe that order is perfectly obvious. I should like to submit that nothing is less obvious than order. But not all agree. The extraordinary Simone Weil wrote: "The first of the soul's needs, the one which touches most nearly its eternal destiny is order." By order she meant a texture of social relationships in which no one is compelled to violate some imperative obligations in order to carry out other ones. Such order is the first need of all. But then she has doubts about her proposition, and so she adds, "Yet we cannot be sure that the idea of an order in which all obligations would be compatible with one another is not a fiction." I should like to reinforce this doubt. If order is defined in such terms as "texture of social relations, typified by the fulfillment of imperative obligations," I think its political significance is obscured while at the same time it is given a utopian twist. For when has there ever been even an approximation to such a state?

Conflicts of principle are at the very essence of political order. Only a glance at the United States or any other Bill of Rights shows that it is full of contradictions in principle. There never has been any resolution of their contradictions, and there never will be any resolution in terms of an order of priority. Is the right of self-expression more important than the right of property? Is either of them more important than the right to education? We have developed in democratic societies elaborate judicial procedures in order to cope with these recurrent conflicts and to redefine imperative obligations so that such a bill can to a certain extent be maintained.

Order, and more especially political order, has undoubtedly, as Simone Weil insists, its soul-satisfying value. But freedom certainly has, too. Which is to be preferred in any concrete situation would seem to depend on the person and on the constellation in which he finds himself. I am inclined to think generally that the weaker the man, the more he values order; the stronger, the more he values freedom.

The conflict over segregation offers an example of the recurrent dialectic of order and freedom. It is usually cast in terms of what is just. Politically one notes that each side in this controversy insists on its own notion of justice and that in this connection the maintenance of the legal order is juxtaposed to the preservation of the social and cultural order. Most men in the North are on the side of the legal order, whereas the South generally is on the side of social and cultural order.

Another suggestive illustration is provided by freedom of religion. Among the earliest human rights, it has undergone a steady evolution. I think that the tendency has been to conceive it ever more broadly, whereas at one time it was rather narrowly restricted. For Locke, it did not cover the right to be a Roman Catholic. His notion of toleration moved within rather narrow limits. Today the tendency is to construct it philosophically. In some of the new constitutions it is simply stated as the right to one's conviction. Your fundamental conviction need not, in other words, fit some pattern of established theology, in order to be entitled to this protection. It has, in fact, come to cover disbelief, such as atheism.

Related is the issue of conscientious objection. Conscientious objection, which is recognized on convictional grounds as a matter of conscience, is in the more advanced states no longer made dependent upon participation in any particular ecclesiastical organization. In normative terms, what should be the conception? I cannot explore this question fully, but let me here make one comment. I think we professors, academic people, students in this country would have been very well advised in linking our cherished academic freedom to freedom of religion (conviction). In academic freedom, freedom to study is just as important as the freedom to teach. It is the general freedom of scholarship, of teaching and learning. If it had been linked to freedom of religion as guaranteed in our Constitution rather than to freedom of speech, it would have been much better; because the core of the academic profession is a man's convictions, rather than his "speech." We need the freedom to speak, certainly. But, even more, we need the freedom to search for the truth, and when we have found it to state it without having anyone interfere with us. This is what is needed. The mere freedom to speak is the freedom of the marketplace, and that is less important to us than the freedom to communicate to students what we really believe to be true, and for them to respond in the same spirit. Without that, the academic profession becomes propaganda, as we would become mere transmitters of somebody else's views and point of view.

Such controversies suggest that there exist various understandings of what constitutes order in a politically relevant sense. There have been four primary definitions, or delineations, as I prefer to say of political order. According to the first of these, order is a structured arrangement of parts, and hence political order would be a structured arrangement of political units. The second way of defining order claims that order is a systematic arrangement of parts. Political order, then, might be an integration of political units into a coherent whole. Peace is the focal point of the third characterization. An ordered political community, then, is one in which peace prevails, and, since law is the precondition of peace, an ordered community is one in which law is maintained. This implies also, of course, the absence of physical violence and the threat thereof. And restricting the delineation to this last point, the fourth interpretation stresses the absence of nongovernmental violence as the criterion of political order.

The vast literature that has been devoted to order largely reduces itself, insofar as it deals with *political* order, to these four characterizations. The difficulty with all of these is that they do not relate order to the values, interests, and beliefs of the community. They do not emphasize, as I think they must, that the realization of a political community's values and interests in terms of its beliefs is an essential aspect of a viable order.

A rather homespun analogy may help us. All order, I would submit, is related to the ends for which any congeries of entities is assembled: the tools in the tool shop, the books in the library, the soldiers on the battlefield. Unless one takes into account what is the object, what is the purpose, of the person in charge, one cannot discern the order although the order is there, and one is very likely to consider it disorder. The most familiar situation to mention here is the study of the scholar in the midst of writing a book at the point at which his wife arrives to clean the room. She will exclaim about the terrible disorder; he will exclaim about the disorder that she creates by going in and straightening up the room. Since she is alien to the purpose for which this particular disarray has been created, it seems to her, looking at it from her point of view, that this cannot possibly be an order; but to the man at work it is an order. You have this same situation in the tool shop. If on a farm a tool shop is terribly neat, with everything in its place, you can be sure that it is rarely used. The tool shop in which everything seems to be in disarray is the one where there is somebody working who really uses the tools. He knows where they are. And he also knows why they are where they are. But someone else coming in from the outside does not.

To return to the general analysis, the usual delineations of order without regard to the values, interests, and beliefs of the community fail to reflect the fact that in the actions of various representatives of different groups of the community, pursuing a plurality of goals, disorder is inescapably necessary. The political community, by organizing itself into a political order, is required to allow for a measure of disorder. Indeed, I submit, any dynamic order is characterized by emergent disorder. The conventional attempts at stating the nature of order by stressing its normativity fail to allow for the value of disorder in the ordering of the political community.

This proposition may also be stated as the principle of the interrelation of communal values. Order is one value among several, and it may have to be restricted or even sacrificed when conflicts occur. Not only freedom has such a dialectical relationship to order, but justice and security may conflict with order. To make order supreme as the one predominant consideration of a political community's arrangement, as many political theorists have done, is not only normatively but existentially in error. Experience has shown, I believe, and historical records prove that men have rarely if ever preferred order to all other values. And I believe that theorists like Marsilius of Padua and Hobbes are basically in error in their preoccupation with order and peace.

There does not exist in point of fact any universally recognized *summum bonum* in the political experience of mankind. Human beings pursue a variety of goals and keep rearranging these goals as the situation changes and as the necessities that motivate them in their action programs impose themselves.

If I therefore were to define political order, I would say it is a term suited to designate the political situation of the community in which component parts, or units, are arranged in such a way that the actions required for the attainment of the purposes of the community will be taken. The crucial issue is whether things are arranged in such a way that there is enough order so that the actions occur which are needed in terms of the values, interests, and beliefs of the community. Even that amount of order is never fully achieved. When men criticize their government for not doing this and not doing that, there almost always is implied some more basic criticism in terms of the functioning of the system itself, once the problem is thought through. This is particularly true in the field of foreign policy. The trouble with our own situation in this field, and it is a very grave one, is due to the fact that the political order that suits us domestically has turned out to be wholly inadequate to the kind of situation for which it was designed. There is little sense in continually criticizing individuals, such as the secretary of state, who struggle desperately to try and make a go of an inadequate, obsolete, and antiquated order instead of searching for the alterations that would have to be undertaken to make it manageable.

Let us then return to the dialectic of freedom and order. For that the value of order has limits has always been apparent enough to those who valued freedom. Freedom in turn depends upon a certain amount of order. This has been stressed by all who have argued about freedom under law. In discussions about world order under law this is the central consideration. This freedom which is at the heart of such a large portion of political thought and action, while fundamentally one, has a number of dimensions, and I think we ought to look for a moment at the problem of freedom in relation to order from this point of view. Many answers have been given to the question, What is freedom, or liberty? I have never been able to tell the difference between these two words. They seem to me true synonyms, as John Stuart Mill thought.

Any inquiry into the problem of political freedom usually carries the implication that we are prepared to say men ought to be free. Just what this means often remains rather vague. Discarding the absolute dichotomy of fact and value, let us accept this normative proposition: that men ought to be free. We can then ask, what is the political situation that is referred to when we talk about freedom? It has for a long time been recognized that it cannot mean that all men ought to be free in regard to all actions they may wish to take, since these actions clash and are incompatible. Various qualifications have been proposed in the past, perhaps the most famous that of Kant, echoing Locke, that each man's freedom must be compatible with every other man's freedom. But this is an inadequate formula involving a *petitio principii* because it leaves us still in the dark as to what this thing is that must be compatible for all persons.

Now my own inclination is to believe that in politics, and the same thought applies, I think, to other realms of freedom, the question of freedom, political freedom, arises in power situations when the power of some participant persons to act as they would prefer to act is subject to interference by the power of other persons. I would therefore say that noninterference by another human being is the elemental notion of political freedom. In my terms I would say that, whenever and to the extent that a political actor appears to act without interference from another political actor, he shall be said to be free. To use an ordinary illustration, like the function of voters, voting is free when a man can go and vote as he sees fit. One reason why secret ballots are universally adopted is because it was readily discovered that when the ballots were open a very large number of people were psychologically, if not otherwise, interfered with. The freedom to vote did not exist. And I think that holds true for many other situations.

I think it is important to realize that I just said that he is considered to *be* free. This being free should be distinguished from feeling free. It is evident that one might *be* free and not *feel* free, and that one might feel free and not be free. In other words, feeling free and being free are two different things, and failure to distinguish these two states clearly is at the core of much confusion in the writings on freedom. A great many people who seem to be writing on freedom as an existential fact are actually writing on various feelings that people might have about their freedom.

A further thought that I would like to offer in this connection is that it is likely that no one will be completely free. There will always be some interfering of one sort or another. One's independence is limited by the very fact of one's being a member of a political community. Political freedom involves limitation.

With this problem clarified, the question of the dimensions of freedom becomes answerable. I believe that there are essentially three such dimensions. Starting from the basic experience of which I have spoken, I think you can say that these dimensions constitute spheres, and that there are the spheres of independence, of participation, and of creation.

Let me begin with the first two of these. There is a very great deal of difference between them. Our ancestors, at the time they made the Constitution and even more before that time, were primarily concerned with the freedom of independence. They were primarily concerned with how they could keep the government from interfering with the way they wanted to think and act. Hence the early rights, the rights that were primarily talked about in terms of the Lockean rights of life, liberty, and property, were conceived in terms of such independence.

There is a very different sphere of freedom, which comes to the fore in the nineteenth century and which I have just called the freedom of participation. It emphasizes the active relation of man to his government. It is no longer a question of keeping the government out. It is a question of getting into the government and taking part in it. This freedom of participation manifested itself in the nineteenth century, if I may just remind you of this by emphasis on civil liberties, that is, the emphasis on those things which one needs when a man is to be an active citizen in a democracy.

In our twentieth century, this sphere yielded to yet another kind of freedom which I call the freedom of creation. This freedom of creation is today for many human beings more important than either the freedom of independence or the freedom of participation. On the most elementary level, every regime accepts it; on the procreative level there is no really serious problem though some of the totalitarian powers have tried to do something about it. As Gaetano Salvemini used to say, "Even Mussolini can't put a policeman behind every marriage bed." Thus, generally speaking, we can say that on that level all regimes, no matter how unfree in other respects, have to accept human freedom. But there are other spheres, particularly the political sphere itself, in which this freedom of creativity which is the freedom of invention and innovation is tremendously important for the development of the community, and for each individual human being it implies the problem of self-development. You may recall that, among the four freedoms of Franklin D. Roosevelt's famous proclamation, the last two are the freedom from want and the freedom from fear. These do not involve keeping the government away, nor getting into the government and taking part, but making the government do something so that men may be able more fully to develop as human beings. Thus the freedom from want refers to the problem of job protection. It turns up as "the right of work" in 1848. But it has now, for example in the Universal Declaration of Human Rights of the United Nations, become a distinct and very important part of these human rights and hence of those freedoms which presuppose action by the government.

One might even go so far as to say that a maximizing of this freedom means a maximizing of governmental activity. With such a statement one reaches the heart of the dialectic of political order and political freedom because, as the patterning of rights and freedoms has unfolded in the Western world, the conflict between freedom and order has become ever more pronounced. If you want, as of course these social and economic freedoms ask, full employment, as much education as possible, peace, you have to "organize" a great deal of order in order to get more of this freedom. This is the most interesting part of the topic, outlined here in the most general way. It is but very little understood by people who talk about freedom that these freedoms limit one another. You cannot maximize them all at the same time. If you want to maximize the freedom of independence, you are necessarily going to reduce the freedom of creativity, and the freedom of participation in the bargain. This conclusion could be put in another way by saying that maximizing freedom is a relatively empty formula because, until you reach agreement in the particular community on what freedoms you are talking about, that is to say, agreement on the relative importance of the several spheres, you cannot find answers to the questions that need to be solved. The debates over the civil rights bill illustrate this well. The property right, which is one of the old rights of the freedom of independence, is pitched against the right of education, which is typically related to the freedom of self-development, the freedom of creativity.

At this point I want to introduce a cautioning that is important in order not to get off into a Utopian and to some extent even romantically Utopian slant, which has bedeviled a great deal of the discussion of the problems of freedom. It underlies a good deal of the less sensible writings of liberals in the past. This is the assumption that all human beings want a maximum of freedom. It is quite untrue. So, in reaction to it, some people have gone so far as to say that most human beings do not want any freedom at all. Or they have said it with reference to a particular community. Think of Erich Fromm's *Escape from Freedom.*

These are just more limited variations on the same theme of assuming that there are many value positions that human beings are inclined to take, putting now one, now another value first. Among these is freedom. We all have acclaimed Patrick Henry who cried out, "Give me liberty or give me death." In fact, there are rather few people who are willing to say this and really mean it and act in accordance with it. There are quite a few people who might say, "Give me liberty and I'll pay a thousand dollars," or even, "I'll take considerable infringement on my job opportunities rather than surrender my freedom of choice," and they will actually act in accordance with it. But "Give me liberty or give me death" is going quite far. Even the old formula about the right to life, liberty, and property, left the question open of which came first; indeed, it rather suggested that the right to life was just a little more important than the right to liberty, let alone the right to property.

If, then, we recognize that human beings generally speaking do not really want to maximize freedom for a variety of reasons, and recognize as well that it is equally untrue to say that either particular groups such as the Germans, or the Russians, or the Chinese, or that mankind in general, do not want any freedom, I should like to suggest that most human beings want a minimum, not a maximum of freedom. One of the interesting questions is, what is this minimum in light of the three dimensions? The answer must be highly speculative. But into this minimum belongs, for many human beings, the choice of their mate for purposes of procreation. It happens to be within the realm of creative freedom. I think that beyond that a very considerable though perhaps a somewhat lesser, number of people are very keen about having the freedom of choosing their job, what they are to do. If you make investigations among people who have lived under totalitarian regimes, e.g., Soviet escapees who have been interviewed, what they most objected to was that they were not free to determine their kind and place of work. Sometimes one can sell people on a particular job, but generally speaking the choice of work is another part of the minimum, again in the realm of creative freedom. It is probably true in our Christian tradition—I do not know how far this carries beyond the Christian tradition—that most people desire the minimum freedom in connection with their religious convictions. This freedom has always been recognized in Christian theology, although by no means practiced by Christian practitioners. Human beings everywhere tend, in the Christian tradition and in keeping with the theology, to desire this as a minimum. They do not want to be coerced in basic convictional respects. Machiavelli acknowledged this, and he warned princes against tampering with their subjects' religion.

There is no time, nor is it necessary, to explore this in further detail. Our problem really is not how to maximize freedom. Our problem really is how to order the community in such a way that as many people as possible come into the enjoyment of the minimum of freedom that they actually desire. If we can go beyond that and order our affairs in such a way that there is a certain flexibility, so that those persons who have greater need of freedom are in a position to secure a greater amount of freedom, so much the better. We are members of an academic community. I think there are among us a certain number of people who are passionately interested in the freedom to search for the truth. And, again, of these a certain percentage cherish the freedom to tell others about what they have thought, the professors. This country has a lot of trouble with academic freedom, because its Puritan forebearers in New England did not think much about this particular facet of freedom. They thought people ought to toe the line and stay within orthodoxy. By contrast a country otherwise not particularly noted for its concern with freedom in its political order, Germany, has been keen about this particular freedom. It has been steadily recognized, and was so even back in the nineteenth century, and the great flowering of the German universities hangs together with the fact that German rulers for a variety of reasons were willing to recognize academic freedom.

This remark leads to another point. I have already remarked that every regime, no matter how structured, will accept some freedom. There is no such thing as a political regime that can do away with all freedom. From this it follows that an increasing readiness on the part of the Soviet Union to permit creative freedom in the arts and in science, while an interesting development and conceivably a very important development, should not be mislabeled as a step toward democracy. It has no necessary relation with democracy, but is a particular way of patterning the social order in response to needs that order has: whether such a development is related to democracy or not is quite a different and separate question.

There is one final point. So far I have spoken entirely in terms of individuals and the problem of the freedom of individuals within the political community and its order. There is another problem of freedom, which I must mention here because it has been questioned recently, and that is the freedom of communities in rivalry with other communities. In a way, of course, the whole revolutionary upheaval in the colonial world springs from precisely such demand for communal (national) freedom. These peoples, large and small, are fighting for this liberation. Let me remind you that the Greeks, who proudly called themselves *hoi eleutheroi,* the free, were thinking primarily of this freedom of a community to order its own affairs. A tyranny, as long as the tyrant was of the community, was still in that sense a free community. I think this is the freedom that means most to a good many of these new nations, these nations in the state of developing a political order. Yet in several very significant writings in England and France one finds such remarks as: "Look at this terrible situation—in Algeria, in Ghana, in Tanganyika. The natives there were much freer before their independence. We maintained an order providing the personal and social freedoms, freedom of speech, freedom of education, and so forth. Their new rulers pay little heed to such personal freedom." What is the reply to such a comment? Their leaders, men like Nyerere, the prime minister of Tanganyika would say: "All you Westerners have always recognized that in an emergency situation, these freedoms must be curbed. The Americans suspended habeas corpus during the Civil War. We are in a state of constant emergency. We are emerging. We have problems to solve that are of a magnitude that obliges us to subordinate personal freedoms for the time being to the paramount task. But *we* are doing it *ourselves!* This is the freedom we cherish. We do not care for the freedom that the French maintained in Algeria."

Freedom is not something about which these people in developing countries deceive themselves. They have the hope that eventually their social order and economic well-being will permit it. The first article of the Draft Covenant of the United Nations states the right of self-determination for any and all people. It is a very difficult task to convert this proposition into political reality. But, in terms of freedom and order, one can see that it springs from the conviction that a people's freedom to determine their own affairs is their most vital one. This is the attitude, and I think it is very important to realize it, particularly when one considers world order. The freedom of the group, as contrasted with the freedom of the individual, is as much part of the dialectic of freedom and order, when we think in terms of world order, as is the freedom of the individual. And yet Americans, with their long tradition of effective, constitutional order, have good reason to be concerned. When they look at the constitutions in the Communist world which contain long catalogues of rights and freedoms, and observe that the actual political order does not work in accordance with the constitution and that there is little prospect of its doing so in the future, they have a right to worry.

On this higher level, the dialectic of freedom and order presents the same problem, the same dialectics, as it does in the parochial political order. There is no freedom without order; but there is also no order without freedom. If one tries to force one at the expense of the other, disregarding the prevailing values, interests, and beliefs, he is bound to fail. And I think this is ultimately the task that faces us. It is a task to which there is no answer that could be recommended as a possible panacea at this time. It is an open question, how we can structure order in the world community when, knowing that such an order cannot be achieved except in response to values, interests, and beliefs, we find the communities composing the world torn by the most profound conflicts between their values, interests, and beliefs.

This is the question, and, as I said to you, the first step in the direction of wisdom is to recognize what the question is, even though you cannot give the answer.

STANLEY HOFFMANN

In Search of a New International Order

All the international problems of today come to a single question: What will be the international order of tomorrow? In the competition between East and West, in the movement that leads former colonies to independence, it is the nature of this order that is at stake. International order corresponds in the realm of world politics to what is at the national level the constitution, in the broadest sense of the term: the aggregate of rules, customs, and processes that defines the competition of political forces, determines the conditions under which the norms of law will be elaborated, and even to a considerable extent defines the nature of this law. As is true at the internal level, international order consists only in part of judicial rules; the rest—the essential—is the product of political, economic, and ideological relations.

I should like to sketch a sort of outline of international law and

STANLEY HOFFMANN, born in Vienna, educated in Paris, is now professor of government at Harvard University. He is an authority on international organizations and French politics, and is also working on United States foreign policy. *The State of War: Essays on the Theory and Practice of International Politics* appeared in 1965, *Gulliver's Troubles, or the Setting of American Foreign Policy* in 1968. Professor Hoffman was Rosenfield Lecturer at Grinnell College in 1964.

This paper appeared originally as "A la recherche d'un nouvel ordre international," in *Esprit*, XXVIII, No. 282 (March, 1960), 478–94. It was translated by Jean Scanlan with the encouragement of the author for publication in this volume.

organization at the present time, and to suggest some directions for progress. It seems to me impossible to understand the present crisis of international law and the difficulties of the United Nations if the following considerations are not taken into account: classical international law is bound to an order which has disappeared—that of the system of relations between states which reigned in the eighteenth and especially in the nineteenth centuries. Entire sections of law collapsed along with this order. Statesmen sought to substitute for these ruins a new order in which law would play a much more ambitious role, and which the international organization would both symbolize and consolidate. The attempt, too bold and too precariously balanced with respect to the political forces present in the world, has largely failed. So, in order to understand where we are and where we can go, we must first go back over the road leading from an order which many remember nostalgically to an ideal which turned out to be a utopia. Today's international law is the dialectic of the obsolete and the premature.

I. YESTERDAY'S ORDER

The golden age of international law was the century of relative peace from 1815 to 1914. The order which then served as a basis for relations between states was characterized by the following features. In the first place, the structure of the international setting comprised at once a number of major powers greater than two, a certain balance of power among these states, and a very strict international hierarchy; the greater part of the world served as space for the expansion of the Europeans. In the second place, fairly strong ties existed among the major powers: the agreement on the rules of the game, a kinship of thought and of caste among the diplomats. In the third place, these powers, without having the same regimes, nevertheless displayed important common points in their internal orders: the conduct of foreign affairs remained for a long time divorced from domestic passions and pressures, and the separation of state and society allowed the members of the latter freely to establish bonds over the borders. In the fourth place, the relations between states which were established in such a universe remained marked by a double limitation. First, that of the realm of interstate relations: it remained restricted, both because numerous international activities were the work of individuals and not of states, and because enormous territorial zones were policed by colonial administrators, hence annexed to the internal competence of European powers. Second, the moderation of the objectives and methods of these powers in their reciprocal relations: the system of balance, the reign of ideologies all of which emphasized moderation, the compromise or even the progressive obliteration of borders were to make of the age of European concert a period when the life of the major powers was never at stake.

International law as we know it expresses this order beautifully. On one hand, since it was based on the mechanism of balance, there was no need for a rigorous institutional framework: as a result the political framework—the European concert—burdened itself with a minimum of judicial rules and resorted mainly to the delights of relations of force. But a law system based largely on reciprocity was able to develop within this framework. First there was the matter of defining exactly the competence of each state over its territory and over the people living in it: hence the law of territorial and personal jurisdiction. Then there was the matter of assuring orderly relations between states: hence the laws of recognition and of diplomatic immunity. In the laws of war and neutrality one could find most of the features of international order: the absence of a power superior to the states, and even of an international organization, corresponded to the right of each state to resort to war; consequently the latter received an actual judicial status. But the concern for moderation reappeared in the regulations: as a relation between states, war was to affect the nonbelligerents as little as possible. As a momentary interruption of the usual relations, as a method of settling a litigation but not a means of exterminating the opponent, it was to have a minimum effect on international economy, insofar as the latter was largely in the hands of individuals; hence the protection of neutrals, considered as fulfilling a true international public service. The international law of commerce also reflected the tendency toward *dépolitisation* of this enormous sector, and the development of arbitration could be explained to a large degree by the fact that many litigations which were submitted to it by states were concerned essentially with private persons established abroad, rather than with fundamental political interests. Thus a jurist of the time could write that international law amounted to establishing the principle of the sovereignty of the state and drawing inferences from it. There was no paradox there: the law organized, defined the limits, the coexistence, and the cooperation of sovereignties; and succeeded harmoniously because these remained moderate—both voluntarily and because the balance system forced them to.

All the features of the former order have disappeared. The structure of the world has changed radically. There are only two superpowers left, but the number of states is increasing at an incredible rate. This fragmentation of the world is accentuated by the increasing diversity of political regimes and the weight of the considerations of an internal order in the elaboration of the foreign policy of each country. Relations between states have suddenly become extended over domains which were formerly largely apolitical. The problem of development, formerly ignored, or treated by private investments, or regulated within one colonial empire, comes for the first time to the center of world politics. The economic zone left to individuals is reannexed by the states owing to the clash of ideologies: the constant concern for well-being assured by public power, and the necessities of an anticolonial struggle. The limitation of objectives and means has almost completely gone under. The birth, the existence, the form of states are put at stake by the revolution of nationalisms as well as by the competition of the great powers, each of which, as Raymond Aron has pointed out, offers the world a more or less vague picture of a type of domestic order and of a type of international order. If the technological revolution imposes a very important restriction in the use of means—both blocs shrink from a recourse to nuclear weapons—it provokes at the same time a headlong race toward impossible military security and contributes in so doing to the ruin of the moderation of old.

Under these conditions, the international law arising from the old order suffers three serious wounds. Parts of the rules have collapsed. The irruption of techniques of "hyperbolic war" in the strategy of states and in the spirits of men has brought with it the massive destruction of the laws of war and neutrality. The traditional rules of immunity have lost much of their justification now that the state has become industrial and commercial. The search for security and new resources destroys many of the limits that classical law imposed on territorial and personal jurisdiction. Next to these ruins there are gigantic gaps; for classical law had obviously not foreseen modern destructive weapons, nor the new methods of subversion and of intervention by propaganda and terrorism, nor the use as weapons in diplomatic war of competences traditionally considered purely internal, such as nationalization and the attributing and retracting of nationality. Here we touch the last wound: classical law, the product of an order with very precise rules of the game, rested on fundamental distinctions which no longer make sense—the distinction between internal competence and the domain of international law, the distinction between public and private, between the civilized nations and the others, between peace and war. Today, the choice of a regime always runs the risk of modifying the world balance (cf. Egypt and Iraq); transnational private groups (students, parties, syndicates) propagate ideologies and serve politics; big international or foreign private companies sign with the state contracts of which the judicial nature remains the object of violent controversy; armistices are carried on without peace treaties. Classical law prohibits submarines from sinking commercial ships, but does not contain the slightest arrangement for the judicial rule over aerial space; here the Alices of law departments find themselves wandering through a land of ruins and question marks.

II. THE INTERNATIONALIST UTOPIA

They are also wandering through a land of mirages. For this classical law which reflects nothing but nostalgic reminiscence of better days, a new law has been substituted which, aiming too high too soon, has accumulated disappointments and spread cynicism. To tell the truth, the concept of Woodrow Wilson and his successors is suffering from a redhibitory internal weakness. On one hand, it decides that since the former order had resulted in its own destruction and that of classical law, by leaving to the states far too much liberty of action (and in particular that of waging war), it is necessary to substitute for it a new order, dominated not by calculations of equilibrium, but by the rule of Law—an order characterized not by the absence of any permanent political institution, but by an international organization, the purpose of which is to preserve peace; an order marked by the limitation or even the prohibition of unilateral recourse to war and by the transferral of the power of legitimate war to the organization itself. But, on the other hand, this new community substituted for the former anarchy is not a power superior to the states: it is just a community of law, it is just the gathering of the states within one enclosure. Thus the restrictions connected with their sovereignty, which the new order implies on paper, will hold only to the extent that the states want them to; the law, which from now on claims to constitute the political framework itself, yesterday maintained by relations of force, remains nevertheless at the mercy of these relations. Hence a universe of fictions (which the theories of law of Hans Kelsen and Georges Scelle reflect admirably) ; there will be from now on an executive, a legislative, a judicial power of the international community, just "as if" the latter were a world state; but in reality this community does not exist any more than it did before. If its members behave badly, the fictions will burst like soap bubbles. If their behavior is reasonable and moderate, we will return in fact to the world of yesterday. And, as everyone knows, it is the first hypothesis that came true.

The attempt to submit the states to more restrictive obligations can be analyzed in two parts. There has been, first of all, a more purely judicial effort. It comprises the creation of an international jurisdiction which, it was hoped, would allow for the settling of an increasing number of litigations, not by force, nor by the uncertain and arbitrary procedures of diplomacy, but by law. This effort also included the attribution to individuals—and no longer just to states —of rights and responsibilities, in order to bring international and internal law closer together in this area as well, by obliging those in power to respect the rights of man in peacetime (hence the negotiation of international conventions on the rights of man), as in wartime (hence, after the Nuremberg trials, the efforts to create an international penal law, of which the 1948 convention against genocide constitutes a part).

That particular attempt was to a large extent shattered against the reefs of a world in revolution. Cold war and anticolonial revolts, so to speak, joined forces against the dream of a judicial community. The Communist block objects to international jurisdiction, and at a time when litigations between states so often implicate their very existence, the acceptance of the obligatory jurisdiction of the court of The Hague is definitely on the decline, in that either the states refuse it entirely or (like the United States) they surround it with paralyzing reserves. Recourse to arbitration has likewise decreased. When the greater number of states aims to change the law, not to interpret the existing law, then international justice cannot but suffer an eclipse. As for the efforts to protect human rights not only do the major states—the U.S.S.R., the United States, and Great Britain—agree in refusing all right of petition by individuals against their governments, but also the cacophony of divergent judicial traditions and competition of ideologies has made of this realm one of supreme mystification: the ideal of the defense of human rights serves as a choice weapon in the arsenal of the blocs, and to the already existing accusations is henceforth added that of genocide. As long as the mechanisms of implementation of human rights which the experts discuss are left entirely in the hands of the states, these mechanisms run the risk of becoming a new source of subversion and tension.

If the absence of a political community among states has reduced to almost nothing the ideal of a judicial community, it has also to a large extent caused the failure of the second great attempt: the transfer of part of the powers formerly held by sovereign states to the international organization. To simplify, the United Nations can be reduced to three main functions: first, the institution of collective security, a secularized form of the medieval conception of just war; second, the peaceful settling of differences and planning of procedures for the "peaceful change" of situations that have become dangerous to international security; third, the organized cooperation of the states in economic and social matters. In other words, it was a question of re-establishing a world order by substituting for political automatisms (balance) and economic ones (an international economy of free trade) a deliberative organization, endowed with sufficient powers.

We are far from that. If there is one point on which most of the states agree, it is the abandonment of the United Nations' functions of collective security. The United States, by organizing in 1950 the transfer of the powers of the Security Council, paralyzed by veto, to the General Assembly, thought to revive these functions in so doing. But at the present time, the principle on which collective security is based—everyone against the violator—remains blocked by the play of coalitions. Applied literally in an East-West conflict, it might lead to a third world war (cf. the Hungarian crisis of 1956) ; the small states are almost unanimous in emphasizing the conciliatory and not the repressive role of the United Nations, and the great powers prefer to count on their regional alliances. As for the explosions that occur in other parts of the world, the interferences of the cold war are such that the great powers tacitly prefer to localize the conflicts rather than to generalize them by collective security. For that matter the latter assumes a definition of aggression, which still does not exist.

In areas concerning the adjustment of situations and the settling of litigations, the gigantic changes that have taken place in the past ten years have seldom been peaceful, and the organization has been running after them much more than it has been able to channel them. The disputes settled basically by means of the mechanisms of the United Nations have been rare: Kashmir and the disputes between Israel and its neighbors remain hotbeds of tension. Basically, this absence of solution condemns the United Nations to playing a Sisyphus role, for it ends in constantly renewed incidents which the United Nations can stifle only by hastily improvising temporary arrangements each time.

Economic and social cooperation has met with various defeats by reason of opposition of interests. Whether it has been a matter of aerial transportation, of stabilization of raw materials, or of border disarmament, rich powers in favor of liberty which would have consolidated their predominance have constantly clashed with less favored powers seeking their safety in a certain degree of protectionism. The funds placed at the disposal of the United Nations for technical assistance and economic development have remained very limited. The organization had been built on three postulates which turned out to be false. The first was the hypothesis of the continued collaboration among the great powers, victors in 1945; the functioning of the entire mechanism of collective security and of ruling of disputes in the charter depended on their consent. The second postulate waś, so to speak, the heritage of the liberal vision of international relations: the idea that most litigations would not be so serious that they could not be settled by elaborate compromises between the parties, with the help of international mechanisms, according to traditional diplomatic procedures and without attacking the zone of internal competence of the states. Finally, there was the hypothesis of a fairly prompt return to normal in international economy: after a period of transition and reconstruction, we would come back to a world with no serious monetary imbalances or structural troubles in the balance of payments, where private capital would again take over the essential role in international investments, and where a world commerce freed from the restrictions accumulated since the great depression would again become possible. However, instead of this harmonious and uncomplicated order, the United Nations has had to face the worst storms; in order to remain afloat in spite of the wreck of the San Francisco Charter, the General Assembly has attempted to behave as a sort of world parliament, adopting from the majority to two thirds of the resolutions, often comminatory, on all things. Unfortunately the given facts themselves, which had made the initial postulates weak—the absence of community, the immensity of the stakes which the cold war emphasizes, the revolution of nationalisms, and the quest for economic development—at the same time took away from the General Assembly any chance of making itself obeyed easily.

Indeed, the United Nations remained without a grip on three groups of factors that condition the behavior of states. The internal circumstances that determine the choice of a regime, the form of institutions, and the nature of political forces totally escape the world organization. The major directions of the foreign policy of a state, its alliances, its economic and military potential are so many given facts which the United Nations must put up with. And finally, as long as the conflicts and the distrusts of states hinder the setting up of collective mechanisms that will replace unilateral recourse to force, the states that consider themselves injured will not be able to give up the traditional *ultima ratio,* even if it means disguising it as reprisals, police operations, or legitimate defense.

III. PROBLEMS AND PROMISES: AN AMBIGUOUS LAW

Nevertheless, in a world that is transforming itself before our eyes an ambiguous international order is emerging little by little, an order that is certainly neither the same as that before 1914 nor the one of which Wilson dreamed. While the cold war has regularized itself into competitive "coexistence," while the mass anticolonial uprising reaches its peak, having triumphed almost in its entirety, it is appropriate to examine the few new shoots that appeared during the most revolutionary postwar phase before describing the order one could wish to establish in the phase now unfolding. For it is from what exists today that we will have to start.

Along with what remains of classical law, an original law has developed little by little: that of interdependence. The realm covered by law has increased immensely: innumerable multilateral conventions, at a worldwide or regional level, deal with innumerable technical, scientific, economic, and social problems; specialized public and private organizations add to these treaties a mass of regulations that little by little define norms of conduct applicable to the states (as in the matter of working conditions). Certainly, the greater the number of subscribers or participants, the vaguer the obligations; the easier it becomes to agree on a multilateral treaty, by substituting for the old principle of unanimity conditions less weighty with elaboration, ratification, and revision, the more the accumulation of reserves by the states is in danger of transforming conventions into distinct and contradictory slices. Progress in extent pays in loss of solidity; but we should take a good look at both sides of the coin.

Similarly, the law of reciprocity and of delimitation has made some ambiguous progress over the ruins of classical law. The states assert their rights acquired over the sea that surrounds them, over the subjects who live in their country; but efforts develop to come up with a new definition of these rights, acceptable to the majority of the states. The recent conference on sea rights and the even more recent agreement on demilitarization of the Antarctic indicate that compromises are not impossible, although on essential points the agreement either could not take place (extent of territorial waters) or it only registered the appetites of the states (continental shelf).

The ambiguity reappears, in the highest degree, in the United Nations. On one hand, instead of being the organ of a universal community, it is one more instrument at the service of the states. The great powers seek their clients there and use it as a forum of propaganda; the small states—thanks to the transfer of authority from the Council to the Assembly—have been able to use it as a sort of compensating power: they have been able to group together at the heart of the organization to hasten the decomposition of colonial empires and accentuate the pressure on industrial powers for economic development; in short, they have been able to make the United Nations a catalyst and an accelerator. To the extent that postwar international politics has been called a universal civil war, the United Nations is its microcosm.

But on the other hand, above and beyond this war, the United Nations plays a triple constructive role which is too often neglected in France, where irritation in the face of flagrant injustices or hypocrisies of which our country has sometimes been the main victim tends to bias judgment. In the first place, in the immense problem of decolonization, the United Nations did not simply give free rein to conflicts of interests, put a premium on violence, and multiply the number of sovereign states of doubtful viability. The organization also tried to reach a convergence of interests between colonial powers and anticolonial movements in territories under tutelage and, above all, succeeded in obtaining from industrial powers constantly enlarging programs and new institutions for technical assistance and development. Much more—in this realm, each political bloc is so afraid of leaving to the other the monopoly and the benefit of aid that the Soviet camp, after years of hostility, has joined in the new programs and in various specialized organizations; far from "subverting" them, it has had to put a damper on its efforts at pure propaganda and contribute to the creation of a more stable order among states—perspectives certainly poorly suited to the apocalyptic vision of Stalin's time.

In the second place, in the only area where the interests of all the states are identical—the prevention of a general war—the United Nations has played a modest but important role. By pressuring the United States to limit the war in Korea, by setting up various mechanisms whose purpose was to stop the conflicts arising in the zone of decolonization (military observers, police force at the Egyptian border, armistice commissions), the United Nations has consolidated the tacit agreement of the great powers not to resort to total war among themselves, and not to allow the lesser powers (even if they are their allies) to endanger world peace.

Finally, and most important, the United Nations plays a psychological role, but an essential one. It is to some extent that of holder of a sort of international legitimacy; we might smile at this, but no one can really do without it (does not the proclamation of the right of the Algerians to self-determination recognize this?). The true criterion of the state today, more than the classical characteristics (territory, population, government), is admission into the United Nations; the Suez fiasco showed that it is not good to rise too brutally against this legitimacy. Many things could of course be said against the "majoritarism" that reigns in the General Assembly, but each member seeks a favorable vote and tries to avoid a hostile vote. Certain practices, certain traditional weapons of states have become much more difficult to use (such as "cannon diplomacy," a too obvious intervention in the affairs of others). It is certainly true that this constitutes a premium on more subtle but no less unjust methods, and that the Soviet bloc is not loath to resort to the traditional techniques. But hypocrisy is sometimes an improvement, and the U.S.S.R. pays dearly in loss of influence for the brutality of its methods (as is also the case today in China).

To another extent, the psychological role of the United Nations is that of a unifier of the states' preoccupations. Of course their reactions remain violently divergent; but for the first time all, by virtue of their participation in the United Nations and by the role of the Assembly, are obliged to take a stand on problems many of which do not affect their immediate interests. The attitude they take in these cases is often dictated by considerations of ideological solidarity, not by calculations of direct benefit. This political mobilization of statesmen on the problems of humanity leads thus to the formation of multinational groups and transforms the notion of national interest: it can no longer be defined without taking into account universal principles and objectives. Compared with the world of 1920 or 1930, this constitutes a revolution. The role of the secretary general of the United Nations in this area has been remarkable.

IV. TOWARD A NEW INTERNATIONAL ORDER?

In international politics as in other areas, one can command nature only by obeying it. We must start from the world as it is. Since international utopia has failed, it would be catastrophic to attempt to stick to it. It would be just as vain, for the same reasons, to aim at a world government that would perhaps be more effective in making law rule than the simple juxtaposition of sovereignties in an organization of states, since it is difficult to see how one would succeed in setting it up. Surely, a new order worthy of the name presupposes an overstepping of the traditional sovereign state. In a world politically more and more fragmented, where the state has lost its classic justification, to assure military security; where territory is less and less sufficient for the subsistence of the inhabitants; where nationalism often threatens individual liberties; the sovereign state as it was defined by nineteenth-century doctrine is an absurdity. But to arrive at a new order it is necessary to go through the states as they are; there is no value in opposing some "real" world composed of economic networks that have no respect for borders, to the obsolete "legal" world which resists unification, as François Perroux too often does. An economist's utopia is no better than a jurist's utopia. An analysis of European integration shows that it is only to the extent that the states and political forces confronting one another see their interest in the overriding of sovereignty, that this will have a chance of occurring.

Our first task consists of defining objectives. It seems to me that, just as the image of internal order proposed by Western countries is that of a pluralistic society, the international ideal to be sought is the vision of a world where security and order would be assured not by any kind of imperialism, but by cooperation of nations. To the peace of domination we must oppose that of association. Not only does this ideal correspond to our whole philosophic heritage, but it also agrees with the fundamental reality of the international setting: a new order can be built only from the national state up, because the independent nation constitutes the essential aspiration of most men. Without a doubt the state is no longer a fortress, but it has become the melting pot of citizens, the framework within which they affirm their identity, as Rousseau foresaw. It is patriotism which, in many places (Iraq, Indonesia, Egypt), stopped Soviet expansion. Thus, the image of a world of free nations constitutes without a doubt the best answer of the West to the Communist vision; and all our efforts to preserve, in any form, ties that hide surviving traces of colonialism are in danger of collapsing under the combined blows of nationalism and communism.

But the proclamation of the right of peoples to govern themselves freely is not enough. A world of multiple sovereignties left to themselves might lead to chaos and provide a choice field for Communist progress. Our objective must be to gather the states, little by little, empirically, in a network of ties and institutions capable of providing for their citizens the possibilities for developing which are lacking within their borders, and capable of subjecting states to more and more restrictive common rules. The national state would thus remain, in law, the supreme formula of social organization, but the content of the sovereignty would little by little be made more flexible, lessened, devalued.

What methods are likely to serve such an objective? Let us begin with the attempts to be avoided. It is useless, first of all, to put one's hopes right away in a grandiose settling of differences between East and West; it is useless to try to entrap too soon, in a judicial code, relations which remain basically relations of force. It is possible, of course, to affect these relations in an oblique manner, to change their nature gradually, notably by engaging the antagonists in common positive tasks; it is perhaps not impossible to reach limited agreements in matters of armament, for example, an agreement on the suspension of nuclear tests or on the prevention of surprise attacks; it is likely that, on precise points such as Berlin, it will be possible to negotiate a *modus vivendi,* and that in various matters the agreement will be tacit rather than explicit, taking the form of unilateral parallel measures rather than treaties. But, in a realm on which depend ultimately the life and the death of the planet—that of East-West relations in political and military matters—it is useless today to seek more than partial accommodations. It is also useless to think that these will suffice in assuring peace, for only the assurance of absolute security for each political bloc would be able to elimi- nate the risks of conflict; and it is of the essence of international politics (particularly in a period of technological revolution, which creates a permanent instability of armament systems) never to offer the states such a guarantee.

In the second place, it is just as useless to begin in the sector of human rights and international protection of individuals. The es- sence of sovereignty is found today in the personal tie of loyalty that binds the citizens to the state (a tie that becomes more and more demanding as the state deals increasingly with welfare and, para- doxically, depends more and more in this respect on resources which are to be found elsewhere). That is why it is absurd to seek to provoke the states in the area of their maximum resistance to outside intrusions. Contemporary history does indeed teach us that the most spectacular failures in international or regional coopera- tion have occurred when a state believes its image menaced from the outside, that is, the image it thought its citizens should have of their nation or of the common good: the examples of South Africa, of France at the time of the Communauté Européene de Defense or since the beginning of the Algerian war, of the fiasco of the United Nations' pressure on Spain right after the war, remind us of this. The best way to improve the lot of human rights is to act on the international causes of the violations: insecurity, misery, disorder of borders; the internal causes are still out of reach in the disjointed world of today.

The tasks that can be undertaken without risk of producing more evil than good are, I believe, of various orders. If we are to create throughout the world communities more vast than the states, we should be working at a level lower than the planetary. It is impossi- ble at the moment to obtain a really integrated system of universal law: the deepest interdependence does not yet manifest itself at the level of the entire earth. Hence we should encourage the creation of political or functional institutions, the signing of all sorts of agreements of cooperation in all regions of the world, and particularly in the regions formerly colonized. To avoid having the new states isolate themselves from one another, become totally separated from their former masters, and delight in a distracting retrospective anti-colonialism, it is essential that the industrial powers of the West coordinate their plans for technical and economic aid and favor a regional rather than national development in Africa and in Asia. The ideal would be to establish contractual ties of association among the new states and the former colonial powers, and closer ties among the new nations whose administrative and economic foundations, and even at times borders, are doubtful.

In the second place, since it is a world order that we are trying to establish, it is also important to give thought to the construction of a universal law, while being resigned to the fact that the ties which will be established in this manner will be less intimate than under present conditions, will be based on reciprocity rather than on common interests, and will correspond to a lesser solidarity. Three kinds of measures appear particularly useful here. The first, in view of the common interest in avoiding a global war, is a considerable reinforcing of the alarm bells put in place by the United Nations: the establishment of a permanent international police force which could be sent as soon as serious trouble breaks out, and the extension of the recourse to observers, even, as much as possible, in litigations that bring East and West directly into conflict, like that of Berlin.

Then, in order to make the irruption of new states on the international scene as orderly as we could wish, the United Nations should play a more effective diplomatic role, and should develop to this end procedures for dealing in the litigations other than interminable explanations in a public place. Thus the secretary general, who tends to play this role alone, could be relieved. Then the United Nations could seek systematically (and no longer intermittently, after each explosion) to obtain a fundamental solution to the litigations that oppose the new states to themselves or to others. Finally, and above all, we must act in the immense area of converging interests of the states: economic development, scientific cooperation, international communications. Our concern must be to pursue the work of delimiting the competence of states on the space surrounding them, and particularly of defining their rights on aerial space. In addition, we must multiply common programs, public and private, of exploration of that space, and common programs for the exploitation of marine resources, in order to avoid the disastrous competition of purely national projects. The creation of a vast international public domain, including, along with the matters already mentioned, the waters of the great river basins and later maybe interoceanic canals, will be essential if we want to achieve a world order of interdependence. An international authority for development should be instituted, coordinating the programs already set in motion by the United Nations, having at its disposal increased supplementary resources and completing the plans undertaken unilaterally by various states, or simply regional plans. Under the aegis of the secretary of the United Nations, programs for the development of civil servants for the new states should be elaborated; a true international public service, a "pool" of international functionaries should be built up to be placed at the service of the new states.

V. THE SHORT-SIGHTEDNESS OF THE WEST

As is demonstrated by the present anarchy of the law concerning space (particularly the reluctance of the great powers to give up the use of space for military purposes), and by the timidity of the agreement on Antarctica, which creates no common organ, the increasing fragmentation of the world and the rivalry of the blocs constitute immense obstacles to such a program. But, to take an example, multilateral programs of economic aid have better chances than bilateral plans to make effective the economic policies of underdeveloped states, or to obtain guarantees for private investments, or to create ties of solidarity between rich and poor states without humiliation or bad feeling; this has been proved by the experiment of the International Bank. Similarly, the presence of the U.S.S.R. in multilateral programs has the advantage of submitting Soviet aid to common principles and procedures, of purging it thus of its ideological content, and of constituting the beginning of a remedy to the fragmentation of the world. To pass on to the political domain, while it is certain that recourse to the United Nations will restrict a state's freedom of action, nevertheless, the choice is no longer between free use of force and its complete abandonment, but between the unilateral use of force and the possibility of having it endorsed—and channeled—by international organisms. It is only if we take seriously an institution that reflects a part of our ideal of a universal order that we will be able to bring other states to serve this ideal. After all, the United Nations expresses—although certainly imperfectly—the world as it is: fleeing battles in the heart of the United Nations, we only end up finding the same belligerents and the same stakes outside of it.

To take the measures that we suggest, statesmen nowadays have at their disposal powerful levers: the universal quest for development is the very type of interest to which one can turn to establish institutions and rules that transcend the states. The fact that the African nations have attained independence under conditions generally less violent than in Asia, and the vagueness of the territorial limits of African nationalisms, are also assets to be exploited. We can hope that after the end of the decolonization a good part of the international litigations will lose some of their virulence, and that a return to diplomacy will be thus made easier.

What slows down the race is above all the apparent incapacity of the main states of the West to think in terms of a world order. France, of course, has had trouble considering the postwar world other than in terms of internal and colonial troubles; at best its horizon extends, for some of its people, to the limits of little Europe: a regrettable provincialism. If the *"politique de grandeur"* could make the French take an exact measure of the world after years of pathological withdrawal, it would have rendered a great service—but of course we don't know this for sure; as for the United States, brutally called to leadership of a coalition after a long period of isolation, led to create a new world order after having profited by the old one, but without having ever taken an active part in it, it has analyzed the world situation almost exclusively as a function of the cold war and in terms of tactics. Actually, the major obstacle in a world where international problems dominate internal politics is that, by a paradox easily understood, the reactions of each state to international problems remain determined by its internal experience, by its traditions, by the frustrations to which the weight of history or of geographic location condemns it, and by the difficulties of the moment.

Soviet leaders appear to have a global and long-term strategy. It is time that the leaders of the Western powers understood that each of their decisions engages them, and engages the world, in a certain direction for the future; each decision implies a choice between a world of closed sovereignties and a world of associated nations, whether this choice be conscious or not. If we adopt measures incompatible with the universal order we want to achieve, we will never reach the brink of a world where the life of the states will not be perpetually at stake, where resort to force will no longer be the most profitable solution for the settling of litigations, and where the borders formerly impassable will be broken down, peacefully, by many transnational organizations, services, and norms. To trust in unconscious actions today, or to do nothing but follow day-to-day tactics, is to deliver the world to chaos.

TALCOTT PARSONS

Order as a Sociological Problem

In this exceedingly comprehensive series of considerations of the problem of order in many different connections, I can deal only with a small bit of the spectrum, order in human society, but I think very few of us would deny that this has some importance for its members. Order is a sociological problem because the unlimited and random desires of man might lead to the state which is described by Hobbes: "a life poor, solitary, nasty, brutish and short." If our lives are not poor, solitary, nasty, brutish, and short, why are they not? So Hobbes presented a problem: explain how man's life in society is more satisfactory than in a state of nature.

The question may now be about contemporary opinion, particularly among intellectuals. I think a good many of our fellow citizens of the intellectual community would come closer to agreeing with Hobbes than is comfortable to most of us, though I really question at times whether they fully understand the utter seriousness of Hobbes's position. One of his adjectives regarding life in the state of nature which the modern cannot altogether accept as describing our

TALCOTT PARSONS became known as a translator and interpreter of Max Weber. He has taught sociology at Harvard University since 1927, serving as first chairman of the Department of Social Relations (1946–56). He is best known for his theory of action and social organization and is also known as the outstanding theoretician among social scientists, who are often empirical in the sense of avoiding systematic reflection on the social order.

time is the word "short," because since Hobbes's time the average span of human life has very nearly been tripled. And if Hobbes felt it was less short in the actual society of his time than it would have been in the state of nature, then I think you cannot say that we have retrogressed since the seventeenth century in that respect. But many find it nasty, many find it brutish, and David Riesman, for example, finds it solitary. We are lonely in the crowd.

I tend to take a rather more optimistic view of the situation, but it is a matter of exceedingly difficult balance. I want, however, to address myself to the more strictly theoretical problem: not whether we like the kind of order we have, but how do we account for it—and by most indices it is a kind of order. Length of life is not merely an incidental matter, but a rather deeply important one. State of health is certainly another one. The various freedoms we treasure in our own position and in our association with others also belong in that area.

The point of view from which I approach the above problem is very definitely a Hobbesian one. The mere fact that we have order is not to be taken to mean that it is somehow given in "nature," but it is a problem to explain how it is in fact maintained. One recalls Dr. Johnson's remark about the lady preacher: "The remarkable thing is not how well she preached, but that she preached at all." From my point of view, the remarkable thing about social order is not how perfect it is, but that it does exist at some sort of reasonably tolerable level. And this is true of a century that has seen two world wars and is threatened by the atomic bomb.

There was a very common formula in the last generation, namely, that somehow one's attitude toward problems of order was a simple function of one's conception of human nature. This is not an adequate expression of the situation, simply because it omits consideration of the structural conditions that have to be met. I think a very simple example is very illuminationg. I do not think the average driver of a motor vehicle is a particularly aggressive creature. He is not fundamentally bent on injuring his fellow drivers, much less killing them. Among other things, he might expose himself to injury rather seriously if he made a practice of being so bent. But the problem of order in traffic systems is a very serious one, not primarily because of the nature of the driver, but because of three basic problems: first, the fact that space on the roads, especially at intersections, is distinctly limited, and we would not care to face the public expense of virtually removing all limitations from road space; second, the fact that there is a high volume of traffic; third, the fact that if traffic is to be satisfactorily organized it must be on a basis that does not require each driver to coordinate his particular intention as to where he wants to go, when, at what speed, by what route, with that of every other driver. In other words, the advantages depend on mutual independence of intention. Given these conditions, I submit that high traffic volume on a limited system cannot move effectively unless there is an effective system of traffic control. It cannot simply be left to the optional adjustments of particular drivers to particular situations.

Now some of this control is by centrally planned and organized direction, but a very important part of the control is by conventions and rules of the road, some of which are enacted into law or promulgated by authorized agencies, some of which are essentially informal. In any case, it does take the form of normative regulation; that is, there have to be rules and norms governing the movement of traffic, and there have to be some agencies that will implement some of them and enforce them.

This is a very simple example, but I introduce it to bring home the fact that this problem penetrates all sorts of areas of our daily life which we do not think of as presenting, in the deeper Hobbesian sense, problems of order. Now let me state a theoretical proposition which would by no means be accepted by all my colleagues in my own profession or in other social sciences, but which I want to lay as the ground of a general analysis.

This is the proposition that so fundamental is the problem of order that the structure of systems of human social action, whether they be personality systems of individuals or social systems, consists of internalized and institutionalized normative patterns of culture —rules, values, and other normative components.

The emergence of this view of the structure of systems of human social action is the primary outcome of a great intellectual movement beginning approximately at the turn from the nineteenth to the twentieth century. On the sociological side there are two very dominant figures: Emile Durkheim, the great French sociologist, and Max Weber, his great German contemporary, the hundredth anniversary of whose birth was celebrated in the spring of 1964. Another contributing stream was associated not with a single name but with a movement which we tend to call that of social psychology

in the more sociological emphasis. I think the major figures here are
Charles Horton Cooley, George Herbert Mead, and William I.
Thomas, in roughly the same generation. I would add to this an
aspect of the work of Sigmund Freud, that having to do with his
insight into the importance of the internalization of moral norms in
the superego of the personality and of other aspects of the normative culture of the society in the ego as well. These seem to me to be
the primary sources. They in turn go back to earlier traditions and
are flanked in their own time and since by other movements, but
without anything like a comparable degree of theoretical concentration.

Let me just run very quickly through what seem to be the main
structural components at the social level, and then I want to say a
little something about problems of process and mechanism in various respects.

At the top of the hierarchy of normative components I would
place values. What do I mean by values? Commitments to conceptions of a good type of society. These underlie other commitments
to the normative system in that society. I think this sort of thing is
best illustrated in common-sense terms. We are apt to be very
ambivalent about values because we are so acutely conscious that
commitment to a value alone does not solve practical problems. We
are so acutely conscious of this that we sometimes lean clean over
the other way and suggest that it is of no importance whatever. I
regard the constitutional doctrine that has been so prominent in
recent Supreme Court decisions, that every citizen is entitled to
equal protection of the laws, as a fundamental statement of values
about the desirable type of society in which we live. Now quite
clearly, in the civil rights field this value is very imperfectly implemented, but would you really suggest that, in the interest of avoiding hypocrisy, we should stop saying that it is a value to which we
are committed? If we did that, then we would be confronted with
the question, What alternative do we accept? And do we accept the
alternative of there being superior and inferior classes of citizens
from this point of view? Or do we think we can get along by saying,
"Oh, there isn't any general principle that is applicable. Each case
has to be handled on its own merits as it arises."

This is a very common-sense kind of statement, but I think it is a
fundamental one. Values that are part of the structure of a society
are not all the values we hold because we must evaluate many kinds

of objects other than a type of society or subsystem of it, including persons, for example ourselves, societies to which we are not committed, many cultural realms, and so on. But, among the values we hold, those which are constituted of the structure of our society are legitimized by moral sanctions and in the last analysis, I think, are grounded in our religious attitudes. On this let me make only one point, however. This does not mean that those who share the same fundamental values must have the same identical religious beliefs. This is a religiously pluralistic society, but I think we can say that this broad value pattern of the case I illustrated and other parts of it are shared by all the principal religious groups. In other words, there is a convergence on values which is compatible with a diversity in certain aspects of a religious system.

Values in this sense, then, are spelled out and differentiated at the level of what I like to call norms, and make a distinction between values and norms. Actual legal rules and precepts are the principal content of at least the more binding and fundamental of the rules by which we live in a society of this sort. They are differentiated, in a sense in which values are not, by the functions of the actions which they regulate and the situations in which those actions take place. I have in mind here such complexes of norms as those associated with institutions like authority, contract, property, the conditions of association, the liberties and freedoms of the individual, and so on. They are in the first instance the primary subject matter of law, but then spread out into informal aspects in many different respects.

Subject to values and norms we have patterns of association of persons, which can be looked at from the collective point of view or from the point of view of membership or participation of the individual. In the former context I like to use the concept "collectivity" precisely, because it is a technical term and is therefore less exposed to the misunderstandings that come from using such a popular term as group. We would not, in the first instance, regard the federal government of the United States as a group. I would say, quite definitely, it is a collectivity in which we as individual citizens participate as citizens, both as exercising certain rights like the franchise, and as being subject to certain obligations such as the payment of taxes. But we also have an immensely ramified structure of agencies in the legislative and executive branches, and so forth. This is all very familiar. I think a particularly crucial component of collective organization is what we call office, by virtue of which people exercise authority, and I myself, for theoretical reasons, am inclined to define the concept of authority, and therefore of office, much more broadly than usual, and to include such items as the franchise as a form of authority. It is our votes that determine who is to be the incumbent of the particular public office, and this is exercising the authority of the electorate to make binding decisions, that is, decisions binding on the collectivity. This is an unfamiliar usage, but a useful one.

The individual, of course, performs a role. I think the most important single point about the "individual" I want to make is that it is not a name for the total personality of the individual, but for the sector of his action system by virtue of which he participates in a particular set of relations with others. The person and collectivity are not parallel concepts, because of role pluralism. You and I are members of families; we are also members of employing organizations or, as students, of the organization in the framework of which you carry on your study. These roles are not identical; they are in important respects independently variable, but the same people are involved in both. This, of course, is very elementary sociology.

At all of these levels, the broad pattern of normative control of our behavior is part of our personalities. The technical term is internalization, and it is one of the most important outcomes of the broad development of the theory to which I alluded that this has become generally recognized. The most fundamental reason why, so far as this is true—and it is true most of the time of the overwhelming majority of the population—we do not steal, or we do not physically attack other people, is that the prohibition of doing these things has become part of us, part of our personality, and we either could not do them, or we would have to pay an internal cost which is sometimes called guilt for violating these internalized norms.

This is true not only of prohibitions but also of prescriptions on the positive side. The most obvious kind of case is the motivation to achieve. Why do we work hard? Basically not because of the external rewards we earn—they have exceedingly important functions including monetary enrichment, and it certainly is true that a man wants to insure a reasonably good standard of living for his family, and his attachments to his family play a part in his motivation to work—but I think the deepest ground of motivation to work is what my colleague, David McClelland, calls "the need for achievement," which is an internalized need in the structure of the personality itself. I think we can say this is fully established.

Internalization in personality systems is associated with what we call institutionalization in the society. This means that internalization of the same patterns at many different levels is shared among many different people, and here we see a very important reason for the hierarchical ordering of normative components because this sharing can only be on very general levels if the roles and situations of different categories of people differ as much as they must in a very complex and highly differentiated society. Of course they must differ enormously, and therefore, if we share them, we must be able to do so on the basis that transcends the differences of our roles and situations. Sometimes sociologists have said that the sexes have different values. I do not think this is a useful way of putting it. There are always problems of definition in areas like this.

I am sure none of us would say that in order to render a judgment of proper behavior by a woman, it is necessary to be a woman. Men are excluded from being women, and women from being men. Of course, that is not the way it is. We have a sharing of standards and values but a differentiation of roles performance.

This leads to a second very general proposition, namely, that the most fundamental ground of order in societies is the internalization of the normative culture in the personalities of its members and the institutionalization of that in the normative structure of the society. This is certainly a much broader conception of the basis of order than that which is derivable from the tradition of Hobbes, or than that which has tended, I think, to be dominant in our economic and political thinking, perhaps particularly our political thinking, because the tendency there has been to center the problem on such concepts as interest on the one hand and authority and other forms of overt control on the other. In fact, we have been subjected to a very disturbing and even disorienting conflict in our intellectual history over the problems of interests versus ideas. Which is more important? I think the logic of this insoluble dilemma is exactly the same as the one that tore the biological sciences apart two generations ago, the question of heredity versus environment. Which really determines the characteristics of living organisms? Their hereditary constitutions or the environmental influences that play upon them?

Of course, it is now a commonplace of biology that this is a totally false dilemma. The answer is both, in interaction with each other, and I think we must say that the same is true of the issue as between ideal factors and material or real interests and so on. I think we have gained a lot of further insight and legitimation from recent developments, not in the social sciences as such, but in engineering and the physical sciences. I refer, of course, to the most important developments of information theory and cybernetics.

The fundamental proposition here is that systems which are low in energy but high in information can control systems which are higher, much higher, in energy and lower in information. Now, communication systems are typically low energy systems. The amount of electric current that it takes to run a telephone system is minimal compared to what it takes to smelt bauxite into aluminum. Absolutely minimal, but you can convey an enormous amount of information over a telephone system with very, very little energy. You can telephone the engineers in the aluminum plant and tell them how to regulate the process of smelting bauxite.

This is the fundamental principle, and I think we can say it is a general principle, certainly of living systems, for it has been developing very rapidly indeed in the biological sciences recently. I think particularly of the analysis of the mechanism of genetic inheritance, at the level of the total organism species and of the individual set. That is, the protein molecule referred to as DNA is an information processing system, not an energy system. And it is this which enables the continuity of the organization type of the living organism to be maintained and transmitted from generation to generation.

Freud struggled with this problem, and his secondary commentators are still struggling with it, but toward the end of his career, I think, he reached a basic solution of it which is the same one I am advocating here for my own field. He put it in the form of a metaphor. The old problem had been that what Freud called the id, or what are often called the instincts, is, motivationally speaking, terribly strong. Is it not simple common sense that the instincts determine human behavior? This would make the psychology of personality very simple indeed. But this is not the case. It is not that simple. Freud put it in terms of a metaphor. He said he saw it as if the relation was similar to that between a horse and its rider. Of course the horse is enormously stronger than any human rider. But if the horse has been properly trained the rider can control it in the sense that the horse will go where the rider wants it to go at the pace the rider wants it to go, and the superior strength of the horse is not incompatible with this control.

This is the basic sense in which I am pleading that normative culture in fact controls the far stronger economic and political interests that are in this sense the substratum of our social organization. I think we have reached the point of clarification on these matters where the older either-or arguments are now completely obsolete. They are still reverberating ideologically and in the popular press. They ought not to reverberate any more in professional circles.

I shall carry the development of this theme a step or two further. It is very closely associated with what I think is going to turn out to be a very important new phase of theoretical development in the social and psychological fields, closely parallel to what has been going on in the engineering and biological fields. And I believe that a very important reference point here is the new level of understanding of language. Linguistics has at last become a genuine science. This is not to be confused with philology. It is the science of how language operates as a mode of expression and communication.

This calls attention to the operation in our societies of certain generalized mechanisms that facilitate and mediate interaction among people, and, interestingly enough, money is one of these. At one level, every one of us knows all about money. It is what it is good to receive in the form of income, and what you need if you are going to get certain things that you want and/or need through the channels of market transactions of buying and selling. But, as a social phenomenon, money is not so simple and has not been terribly well understood. I will not worry about the semantic question. I think it is convenient and a good pedagogical device to say that money is a language. Some might boggle at that and say it is only a member of a family of phenomena that includes language. I do not care. But I want to make a crucial point: it is a generalized symbolic medium of communication.

It has taken the science of economics a long time to emancipate itself from the view that money really is only a rather special kind of commodity. There is another semantic problem there, but again the point is that its important property is not its value in use, as the classical economists put it, but its value in exchange. And the problem is what does value in exchange, as distinguished from value in use, rest upon? In the same sense, the physical properties of the particular sounds that are issuing from my vocal apparatus now are of no importance to you except as the conventions of the English language which you, knowing that language, can interpret and understand. That is, I am conveying information, not energy, in this technical sense. Value in use is an energy category in the information theory sense, not an information category.

I should like to assimilate not only money, but political power, to this category of the generalized symbolic mechanism, as well as certain others which I cannot take time to go into, but this includes a category that I would call influence, in a rather technical sense, which is exceedingly important in the political process and in many others. With respect to all of these media, there is an interesting and fundamental duality. We can see it in the case of money, I think, very clearly, and it is well understood by economists in this respect. On what does the value of money rest? Not one thing, but two things, which are important in different contexts. When I say two things, I mean two kinds of things. On the one hand, the value of money rests on its relation to real assets, to things that have value in use, whereas land, diamonds, and all that sort of thing are the kinds of things to which holders of money take flight when they think the monetary system is in danger of collapse in the case of a runaway inflation, for example. A very special part has been played by the precious metals in this respect, as the form of money that was closest to a real asset. Keynes, at one point, makes the remark that land has a significance somewhat similar to that of gold in relation to money, and I think this is quite correct.

This is what you might call the security base of monetary systems, but only a very tiny proportion of the money in circulation is covered by metallic reserves, as we are all aware. What, then, does this vast superstructure of paper money and bank credit and deposits and so forth rest upon? There is one general formula. It rests upon the productivity of the economy for its value; this is the flow of goods and services for which it will be exchanged.

This duality of formula can be generalized. Let me just state what I think it is for political power; and here, when I speak of political power, I mean political in the broad sense that includes the functioning of private collective organization as well as governmental. The analogue of value in use in the power context I take to be realistic capacity to coerce or compel, and its political importance derives essentially from the relation to collective action of the bindingness of decisions and commitments. If a decision is binding, then it cannot be a matter of simple personal preference whether the obligation that flows from it is or is not fulfilled.

Effective means of coercion, in order to implement the binding-ness of decisions in case they are challenged, is the analogue of the real asset for the economic case. And physical force has a place in this respect parallel to that of gold in monetary systems. As Karl Deutsch of Yale University put it, I think very correctly, it is a damage control mechanism. When the system is threatened, if it is a monetary system, you rush gold reserves to try to stop the spread of panic and so on; and if it is a political system, you rush police or military forces to try to stop the spread of disorganization and panic, the undermining of order. But this is not the whole of the power system. The old argument of coercion versus consensus is exactly paralled in this field to gold versus productivity, and it has the same logical structure of the other arguments I have been reviewing and the same intelligibility of the either-or alternatives.

Resting on consensus is the fundamental process, the property of political systems. This is what is parallel in political systems to productivity in economics.

The more complex and differentiated a society, the more its functioning must rest not only on institutionalized normative cul-ture in the sense I have outlined, but also on the effective operation of such generalized mechanisms. Adam Smith's famous idea of the division of labor is prototypical of the differentiation of society as an intercomplex unit. In precisely the market sense, or in a sense parallel to it, this is always attended with risk; that is, the money in my pocket does not have value in use. I cannot eat it or wear it. And the power of an organizational office, public or private, is not effective means of coercion. It is a medium by virtue of which one hopes as long as the system is operating properly to have one's decisions effectively implemented. But one cannot go out and beat up the recalcitrant person and make him do it. This would be a deflated power system.

Now, not only is this true, but these media open the door to the most important possibilities of innovation, of creative change, in our type of system. Again, the economic analogy is a very important one, and its parallel in the political and other fields is very impor-tant. Political theorists generally have taken the position that power should be treated as what, on the basis of the theory of games, people call a zero sum phenomenon. Economists fortunately got over that idea with respect to money long ago. Money is not the zero sum phenomenon. It is an expansible and contractible phenomenon as a function of the economic process, and the creation of credit is a fundamental mechanism of its extent. I suggest that the creation of political power is directly parallel to the creation of money through the credit mechanism, and that power is an expansible and contractible medium, but if this is true there are political analogues of inflation and deflation. There is another element of risk, therefore, of the insecurity of order in the nature not only of the economic aspect of society, but of many other aspects.

It seems to me these media are particularly crucial in our type of society because ours is a pluralistic and, relatively speaking, decentralized society. We could not tolerate the centralization of a Soviet Russia or a Communist China. I myself have no sympathy whatever for the conservatives in our political system who say we are already socialistic. This is nonsense from the social scientist's point of view. Of course we have big government, but ours is such a complicated society that we must have it in order for the society to function. But it is a long way from our level of development of government to a socialist state—a very long way, indeed. And we therefore depend tremendously on the kind of mutuality of expectation and trust that is involved in the operation of these generalized mechanisms. I would therefore suggest that, if we are to be concerned with order at the social level, we not only need to understand the basic institutional structures and their relation to the psychology of the individual personality, but we also need to understand—much more extensively than the social scientists now do—the operation of the interaction and communicated processes by which the society goes on, and the conditions of order in those processes.

SAMUEL E. STUMPF

The Moral Order
and the Legal Order

Modern man's life is controlled more effectively, forcefully, and in greater detail by law than by any other agency of social control. His obligations to his fellow man to keep promises, to respect property, and to refrain from injuring others—these obligations, when fully analyzed and expanded, cover an extraordinarily broad range of human behavior, and all of it has gradually come under the domain of law. That many people are not consciously aware of the operation of law upon their lives does not necessarily mean that their lives are being lived in detachment from the law. This unconsciousness about the law could very well mean the opposite—that our lives are so fully encompassed and controlled by the law that only on the occasion of some deviation from it are we made specifically aware of how closely the law hovers over us.

We are usually most sensitive about the rule of law when we feel that we have suffered some injustice or wrong. At such a time we quickly invoke a rule of law, or in the absence of such a rule, express

SAMUEL ENOCH STUMPF, after a successful chairmanship of the Philosophy Department of Vanderbilt University (1952–67), became president of Cornell College in Iowa. He was lecturer in jurisprudence at Vanderbilt Law School and was in 1951 the youngest scholar ever to hold the Gates Lectureship at Grinnell College. His most recent books are *From Socrates to Sartre* (1966) and *Morality and the Law* (Nashville, Tenn.: Vanderbilt University Press, 1966). This essay appears in a different form in the latter.

our anguish by saying "there ought to be a law against it." On the other hand, there are times when certain creative forces in our nature are frustrated by the inflexibility of a legal rule, when modes of behavior suggested by our moral urge are made impossible or difficult to perform because of the requirements of law. When this happens, we are deeply critical of the law, even of the idea of law, and express this criticism with the derisive term "legalism."

This ambivalent attitude of affirmation and criticism of the law may seem contradictory. It may also suggest a pervading egoism in human nature which makes one quickly willing to impose the strictures of law upon others while claiming an immunity from such restrictions upon oneself. But neither the contradictoriness of affections nor the egoism in human motivation is the chief lesson to be learned from man's ambivalent attitude toward the law. There is no real or necessary contradiction between seeking the rule of law in one instance and expressing deep irritation over a law's inflexibility in another. Both of these attitudes spring from the same source, from our moral sensitivity. Even before there is a law, we feel there ought to be one, and even after there is a law, we still retain the feeling that a law ought to adjust itself not only to mechanical considerations but more significantly to the requirements expressed by our moral concerns. This double attitude of affirmation and criticism suggests, therefore, not so much the perversity of human character as the complex nature of law. It suggests that, however we think about the nature of law, we cannot account for what law is without at the same time taking into account man's moral nature.

It may seem paradoxical that, in spite of the pervasive influence and control the law has upon our lives, at the same time we should have so much difficulty achieving a clear concept of law. And no one seems to have more difficulty with this concept than the jurists themselves, who are closest to the working arena of the law. The source of this difficulty is the law's many-sidedness, which no simple definition can fully grasp or contain. In ordinary discourse men generally know what they mean when they refer to law, and, in spite of disagreements among jurists about the technical meaning of law, cases are daily being decided and settled as though the nature of law were quite clear. But attempts to articulate just what is meant by the term "law" or the rule of law reveal deep and serious disagreements over how we shall understand the nature of law. And these disagreements are serious because they affect not only the theoretical concerns of jurists but also the practical enterprise of achieving the rule of law.

The most formidable difficulty encountered in understanding the nature of law is the difficulty of accounting for the moral element in law. Law moves in a strange and imprecise way between the domains of power and morality. While the living law is capable of accommodating these diverse domains in their fluctuating proportions, recognizing the function of power at one moment and the demands of morality at another, the process of conceptual definition is less successful in grasping this double life of the law. The process of definition is, after all, a process of inclusion and exclusion. A definition of law is therefore a statement at once of what law is and of what it is not. If a definition of law is able to account for the element of power but not for the element of morality, such a definition has the effect of saying that law is force and that law is not morality. While we might agree that law is not identical with morality, we do not want to say that law is simply force. To define law in terms of force is to define not law but force! This reduction of law to force is the consequence chiefly of the severity of narrow definition and not the result of a true account of the nature of law. The use of simple definitions for explaining law has very little success and value in dealing with the nature of law. The chief limitation of the technique of definition in this case is that a definition is most successful when dealing with a *thing*. But the word "law" does not refer to a simple thing in the same manner that the word "table," for example, does. There is a marvelous correspondence between the word "table" and the actual table. The jurist would like to achieve this same precision and accuracy when he uses the concept of law. But the single word "law" is incapable of suggesting, by itself, the rich freight borne by the concept of law. For this reason, whenever jurists seek to define law with the same precision achieved in defining a table, there is bound to be some major distortion of the concept of law. For most definitions of law have lifted out of the full phenomenon of law the element that lends itself most easily to a direct identification, as in the case of John Austin, who defined law as "the command of the sovereign," and Justice Holmes, who spoke of law as "what the courts do in fact." Since the moral element is the most difficult element either to identify or to manage in any definition, this element gives most difficulty in fashioning the concept of law.

The separation of law and morals is not a casualty solely of the stringent process of definition. This separation is mandatory if we are to preserve both the clarity of the concept of law on the one hand and the purity of moral obligations on the other. There is the constant danger that, if the identification of law with morals is too close, then the law will become the substitute for our moral standards; if the law *is* our moral standard, we have lost the possibility of a moral criticism of the law. Moreover, the requirements of moral obligations are of a kind which the law cannot in every way encompass or enforce. Hence, the separation of law and morals reflects a recognition of the differences between them.

However, the comparison between law and morals brings to light not only differences between them but also similarities. The similarities between law and morality are as significant as the differences. Moreover, the discovery of these similarities has an important bearing upon how we shall understand what is meant by the concept of law, for, if we discover a close relationship between law and morality, then we can quite legitimately say that law is a moral phenomenon, that the legal order rests upon the moral order.

In the following analysis, the word "law" will be used to refer to the laws of governments. The word "morality" will encompass the conceptions men form of the rules for prescribing human behavior. Whether these rules of morality are based upon a particular conception of human nature, as expressed, for example, by Aristotle or John Stuart Mill, or derived from a theological interpretation of man, or whether the rules of morality are simply the outcome of the considered consensus of the community does not, at this point, make much difference. For our sole concern here will be to consider whether we can argue successfully that law is a moral phenomenon, that in order to understand the full nature of law we need to recognize the intersection of law and morality.

1. The difference that strikes us first is the fact that law *commands* us to act, whereas in morality we *choose* to act. To be sure, there is the commandment to love our neighbor. Still, the moral command or imperative is distinguished from the legal command by the fundamentally different type of force that lies behind each. In morality, there is the force of conscience or even of persuasion. To this force the self reacts with a mixture of deliberation, internal struggle, and a conscious decision to obey or disobey. Apart from the pressure of the community about us, our final decision in the

moral realm is rooted in our personal choice to conform our behavior to the moral rule. The command of the law, however, has an official sound and is never independent of the apparatus of society's organized force. Our immediate reaction to such a command is to consider the physical or punitive consequences of our failure to comply. We obey because we have to. Although we choose to obey the law, for after all we could also disobey it, we did not choose to be subject to the law. The moral law is something from which one chooses to draw the rules of behavior, provided that these moral precepts are sufficiently clear and intellectually coercive. Men move with a subtle freedom through the dim domain of moral discourse, taking and leaving what suits their interests and tendencies, and they do this with no immediate adverse result. On the other hand, while men do from time to time deliberate over whether they will obey the law, neither the substance of the law nor its obligatoriness is in doubt. The legal command at once signifies what should be done and what will happen if it is not done. In this sense, the law commands, whereas in morality we are persuaded.

This certainly represents a fundamental difference between law and morals, the difference between external compulsion and internal affirmation of an obligation. But are we willing to say because of this difference—a difference which by and large is made dramatic by the presence of the threat of force lurking behind the command of law—that this entails a *separation* of law and morals? Do we obey the law *only* because it is commanded? Does the quality of obligatoriness attach to the law only because of its officialness, which is guaranteed by physical power? Is it not more accurate to say: granted that the law gets itself accepted in most cases because of its threat of pain, at the same time the law does not obligate us solely because of this threat? We are willing to be bound by the command of the sovereign because, in addition to the power available for enforcing the command, the content of the command "makes sense," is "reasonable," or is "just." We resent and resist commands that are "arbitrary." We tend to transfer to the domain of law-making a moral criterion; that is, we expect the substance of the legal rule to be morally defensible. The legal "ought" partakes of the moral "ought," and for this reason there can be no thorough separation between compulsion and choice.

2. Another difference is that the law is general and abstract, whereas morality is concrete and personal. The law necessarily has

to be phrased in an impersonal way because it is addressed to hypothetical persons who may or may not fit the category of behavior for which the law is framed. At the same time, the law treats everybody the same when they come under its operation. Although under certain circumstances differences between people are taken into account, by and large the general character of law has the effect of treating everyone alike. This makes the law impersonal and abstract; the officers of the law are made to think in terms of rules and not people, giving at times the impression that the preservation of a rule has a higher value than preservation of human dignity. Morality, on the other hand, stresses obligations not to rules but to persons. A rule for the moralist has no existence apart from the concrete persons who live by it, whereas the abstract nature of law frequently calls for behavior solely in the name of the law.

Moral rules can and do come under the same criticism as legal rules, for moral rules can also be abstract. The injunction "love thy neighbor" still leaves unclear what exactly is meant by love and just who is one's neighbor. A person can very well follow the moral rule out of a greater concern for the rule than for the neighbor. Moreover, a moral rule will often get accepted out of respect for the source from which it issues. Here again the moralist places more emphasis upon the rule, this time its origin, than upon the person in whose behalf it is made. What this shows is that moral rules also possess a general and abstract character, that at times they take precedence over persons and to this extent resemble legal rules. The difference, however, is that the moral rule possesses the possibility of wide flexibility in a way that the legal rule does not. The requirements of morality render the moral rule more supple and adjustable to concrete circumstances than is the case with the legal rule, whose rigor requires its enforcement even when to do so in a particular case clearly seems harsh.

Too much can be made of the abstract and general character of law as the reason for its being different from the rules of morality. Although a legal rule is in fact general, it nevertheless does refer to concrete human beings whose behavior it is designed to regulate. Whoever formulates a legal rule certainly has in mind the possibilities, tendencies, and dispositions of human beings and proceeds on the assumption that these conditions of behavior are common to most men. It is hardly correct, therefore, to say that the law is abstract if this means that the law does not take into account the capacities of concrete persons. We have already said that in this regard morality does not differ from a legal rule, for the moral rule is also general. The moral rule is founded upon the same premise as the legal rule, for the moral rule also assumes that there are basic similarities between all human beings. A moral rule can be general without being abstract, that is, without losing contact with concrete human beings. Even a highly flexible and dynamic morality that puts greatest emphasis upon the peculiar requirements for behavior imposed by the special circumstances of the moment must proceed on the conviction that not only this person or these persons should be treated in this way but that *any* person under these circumstances should get this treatment precisely because this is the *human* thing to do.

Morality has its own way of being general, of abstracting certain stable structures from human nature and assuming that these qualities will be present wherever human beings are present. The very notion of "person" already implies certain determinate characteristics which at once identify a moral agent and at the same time prescribe his obligation. Moral obligation assumes the stability and the primacy of certain human characteristics, and it is possible to speak of these in general terms (as for example, "worth," "dignity," "equality," "freedom," and "rights") without speaking of any person in particular. Thus, both legal rules and moral rules envision a human nature; both are general in their formulation, and both are abstract in that they rise above *particular* persons. But the legal rule, just like the moral rule, is chiefly concerned with the behavior of human beings, and for this reason the category of law is not fundamentally different from the moral category. Indeed, the moral element as here described is built into the legal rule. Many of the same criticisms one can level at the law can be directed at moral rules as well. It becomes quite clear that we are not dealing with a separation of law and morals, we are simply acknowledging that there are some differences between them. The conclusion is, therefore, not that the law is incapable of taking into account the lives of concrete persons the way morality does; it is rather that the law contains reasons for its enforcement which go beyond the special concerns over the persons immediately involved.

The importance of the quality of "generality" in law is not that it deflects law from personal concerns but rather that it seeks to be relevant to many persons and many times. In order to retain the relevance of a law for a continuous period of time, it is necessary to preserve its general character without identifying the law with any particular event. The law against murder does not stipulate anything about the instruments used or the times at which the act is committed, for it must be able to control all the great variety of ways in which the act is committed. But even here the law shows considerable flexibility, for the specific result of killing a person has a wide variety of legal consequences. The law takes into consideration such factors as self-defense, duress, accident, and mistake. Still, it is true that the law will at many points lead to a different action from a solution suggested by morality.

3. Laws are valid in a particular place, whereas moral rules are able to cross over boundaries. A system of laws is effective and applicable in a limited geographical or cultural area. Only under special circumstances does a person in one state or nation have any legal liabilities under the laws of another state or nation. For the most part, laws apply to the regular members of a community or to those outsiders who actually enter the community either physically or through such channels as trade and commerce. A moral rule, on the other hand, does not have any known boundaries. If a person is under the moral obligation to love his fellow man, there is no way of limiting this obligation to a special or restricted group of people. A catastrophic earthquake in Chile creates no legal obligation upon Americans to come to the aid of stricken and homeless victims, but it does lay a moral obligation on them. Thus, legal obligations have a limited scope of applicability, for they apply to a special group of people who have a special and formal relation to the lawgiver. There is, of course, a limited relevance to certain systems of morality and certain moral rules, for not every moral obligation is recognized as universally acceptable or binding. We are all familiar with the relativities of moral standards both in time and place. This fact of moral relativism has the effect of creating limitations upon the applicability of moral rules similar to the limitations characteristic of legal rules. But moral discourse and moral philosophy, by intention at least, deal with human nature and not with local mores, customs, or habits.

The moral philosopher may in fact be influenced by his cultural setting in his quest for the standards of human behavior. But it is *human* behavior that concerns him, and not solely French, English, American, or African behavior. The premise of moral obligation, therefore, is that wherever human beings confront each other, certain moral obligations will always be present, as for example, to be honest, to refrain from taking what belongs to another, and to refrain from injuring another person. Exceptions to these obligations are of course easily conceivable, but there is a virtually universal expectation that these rules will be respected between men. There is no similar universality attaching to any municipal law, for the area of its applicability is set off by specific boundaries. Only when a municipal law is deliberately recognized, as between two nations, does it travel beyond its original boundaries. It is very much to the point here to recall that the jurist Austin would not accord to international law the quality or character of "law." For him these rules governing matters between nations were called "positive morality" and not law, suggesting that the law differs from a moral rule not only by virtue of a different sphere of applicability but rather by whether the rule is a command of a sovereign which alone invests a rule with the quality of law. In any case, we have seen here an important difference between law and morals. This difference, however, does not yet indicate a separation of law and morals; at most it uncovers the limits within which the law moves.

4. Another way of contrasting law and morals is to say that law is concerned with *external conduct,* whereas morality is a matter of *internal motive.* There is an external standard for behavior by which the law measures an act, a standard on which reasonable men will agree. But to get such agreement from reasonable men, they must be offered some evidence of external behavior which they can confidently analyze. The law is capable of making important distinctions between various types of behavior, and it makes these distinctions chiefly on the basis of external facts. The same act can transpire under different circumstances with correspondingly different legal consequences. For example, a man repairing a chimney throws or drops a brick down from the roof, thereby hitting another man and killing him. Three possibilities of what happened could be the following: (1) a passerby climbed over a fence and was walking along the side of the house where there was no path and where no one was accustomed to walk and was struck on the head when the bricklayer discarded a defective brick over the side; (2) the bricklayer had carelessly piled some bricks on the roof, and one of them slid over the other side, striking a mailman who was approaching the side door where he always delivered the mail; (3) the brick-

layer recognized an old enemy and hurled the brick at his head. The differences between these three variations are all obvious to a reasonable man analyzing the specific details of the external act; there is no need to know any more about these acts for reasonable men to understand the different degrees of responsibility and culpability involved.

The marks of morality, however, are not so external and are harder to enforce and therefore are not the immediate concern of the law. There is not only humor in the headmaster's injunction, "Boys, be pure in heart or I'll flog you," but also a dramatic reminder of what the law can and cannot do. The law cannot reach into the subtle wellsprings of benevolence and animate by force what by its very nature must be spontaneous and free. Nor can the law pursue people through all their waking moments and guide and control them as they touch each others' lives in an indeterminate number of ways and in varying degrees of intimacy. The rapid shift from one relationship to another between people renders life highly dynamic and fluid. The gentle suppleness of human existence with its constantly novel experiences, enlarging horizons, and delightful and tragic new turns and surprises cannot at any one moment be adequately anticipated nor fully captured in the form of a legal principle. The law must wait for a particular act, a single event lifted from an endless chain of human behavior before its mechanism of control can operate. But the event that triggers the mechanism of law is an external event, it is some mode of external behavior. Morality is so definitively a matter of internal sentiment and motive that it can rarely be discovered by the apparatus of law. Such subtle acts as those characterized by respect, considerateness, patience, forgiveness, sympathy, and love are deeply submerged in the center of the self at a far remove from the touch of law. While the law can command the payment of taxes, it cannot require the additional element of cheerfulness, and while some aspects of marriage can be controlled by law, there is no way for law to guarantee true tenderness. The efficacy of law seems to end at the threshold of man's internal self, and at this point morality becomes the arbiter of the human act.

Upon closer inspection, however, this distinction between external and internal behavior is not so sharp or clear as it seems at first. External behavior is never unrelated to an internal act or to internal motivations. The same external act can, therefore, be produced by a variety of internal motivations. While the law is concerned chiefly with the external act and, indeed, will come into play where there is such an act, the law does nevertheless take into account the inner life of motivation, usually speaking of this element as "intent." Thus, it makes a difference in law whether there was *intent* to murder, and the law goes to great pains to discover this intent. To be sure, intent can be discovered only if there is some accompanying public act that is objective evidence of intent. Nevertheless, the law is profoundly concerned at appropriate times with the inner life of the actor as the decisive element in determining the fact and degree of guilt or responsibility.

The law reflects the internal working of the moral self in still another way. Even though the legal rule applies ostensibly and in most instances to an external act, it is of utmost importance to bear in mind that the emergence or creation of the legal rule in the first place is an internal act. At its very inception the law is an internal sensitivity to a configuration of external fact. The initial impulse which suggests that "there ought to be a law against it" is frequently a simple moral judgment of an act whose repetition the law is fashioned to prevent or discourage. That workers should be compensated for injuries suffered in the factory becomes a matter of legal obligation only after the internal judgment that this is the "right" or "desirable" thing to do has been made. The moral sense of obligation between man and his fellow man is frequently the energizing factor in the creation of law. Once this moral judgment is fashioned into a legal rule, the legal rule has a life of its own and gives the impression of having a purely legal and not a moral complexion. An employer who violates a workmen's compensation law is not interrogated about his love for his fellow man, but only whether he has met the specific external requirements of the law. Still, a full view of the law which looks not only at its mechanical application but also at the reason and manner for its creation indicates that the law is the embodiment of internal moral sentiments. The law emerges from the comprehensive consciousness of the community and seeks to control the external behavior of men, but, again, the law can do this chiefly because it is addressed and communicated to the internal consciousness of the governed. Whether laws are good or bad, outdated or too far advanced for local public opinion is one thing; but that law, as a rule of conduct, is a reflection of the internal life of judgment seems clear. Hence, even though the law cannot enforce the injunction to "bear one another's burdens," in the sense of requiring every factory manager not only to compensate for injuries but also to express the attitude of compassion and benevolence, the law does in effect enforce the moral injunction in its external aspect.

5. What the above contrast between external and internal behavior suggests is that the law is concerned with *minimum moral standards,* whereas morals envision the truly good or *ideal life.* The scope of law is certainly far more limited than the scope of morality. In most societies the law limits itself to what are considered the basic requirements of social order. This is particularly true in a society that exalts the value of human freedom. The scope of freedom is in inverse proportion to the scope of law, for as the coercive power of law is extended over man's life, to that extent man's freedom is diminished. In a free and open society, therefore, the law is restrained and restricted to guaranteeing the minimal conditions for an orderly and peaceful community. The law provides the structure within which men can live with reasonable assurance that promises will be kept, property will be safe, and people will not suffer intentional physical harm. Once these minimal guarantees are secured, the law can refrain from prescribing man's conduct in more specific detail.

The law has frequently been considered as playing the role of an umpire, watching the race only to insure that nobody is pushed off the track or tripped. It is not the function of the law to make sure that everybody wins the race, but only that the lanes are kept clear. In this view, the law is limited to providing a race course within which various kinds of races can be run depending upon what the people find interesting and compelling. This is to say that the law as such is not the agency for bringing to fruition the full possibilities latent in human nature or its destiny. In this view, also, there may be a deep skepticism over whether there is any particular destiny or discernible structure in human nature whose possibilities should be coaxed into reality by the coercive agency of law. But even if human nature did require special modes of behavior, is it by law that this behavior should be ordered? The law simply liberates man from daily concern over survival so that within this secure context he can turn his attention and energies to those more intricate and personal relations which his moral nature urges upon him. In this context men assemble to marry, do business, debate, study, and worship.

They express ideas about goodness, justice, truth, and ultimate reality. They communicate through speech, the printed word, and various forms of art. They form associations for the production of goods, the education of children and adults, and the worship of God. Out of all these activities are distilled the rules of morality and the system of obligations between man and man.

Here the concern is with the proper conduct through which the full life is to be achieved, hence a concern over the methods and opportunities for successful survival, the maximum fulfillment of intellectual and aesthetic capacities, and the commitment to what is considered ultimate in the nature of things. The way men act in this broad sphere cannot be fully prescribed by law because life in this sphere is too protean. Large areas of life must be left untrammeled and uncoerced in order to preserve the possibility of free and creative discovery of new human values. That this involves risk to older and settled values goes without question. In the economic order, at least, the element of risk is clearly accepted, for here the prospect of loss is overshadowed by the possibility of great gain. In art and literature there is also the need for freedom, otherwise we see the dreary repetition of standard forms and lose the unique contribution of the artist, which is freshness of perception and expression. Education and religion, too, must be pursued under conditions of widest freedom if the deepest values inherent in the pursuit of truth are to be realized. The law is brought into these areas under great peril, for the law, before it can be the guide for the community, must itself be informed by the highest insights of the community. Can the law, however, decisively control those areas of behavior which by their very nature are still in the process of discovery? Can the law define what is truth or how God is to be worshiped? Only on the assumption that ultimate answers are already available to these questions can the law move into these areas with any degree of confidence. But, again, even if reasonably reliable truth is available to a community, is it within the scope of the law to regulate the broad area we have here been describing, or is this to be reserved for the more subtle control of morals?

Does the concept of law necessarily imply a concern with minimum standards of behavior, leaving to morality the role of making men moral? Historically this question has been answered for the most part in the negative, for the breadth of the law's concern is in no wise suggested by what the nature of law is. Whether the law will be used narrowly or widely is a matter not of the meaning or nature of law but a consequence of a society's decision about its use. Aristotle saw in law the instrument for habituating men to the morally good life; Soviet jurists see in law the agency for the remaking of human nature; and in the United States the law has gradually absorbed many areas of behavior that might well be considered the proper province of morals. Law and morals are not successfully separated or distinguished by holding that the scope of law is narrow while the scope of morals is wide. The scope of law changes from one era to the next, and in our era the law has spread its control over a very wide span of human behavior. It may be that the intimate relation between law and morals, and not their separation, is what is indicated by this variation in their relative scope, for if men do not perform voluntarily their moral obligations, these obligations will be enforced by the law.

The law never self-consciously or deliberately enforces an immoral mode of behavior; those who fashion the law, for the most part, believe that the substance of the law is required either by moral considerations or at least by the general welfare of good of the community. The scope of law seems to increase as a society becomes more sensitive to how men "ought" to be living or how the social life of men can be improved. At each step in the march of the law there is resistance to its invasion into previously "free" domains of human behavior; at the same time there is constant pressure for the law to move into these previously uncontrolled areas. What at one time were considered the minimal concerns of the law have been over the years so elaborately reconceived as to proliferate the law's influence with astonishing thoroughness. The simple guarantee that promises will be kept has expanded into a broader control over what kinds of promises or contracts will be permissible in the first place (cf. "yellow dog contracts," *Adair* v. *U.S.*) ; the guarantee of the safety of property has also been accompanied by a radical reconception of what private property means and what rights collective society has in this property (cf. minimum wage and social security laws) ; the protection from injury has also been broadly reinterpreted so that today injury is no longer limited for the purposes of law to physical harm alone, but now includes such forms as injury to reputation caused by slander and injury to personality caused by segregation. The legal rules and decisions regulating these sensitive areas are nonetheless laws for having moved into areas once held more exclusively by morality.

6. The law is *made,* whereas a rule is *discovered* as already there. Early jurists were fond of saying the opposite, that laws are not made, they are found. But by this they meant simply that the obligatoriness of a law was to be found in its moral defensibility. Surely laws are made in the sense that they emerge from a formal process of enactment. Certain modes of behavior are neither just or unjust, nor good or bad, before or until a formal rule is made to regulate them. The laws of traffic transform otherwise neutral behavior into delicts or misdemeanors as soon as these legal rules become official. It is an offense to travel at certain speeds or park in certain locations only after rules declaring these as offenses are made or promulgated. Without such an applicable rule, these acts are legally indifferent. The positing or making of the rule is the only way law comes into being for these acts. But the positive law prescribes our behavior not only in these areas which are morally indifferent before the law is made, for we have already seen that the law as often enforces behavior that is suggested or required by moral obligations. Even here, the law is made and has a positive character because it is the positive enactment of the official lawgiver. Whether the substance of the law is morally neutral or morally freighted, the quality of law attaches to a rule only when such a rule becomes an official part of an official system of rules by the positive recognition by the sovereign, through either the legislative or the judicial process.

Moral rules, on the other hand, are not made but found. There is no way to unmake a moral obligation. A law can be made and can be repealed; a judicial decision can be made and overruled or reversed. But the peculiar quality of a genuine moral obligation is that it is categorical, that it is required by the very nature of man. A person must respect another person, not because somebody made a rule or law to this effect, but because human beings intrinsically ought to treat each other this way. Although there are exceptional occasions when moral responsibilities seem to be waived, such as killing in time of war, there is no way of being released from the demands of morality. Whatever type of moral system we may confront, whether Aristotelian, Augustinian, or any form of existentialism, in any case the assumption on which the moral act is conceived is that our human nature, by being what it is, already contains or prescribes in some way the nature of our obligation to our fellow man. The moral rule is discovered or found in the sense that certain ways of behaving appear fundamentally appropriate, whereas other ways appear inappropriate and in varying degrees damaging to personality. Although human beings are capable of an almost indeterminate variety of conduct without infringing the quality of appropriateness, nevertheless, at critical points, the requirements of human nature clearly call for a particular quality of behavior for no other additional reason than that we are men.

How does this distinction which says that law is made while the moral rule is found help to clarify the concept of law? For one thing, it helps us to isolate from all the many kinds of rules the peculiarly legal rule. Moreover, of the many ways in which the word "law" can be used, we can now limit this concept to those rules which are the official norms of behavior for a society and which are made official in some positive way by the sovereign authority. To say that law is a rule of behavior commanded by the sovereign means no more than that until a rule has this element of positive enactment or recognition; it may be a customary rule, a moral rule, a religious precept, but not a law. When people say "there ought to be a law against it," they are saying that what at the moment may be only a moral obligation ought to be made a legal obligation. The moral obligation may have broken down, and now there is the desire to supplement the moral obligation with a legal obligation which is supported by the apparatus of official force. The moral rule and the legal rule may very well have the same substance, but what transforms the moral rule into a legal rule is its official recognition or promulgation by the sovereign. The moral rule by itself is not a law. But the moral rule can be or become relevant to the process of law. Likewise, laws do not in every instance have a moral basis. This means that, in the narrow view, the quality of law is conferred on a rule by the act of positive recognition or promulgation.

To say that law is made should not confuse the relation between law and morals. It is not necessary to accept the severe conclusion that a person has rights only if the law makes them or confers them upon him. It is one thing to say that to make a legal rule is to create a right, as if to say that until the legal rule is made a person has no right at all. It is quite another thing to say that when the legal rule is made the conditions for dealing with human rights in a legal way have been established. Rights have their initial form in morals, and the legal rule is the official recognition and the technical means of enforcement of rights. That is the meaning behind the phrase, "to secure these rights, governments are instituted." The law does not invest a human being with the qualities of worth and dignity and the other values that flow from these: these values are intrinsic to human nature when viewed from the point of view of morals. Certain behavioristic descriptions of human nature reduce man to a morally neutral status and account for whatever value he may have to the mores, customs, and habits of a community. Again, the moral philosopher, or theologian, while recognizing the relativities of cultures, nevertheless builds upon the common element in human expectations everywhere.

The identification of rights as they are suggested by the human urge that promises be kept, possessions secured, and injury prevented is never complete either in the fullness of their description or in their quantity, for the specific rights involved here come to light as conditions focus upon them. The moral priority of rights, however, does not alter the fact that a right becomes legal only after a law has been made, either by legislation or by a judicial decision. There are times when a moral right has not yet been legislated but becomes relevant for the first time in the course of a controversy in the judicial process. The judicial process involves both finding and making, for where there is no specific statute or precedent governing a controversy the moral norm is sought, and when it is discovered or when the process of judgment has matured under the influence of a moral norm, this moral norm is transformed by judicial recognition, interpretation, and application into a legal norm. The making of law is, therefore, not in every instance the beginning of a right, but in critical areas of human behavior it is the extension and transformation of the moral right into law. It is certainly not the case that every law is the extension of morality. Law in the making reflects all the weakness, selfishness, and predatoriness of which men are capable. There is no guarantee that the law will be made in accordance with man's moral insights or the requirements of his moral nature. But, even where a law has been made in violation of a moral right, the law is subject to criticism only because there is this discrepancy between the law as it is in fact and what the moral right indicates that it ought to be.

7. Legal obligation is not so ultimate as moral obligation. In spite

of the intimate relation between law and morals, the law is not the standard of morality. Law and morals are bound together for the reason that the function of law as an agency for controlling human behavior cannot proceed without reference to moral imperatives. To a large extent, the direction in which the law will lead human behavior is suggested by the moral tendencies of a community. But a community's moral vision is dynamic and is affected and influenced by a struggle of competing interests. The moral quality of law will constantly reflect the outcome of contests of power between representatives of different interests, and not all interests have the same moral quality. A law that seeks to enforce fair trials for all people clearly has a different moral quality from a law that prohibits members of a minority race from owning property. Every legal system is made up of laws that reflect clear moral imperatives, on the one hand, and laws that clearly cannot be justified morally, on the other. If the law were to represent our only standard of right, we would lose the independent perspective moral insight provides from which to evaluate the law. We constantly speak of good laws and bad laws, and we do this from whatever moral position we have taken. When our moral judgment condemns a law as bad, we are faced with the dilemma of obligations contradictory to the legal rule and to the moral rule.

In a democratic system of law there is a double basis for legal obligation. The law is obeyed, for one thing, because of its moral quality. Second, it is obeyed because it is a proper and official part of the structure of law. It may be that not a single law can ever arouse complete or unanimous consent about its moral defensibility. Yet, it is obeyed by virtually the whole community. There is a kind of morality that compels one to obey the law for the sake of the community even when one does not accept the moral substance of the law. To varying degrees the members of a democratic community will always have some criticism to make of the laws. Most of these moral criticisms have the effect of reducing or eliminating for such a person the moral obligation to obey the law in that he will decide that the law simply violates elementary justice, as in the case of an unjustly discriminatory tax. But the fact that a law is morally deficient does not immediately lead to disobedience of the law, for there is still the second basis of obligatoriness, namely, that the system of law, the rule of law that encompasses the remaining rules and procedures, must be upheld. This is particularly important when it is considered that an individual's criticism of the law may not be shared by other members of the community who also presume to be expressing their moral judgments. Again, even the bad law is obeyed under certain circumstances because in this way the structure of the legal order is preserved.

In democratic society there are specific remedies available for dealing with a bad law without threatening anarchy or chaos. Chief among these are the legislative and the judicial processes. It is possible therefore to renounce one's obligation to the questionable morality of the law and at the same time obey the law for the sake of the legal order upon which other important values continue to depend. In such a case one affirms his higher obligation to the moral rule in whose light the law now becomes morally deficient. The degree of "badness" in the law will vary from law to law, and thus the intensity of one's reaction to it will also vary. The bad law can be either superseded by a new law or challenged through the judicial process. If neither of these procedures is available, either because all the modes of power or the predominant opinion is contrary to a person's moral sensitivity, he then must decide whether to continue to obey the law out of a desire to preserve the legal order or whether his moral obligation overrides even this second basis of the law's obligatoriness.

The life of the law involves a continuous process of protest. No formulation of laws can ever be taken as absolute or eternal. The basis of continuity in the law is provided by those accurate and fundamental insights into human nature and its rights contained in the law which history continues to affirm. Legislation and court decisions prevail only as they continue to fit the moral and pragmatic expectations of society. Where these laws have lost their contact with either the practical necessities or the moral sensitivities of the times, they either fall into desuetude or are altered or eliminated altogether. There are times also when the whole structure of law, and not simply a particular law, is looked upon as of secondary importance by some in the solution of grave social problems. The overwhelming sense of moral obligation concerning human relations overrides the more deliberate processes of law. The feeling that the solutions to these problems are immediately mandatory and cannot wait for the inherently sluggish pace of the law or take the risk of a technical diversion or obstruction has often led some to bypass the procedures of law, and they have done this by disobeying the law. The law has learned to anticipate this problem and has made provisions for predictable protest. The objections voiced by those who could not conscientiously bear arms in any kind of war have led to an alternative for them to conscription laws, so that one who "must obey God rather than man" does not face the earlier dilemma which the conscription law posed for him. Still, though there is some postponement of disobedience to law through the double basis of law's obligatoriness and through the availability of regular procedures for challenging and altering the law, the time may very well come when for reasons of conscience a person feels that his obligation to law is not ultimate, that his moral obligation is of a higher order.

From this analysis of the relation between law and morality we can derive at least three major characteristics of law, namely, that law is (a) a body of rules fashioned for the purpose of regulating human behavior and that in the making of these rules there is dependence upon the conceptions of morality; law is also (b) enforced by the coercive power of the state, but this power is not the "essence" of law for it is brought to bear upon persons only in conjunction with a rule; also, (c) law is directed toward ends which the society is trying to achieve. The two main ingredients of law are therefore power and morality; law cannot be reduced to either power or morality. The intersection of law and morality is what renders law a moral phenomenon. Finally, (d) law is here seen as a flexible tool for regulating human conduct, and its flexibility is the outcome of man's ever new insights into what is morally right. The law is also the mechanism of stability and also predictability, and until the law is altered to fit our fuller moral insights the law is the bearer of our social morality.

Order: A Challenge to Contemporary Society

HANS HOFMANN

Order and Chaos:
A Plea for Flexibility

A few years ago, in a sudden flash, the American people experienced the very delicate relationship existing between order and chaos. On November 22, 1963, for a brief moment, the fundamental principle of the American political system was undercut. Whereas we are able to cope with destructive outbursts that arise within the established order, when the very foundation of that order is attacked we experience the reality of total helplessness. We realize how fragile are the structures of our corporate life, and we tremble. Ironically, it is only through an event of such enormity as the assassination of the President of the United States that we became aware that that which provides a context for all our functioning is not invulnerable, but problematic. At the same time, we do not appear to be able to tolerate the awareness of the tenuousness of life's fundamental structures. When they are attacked, as in Dallas, we immediately

HANS HOFMANN, a native of Basel, took his doctorate in theology at Zürich in 1952. Since that time he has taught at Princeton and Harvard universities. Notably, he directed the Harvard project on religion and mental health, 1957–61. Since that appointment he has been in private practice as a psychological consultant. His interest in Reinhold Niebuhr has developed into a deep concern with American culture, particularly with regard to value formation and value changes. He is the author of *The Theology of Reinhold Niebuhr, The Ministry and Mental Health, Making the Ministry Relevant, Religion and Mental Health, Sex Incorporated,* and many articles on psychology and religion.

smooth over the impact, explaining what happened as nothing but the absurd act of a deranged mind. We turn our attention to the details of daily routine, affirming that "life must go on." We appear to need the emotional assurance that there is always order which can dominate the outbursts of chaos. But why do we make such an assumption? Why do we seem to need order and the exclusion of chaos, at all costs? A look at the backgrounds of our culture supports the view that the function of order is to dominate and restrict chaos.

It has been an entrenched assumption in Western culture from the time of Plato that order takes precedence over chaos. The Greek tradition conceived the notion of the universe as a cosmos—a beautiful, harmonious, and beneficent sphere. Human personality was viewed, in potentiality, as the microcosm of the universe. Man's function was to mirror the macrocosm as perfectly as possible in his self, *Nous*. His task was to recognize, identify with, and represent the perfect order. Chaos was excluded as logically impossible.

Though the Hebraic-Christian tradition rejected the Greek notion of the cosmos, especially the idea of cyclical harmony, it, nevertheless, affirmed the view that order takes precedence over chaos. While it did not acknowledge that this world is, in itself, good and beautiful, it understood the Creator and Sovereign God as providing the world with order through His will. The vehicle, in the Hebraic tradition, through which God made viable His lordship among His people, was the covenant. This channel of control depended for its efficacy on the unquestioned faithful obedience of man. The heart of the covenant notion was the recognition that life and corporate relationship with God were indivisible; i.e., to be outside the covenant community was death.[1] However, because they were situated at the crossroads of the ancient world, the Hebrews and their descendants found it impossible to maintain such an exclusive foundation of universal order. Caught up in the international power struggles, they discovered that they did not have the wherewithal to live up to the fundamental demand of the covenant.

At this point, Christianity introduced the concept of the "new man." The real God and the real man, Jesus Christ, and those incorporated in Him, are ultimately freed from the corrupting "powers" of this world. The work of the Holy Spirit in the "new

[1] Cf. J. Pederson, *Israel, Its Life and Culture* (London: Oxford University Press, 1940).

man" enables him to fulfill the original intention of the covenant. As citizens of the *civitas dei,* the Christians have the vocation to manifest God's eternal order. On this basis, order was understood in Platonic terms. Chaos, however, instead of being merely the absence of order, assumed a new and more negative character. For Augustine, it is the product of man's sinful corruption. The result is a shift in understanding concerning how order and chaos are related. No longer could order be viewed as establishing its priority on the basis of cognition. Chaos could not be overcome by the act of penetrating through it to the underlying structure of order. On the contrary, chaos is to be overcome only by volition. The heavenly structure must be superimposed upon what, per se, is chaotic.

A new motif is introduced into the understanding of order and chaos, a motif that receives sublime expression in the medieval Gothic cathedral. Incorporating Aristotelian dynamism, the divine order is regarded as having already overcome and utilized the chaotic. Now, the latter merely serves as the raw material out of which the redeemed man sculptures his aspiration toward final union with the divine order. The Scholastics carried this vision even further, into the Thomistic unification of grace and nature. All the more significant for us is the subtle shift whereby grace becomes identified as order, and nature as chaos. This identification, however, augured the dissolution of the medieval synthesis.

By harmonizing the total universe, the Thomistic system no longer could account for the accidental. Just as the Jews had been unable to answer the pained outbursts of a Job, so the Schoolmen could not account for the sordid realities of pestilence, poverty, famine, and war. Ironically, at the very moment when the capstone of the Christian civilization was being lowered into place, symbolized by the construction of St. Peter's dome, the voluntarists of the Reformation and the naturalists of the Renaissance were uprooting its foundations. Attention shifted from the synthesis to the discovery of the actual.

The Reformers, though they remained medieval in their presuppositions, were convinced that the true battleground of order and chaos lay within man. Faith, viewed functionally, was the means through which man participated with God in the ongoing battle against Satanic chaos. Chaos was neither fully denied nor speculatively eliminated. It, rather, provided the somber background on which its shining dualistic counterpart, the ordering grace of God, appeared the more brilliant. In order that the notion of God as Lord even over the threatening forces of chaos might be maintained, the absolute transcendence of the deity had to be underlined. A truly operative resolution of the tension between order and chaos was thereby precluded. Instead, a dichotomy became fixed between them. The Lutheran wing of Protestantism concentrated its attention on the future kingdom and the church as its foretaste, leaving the secular powers to adjudicate between the earthly order and chaos. Calvinism, focusing on the building of the kingdom on earth, never achieved an immanent certainty of acceptance by the sovereignly transcendent God.

The children of the Renaissance ignored the religious scruples so blatant in Protestantism and the Counter-Reformation. They were highly suspicious that personal religious uncertainty, schism, and religious warfare brought about sociopolitical chaos and were unnatural "fig leaves" on the beauty of the natural. They regarded themselves as the unfallen inhabitants of Paradise, having as their sole task the glorification of God in His wondrous works. Seeking to have the best of both possible worlds, they superimposed the Christian God on the Greek cosmos. They banished chaos to the limbo of those who still linger in ignorance and the unnatural lack of grace. It is from this joyous blending of nature and order that result the faith of deism, the confidence of rationalism, and the curiosity of naturalism.

However, the fatal flaw of this new humanism was its shallow understanding of man. This fact was recognized by those who became growingly concerned with the social order, acknowledging that not all men were of good will, or at least did not act for the general welfare. Yet, it was thought that enlightened man could construct an enlightened society that would contain and uphold self-regulating order. Could it be that our impatience to get on with the details of our public and private lives, so evident at the time of the assassination of President Kennedy, reveals how difficult we find it to outgrow our need of self-regulating order?

Fortunately or unfortunately, man, in a new age, is unable to rely upon the solutions that may have sufficed in a former era. A good case in point is the remarkable shift that took place at the beginning of the modern period. Precisely at the time when medieval man had achieved an encompassing synthesis that would integrate all phenomena, a radical shift of interest took place. Man became dissatisfied with the old certainties, finding them inadequate to account for that which had come to command his attention. In his excellent analysis of the backgrounds to the thought of the seventeenth century, Basil Willey elucidates this point.[2] Quite possibly, we too may be in a situation in which the old order is passing away.

Though it is a matter of conjecture to assert, with any accuracy, that we are today in a transitional period analogous to that delineating the medieval from the modern, the parallels are striking. We can no longer take for granted the verities that have been the unquestioned assumptions of former epochs. The sovereignty of a personal God assuring a personal world order has vanished into the openness of empty space. The scientific theory of relativity has exploded the notion that either the star or the atom can be relied upon to follow a predetermined order. Psychology, since Freud, has undermined the supposition that man is reasonable and able to control rationally his unconscious drives. In short, fundamental pillars in man's construction and representation of order have crumbled. And intertwined with these developments and fomenting them is the perennial question of the relationship of order and chaos. Could it be that our inherited order is so wizened that it no longer hides from us a reality that threatens us? Could it be because chaos is so omnipresent that we try to deny its existence so furtively? Could there be, possibly, another way of understanding and relating order and chaos that would be creative and viable for us?

As blundering and self-defeating as it may appear to the observer, the "moral degeneracy" of the young person, out to get his "kicks" from sex, alcohol, drugs, and so forth, can be interpreted as one way of breaking through to genuine experience. In this respect, he is not unlike the beatnik who senses the lassitude of our societal status quo. Though each expresses his dissatisfaction with society in different ways, neither goes beyond sterile rebelliousness and, thus, is incapable of reaping the benefits of genuine experience. As is obvious from their frustrated yearning, to deny an existing order is not either to overcome it or to come to terms with its opposite—the threat of chaos. A more radical coming to grips with the problem is called for. The purpose of this essay is to suggest that the ancient Semitic myth concerning the beginning can be of real pertinence to contemporary discussion of order and chaos.

---

[2] Basil Willey, *The Seventeenth Century Background* (New York: Doubleday, 1953).

Contrary to popular understanding, the Biblical account of creation is neither a historical nor a natural, scientific account of how
the world originated. The material presented in the two creation
accounts and the other myths of Genesis, though deriving from
earlier sources, represents, in its present form, the attempt of the
already well-established covenant community to universalize its particular religious outlook. Adam means man in the generic sense, not
a specific historical personage. Eve refers to every mother (literally,
"mother of all living"), connoting womanhood as the source of all
human living. Having escaped from state slavery in Egypt and
covenanted together with Yahweh in the desert, the Hebrews used
ancient myths to convey the meaning and significance of these
events. They believed that what was happening to them had universal implications. Their function was to be the vehicle through
which mankind would discover its true nature and destiny.

The fundamental motif of the Hebraic understanding of man is
the insistence that man's existence and his function are inseparable.
Man is the point of contact between the creator God and the created
world. His function is to mediate between the two. This interpretation of man as the juncture of nature and God finds expression in
the fusion of the two versions of creation which together compose
the creation story. In the first account, God creates the context and
places man within it as the capstone. The emphasis, however, is on
the distance between the creator God and the creature man. In the
second account, man is created first and then a context is provided
for him. Here, the emphasis is on the intimacy of God and man.
With God, man shares the life-giving breath. With the rest of
creation, man shares inextricable rootage in nature. What is especially significant in the Genesis myth is the notion that God comes
out of his aseity and hovers over the yet-unordered potential creation. Parenthetically, the concept of *creatio ex nihilo* is a theological
speculation meant to enhance the majesty of God. It is, nevertheless,
misleading, since it focuses attention on the aetiological rather than
the teleological question.

The basic interest of the creation story centers in the work of the
spirit, *Ruach.* The very being of God is comprehended by the
Hebrew in dynamic terms. One does not speak of Yahweh as if His
being and activity are distinct. His activity is His being. He is
known only as He manifests Himself. For example, when Moses, on
the occasion of receiving his commission to go to Egypt and free the

Hebrews, asks who it is that sends him, from the burning bush comes the response: "You will know me by what you see me doing." [3] One recognizes God by His actions.

When God is depicted as breathing life into Adam, this does not imply either man's mere biological vitalization or his formation out of nothing. The point is, rather, that man is addressed by and participates in God's purposeful activity. Such involvement is the essence of creativity for the Hebrew. The notion of man as created "in the image and likeness of God" further elucidates this understanding of the relation of God and man. As Michelangelo depicted so suggestively in the Sistine Chapel, the notion of *"imago dei"* means that God lifts man into direct, face-to-face relationship with Himself. To say that man is created in "the likeness of God" is to indicate that man shares with God the ability to express himself and to be responsive.

It should be pointed out that the word "responsibility," which we use so loosely, means, literally, the ability to respond. The Genesis myth regards this ability as the distinctive characteristic of man. Of course, man also reacts. Like all other animals, he is driven by instinctual needs and is subject to external stimulae. But in contradistinction to the other animals, man is not simply at the mercy of internal and external forces. When we say that man can respond, we point to his ability to evaluate such forces, formulate alternatives, choose among these, and act. This ability is grounded in the human capacity for memory. The other animals store what are in fact reaction patterns, as, for example, the hamster "learns" the action that will secure it food. In addition, however, man remembers events in the past, his reaction to them, and their meaning for him. He does this consciously and unconsciously. On the basis of his recollection, which involves fact, feeling, and meaning, he projects more broadly into the future than do other animals. His hopes and fears encompass not only the meaning of future events for him, but also how they will relate to his self-image. This is what we mean when we say that man is able to respond, and not just to react.

According to the Genesis account, man's capacity for response is the means whereby he exercises his function as mediator between God and creation. When he is told to make full use of all that God has provided, it is not intended that he obstruct the free interplay of

3 Exodus 3:13–14 (freely translated) .

God and creation by exploiting the latter egotistically. Rather, he should be an unobstructed medium. His function as mediator is mirrored in the fact that he, himself, is not created as a single, closed entity. It is only in the coming together of male and female in naked openness toward each other, that man finds his fulfillment. As distinguished from life understood as mere biological functioning, human existence requires for its fulfillment that man experience the awareness of another and enter into a responsive relationship with him. To survive alone on a desert island is possible for man, but to do so is to fall short of the full meaning of being human. New life, itself, comes into existence only through the mutual encounter and cooperation of male and female. Neither partner is creative in isolation from the other. Further, in coming together, the spouses do not only cohabit and become the medium of new life. They, themselves, are changed by the encounter. As well as creating life, they discover a new identity in being the channel through which the infant is related to the world. The failure of either parent to play his proper role in this symbiotic relationship is a significant cause of emotional illness. In short, man is created to live in face-to-face relationship. Human life arises and unfolds between people, drawing them into a new existence.

Just as the function of parents is to draw out and free the infant for relationship in the world, so man's task as mediator between God and creation is to recognize and unfold the potentials of nature, recreating them from the wilderness of chaotic expanse into the vineyard of ordered fruitfulness. This is *homo qua faber,* the product of which we call civilization.

However, man as fabricator does not exhaust the meaning of being human, nor of his mediatorial function. As well as fabricating, he needs to evaluate. To do this, he must step back from his immediate involvement in mere production and survey the whole. To be fully human, man must attempt to comprehend and express the encompassing meaning and purpose of what he is and does. This is the task of *homo qua creator,* the outcome of which we call culture.

As man moves constantly between the activity of civilization and the reflection of culture, he recognizes that he is animated by that God who breathes His life spirit into the creative awareness and activity of man. Man responds to that recognition by spontaneously and joyfully acknowledging the presence of God. Worship is the name that is given to this expression. True worship is neither a dutiful obeisance nor a desultory habit. It is, rather, the liberating expression of the inner vision that "wells up" in the free man.

In giving utterance to such inner awareness, man recognizes that true freedom is possible only when there is acknowledgment of limits. He knows the truth of the phrase: "whose service is perfect freedom." Such an insight shines through the Genesis narrative. In that narrative, the limitations of man's activities are intended as a gracious safeguard of his freedom. Created to live responsive to God and nature, it is not necessary that man decide for himself what is *tab* and what is *rah*. These words, which are usually translated "good" and "evil," and thereby are made to carry a moralistic overtone, should be rendered "constructive" and "destructive." They signify a basic motivational attitude. The tree of knowledge is not intended to be a seductive trap, testing man's obedience. Rather, the knowledge of what is constructive and destructive for man arises in the immediacy of his relation with God and nature. He does not need to have the knowledge of what is constructive and destructive in abstraction. Such knowledge is really impossible. For it is only in the process of actualizing, again and again, the purpose of his existence as mediator that man can discover what is constructive and destructive. To covet and pursue such knowledge in abstraction is to desire autonomy and thereby to pervert the very end for which man is created. By implication, any ethics, philosophical or otherwise, which attempts to construe an independently permanent structure, is ruled out by the Biblical perspective. Indeed, to evisage such an ethics is to commit the basic sin. For, if one is to carry out this enterprise, it is necessary to remove oneself from the immediacy of his context. He has to abstract himself from the uniquely human function of mediation. The result is a radical distortion of man's understanding of himself, God, and nature.

However absurd it may appear in the light of the foregoing that man should ever desire to possess a knowledge that must inevitably corrupt the very reason for his existence, man always finds himself already in its pursuit. In this connection, it should be noted that the account of man's "original nature" was conceived by men who already found themselves "fallen." The creation story is misconstrued if it is interpreted as implying a chronological sequence of events from "original" to "fallen." The story of man's "original nature" was arrived at in response to the Biblical writers' inquiry concerning the nature of human life when God, rather than man, is sought and served.

As was stated above, the consequence of man's lusting after autonomy is the corruption of himself, his understanding of God, and his relationship to nature. With regard to himself, the effect of his attempt to establish himself as the bearer of absolutely dependable knowledge takes the form of being unable to acknowledge and live in interdependence. The first consequence of the "fall" is that man hides his sexuality in pretended innocence. The fig leaf represents the wish to be natural without having to acknowledge interdependence. The illusion is thereby created that the individual can be self-sufficient. In nakedness, sexuality reveals unmistakably that man is created to discover himself in face-to-face encounter. Hence, he clothes his sexuality in order to assert the pretense that he is sufficient unto himself.

Falling prey to the illusion that independence is superior to interdependence, man concludes that to live independently is to be like God. He desires to have that absolute knowledge which he assumes to be what distinguishes God from everything else. In competitive jealousy it occurs to man that God may have kept such sublime knowledge to Himself in order to keep man in a subservient position. Thereby, man misunderstands the ethos of the creation. His assumption that it is of the nature of the Deity to possess such knowledge reveals how wide of the mark is his conception of God. The Biblical notion of God is not that of a self-sufficient Narcissus, eternally complacent, admiring His own splendor. To the contrary, He forever wells out of Himself in order to enjoy the response that returns to Him from creation through man. Such a dynamic conception of God undergirds and brings to life the Biblical emphasis on creation, covenant, incarnation, resurrection, and eschatology. It is not in the idea of self-sufficiency that God's nature is to be understood, but in the notion of interdependent involvement. Parenthetically, to suggest such an understanding of God does not violate His aseity, as some theologians assert. Little confidence is shown in the majesty of God, when there is fear that it may diminish as a consequence of emphasizing the reality of His involvement in the world. To be excessively concerned that the notion of God's self-sufficiency not be violated by any suggestion that He "needs" the creation, may only reveal an underlying adherence to the illusion of human self-sufficiency that has been projected surreptitiously onto the divine nature. This is, however, but one example of what can result from mistaken human self-understanding. More graphic consequences are to be discovered from an examination of man's activity in the natural realm.

It will be recalled that, for the writers of Genesis, man is intended to function as mediator between God and the world. Being aware that he exists for a purpose, man realizes that there are God-given potentialities in the rest of creation. His appreciation of the presence of God in creation, himself included, precludes man from distinguishing and separating God's intentions in creation from the potentials of nature as such. His role is to discover both God's purposes in nature and how nature's resources can be employed to give expression to God's designs. The ability to carry out such an assignment presupposes human conscience. As the Latin root connotes, "con-scientia" means knowing, simultaneously, two parallel actualities in their reciprocity. Contrary to popular misconception, conscience carries no moralistic overtones. It merely suggests that, through the "knowing together" of God's intentions in nature and their potential actualization, the truly ethical question arises and its moral resolution is foreshadowed. To allow conscience to play its role, imagination (interpreted as the anticipation of the possible) and independent decision (understood as the willingness to choose and stand by one's choice) are mandatory. The only pseudo-alternatives to such a dynamic view of conscience are a sterile, rigid dependency on the assumption that God has spelled out, once and for all, the moral solution to all human problems, or a presupposition that nature's "laws" are so comprehensive, interlocking, and infallible that human choice is eliminated. They are pseudo-alternatives because neither can in fact deliver what it promises. The former, fundamentalism, denies the crucial Biblical notion of God as a free agent, whose purposes for the world are to be fathomed only in the context of genuine human decision. The latter, naturalism, misunderstands nature by presupposing an orderliness that does not exist apart from man's ordering decision. Obviously, both give no place to genuine human choice.

Man's ordering involvement with nature implies, of course, that work is not toil. Similar to the child extending himself as he reaches out in curiosity, grasps in wonder, and harbors with delight, so it is with man. His daily work is intended to be the adventure of exploring nature, discovering its intricacies, and cherishing its "secrets." The richness of such living exhausts man's vitality, permitting him to accept death as the fulfillment of life. Instead of experiencing life as a work of labor, as an unending sequence of chores to be done and good deeds to be carried out, man knows the reality of play in all its wonder and potency. Significantly, play is a word that has lost its primal, positive connotations for modern man. All too often, it is used as a synonym for wasteful, and hence irresponsible, leisure. Though of dubious connotation, the word "play" points to the ease and grace of that style which bows to what is at hand, invites its possibilities, and allows for the unfolding of its genius. This style manifests itself most expressively in the ballet. Such an artful quality frees work from its bondage to drudgery and enlivens leisure with a sense of adventure.

Why, however, does man find his work so tedious, his leisure so senseless, his play so unfulfilling? Put most simply, man's inability to work, rest, and play creatively is the consequence of his having lost his place in the world. Driven to establish his autonomous self-sufficiency, he abuses these activities, employing them in his self-justification. But why is man so intent on justifying himself? It will be recalled from our earlier discussion of the Genesis account that this compulsion is the result of man's refusal to serve as mediator between God and the world. He chooses, instead, to set his own terms for his existence. Yet, he does this with the dim, unadmitted awareness that he is attempting the impossible. Having chosen to be master of his destiny, he is bound to the consequences of his action. Removing himself from his natural habitat, he no longer can work and play creatively, bringing nature to its fulfillment. Having projected a picture of God as a being "up there," he attempts to rise to equality with Him, failing to realize that such a God is a caricature. Dimly suspicious that he cannot carry off his Promethean enterprise, he battles unquenchable thirst for security. He compensates for such insecurity by husbanding furiously all his forces. Ironically, this results in his being less effective and more insecure. Since he is unable to face honestly his predicament, he inverts reality, imagining that he is the unfortunate victim of hostile circumstances. The net result is inescapable confusion of belligerence. The myths of Genesis are superb in their depiction of human living under the curse. Cain's killing of Abel is suggestive of the frenzied rage that engulfs one who sees a brother succeeding where he fails. The same inability to acknowledge that one has missed the mark is manifested in Adam's placing the responsibility for his disobedience squarely on his partner. Another way of avoiding the realization that one falls short of his presumptions is taken by Noah's associates. They heap biting ridicule on the one who discerned the signs of the times realistically and planned accordingly. But the most glaring instance of self-defeating hubris is the story of the Tower of Babel. Grossly misusing the resources of nature and man, the citizens of Babel set themselves to the task of climbing to the heavens to displace the deity. Not only do they make the consummate error of assuming that they could accomplish such a feat, but they reveal their supreme ignorance in thinking that such competitive self-assertion would bring them into the presence of the real God.

What, then, is the curse under which man labors? In the Genesis account God makes clear to man that, if he insists on proving himself through the grime and sweat of toil, he misses the opportunity of being human. Not only is he doomed to fail in his assigned role as mediator, but he misuses nature, drawing it into the swirl of his self-defeating ambitions. In addition, he must live his years with the sword of Damocles, death, suspended tenuously above his head and certain to descend. What could have been the fulfillment of life's ripeness now stands as the ultimate, unavoidable threat.

There is a two-sidedness in God's action of withdrawing from man the fruits of the tree of life. On the one hand, this action reveals God's judgment on man's rebellious self-aggrandizement. If man presumes that life is, unquestionably, his possession and can be used for the ground of his self-justification, God points out to him that life is always a gift of surprise. It can never be clutched in calculation, but only received in childlike awe and gratitude. On the other hand, God's denial of unending life does not signify only termination. Since "fallen man" is so intent on justifying himself, he would never have the grace to relinquish his desperate hold on life. In this context, God's action in limiting life represents a gracious liberation of man from the vicious circle of futile toil. This latter motif, of course, is a foretaste of the promise of God to man that there will be a new creation.

Our reason for having given considerable attention to the Genesis narrative is our conviction that its understanding of man is of crucial significance for contemporary discussion of the relation of order and chaos. On the basis of the Genesis myths, we can perceive what underlies our tense adherence to order and fearful aversion from chaos. Genesis implicitly suggests, on our reading, that at the heart of contemporary concern with order and chaos there lies a perverted understanding of their nature and relation to each other. The existing order distresses us so much because we fear it is unable to contain the explosive outbursts of chaos. But this is because it is built upon what is, in fact, an illusion. It is rooted in the perverse notion of autonomous human self-sufficiency. As we have seen, Genesis indicates that only anxious insecurity, abuse of nature, and a distorted view of God can result from such a warped basis. An order that is contrived to support and encompass the universe as man wants to see it is doomed from the start. However, the problems created for man by his grandiose scheme of structuring reality do not remain on such a simple level. For, once having given birth to the freak of his ambitions, man cannot help attempting to reshape the world to fit his creation. Such an endeavor involves him in cutting and patching in those areas in which reality threatens to break through the thin weave of his synthetic fabric. He is also driven by the incessant fear that his order will collapse if he does not attend to it constantly. In so doing, he finds that he must continually compensate for his nightmarish apprehensions by upholding, Atlas-like, his fabricated order. Thus, ironically, what man intends as the exhilarating expression of his creative potency turns into the oppressive genii which tyrannize their own maker. But man cannot wholly escape from the realization that he has made and is bound to an idol with feet of clay. Such a realization is the seed of his destruction. Nevertheless, he parries its unsettling thrust by frantically clutching the shaky scaffolding of his order. His insecurity, though, breeds the paranoid fear of those imaginary forces of chaos about to attack his world. He reacts to this fear with such pathological intensity that he fails to realize that the real danger is not without, but within. He completely overlooks the simple fact that no order can remain inviolate in a world of change. Missing this point, he is oblivious to the insight that what is first to crumble is that which resists change by turning its back. He repeats the folly of Lot's wife. And, as she was changed into a pillar of salt when she looked back, so any reactionary order soon becomes petrified. In other words, any order that does not allow for change invites its own destruction. It, too, misinterprets chaos.

The misunderstanding of chaos that arises from too rigid a view of order is best demonstrated by making reference to the dynamics of the paranoid personality. The paranoid has a deep, unconscious deficiency as regards the ability to trust himself and others, and this results in fear. However, he is unable to admit this presence of fear to himself. Hence, it is projected out onto the environment. Not only is the environment interpreted as hostile toward him, but his very behavior elicits rejection by others. In this manner, the paranoid achieves his neurotic goals, thereby instituting an atmosphere that continually satisfies his pathological needs. The fact that the environment is quick to reward his antisocial behavior with hostility confirms the sick person's illusion and makes him feel justified in his own behavior. Any suggestion to such a person that reality may be different from his perception of it is treated with righteous indignation. His order is the only possible norm for him, and he defends it at all costs. Likewise with "fallen man" and his interpretation of order and chaos. Since he really does not have complete confidence in the order he has superimposed on reality, he constantly fears its collapse. Not only is he unwilling to face such a possibility, but, even more, he refuses to acknowledge that he would be the cause of his order's demise. On the contrary, he sees the forces of chaos lying in wait for the right moment to destroy him and his order. In his defensiveness, haunted by the realization that he must be eternally vigilant, he cuts himself off from all meaningful exchange with his environment and so unwittingly precludes any possibility of evaluation and improvement of his order. Such a lack of flexible open-mindedness irritates, of course, those who do not perceive order in the same fashion as does he. They grow critical and attack his petrified structure. He, though, understands such behavior as the representation of chaos. He senses a threat of destruction of the only order that he can visualize. He reacts to the challenge with blind force, summoning all his feelings of righteous indignation. Since he is captive to his private understanding of reality, he attacks all alternative interpretations of order as cancers to be totally eradicated. Ironically, he overlooks the evidence of history which records, again and again, the demise of defensively closed order. The destruction of his tenaciously held view of order is unavoidable, because he has not appreciated the nature of chaos.

The perverted understanding of chaos operative in "fallen man's" attitude is its being construed as an external force in diametric opposition to the ordering principle. It is tacitly assumed that order and chaos are mutually exclusive absolutes. Not only is he mistaken in viewing them as discrete entities, but he fails to see that they do not exist on their own. He misses the point that they are tentative projections of man, coming into play when he seeks to organize and interpret his experience. What "fallen man" apprehends as chaotic in his experience is, in reality, no more and no less than an ongoing life process of historical change which forever eludes embalming. Put positively, chaos is the ever new upsurge of the forces of life into human awareness. As such, it is neither good nor evil. It calls for sculpturing on the part of man, though, if it is to bear good fruit. To be sure, when man encounters its reality, he feels threatened. But it is the threat of challenge, of possibility. Man knows that what lies before him, awaiting his decision, can become destructive as well as constructive. The dread of which he is aware is, thus, located in his freedom. Further, the choice that he makes, as well as resulting in constructive or destructive consequences, will reveal his understanding of himself and his purpose in the world. How he chooses, in short, manifests who he is in the fullest sense. As such, it is bound to be anxiety producing, however much he may be conscious of what is going on at the time. The nature and quality of the trust that undergirds his life will be clearly seen from how he chooses.

Tremendous resources are necessary if man is to employ his freedom for constructive ordering. Though a full discussion of this point would take us far beyond the scope of this essay, it should be pointed out that wider and deeper support is needed by human personality than can be provided by the immediate familial setting, if man is to act constructively. For example, one of the chief purposes the notion of covenant served in ancient Israel was that of making the trust relationship more inclusive, with the result that a more adequate conception of order could be maintained. Similar, and still more universal, is the concept of the "Church" and its function of providing a solid context for constructive ordering. In short, wherever man has understood himself as carrying out a constructive ordering function in the world, he has found it necessary to ground himself in a principle of benevolent protection, be it God, nature, society, and so forth. Only so has he been able to feel himself free to explore, design, and test what might prove to be temporarily useful order.

In the light of the foregoing, what, then, can we say concerning an order that incorporates change? Is it possible to develop and maintain an order that would be flexible, dependable, and realistic?

In answering the above question one very important point must be kept in mind, namely, the impossibility of delineating, once and for all, a perfect, all-inclusive order. For life in its very essence is dynamic, open-ended, novelty-producing process. One of the chief reasons why all utopias are illusions is their failure to appreciate the significance of change. Further, and corollary to this inability, is their failure to take cognizance of man's determinative function as the agent of change. For them, man plays the role of either the revolutionary who vehemently destroys the existing order, or the reactionary who desperately seeks to maintain the status quo. In reality, man lives by change, discerning its signs, perceiving its trends, and reshaping what is into what may be. Parenthetically, speculative discussion of man's basic nature as good or evil is futile. Having the capacity for acting constructively or destructively, man becomes destructive only when he is frustrated in his attempt to participate freely, and thereby find himself, in the process of change. At the same time, it should not be asumed that man is by nature constructive. Rather, he discovers and unfolds his propensity for constructive action through his active participation in change. In short, it is a serious error to concern oneself with the nature of order apart from the ordering man. It is only flexible man, knowing his true dependency, who can realistically order.

An outstanding example of man as mediator, of one who combined in his own personality the ability to trust, to cut through sham, and to elicit genuine response, is Jesus of Nazareth. Trusting in his "heavenly Father," he was aware that his existence found its fulfillment in his being a sensitive and penetrating medium of that force of life which we identify as God. For that reason, he was able to see through the pretenses and rigidity of the existing order. Yet he refused to play the revolutionary and substitute the Zion of an earthly Messianism for the cynical despotism of Rome. His attention was focused on the motivational roots of human behavior. He knew this to be the locus of man's mediation between God and the world. As a Semite, he viewed the heart, rather than the brain, as the transformer of the divine intention into human action. He knew that it was here that man decides whether or not he will function as mediator. It was for this reason that Jesus focused his attention on the heart. Further, he was aware that how man chooses, accepting or not the role of mediator, determines in what light he will view order. Man's fundamental choice is either to accept his function as mediator or to try to escape from it into the illusion that he is the autonomous guarantor of order. Depending on his choice, man either views order as an open-ended process that welcomes change and demands of him flexibility, or he clutches the existing order as inviolate and frantically attacks any who would question it.

In his teaching and living, Jesus not only posed the fundamental question of the heart for his contemporaries, but in his very presence and person he forced the issue. He was the man of mediation through whom flexible order came to expression. The Jews of his time were forced to decide whether they would accept his challenge or eliminate him. The fact that, when the issue was joined, Jesus had to struggle with it and face its consequences alone, should give pause to those who think it a simple task to be an agent of flexible order. The difficulties inherent in maintaining an attitude of trustful openness and creative flexibility are amply documented in the history of the Christian church. Especially in times of basic change, such as may be ours, the plea for flexibility should be heeded. However, such a response should not prompt us to overlook the substantial difficulties, as well as promises, inherent in such an endeavor.

What, then, are the characteristics of a flexible order that would be meaningful for contemporary man? Given the present cultural mood, it seems to this observer that our most pressing need is to view order as a dynamic process, rather than as a static system of timeless truths. It is especially unfortunate, though understandable, that Christianity, which has provided Western culture with its frame of reference and symbols of ordering, has frozen the vital spirit of openness so manifest in its founder. To some, it appears that the crisis facing the contemporary Christian church is even more serious. They would assert that the church has not only become bound to a once viable but long since outdated conceptualization of order, but that it actively resists even a sympathetic attempt to reopen the quest for a flexible order. It could be argued that the most that organized Christianity appears willing to tolerate is a rephrasing, in apologetic fashion, of the content of the traditional symbols. It seems as if the church is still caught up in the medieval mentality of regarding theology as the "queen of the sciences" and of interpreting all reality exclusively on the basis of its doctrine of God. Such a mentality is in striking contrast to the approach of modern science and undoubtedly creates innumerable problems for those who would seek to live and work within the context of both.

In seeking to delineate what might be the characteristics of a contemporary flexible order, it is interesting to note that the scientist, not the theologian, displays the tough, open-minded spirit of discernment so paramount in the life of Jesus. The scientist utilizes the existing order which correlates and interprets facts merely as a hypothesis to be verified, i.e., as a stepping stone for further insight and discovery. Whenever the data no longer jibe with the formulated construct of order, the latter is immediately either revamped or discarded. Historically, the growth of scientific knowledge can be seen as a succession of fresh data breaking out of the confines of established hypotheses, thereby giving birth to new, though tentative, constructs of order. Such an approach commends itself as of far wider application than exclusively that of natural and applied science.

Of course, the methods and techniques of science are not directly applicable to the phenomena of man in his sociohistorical setting. This is because human experience, out of which come the dimensions of meaning and value, cannot be measured with scientific precision or reproduced at will in laboratory tests. Furthermore, the variables of human expression are at once so manifold and so diversified that scientific comparison and categorizing become impossible. The social and behavioral scientists are well aware of these problems and are endeavoring to develop a more appropriate methodology.

If we were to attempt to visualize what, today, is still most needed in order for there to be a flexible human order, it would be the creative interplay of the scientific, the artistic, and that aspect of human awareness which heretofore has been the exclusive domain of religion. To unfold and refine the human ability to experience and express what we have in this essay classified as man's mediation between Divine intention and the potentials of nature is a task that confronts us with urgency.

Obviously, man must come to grips with himself. And he must do so in terms that avoid the lofty escape of otherworldliness and the stunted captivity of scientism. If it is no longer possible for man to see himself as basking in the protective glory of God, it is, likewise, nonsensical for man to view himself as merely a child of nature tinkering with thermonuclear energy. A comprehensive understanding of man's nature and function must be attempted. To accomplish this, the fragmentary insights of the various human sciences must be brought into fruitful interaction. The goal is to stimulate the growth of human personality and corporate human living. They, in turn, will be the leaven of a flexible order understood as process.

IREDELL JENKINS

The Modern Distemper:
The Failure of Purposiveness

The general subject of this series, the concept of order, is a rather broad and inclusive notion, as the preceding essays have amply shown. I am going to cut down this ambit somewhat by centering my attention on a particular theme: namely, the challenge that man confronts of composing order. It is characteristic of the human enterprise that it faces this task in virtually all of its undertakings: in our individual lives, in our social and economic affairs, in our political activities, in scientific and philosophic inquiry, in literary and artistic creation, in our search for peace, in such very specific efforts as those to control traffic, market prices, or the population explosion—in all of these cases, what we are trying to do, in one way or another, is to bring order out of disorder. Indeed, I think it might be said that the challenge of composing order constitutes the very essence of the human situation. Finally, I shall try to give a sharper and more definite thrust to this theme by espousing a very explicit thesis: namely, that modern man and modern society have

IREDELL JENKINS has long been professor of philosophy and chairman of the department at the University of Alabama. He has contributed notably to legal philosophy and to aesthetics. His basic commitment is to metaphysics, in which the concept of order is most prominent. He is author of *Art and Human Enterprise* (1958). He has held distinguished fellowships, among them a Rockefeller Foundation Research Grant and a fellowship in law and behavioral science at the University of Chicago.

not risen adequately to this challenge. What is worse, they have not even accepted the challenge and attempted to deal with it. Instead, they have evaded or denied the issue, insisting that it does not exist or will somehow automatically resolve itself. I shall argue that deep beneath all of our more obvious and superficial ills, this refusal of the challenge of order constitutes the heart of the modern distemper.

The line of argument required to support this thesis must contain three major steps: first, an analysis of the concept of order. This is certainly a familiar notion, which we daily use in such phrases as "the social order," "the order of nature," "law and order," "an orderly life," or "a disorderly house." But it is extremely difficult to find anywhere in the literature of the subject an explicit and precise analysis of the concept. It seems that familiarity blunts our critical sense, and the common idea of order is itself extremely disorderly. So my first step will be a systematic analysis of this concept. Second, an explanation of just why it is that man faces the challenge of composing order. For other entities and creatures—e.g., atoms, molecules, stars, plants, and animals—order seems to be assured to them automatically: they do not have to devise careful plans or establish complex institutions to bring order out of disorder. Man does. Why? We need to investigate the human situation to see exactly what distinguishes it from other modes of existence and creates for it the problem of composing order. What is particularly required here is a close analysis of this problem itself, exposing its various facets or aspects. Third, an examination of the character and cause of our failure to rise to the challenge of order. We must marshall the evidence to establish the fact of this failure. And we must identify the causes, or factors, responsible for it. Fourth, and finally, one might expect some indication of the way in which this failure can be corrected. This would require, for one thing, a theoretical solution to the problem of composing order, as this will have been explicated under the second heading above. It would further require an account of how this solution can be implemented in practice. How much can be done with this aspect of the matter depends on the time and space available, and I rather fear there may not be enough—in fact, to be honest, I rather hope there will not.

And now to develop this argument.

I

When the notion of order is under discussion, its meaning seems always to be regarded as self-evident: it is never explicitly analyzed, but is simply assumed as a primitive term that neither requires nor permits explication. And indeed the common ostensive meaning of the term is clear and simple. The concept of order embodies our discovery of pattern and regularity in the world. It announces the similarities that hold among things and the sequences that run among events; it summarizes the fact that we find threads of uniformity and connectedness that bind together discrete objects and occurrences. To say that "order holds" is to say that we are in the presence of some stable body of relationships, some systematic structure, such that we can count upon spatial arrangements, temporal recurrences, and logical inferences. "Disorder," of course, conveys the converse of all this; it announces the presence of the arbitrary and erratic, the irregular and unstable, the amorphous and haphazard.

These rough-and-ready common-sense meanings are adequate enough for a good many practical purposes: if we are trying to arrange a class schedule, or the furniture in a room, or a table of high and low tides, or a filing system, these notions will serve us reasonably well. But they evidently leave a good deal to be desired in the way of analytical precision and theoretical coherence. If these desiderata are to be realized, and the concept of order is to become a really fruitful basis for inquiry, it must be given a more exact and systematic analysis. This effort can best be launched with a brief definition, which can then be expanded and explained. So I suggest this: Order is the name for that state of affairs in which we discover regular and determinate sequences that are exhibited in the activities and behavior of distinct entities that together form a series of organized wholes. The situation required by order thus has four basic aspects or dimensions: a plurality of distinct entities, the organization of these into a series of higher order entities, energy expended and activity engaged in by these entities, and all of this taking place in a way that exhibits coherence and continuity of relationships. These dimensions I shall identify respectively as the Many, the One, Process, and Pattern. And these dimensions, I would argue, together constitute the framework, or matrix, of all reality and existence. Whatever region of the world we examine is at once a manifold, a universe, an arena of change, and a structured system. Every particular thing whatsoever is at once an element in various fields or wholes, a unique entity, a locus of energy that is engaged in constant transactions with other things, and an item that occupies a definite place in a complex scheme of relationships.

This completes the first stage of my argument: the analysis of order. I think it is obvious that the terms "order" and "disorder" are correlative and express differences of degree. We refer to some context of reality (some phenomenal field) —e.g., a room, an individual life, a society, a train schedule—as orderly when the entities that compose the Many are distinct and identifiable; the Ones, or wholes, are organized and effective; the Processes that take place are uniform and constant; and the Pattern of relations is regular and stable. We regard a context as disorderly when the entities are amorphous and transient, the wholes are vague and vacillating, the processes are erratic and haphazard, and the relationships are tenuous and unstable.

II

We come now to our second major question: Why does man face the problem of composing order? Or, put differently, what in essence distinguishes the human situation from that of all other creatures and so confronts man with the challenge of order? In answering this question I shall at the same time offer a precise and systematic analysis of this challenge itself, indicating its major facets and so exposing the significant specific tasks that its solution requires. My approach to these matters has as its fundamental assumption the theory of organic evolution, which tells us that man, in common with all other living things, is the product of a complex developmental process. From this theory we can infer that certain important changes occur in the long course of time, finally marking off human nature and the human situation as a distinct local context of reality; these changes place man in a novel condition, and confront him with a radical challenge, namely, that of composing order; and if his further evolutionary success—or even survival —is to be assured, he must rise successfully to this challenge. Further, relying upon the preceding analysis of order as the framework of all reality and becoming, including evolution, we can infer that these changes occur within the dimensions of the Many, One, Process, and Pattern; that is, as the movement of evolution proceeds, gradual but important changes take place in each of these dimensions. The problem, then, is to discern the precise nature of these changes and the outcome in which they culminate at the human level.

The way in which I propose to deal with this problem can be expressed in three synoptic statements, which will be developed more fully. First, I shall posit the presence, and the continual compresence, of three different regimes, or sets of conditions, that I shall designate as Necessity, Possibility, and Purposiveness. Each of these regimes is constituted as such by certain significant traits that characterize the dimensions of Many, One, Process, and Pattern: that is, each of them refers to a certain type or mode of order. Hence, to say that things exist under the regime of Necessity is to say that the dimensions of its existence exhibit certain distinguishing features and structures; and similarly for the regimes of Possibility and Purposiveness. Second, these regimes do not have any separate and independent being; they are not radically distinct or isolated from one another; they are commingled throughout reality and interpenetrate one another. But the conditions that these regimes summarize are present in different proportions in different regions of reality. And that is precisely what distinguishes these regions. Third, the direction of evolution, as it proceeds through the realms of the inorganic, the organic, the vital, the sentient, the psychic, and the social, has been from the regime of Necessity through that of Possibility toward that of Purposiveness. As we move from the fields of physical and chemical phenomena, which are dominated by the conditions of Necessity, toward the fields of biological, psychological, and cultural phenomena, we find a continually larger infusion of the conditions of Possibility; and we find, concurrently, that this latter regime requires to be completed by a corresponding infusion of Purposiveness. That is, we find that the earlier type of order dissolves, threatening disorder, and challenging man to compose a new and higher type of order. The course of this movement, and its culmination, can now be elaborated by tracing the changes that it introduces into the dimensions of order, and the problems that these changes create for man.

In many regions of reality, where Necessity is preponderant, the following general conditions hold. Within the dimension of the Many, the outstanding feature is the close similarity of things of the same kind. Entities exhibit the characteristics of their class or species in such a uniform manner that they are virtually identical. The actual uniqueness of things makes little contribution to their existences. Furthermore, these entities are largely dominated by the fields or systems, the Ones, in which they occur. Things are engulfed by their milieus of existence, and their self-assertion is severely limited. Concomitantly, the Processes in which things take part fall under the formula of action and reaction. The course of the actual occasion is controlled by antecedent events and prevailing conditions, so that the effective intervention of things is slight. Entities transfer and release energy, but do not direct it. Finally, the Pattern of relationships that pervades such regions is detailed and rigid. A prior system of connections absorbs things as they come into existence and holds them fast throughout the course of their becoming. This monolithic web of relationships leaves little room for things to establish their separateness or make their own arrangements.

These four conditions of Necessity—similarity, domination, action and reaction, and rigidity—nowhere hold absolutely. But they do appear to be the prevailing characteristics of many regions of nature, and we confront them directly in significant areas of our own lives. That is, our own mode of being is strongly colored by Necessity. But there are other conditions that are also present throughout reality and that gradually become more prominent and influential in certain regions, notably that of man. As this occurs, Necessity is supplemented—but not superseded—by Possibility.

Men now become differentiated and distinctive persons. With regard to our more complex functions, we become capable of a wide range of activity: though we still share a common nature and situation, there is room for variations of capacity, temperament, and interest, so that individual differences make a real difference. We find that our endowment is extraordinarily plastic, permitting of various realizations but guaranteeing none of them. Concurrently, we attain to a larger measure of sufficiency and independence from our surroundings: we can control these within limits, instead of being altogether at their mercy. We become members rather than parts, we view ourselves as ends as well as means, and we participate in the affairs of the wholes that are our milieus of existence. Further, we now exercise a high degree of self-determination: the nexus of action and reaction loosens; the present becomes an actual occasion rather than a sheer passage from past to future; and there is room within it for spontaneity and initiative. We can buffer circumstances, can delay response and deliberate our decision, and so can determine for ourselves what we are to do and be. Finally, the Pattern of relations that runs through much of human existence is quite flexible: many of the relationships in which we stand to other persons and situations are open, fluid, and only generally defined. So in these contexts we have discretion as to the positions we are to occupy, the transactions we are to carry on, and the courses we are to follow.

The outstanding features of the regime of Possibility are its incompleteness and tentativeness. The conditions of differentiation, participation, self-determination, and flexibility inaugurate a state of affairs that is markedly unstable and unoriented. As we encounter these conditions, they solicit us to give them a form, a content, and a direction that in themselves they lack. It is of the essence of Possibility that it requires that we make a use of it: it presents us with opportunities, but it is up to us to exploit these. The regime of Purposiveness is constituted by our response to this appeal; it is here that we use existence to make of this what it is not yet, but can be and ought to be. Purposiveness is the intelligent and intentional exercise of our powers, through which we direct existence toward some possibilities and away from others. The exact ideal manner of this exercise can be made explicit by tracing it through the dimensions of order.

In the dimension of the Many, Purposiveness appears in the guise of cultivation. Differentiations are not neutral: some are advantageous in the present and fruitful for the future, while others are the reverse. Thus the plasticity that we discover in ourselves imposes on us a double task: first, we must decide among the various outcomes that our powers lay open to us; second, we must nurture these powers toward their realization. In the dimension of the One, we act purposively to define and institute authority. Participation permits individuals to exploit the resources of the whole—the environment or the group or the state—for their own interests; thus it carries the germs of inefficiency, conflict, and divisiveness. It is the function of authority to protect the public good against these private depredations: it restrains recalcitrance, assigns roles, and coordinates functions, and so preserves the milieu of existence against dissolution. Our exercise of self-determination, in the dimension of Process, means that we give to the course of events a content and direction that it would not otherwise have had. What we decide has repercussions, both for ourselves and for others. The uses we make of self-determination must therefore be guided by a sense of responsibility, which leads us to anticipate the outcomes we are preparing, to be sensitive to their total consequences, and to acknowledge ourselves accountable for the differences we make. Finally, in the dimension of Pattern, we act purposively to ensure the continuity and coherence of our physical and social environments. The separate undertakings in which we engage, and even more the joint enterprises that we carry on together, require that we be able to rely upon certain uniformities and regularities. It is only in this way that individual efforts can be wrought into a form that permits coordination and exchange.

In concluding this phase of my argument I would again emphasize very strongly that these three regimes have no real independent existence. What I have been describing are abstract types: in their actual occurrence, these sets of conditions are everywhere commingled. This is notably true of the human context, since it is here that the compresence of these regimes makes itself felt most forcefully. Man falls under definite necessities; he confronts certain possibilities; and he exercises a measure of purposiveness. Men are limited, both by their intrinsic natures and by the established order that holds around them. Men exploit opportunities that the world and their own resources present to them. Men lead careers that have momentum and orientation. These are simple and ineluctable facts. The basic problem with which existence confronts man is that of finding the proper balance and reconciliation among these three regimes.

III

We can turn now to the thesis that is the crux of my argument: that the refusal of the challenge of order lies at the heart of the modern distemper. In the light of the preceding discussions, I can specify this thesis more closely. For I would argue that our refusal of this challenge resides primarily in a failure of Purposiveness. As the movement of evolution has brought man into the regime of Possibility, he has shown a vast enthusiasm and ingenuity in exploiting the advantages thus put at his disposal. But, unfortunately, he has shown an exactly corresponding reluctance to move systematically onto the level of Purposiveness, and so to give a coherent direction and content to the uses that are made of these possibilities. That is, he has welcomed the privileges of his position but has evaded its obligations. I must now try to expand and support this thesis.

I can best approach this task by an exercise in cryptohistory. I think it would be acknowledged that until the dawn of history— and even considerably after that—the conditions of human exist- ence approximated very closely to those that I have described under the regime of Necessity. Throughout this time, individual differ- ences of status, function, training, opportunity, and achievement were relatively slight. Men lived in small and cohesive groups that exerted a pervasive influence over their numbers. The margin of safety with respect to the environment was small, so that the way of life was largely dictated by the pressure of external circumstances. As a result of this, the goals and patterns of life were closely defined by the exigencies of survival: they were seized upon not so much as positive goods, but rather as the avoidance or minimization of ills. Man could see only shortly into the future and would envisage little in the way of alternatives to the present. Under these conditions, the direction and course of men's efforts, both individual and social, were to a great extent determined by the sheer demands of exist- ence. As has frequently been remarked, the primitive mentality, whether paleolithic or contemporary, tends to confuse what is with both what must be and what ought to be.

It is only with the dawn of historical time that the grip of Necessity relaxes appreciably, and Possibility becomes a significant feature of the human context. For a good many millennia after that, this infusion is quite slight; and, what is more important, even then it affects only a small proportion of the human population. It is not until strictly modern times that Possibility—in the systematic sense defined above—seriously colors the lives of any large numbers of men. But during the last century or so this movement has been both accelerating and spreading at a steadily increasing rate. At least for us of the Western world, Possibility now pervades all the dimen- sions of our existence.

I have argued above that the outstanding features of the regime of Possibility are its incompleteness and tentativeness. It requires that we make a use of it by the intelligent and disciplined exercise of Purposiveness; that is, it requires that we devote ourselves seri- ously to the problems of cultivation, authority, responsibility, and continuity. This means that we must make an inventory of the possibilities open to us, anticipate their future consequences, evaluate these, establish a consensus of opinion, organize a common pursuit, and then commit ourselves. Yet, as I have claimed, this is precisely what we seem incapable of doing. Until quite recent times, when the grip of Necessity relaxed, almost any opening it offered promised an improvement; thus the goals of action were simple, obvious, immediate, and compelling. But, as possibilities increase, this ceases to be the case. Many goals are available; they stretch into the future; their outcomes are obscure; and they are irreconcilable with one another, so that each at once attracts and repels us. This places the burdens of choice and commitment upon us, and they seem more than we can bear.

Rather than accept the challenge of Purposiveness, we have immersed ourselves in the regime of Possibility. Much of the behavior of modern man seems evidence of his adopting the view that all possibilities are equally and absolutely desirable. Or, to state the matter differently, whatever *can* be done *should* be done. These propositions, I believe, convey the essence of what has been called the technological spirit. Surrendering all claims to evaluation, this spirit trusts to the sheer exploitation of possibilities somehow to issue in the creation of order and value. It is hardly surprising that this hope is often disappointed; the random choice and unregulated use of possibilities must frequently breed confusion. But, even when this occurs, we are reluctant to exercise Purposiveness, that is, gradually to transform the present state of affairs toward an envisaged and contingent future. Instead, the usual recourse is a reversion to the regime of Necessity: we seek to perpetuate one actual possibility and eliminate all others.

It is time to muster evidence in support of this thesis. For the sake of clarity and completeness, I shall present this under two headings. First, evidence drawn from the theoretical or intellectual plane: this will seek to show that modern culture tends to think and to interpret the world in terms of Necessity and Possibility, not of Purposiveness. Second, evidence drawn from the practical plane: this will seek to show that modern culture tries to solve its problems, and escape its difficulties, by action on the levels of Necessity and Possibility, not of Purposiveness.

With respect to the intellectual climate, it is proper to start at the most abstract level, with a consideration of the currently influential philosophic doctrines. I think that these clearly fall into two groups.

One, composed of the positivists, the naturalists, and the "scientific" philosophies, is committed to the view that all of reality and existence can be accounted for in terms of the conditions of Necessity: these schools are deterministic, mechanistic, materialistic, and reductionistic. The most prominent members of the other group are the existentialists and pragmatists: these throw the major emphasis upon Possibility, with their insistence on freedom, futurity, choice, and goal-directed behavior. But even these schools refuse, on the whole, to acknowledge any objective values by which man's use of freedom can be disciplined and directed. They certainly stress the employment of intelligence and the acceptance of responsibility by the individual in his role as decision maker—and so as maker of the future. But they have virtually nothing to say regarding the form and content of this future; they leave the selection of ends to individual discretion and concern themselves only with the mastery of means.

The impact of these abstract philosophic doctrines is most apparent in the relativism and subjectivism that are so characteristic of the modern distemper. It is widely held that there can be no way of establishing opinion on any question that is not matter of fact— where "fact," I think, is defined by the conditions of Necessity. This means that only descriptive predictions of *what will be* can legitimately run into the future. Normative judgments of *what ought to be* are regarded as nothing but the projection of private preference, having no solid ground save to the extent that they can muster numbers of their side and so become the expression of public opinion.

Finally, this subjective and relativistic mood becomes an influential cultural force through various specific beliefs and practices that derive from it. Perhaps the most conspicuous of these is the doctrine of ethical emotivism as developed by Moritz Schlick, A. J. Ayer, Charles Stevenson, and others. As an analysis of the ways in which our moral motivations are perverted, and our moral judgments distorted, the work of this school has a good deal to offer. But as pretending to be a full account, rather than a pathology, of the moral life, it strikes me as both a travesty and a tragedy. It fails altogether to do justice to the phenomena of obligation, conscience, duty, and guilt; and it makes virtues of egoism and expedience. A similar manifestation is the movement of legal positivism, which reduces law to legislative enactment and court decision, denies the ideal element in law, and so introduces a radical separation of law from justice. The political analogue of this movement is the widespread tendency to define democracy in procedural rather than substantive terms; the meaning of democracy is found not in the values it holds and the ends it seeks, but sheerly in the techniques by which decisions are made and carried out. Extending this line of thought one step further, I would say that ethical emotivism, legal positivism, and political operationalism are themselves expressions of the more basic phenomenon of social—and perhaps even metaphysical—egalitarianism; and the heart of this doctrine is the avoidance of all qualitative judgments and the insistence on making all decisions in quantitative, or numerical, terms.

As a final, and more concrete, example on the theoretical plane, we can take the contemporary attitude toward the idea of rights, as it is found in numerous recent declarations and manifestoes. The most popular and widespread view of this matter regards these rights of man—or natural rights—as absolute and autonomous; they simply inhere in man as such, and are subject to no qualification or denial. This view is, of course, excessively naïve, and it undergoes modifications at a more sophisticated level. The most obvious such step is the recognition that rights cannot be conferred without a corresponding imposition of duties: we can enjoy the opportunities our rights promise only if we accept the duties they demand. A further step is taken when it is realized that rights are empty unless they are supported by the proper powers, or capacities: the right to do something is purely abstract until we have at our disposal the concrete training and skill and tools to exercise it. It is now widely acknowledged, in legal, political, and social theory, that rights entail duties and powers. But there is, I think, yet another step in this argument: this is the recognition that rights find their ultimate meaning only in the goods, or values, that they promote. Rights must not only be conferred, protected, and implemented; they must also be directed toward the ends that embody their consummation. For a right that reaches no good is worse than empty or useless—it is vicious. But this step of tying rights finally to goods—the right to the good, means to ends, powers to values—is precisely the one that is now neglected and even deprecated. To state this in the terms developed above, we willingly wage war against Necessity, and exploit Possibility, but we are reluctant to explore and employ the regime of Purposiveness in our understanding and ordering of ourselves and the world.

We can move now to the practical plane. What I am interested in here is evidence indicating that we respond to the pressures of life, and try to solve its problems, exclusively at the levels of Necessity and Possibility; and that we are unwilling to deal with these issues by a systematic exercise of Purposiveness. Among the simpler and more obvious instances of such behavior are the uses we have made of drugs and pesticides. We employed these in the pursuit of obvious and immediate goals; and we did this with little envisagement of further consequences, with no sense of the responsibility of power, and with little thought for the coordination of our actions with the total pattern of life. The same is true of our handling of the population explosion that has followed our success in lowering the rate of infant mortality and extending the life span. Taken in conjunction with recent advances in genetics, this opens the door to a purposive cultivation of the genetic endowment of future generations. Indeed, as many scientists have pointed out, man is now in a position where he can largely supplement—indeed almost supersede —the blind operations of natural selection with the enlightened direction of intelligence. That is, we can substitute purpose and plan for struggle and accident. But, instead of this, we use our powers merely to increase the range and rate of possibilities.

Turning from these relatively casual and local examples, I would say that such highly institutionalized and intentional pursuits as those of education, religion, and science exemplify exactly this same attitude. Traditionally, education was deeply concerned with the inculcation of a sense of values and a way of life. But in recent decades the employment of education in these tasks has been increasingly frowned upon, until now it has been totally surrendered, save in certain rare outposts—or, as most would put it, vestigial survivals! As presently conceived, education is almost altogether technological in spirit; it equips its students with certain knowledges and skills, but leaves quite undefined the ends to which these should be put or the manner of their use. Education, so to speak, has ceased to be a discipline and has become an investment. As has been often remarked, churches have all too frequently followed a similar path; they seem more interested in promoting individual peace of mind and a harmonious social environment than in calling their worshipers to an arduous self-examination and rededication. Finally, it was not until the explosion of an atomic bomb that science, in any institutional sense, became concerned with the uses to which its products were put. And even now such men as Linus Pauling and H. J. Muller are rather rare exceptions to the general rule of axiological apathy.

In concluding this survey of the evidence, let me refer briefly to two concrete cases. One of these seems to me to be the most dramatic, ironic, and tragic of all of our failures of purposiveness: namely, our economic dilemma. For long millennia man struggles to escape the hard necessities of labor and scarcity, and to achieve the goals of leisure and abundance. At last, thanks to technology, he breaks through the last barriers: and at once this promised land turns into the desert of overproduction and unemployment. Man, in the more favored societies, is finally in a position where he can satisfy all of his material wants and still have time and energy to spare. One would think that this is the ideal invitation to the employment of purposiveness; here, if ever, man should be challenged to explore new goals to which to direct life and new values to achieve. But our response is exactly the contrary: we meet this challenge by limiting the production of goods and by seeking blindly for new *needs* for labor. That is, we take refuge in the regime of Necessity, hoping in this way to find an order that escapes our purposive activity. My other case is less serious, but perhaps even more typical and illuminating: I am thinking of our widespread addiction to gambling. For gambling, I would say, represents the supreme case of man's willful surrender to Possibility: with forethought and intention, man divests himself of all control of the outcomes he attains. When we gamble, we hope to get something for nothing, and so to escape Necessity. And we hope to get this without any planning or direction on our part, and so to escape Purposiveness. To gamble, in a word, is to immerse one's self in pure Possibility.

IV

In the preceding discussions, I have tried to present a careful analysis of the challenge that man confronts in composing order. Further, I have mustered evidence to indicate that the heart of the modern distemper resides in the persistent refusal of this challenge; not, let it be emphasized, in the failure to master it, but in the refusal to accept it. This diagnosis gives rise to two obvious questions. Why has this refusal occurred? How can it be corrected? To these I can give but a moment's attention.

I would suggest that the basic cause of this refusal is our fanatical devotion to the exactitude and certainty of scientific method. The accomplishments of the physical sciences, both in theory and in practice, have persuaded modern man that truth and knowledge reside exclusively in propositions that can be couched in the vocabulary of science and verified by its techniques. That is, we have come to expect precision and proof, and to reject all arguments whose conclusions cannot meet these demands. But when we pass value judgments, project future purposes, and commit ourselves to unrealized goals, these demands are inapplicable: not only in the sense that they cannot be applied, but in the more basic sense that they do not apply—that is, they are inappropriate.

If we are to accept the challenge of Purposiveness, the indispensable first step is to accommodate ourselves to the fact that our judgments on this level must be tentative, contingent, and continually correctable. To demand precise and provable answers to the problems that Purposiveness poses is to forfeit all intelligent answers, and to leave the outcome to chance and circumstance. I think that we now have more than enough knowledge and skill to make reliable—though clearly not exact and certain—judgments about the ends to be sought and the means to achieve them in the areas of cultivation, authority, responsibility, and continuity. But we stubbornly postpone the exercise of these powers until they will have attained a perfection that is altogether beyond them. In this field that is riddled with paradoxes, none is more ironic than the fact that pragmatism, positivism, and scientism, which arose to free us from a body of supposedly achieved certitudes, should end by enslaving us to a new quest for certainty. But even this achievement threatens to be surpassed by existentialism, which, in seeking to save man from this status as an object bound to the world, has placed him in a subjective vacuum where there is no reason at all why he should do one thing rather than another. I think that our salvation depends upon finding a path between these extremes. This means that we must accept the fact that our projections of value and our commitments to life are neither rigid deductions nor random whims: mixed, they are free but responsible **decisions**.

HELMUT KUHN

The Case for Order
in a Disordered Age

"Order" belongs to the basic concepts of our thought, not only in philosophy, but also in all branches of science, and in all phases of our life. Corresponding to the importance of order for human thought are the age and dignity that accrue to this concept in the history of philosophy. The fragment from Anaximander conceives the generation and destruction of things, through which they pay penalty and retribution to one another, as happening "according to the order of time" (*Kata ten tou chronou taxin*). The connection of order with time also anticipates a later linguistic usage. Among the Romans, *secundum ordinem* usually means "in succession," or "one

HELMUT KUHN has had a distinguished career in Germany, in the United States (at North Carolina and Emory universities), and again in Germany, now as Ordinarius Professor in the University of Munich. His considerable work in aesthetics is best known to English-reading philosophers in *A History of Esthetics* (with K. E. Gilbert, 1950 and subsequently). He has worked in the existentialist vein, as historian of thought, as methodologist, as well as metaphysician. This essay appeared in the *Transactions of the Sixth German Congress for Philosophy* in 1960.

This article is a translation of "Ordnung im Werden und Zerfall," pp. 11–25 in *Das Problem der Ordnung* (Meisenheim am Glan: Verlag Anton Hain, 1962), the proceedings of the Sixth German Congress for Philosophy, held at Munich in 1960. The article is also published in a French version as "Le concept de l'ordre," *Gregorianum*, XLIII (1962), 254–67. The English translation was done by J. Michael Young in a project with Professor Paul G. Kuntz of Grinnell College. The translation was undertaken with the author's encouragement and was submitted to him for corrections.

after another." But this does not signify a restriction of the concept of order to that of temporality. If, using scholastic terminology, one denotes the highest universality—that which follows directly upon Being and which surpasses all boundaries of genera—as "transcendental," then one must wonder whether order does not belong to the realm of transcendentals, or at least stand in close relationship to them. With this high degree of universality is combined a high degree of hierarchical gradation, as in the similar case of the concept of the good. Among one another, variously constituted orders can be thought of as being themselves mutually ordered in such a way that they stretch upward to the uttermost prominence. For the Greeks, intellect (*Nous*) was both the source and the essence of order. This prominence, indeed this divine stature, of the concept of order characterizes its history through the centuries. Dante writes, for example, "All things whatsoever have order among themselves, and this is the form that makes the universe resemble God." [1] And Jacopone da Todi sang praises of the love of God, which "crowns itself with order." Even in the thought of the European people who are furthest removed from the Greeks—namely, the Russians—this greatness still characterizes the concept of order. Thus, in the writings of Dostoevski, Dimitri Karamazov sees his inability to establish the "higher order" within himself as the tragic flaw in his existence.

Only recently has the concept of order acquired a bad connotation. Kant still spoke of the "Order of Nature" and the "Order of Things" in the grand, traditional sense; [2] and Hegel developed the dialectic of the concept of order with consummate mastery. [3] In the following period, however, the concept of order became less and less common in philosophical circles. [4]

In the meantime the concept had been discredited through misuse. Advocates of the totalitarian movements and forms of govern-

---

[1] John D. Sinclair (trans. and comm.), *The Divine Comedy of Dante Alighieri* (London: Bodley Head, 1958), "Paradiso," Canto I, pp. 103–5.

[2] Immanuel Kant, *Prolegomena to Any Future Metaphysics That Will Be Able to Present Itself as a Science*, trans. Peter G. Lucas (Manchester: Manchester University Press, 1953), Sec. 38, pp. 82–84; and *Critique of Pure Reason*, 2nd ed., p. 576 (see translation by Kemp Smith [London: Macmillan & Co., 1964], p. 473).

[3] G. W. F. Hegel, *Phänomenologie der Geistes*, 6th ed., edited by J. Hoffmeister, in *Sämtliche Werke* (Philosophische Bibliothek; Hamburg: F. Meiner, 1952), V, 267–74.

[4] Johann Hoffmeister's carefully prepared *Wörterbuch der philosophischen Begriffe* (2nd ed.; Philosophische Bibliothek; Hamburg: F. Meiner, 1955) does not even mention it.

ment emblazoned order upon their banners—order, that is, in *their* sense. Thus "order" fell into the wake of a questionable enthusiasm for discipline, finally to founder in its connection with regulation. Following this discordant praise a critical judgment was passed upon the concept, in the name either of individual freedom or of the future that surpasses all reasonable expectations. In fact, if the unbounded freedom of individual existence is made the One and All, then order, which limits, can mean nothing but compulsion and estrangement. The love of order turns to hate for order, and the "sacred Order," the "blessed daughter of Heaven in whose employ / Like is bound to like in light and joy," [5] is transformed into a work of the devil. In Jean-Paul Sartre's *The Flies,* Zeus, the tyrant of heaven, and Aegisthus, the earthly tyrant, recognize that they are related by a fanatical hunger for order. The saying, *"fiat ordo, pereat homo"* ("Let order be done, even if man perishes") characterizes them both.

Another French student of German existentialism, Jean Beaufret, teaches us that we cannot dismiss this neognostic attack on order as poetic license. In order to show that order is the central concept of the philosophy of Leibniz, Beaufret begins with the notion of the infinitesimal calculus, showing that Leibniz made this notion fruitful for metaphysics by the use of an analogy. As in the calculus an infinite series can be defined by a functional formula, so in metaphysics we can conceive of a series of contingent truths, infinite for our reason, as unified and arranged in advance by the vision of a divine intelligence. In this way would be attained a maximum of determination of the order of reality. Thus Leibniz writes, "Order may be measured insofar as there are many things in a multitude to be observed." [6] That is to say, the greater the number of components that are linked together in a unity, the more perfect the order. Beaufret observes that this sequencelike polyphony which Leibniz envisions, and which is equally far removed from both monotony and cacophony, excludes the unexpected, since in it everything has been taken into account. Not bothering with the observation that this exclusion of the unforeseen is characteristic only of the vision of God, which is unattainable for man, he continues: " 'Order' is the

[5] Johann Christoph von Schiller, "Das Lied von der Glocke," in *Sämtliche Werke,* ed. Eduard von der Hellen (Stuttgart: J. G. Cotter, 1904), I, 45 ff.

[6] *Die Philosophischen Schriften von Gottfried Wilhelm Leibniz,* ed. Karl Immanuel Gerhardt (Berlin: Weidmannsche Buchhandlung, 1887), III, 558.

ascendancy of the complete preparation of ready-made clothes over the improvisations of 'made-to-measure' clothing; and thus the certainty of planning which dominates in complete preparation better fulfills the aim of 'suitability' than does a stumbling-about from case to case." [7] According to Beaufret, then, the Leibnizian notion of a *"planification divine"* leads along the path beyond Hegel's *Phenomenology of Mind* and Nietzsche's *Will to Power*, to the dominance of the modern thought of organization. In the present world, our French contemporary thinks, Americanism and communism are nothing more than especially striking empirical manifestations of just this dominance.

Thus the suggestion that we may discover the source of the malady of our times in the rage for order that characterizes Aegisthus and Zeus comes not only from the nihilistic drama of existentialism, but also from the history of philosophy, when interpreted in a fitting way. But, if one ventures into etiology at all (which kneads the recalcitrant material of the history of philosophy for use in propaganda), then why stop with Leibniz as the corrupter of the ore? Why not go back rather to the Greek beginnings? In fact, one can find a wealth of evidence there for the proceedings now being conducted against order. Even the Greek word for order, *taxis,* can be viewed as treacherous. It is derived, after all, from the verb *tasso* (meaning "to place," "to set up"), and it means primarily the setting up of an army in order of battle. Order is thus that which is ordered. But there is an ambiguity here, since "ordered" means either "possessing a pattern" or "having been forced into a pattern"; and this ambiguity has its prototype in the use of *taxis.* Thus everything suggests that the meaning of "order" originates from the sphere of human activity, inviting its interpretation as the "Will to Power." In Greek thought—or, in any case, in post-Socratic Greek thought—the desire to know corresponds with the desire to order. Through large-scale application of the new formula for interpretation we thus arrive at the following verdict, which is above all interpretations: the *homo technicus* of our century turns out to be the rightful heir to the *homo academicus* presented by Plato; and the Neoplatonic doctrine of being, which stands beneath the banner of the concept of order, is thus transformed into a gross mistake, whose fateful meaning was brought out by Nietzsche's theory of the

[7] Jean Beaufret, "La Fable du Monde," in *Heidegger zum 70 Geburtstag* (Pfullingen, 1959), pp. 11–18.

"Will to Power." The history of metaphysics reveals itself as the progressive history of nihilism.

The result of our survey of the present and past is disconcerting. "Order is heaven's first law" [8]—thus had Alexander Pope summarized Western thought in a moment, at a time when it was already facing the shock and renovation of romanticism. But then, in our age, the star that had shone for two millennia suffered a downfall comparable to Lucifer's. What was good has, in the opinion of contemporary thinkers (both thoughtful and brash), become bad. Once, when asked for what purpose he really lived, Anaxagoras had replied: "For the contemplation of the heavens and of the order which governs all." [9] And the Christian *theologia gloriae* had sounded the Western hymn to order with still greater force. For some of us today, however, the mere word has an evil sound in our ears, as if concealed within it were an attack on the very humanness of humanity. We exist in the midst of a great disorder of concepts, as well as of private and public life. If philosophical spokesmen think and express what others feel, however, the consciousness of this situation does not seem to have evoked any ardent longing for order, but rather a hatred for order. How is this sudden change to be explained? Can the possibility for revaluation be found within the concept of order itself? Or should we seek the reason not in the concept, but rather in the subject of the concept? We speak of the fact that an order grows, and again of the fact that an order decays. Does the theoretical distrust of order perhaps indicate the decay of a real order—of an order so comprehensive that it contains within it the order of thought, and so comprehensive that the order of thought is destroyed in the decay of this order? These are the questions that arise from the breakdown of thought in matters of order. Yet they all press toward the prior question, What is order?

Order is a relational concept. One can imagine an indeterminate, simple, self-contained being, which is prior to, or outside of, all order. A temporal being, however, is already ordered by virtue of its temporality: the succession of situations, in the sense of before and after, represents an order—namely, the temporal order. Similarly, wherever a plurality of objects (ranging anywhere from two to infinity) arises simultaneously in a field of vision, an order already exists. To formalize, we might say that order is a mode of "together-

---

[8] Alexander Pope, *An Essay on Man*, Epistle IV, 1, 49.

[9] Aristotle *Eudemian Ethics* 1216a15.

ness." Things are brought together by order. Now just as the basic mode of "togetherness" consists of the relationship of the whole to its parts, so also is order a relation in virtue of which many things function together as if they were but one. And all of these statements hold true in like manner for the spiritual and the intellectual, as well as for the corporeal, for concepts and thoughts, as well as for things and beings. In short, with these statements we are already moving in the sphere of strict, transcendental universality.

But what is disorder? For the present level of consideration it is a mere negation, to which nothing in reality can correspond. After all, the copresence of many things, however this be determined, represents an order, however elementary. Even chaos is imaginable only insofar as it bears traces of order. But the range of this elementary concept of order is at once an intimation of its provisional character.

Order is a relational concept. Now we distinguish between accidental and essential relations brought about by order. Corresponding to this there may be two types of order: *ordo extrinsicus* ("external order") and *ordo intrinsicus* ("internal order"). It is not a matter of two sharply differentiated classes, however, but rather of a scale between two extreme possibilities. On the one hand there does not exist a totally external order, but there probably are approximations to it. Even a pile of rubbish can contain only spatial objects, and thus objects that essentially belong together in the spatial order. We are here considering, however, only the essential spatiality of objects, and not their specific characteristics. At the other end of the scale we imagine a living organism that is adapted to its environment. But this type of essential order—in which, for example, the nature of the living organism is adapted to the nature of the accompanying environment—still leaves a degree of independence to the component in the order; and this degree of independence can fall far below that of a living organism, without yet reaching the zero point. It should also be noted that what is ordered only externally (and without adaptation), like the object in a pile of rubbish, can nevertheless possess an internal order. But then this internal order stands in no particular relation to the totality—in this case, to the pile of rubbish in which it is located. It is quite the contrary with essential order. Here, too, the individual component in the essential order can probably be viewed as something ordered internally. But this internal order of the component is related to the comprehensive order. In this case, then, we have not merely an order, but an order of orders; and a like statement can be made about the comprehensive order, with reference to a *more* comprehensive order.

Thus we have found two distinguishing characteristics of orders: intensity (or essentiality) and potentiality (or richness). And these two characteristics have one thing in common: both individually and mutually they assume differences in degree, in the sense of "higher" and "lower." They are the principles of hierarchical order. They constitute that order above orders, the extension of which is expressed by the polar opposites of position and privation—or, symbolically, by "above" and "below." A maximum of intensity can be imagined in a system of thought: the totality of thought, with the multiplicity of its components, forms a strict unity, which can be comprehended with *one* glance of the mind's eye. On the other hand, something that is not thought, but that rather is real, illustrates potentiality. It expresses the richness in the order of orders, as this property is represented in every organism, and even in every atom. But these illustrations already show, after all, how little these two principles can actually be separated—they permeate and limit one another.

We have yet to define "growth" and "decay." With the introduction of the thought of graduated order, however, we can now give a clearly outlined meaning to these two concepts. "Growth" means the generation of a higher order; "decay," on the other hand, means that a higher order is replaced by a lower one. A people, for example, can become a nation. Out of the population, which is itself a mutual ordering of men in relation to a society, grows the higher order, animated by faith and thought. Yet this occurs without the destruction of the primary order, the people. On the other hand, the people can become a mass. That is to say, they can sink to a lower form of order and then, as we know from experience, become manipulable—material for an authoritarian order that is imposed upon them.

The illustration from the life of society could be replaced or supplemented by an example from organic life. As in the former example, it is apparent here that growth and decay, when expressed with regard to order, are defined as a change in order, as read off on the scale of "higher" and "lower." A further profit also accrues to us: since we have familarized ourselves with the thought of "more" and "less" in order, we can now give to the concept of disorder a meaning which far surpasses that of mere negation. Disorder is something other than the mere negation of order. Neither is it a barely imaginable minimum of order. Nevertheless, it is in fact a function of order, namely, the inverse of the principle of potentiality (or richness). It is the permeation and juxtaposition of mutually inconsistent orders, i.e., orders that are not mutually ordered. The explanation of disorder as the perversion of order affords the basis for the statement, *corruptio optimi pessima*—the higher the orders that have come into conflict, the greater the disorder.

With the help of the elementary analysis now complete, we are able to depict the great scheme of order that lies at the basis of the many variations of classical metaphysics and was revived by Leibniz with unique subtlety and insight, perhaps for the last time. We imagine a multiplicity of substantial creatures, whose being consists in their effects or actions, and which form an organically related and structurally gradated whole. Without denying the individuality and multiformity of these beings in their respective positions in the hierarchy of order, we may say of them all that in their very existence they are all guided by the command, *suum esse conservare* ("preserve your own kind"). And for all of them the drive for self-preservation has at the same time the meaning of a principle of development. The ontological imperative just given is inseparable from a second, evolutionary imperative: Become what you are. But now the totality of beings—let us call it the "world"—so well illustrates an order that is both intensive and rich, that the efficiency resulting from the commands for self-preservation and self-development provides at the same time a basis for collaboration and cooperation within the great society of the creatures of the world. A harmony persists between the preservation and the unfolding of the condition of the world, and the self-development of the creatures that constitute this world. The creature that entirely "becomes itself" fulfills through this very act of self-fulfillment the place that was assigned to it in the order of the totality. Creaturely uniqueness and the value of individual positions within the order crumble away. This scheme of order will naturally be fit to serve as a scheme of the world only if it is conceived of as subject to imperfections. It is both necessary and possible that there be room for disorder, as well as for the destruction of worldly creatures. But these negative moments, along with the grief they cause, must be made comprehen-

sible within the scheme, as the price that must be paid for the
preservation and development of the whole. And that seems reasonable enough. In the realm of the living the old, who must make
room, pay with their death for the good fortune of the young—until
these in turn are called upon to pay their fee.

This sketch of the scheme of order leaves unanswered the question regarding the source of order—the question of transcendence.
It was precisely this question that was raised by Aristotle as he
reflected upon his daring outline of order in Book Lambda of the
Metaphysics:

> We must now consider also in which of two ways the nature of the
> universe contains the good and the highest good, whether as something
> separate and by itself, or as the order of the parts. Probably in both ways,
> as an army does; for its good is found both in its order and its leader, and
> more in the latter; for he does not depend on the order but it depends on
> him.[10]

To put the Aristotelian question in our own terms, if every individual creature has its cause and its purpose outside itself (i.e., in the
totality of the order) , then must the same thing not be true of this
totality itself? Must it not depend, both for its origin and for its
fulfillment, upon a transcendental, self-grounded good? But we need
only ask this question in order to realize how badly we are equipped
to answer it. Do we even know the meaning of the Aristotelian
phrase *to eu?* Do we have any right to connect the formal principles
of hierarchy (intensity and potentiality) with the good? As these
questions leave us perplexed, it becomes clear that our previous
reflections on order have not brought us noticeably closer to the aim
of our questioning. How was it possible for a breakdown of thought
to occur in matters of order? How was it possible that first there was
a confirmed glorification of the concept of order, and now there is a
complete rejection that has not even been fully grasped yet? Just
how is this breakdown to be overcome? We still have learned
nothing about these problems. We still lack a further step of
thought that will transport us into the midst of our difficulty.

We begin with an observation made earlier. The Greek word *taxis*
in no way denies its descent from a verb that means "to place" or "to
set up," and it thus indicates a human action. By virtue of this
origin it lies within the range of meaning of the word *techne.*

[10] Aristotle *Metaphysics,* trans. W. D. Ross (London: Oxford University Press,
1924) Book Lambda 1075a11–15.

According to Plato's *Gorgias,* the generation of art is characterized by the order that governs it and is differentiated from an act at random *(eike,* 503e). The same is true of the succeeding Latin word *ordo.* As an "age-old technical word of the weaving trade," [11] it not only replaces the Greek term but lives on by virtue of its own strength, and that of its derivatives in modern languages. This "technological" origin of the word might well express something about its meaning. One need only enlighten himself about the content and bearing of this expression. Instead of attacking the question with a philosophy of history inspired by Nietzsche's *Will to Power,* however, and instead of suspecting inclinations toward the taboo "desire to order" (a Greek prelude to the atomic age), we could seek more modestly to obtain an explanation from the nature of things. And this explanation will lead us to that aspect of the concept of order which we have thus far neglected.

The meaning of art is not sufficiently understood if we describe it as production with the aim of controlling a certain material of the environment. We are nearer the truth if we speak of an attentive and formative intimacy with nature, with regard to a work which is to be consummated. This intimacy facilitates an acquaintance with nature; and it is the merit of Socrates to have made this acquaintance fruitful for philosophy. Art proceeds in an orderly fashion; i.e., it does what it does in reference to an anticipated goal, and it does so step by step, according to a plan adapted to that goal. But this orderliness of human action is not a weapon discovered by man in his struggle to subject nature; it is gained from, and adapted to, nature itself. Even the fruits do not ripen at random, but rather in accordance with the order of the seasons. Thus human technology, in the role of the farmer, must adjust its attentive action to this order, just as in the role of the doctor it incorporates the rhythm of the body, and in the role of the architect it incorporates the rhythm of the climate, the landscape, and the society. Thus, in the order of the artistic act the order of nature also appears, as the common ground upon which intercourse takes place between the human demiurge and its natural partner.

We must further bear in mind that the one who engages in the creation of a work, as a man, embodies an order. By virtue of this order the human artist is always *just* an artist. As a man, he does not

[11] F. Kluge, *Etymologisches Wörterbuch der deutschen Sprache* (17th ed.; Berlin, 1957), *s.v.* "Orden."

assume the role of *homo faber* ("Man the maker"). He is never totally engaged in the attentive and formative intimacy with his partner, nature; indeed, even the engagement through technology is always directed from a point of freedom outside the paternal, yet bellicose, embrace of nature. As a creature of both body and mind, man is not only the partner of nature; he also stands opposite the entirety of nature as a "world." He is able to think; and hence he is able to see everything that happens as an object, and to determine his actions on the basis of this view. Thus it is given to him to see the world as a collective order that avoids his molding grasp. And he can differentiate from it the orders that he himself has formed, or that he has cooperatively formed, either as the demiurge of his natural environment or as an associate in the forming of his own life and the life of the society that sustains him. And thus he cannot help asking how the order formed by him, either individually or in cooperation with others, is related to the prior order of nature. This problem, if pointed out to questioning individuals, reduces to two different, though interrelated, questions: (1) How is man related to the order of the whole (the "world") into which he is placed, or in which he is located? (2) How is man related to the order (or orders) of the historical world, into which he, as a participant in human history and as a creature of society, is born?

Both questions show the nature of the thought process that now confronts us again with our initial dilemma, the breakdown of thought in matters of order. We no longer see order as something given, but rather as an undertaking in which man participates—as individual, as nation, as humanity. Even where he cannot engage in ordering, or in causing disorder, man is still called upon to accept or reject the order that confronts or encompasses him. He is called upon to adapt himself to it in one way or another.

Out of man's inclusion in order, now considered as an "undertaking," comes the following basic proposition, which appears from an analysis of the "breakdown" of thought in matters of order: Every order that affects man may also imprison him. It belongs to man, however, to preserve the freedom to rebel against the order that he discovers in the world, and against the order that he has created in his historical existence. He is not only a creature who is bound by order, and who creates order, but also a rebel. And in the historical life of man we find him constructing orders that suit him and destroying orders that do not suit him; hence the pattern of history displays an alternation of phases. Within the framework of this activity, the shedding of the yoke of order can be creative, insofar as it is done not merely as a denial of order, but rather as a denial of this particular order in the name of order in general. In the historical wear and tear of orders, the *ordo ordinans* ("order ordering"— order as an active force in creating patterns) confronts the *ordo ordinatus* ("order ordered"—order as already existent patterns). Thus the possibility of rejection also belongs to the history of Western thought on order. Many are of the impression that the irate protests of our contemporaries represent a novel occurrence in history; but this is a misconception, and it must be eradicated. They are the most recent phase in a long tradition. Albert Camus, in his *L'Homme revolté*, has traced this tradition back to the eighteenth century. In reality it goes back even to the formulation of the principle of order. To the extent that a beginning can be recognized at all, we can find it in the history of the dishonored heroes, as told by Sophocles. Ajax seems ready to submit to the ruling order:

Let us learn to pay homage to the sons of Atreus. They are the lords, and to them we are permitted to yield. Indeed, how could it be otherwise? Even the frightful and over-powering ones yield to sovereignty. Winter gives way to summer, night to day, the storm to the still of the sea. Should we alone fail to be wise? [12]

But these words are deceptive. Even as he utters them, the speaker had decided to turn his back on this world of political and cosmic order by hurling himself upon his sword. Here begins the long tradition in which suicide acquires the meaning of a protest against the prevailing order. In other respects, this tradition has also been characterized, from its early beginnings down to the present day, by two counterbalancing symbols, the one Greek-mythological and the other Biblical: the Prometheus symbol, and the symbol of Lucifer as given by the prophet Isaiah.

How is man related to the total cosmic order in which he finds himself? This was the first of the two questions that appeared from our new point of view. A thorough examination reveals that there are two possible answers to this question, which differ radically. The first answer, which we might briefly call the metaphysical one, maintains that man's station in the cosmic order is designated to him. To fulfill this position properly is his only chance; to fail to do

---

[12] Sophocles *Ajax* 667 ff.

so is his true danger. Even the most daring stretch of his powers must still be governed by the spirit of obedience; even his highest creativity does service to conformity. In terms of this answer to our question, order can mean for man only the taking of his designated place in the cosmic order.

This answer, which might well be called a classical one, rests upon a series of assumptions which, though unchallenged since antiquity, are being more seriously doubted today than ever before. First of all, the cosmic order, to be capable of encompassing man without encroaching upon his nature, must be "meaningful." But, in demanding that the cosmic order be meaningful, we have already decided that there must be a divine being transcendent to the order. For an order that is meaningful, and thus in the position of the highest order, and one that we know by experience, cannot possibly be attributed to the interhuman *ordo amoris* ("order of love"). Furthermore, it must be possible to assume that the order in question can be recognized, however limited the human possibilities for recognition may be. Finally, it must be thought that this recognition is guided by the "emphasis" of the soul, aiming at the perfection of its own being. And this guiding must take place in such a way that the obedient submission to the established order is one with the freest act of man. If we reject metaphysics, then perhaps we do so because we recoil with shock before the demand of the truth that shines forth from these assumptions.

But now we come to the second answer to the question before us, which directly opposes the metaphysical answer just examined: there exists no essential reltionship between man and the cosmic order. In Nicolai Hartmann's formulation, man's task is "to come to terms with a world not planned for him." [13] Or, to use the gnostic phrase, which has been transformed into a curse by Heidegger, "Man is thrown into the world." This answer commends itself morally; it is clothed with a luster acquired from the tradition of Prometheus and Lucifer. Man's self-preservation against a world that is foreign to him is, as Hartmann continues in the passage cited, a task "by far greater and more worthy of his power for self-determination." In addition to this, the answer commends itself intellectually: no superhuman effort is required in order to make sense out of it.

[13] Nicolai Hartmann, *Neue Wege der Ontologie* (Stuttgart: W. Kohlhammer, 1949) , pp. 70–71.

More closely viewed, however, this second answer is seen to be lacking intellectually. In spite of its apparent value, it is doubly absurd in its consequences. If we attempt to imagine man, gifted with the power of self-determination, placed in "a world not planned for him," then we necessarily forfeit any understanding of human nature; for such an understanding can be gained only from the interweaving of man and nature. If we forget to consider his corporeality, or his position in the hierarchy of creatures, then we can understand nothing more. But, worse yet, if we accept this much celebrated position, then we necessarily forfeit every concept of that entire world against which man in his solitude supposedly stands. Since we are men, we can be aware of the totality of the world only from a human perspective; and this awareness can uncover reality only if the human perspective possesses a natural relationship with the totality around it. Thus, whoever removes man from the world and views him as a stranger to nature necessarily throws away the key which alone can unlock this world. In the wake of Nietzsche, much has been said of the world-disrupting effect of Platonic-Christian dualism. But if dualism is what does away with the concept of the world, then the true dualists are those who view man as disconnected—as a creature thrown out of his union with the world. These are in fact the true heirs to the gnostic tradition.

Let us now discuss the second question that arises from the inclusion of man in the concept of order: namely, "How is man related to the order (or orders) of the historical world, into which he, as a participant in human history and a creature of society, is born?" Here again we shall discuss two mutually opposed answers, but this time placing the critical one first. Whereas it was possible in the former question to deny the existence of an essential relationship between man and the natural world, no such thing is rationally possible in the case of the relationship between man and the orders he has created. Therefore the critical answer can maintain only this: the self-preservation with which man is charged demands of him that he conquer his freedom from the traditional orders into which he is born. His historical task, and thus the meaning of history, consists in progressive emancipation. But this leads to a further question: does not the critical destruction of historical orders, and the emancipation from their control, lead necessarily to a future order? In other words, is it not necessarily the case that the princi-

ples upon which outmoded orders are criticized turn out to be the
constructive principles of a new order? Radical criticism of traditional orders aligns itself naturally with the thought of progress in
the philosophy of history, and thus with utopianism. By this I mean
that the future order, at which the criticism of the existing one aims,
is regarded more as a self-given result than as something toward
which to work, and that furthermore nothing definite can be said
about this future order. This future order stands out as the entirely
"new and different"—as the true fulfillment of history, as opposed
to the orders that merely come to pass in history.

This philosophy of emancipation, still a prevailing mode of
thought today, has reached a point at which our original distinction
disappears. The dichotomy between man's relationship to the world
and man's relationship to history reduces to one and the same basic
attitude. Since it is given to man neither to flee from nor to mimic
the cosmic process, which is essentially foreign to him, but rather to
do battle with this process, he thus stands over against the established historical orders as a Promethean revolutionary. Man philos-
ophizes with crushing hammer in hand. Thus we need not merely
an idea of the character of the human attitude, but rather a radical
concept of human authenticity. We have previously spoken of this
world naïvely, as if it were something naturally given. But now we
are called upon to imagine that this world exists only as a "world-
for-us"—i.e., to imagine that it exists, in its actual construction, only
through man, who is engrossed in his actual, historical situation.
We are challenged to view this world as an order created by man in
history. And in the midst of this temporal world, which is uniformly
structured yet not definable by any universal concepts, stands man
as "world-shaper"—as the creative center, or source of order, in the
sense of *ordo ordinans*.

But his greatness is burdened with an ambiguity. The demiurge
of the orders of the historical world is at the same time the victim of
history. It contains him entirely; it is the overpowering *vis a tergo*
which, without his awareness, dictates completely the order man
creates. Thus he is free upon the basis of his lack of freedom; he is
both a creature that orders and a creature that is thrown into an
order. In short, to accept the critical interpretation of the relationship of man to historical order is in fact to destroy man. And this
theoretical self-destruction is uncannily suitable to a situation in
which the means for actual self-destruction are present. This posi-

tion fulfills all too well the Hegelian precept according to which philosophy is "its age, captured in thought."

Thus only the affirmative, or metaphysical, answer remains. This answer shares with the critical reply the common characteristic of reducing the twofold question to a single question. If, as we have seen, the culmination of all wisdom lies in submission to the total order, then the source of all order and the *principium ordinis ordinantis* ("principle of the order that orders") for this supreme wisdom is not the totality of the natural world, but rather its transcendental ground. For man, the first and last determination of order lies in the fact that he is *capax Dei* ("capable of understanding God"); and from this relationship to the transcendent follows his submission to the totality of the world, as well as to the historical world. Nevertheless, new questions arise about the relationship of man to the historical orders—questions that have thus far scarcely been touched. Nothing is gained by applying the general thought of meaningfulness to the historical world. Yet a political traditionalism still follows from the metaphysical and theological piety toward order. And admittedly there does not follow that "revolutionism" which we have come to recognize as the practical-political counterpart to the "critical" answer to the question of order. But the major difference between these two answers lies rather in the fact that the metaphysical answer results neither in an interpretation of the "contemporary situation" by a philosophy of history nor in an application to the currently demanded attitude toward historical actualities. On the contrary! The metaphysical answer makes intelligible the fact that traditional order can be maintained only through continual renovation, that preservation and criticism belong together, and that even an order which is functioning excellently at present may be in truth a perverted order, and thus an organized decay.

The metaphysical answer, far from diverting our gaze from the realities that confront us, leads us to concrete judgment and vision. Hegel wanted to attain concrete judgment and vision by scientifically deciphering providence, using the dialectic of reason. Analysts of the current situation who were inspired by Hegel strive toward the same goal by using the dialectic of anxiety toward the future. But in this way one outlines and schematizes the present, instead of living in it and thinking from within it. Concreteness of vision in the area of human historical action (and thus in the field of the "practical reason") can be attained only if the principles of order that guide us free our gaze for an intuition saturated with experience—an intuition of what is now happening, together with the horizon of the past and the chances for the future. The post-Hegelian construction of the present leads partially to fanatical actions and partially to an eschatological paralysis of action. But the concrete vision not distorted by a philosophy of history—that vision which comes with the metaphysical answers—leads always to reasonable action. Since man is inserted into human history as one responsible being among others, his mode of vision within this area will be "in order" only when it is determined along lines of judgment and cooperation, and when it is in this sense "political."

To give an example, capitalism and communism as historical phenomena can be identified and judged only according to their respective principles of order. When this analysis is made, it becomes apparent that the capitalistic system contains a force that tends toward the perversion of order, insofar as it grants the economic motive an unfitting position of prominence. Yet it is also apparent that this perversion is open to alleviation; it is not fateful in the same sense that totalitarian communism is, which violates both conscience and person, and thus the base of human society. This judgment, which is indispensable for the comprehension of the phenomena, frees the gaze for the unfolding of a historical perspective, in which historical realities appear in their concrete interdependence and their causal relations. And between principles of order and intuitive comprehension of the situation the full scope presents itself in which we live our active existence and suffer our fate in mutual responsibility—the sphere of inilluminable twilight, in which human freedom, groping and grasping, seeks its way.

In the midst of the historical growth and decay of orders runs the path between the two extreme dangers: between the temptation to allow intellectual freedom to become intoxicated in destructive criticism, and the temptation to establish an indolent peace with the powers of the age. This path can be traveled only because growth and decay, and the extremes of temptation that appear from the interweaving and the causal dependency of the two phases, are bridged by a meaningful—that is, equitable—cosmic order, the *ordo divinae sapientiae* ("order of divine wisdom"). Admittedly, the unity of freedom and order, which lies hidden in the depths of the divine, remains impenetrable for the patchwork of our knowledge.

We must be content to contemplate the growth of freedom out of subordination—a fulfillment ultimately incomprehensible, yet still actualized from time to time. It was precisely this process of growth which drew from the Psalmist these famous words (Psalm 118):

> I will praise thee: for thou hast heard me
> and art become my salvation.

JOSEPH F. WALL

The Historian's Approach to Reality

Why have many historians in the past one hundred years felt obliged to call themselves scientists? Can the question of science and history be reversed; that is, if history does not have a place in science, does science have a place in history? I shall hope to give an answer to both of these questions as I develop my interpretation of the meaning of reality.

I should like to approach this question of reality in its universal aspect in a tangential manner by relating how in a seminar in American Studies, as prefatory to a study of Herman Melville, I asked the question, "What is the most shocking idea you can conceive of holding in regard to God?" I at once received the answer I had expected when a girl answered, "The idea that there is no God." I then assigned to this student Melville's short novel, *Billy Budd,* and suggested that she might be interested in looking into Lawrance Thompson's interpretation of that novel. Thompson's thesis in his book *Melville's Quarrel with God* is that Melville in *Billy Budd* symbolizes in the ship's captain the utter depravity of

JOSEPH F. WALL, a graduate of Grinnell College, has taught there his entire career, serving in many capacities including that of Chairman of the Faculty. He is the author of a distinguished book, *Henry Watterson, Reconstructed Rebel,* and is preparing a biography of Andrew Carnegie. He has been a Fulbright Scholar at the University of Edinburgh and a Fulbright Visiting Professor in American Studies at the University of Gothenburg.

God. God is totally evil. Hence Billy Budd must be destroyed, for his is the innocence of Adam before God taught him evil. The next week the girl made her report. She admitted that the idea of God's being totally evil was a more shocking concept than the idea that there was no God. I did not suggest to her that there might be an even more shocking view of God than either the atheistic or the Melville-out-of-Thompson interpretation of God as evil apotheosized—more shocking even than Bernard Shaw's making of heaven and hell frightfully dull places with both God and the devil as dreadfully talkative bores. Quite simply put, it seems to me that the most disturbing concept possible would be to hold that there is a God and that He is an idiot—most disturbing because this would be simply another way of saying that there is no order or, if you like, purpose or plan in the universe and in the affairs of man.

Men have been successful in replacing God with other concepts of order and still finding meaning in the universe. It is even possible to find order in evil. Both Dante and Milton picture hell as a well-run place. (One might add parenthetically that Milton implies hell is better run than heaven for it has never known a revolt.) But to say that God is an idiot is to abnegate all reason for existence. If the denial of any order in the universe is the ultimate in nihilism, then it would appear that the concept of order is the essence of reality, a universal quality of reality meaningful to and known implicitly by all men.

That order is an essential of reality does not mean that men have not at times denied order, for there can be no idea, no matter how basic, that is not subject to contradiction. Throughout history, there have been those few who could dare to imagine the absence of order, who insisted upon taking a hurried glance through the curtain of reality into that vast auditorium of chaos. The Flemish painter Hieronymus Bosch, at the end of the fifteenth century, attempted to paint the portrait of chaos in great frightening canvases whose meaning was incomprehensible to his contemporaries, but in the end this nightmare vision of unreality was too frightening even for its creator, and Bosch returned to the painting of a world of religious order, of the Prodigal Son and St. John the Baptist.

Shakespeare, too, could speak of unreality, of the orderless world of the idiot. Macbeth in the last act speaks Shakespeare's most frighteningly nihilistic line:

Life's . . . a tale
Told by an idiot, full of sound and fury,
Signifying nothing.

But Shakespeare did not always maintain this nihilism, and in the
last act of *Hamlet,* Hamlet says:

That should teach us
There's a divinity that shapes our ends,
rough'hew them how we will.

This questioning of order, these brief glimpses into chaos seem to
occur most frequently in those historic periods which mark a transition from one order to another, and it is significant that our own
century has been marked by such questioning. The popular American playwright, Robert Sherwood, wrote a play called *Idiot's Delight,* which opened in March, 1936. In this play, which is set in the
Austrian Alps, an aging American hoofer with a troop of American
dancing girls meets his former mistress in a resort hotel; she is
posing as a Russian countess in exile. It is on the eve of what proves
to be the beginning of World War II, and the play is concerned
with rumors of war. Irene, the bogus countess, speaks the lines that
give the play its title and express the essential philosophic nihilism
of the play. Irene says of God: "Poor, lonely old soul. Sitting up in
heaven, with nothing to do but play solitaire. Poor, dear God.
Playing Idiot's Delight. The game that never means anything, and
never ends." The play concludes with the first bombs of World War
II being dropped on Austria. When all of the other guests and the
staff of the hotel hurry to the basement for shelter, the American
dancer and Irene refuse to go. They invite the chaos they see in life,
and the curtain falls with the two of them sitting at a grand piano.
Harry is playing a jazzed-up version of "Onward Christian Soldiers"
as the walls collapse around them. So Sherwood viewed the world in
the year Hitler marched into the Rhineland and Mussolini grabbed
off Ethiopia.

Four years later, however, when the nightmare vision of 1936 had
become a reality, when the bombs were falling and World War II
had begun, Sherwood renounced his earlier nihilism. A new play of
his opened in April, 1940, with the significant title, taken from
Revelation, *There Shall Be No Night.* That play ends with the wife
of a Finnish Nobel Prize-winning scientist reading a letter from her
husband, which was written just before he was killed in battle with

the Russians. Her husband states Sherwood's own reaffirmation of order and reality when he writes to his wife of "man's unconquerable aspiration to dignity and freedom and purity in the sight of God."

This same questioning of reality followed by a disavowal of unreality can be found in two novels—E. M. Forster's *Passage to India* and Franz Kafka's *The Trial*—both complex and certainly not restricted to one theme, but both concerned in some way with order. In *Passage to India*, Mrs. Moore, an elderly Englishwoman in India to visit her son, accepts an invitation from a young Hindu to go with him and a party of friends into the famous Marabar caves of central India. Mrs. Moore looks forward to the trip with the mild excitement of the tourist who is expected to see the notable sights in an alien land. But, when she finds herself inside the dark cavern, she experiences what she had not expected. The heat and the stench overcome her, but mostly it is the echo, a monotonous sound of *bou-oum,* that drives her to distraction. For a moment, she feels she will go mad as she tries to fight her way out through the crowd. Outside she sits down to rest and to write a note to her two children in England. But she discovers she cannot write. Forster describes her reaction:

The crush and the smells she could forget, but the echo began in some indescribable way to undermine her hold on life. Coming at a moment when she chanced to be fatigued, it had managed to murmur, "Pathos, piety, courage—they exist, but are identical and so is filth. Everything exists, nothing has value." If one had spoken vileness in that place or quoted lofty poetry, the comment would have been the same—"ou-boum." If one had spoken with the tongue of angels and pleaded for all the unhappiness and misunderstanding in the world, past, present and to come, for all the misery men must undergo whatever their opinion and position, and however much they dodge or bluff—it would amount to the same, the serpent would descend and return to the ceiling. Devils are of the North, and poems can be written about them, but no one could romanticize the Marabar because it robbed infinity and eternity of their vastness, the only quality that accommodates them. . . . She tried to go on with her letter. . . . Out suddenly, at the edge of her mind, Religion appeared, poor little talkative Christianity, and she knew that all its divine words from "Let there be Light" to "It is finished" only amounted to "boum." [1]

Mrs. Moore never recovers from this brush with unreality, with an orderless universe. She leaves India soon afterward and dies on

[1] E. M. Forster, *A Passage to India* (New York: Modern Library), pp. 149–50.

the ship after a few days at sea. But Forster does not permit chaos to win out. Mrs. Moore is not forgotten by her Hindu friends. She becomes something of a legend and in time is transfigured into Esmiss Esmoor, a Hindu goddess in that wide and accommodating pantheon that is the Hindu mythology. She finds a place at last in an order she never knew.

Kafka's *The Trial* is a much more difficult novel. It can be read at many levels for many meanings. One level certainly is concerned with the question of order, which is also the question of reality. The key to this reading is in the opening line of the novel: "Someone must have traduced Joseph K., for without having done anything wrong, he was arrested one fine morning." The important phrase here is "without having done anything wrong." Here is the clue to K.'s dilemma; one fine morning he discovers himself living in an orderless world—an adult Alice in a nightmare Wonderland. He is on trial, but cannot discover for what. He tries to deal with the court as if it were a court of law in a universe run by law. He hires the best lawyer possible; he tries to influence the court through influential people; he is willing to try bribery—all of the little tricks that have meaning in the well-run system of a sane world. But at the first session of the court, upon taking a hurried look into the imposing records and law books of the court, he discovers that they are filled only with pornographic pictures. He visits the court offices, located in a garret, and finds he has invaded an insane asylum. Only in the end does the realization come that this trial can have meaning only if he admits to a guilt—the guilt of the disorder in the world for which all men are responsible. He then goes willingly, although he has the opportunity to escape, to his own execution. Only then does the nightmare of chaos take on a purpose, a reality, without which there is only insanity. It is a disturbing and significant book, and in its own way it is an eloquent plea for order in what appears to be a disintegrating world. Not even Kafka can accept the surrealistic chaos he so graphically portrays.

There have been many concepts of order in man's history from the animism of the primitive tribe to the scientific world of the twentieth century. How these major concepts arise and how they are replaced by other major concepts are the problems of approaching reality with which the historian must be concerned. Within every order there are a few great seminal minds who give to these concepts their meaningful forms. To quote Isaiah Berlin from his provocative essay, *The Hedgehog and the Fox:*

There is a line among the fragments of the Greek poet Archilochus which says: "The fox knows many things, but the hedgehog knows one big thing." Scholars have differed about the correct interpretation of these dark words, which may mean no more than that the fox, for all his cunning, is defeated by the hedgehog's one defence. But, taken figuratively, the words can be made to yield a sense in which they mark one of the deepest differences which divide writers and thinkers, and it may be, human beings in general. For there exists a great chasm between those, on one side, who relate everything to a single central vision, one system, less or more coherent or articulate, in terms of which they understand, think and feel . . . and, on the other side, those who pursue many ends . . . who entertain ideas that are centrifugal rather than centripetal. . . . The first kind of intellectual and artistic personality belongs to the hedgehog, the second to the foxes. . . .[2]

Interesting as Berlin's thesis is, it should be qualified to the extent of pointing out that even the foxes must run in an orderly fashion and leave behind a perceivable spoor. And, as for the great hedgehogs of history, they themselves can know the one big thing only if it is plausible within their particular concept of order. To illustrate, St. Bernard, crossing the Alps into Italy in the year 1135, might well have observed, as he ascended to the high passes and then descended into the deep valleys, those many forms of vegetation that surrounded him. Had he observed how certain wildflowers and trees could grow at certain altitudes but not at others, he would have had the data that Darwin needed to formulate a theory of evolution. Had he made these observations, historians of the next century might well have been discussing the impact of social Bernardism on twelfth-century thought. But of course Bernard made no such observations. His letters reveal that he kept his thoughts on God and his hands folded in prayer. It is quite inconceivable that he could have done otherwise. Darwin had to wait until the nineteenth century. Science is a part of history and cannot anticipate a new concept of order before its time.

For over a thousand years, in western Europe, the prevailing concept of order was theocentric. Within this order, society accommodated itself. The great hedgehogs of this period might dispute

[2] Isaiah Berlin, *The Hedgehog and the Fox: An Essay on Tolstoy's View of History* (New York: Simon and Schuster, 1966), pp. 1–2.

dogma and doctrine, but not the order. And if, on occasions, men felt they were dealing with a somewhat capricious God, they did not question the order, but only their own feeble understanding of it. The ways of God are inscrutable, and man cannot hope to understand all. Faith alone was the only answer to many questions, and Augustine and Luther were the greatest of the hedgehogs because they based their concept of order on faith alone. But in time some men wanted other answers to some of the questions asked. If you wish God to remain inscrutable, do not try to make him logical on man's own terms. Aquinas and the Scholastics, and later Calvin, made logic too attractive, and in effect they unwittingly invited a new order. Descartes accepted the invitation.

Since Descartes, Western man has lived within an order that has had natural science as its center. It is significant that the greatest hedgehogs of the past three hundred years have all been natural scientists: Newton, Darwin, and Einstein. This is not to say that there have not been suborders within the order of science, and other men who have known one big thing. But even these men have put their one big idea in terms of science. Marx, rejecting the earlier socialistic experiments of his century as utopian, called his socialism scientific. Freud, who at first appeared to his contemporaries to be deserting the rationality of medical science for the irrationality of sideshow quackery, eventually proved to the world that he had in fact extended the order of science into regions that orthodox science had never imagined it might invade. He made rational the irrational, gave reason to hysteria and purpose to dreams.

It is hardly surprising, then, that historians in the last two centuries, living in and recording their order, should so identify themselves with that order as to assume the role of scientists.

If the concept of order has about it that universal quality of reality, and if it is the duty of the historian to interpret and explain that order in relation to other concepts that have preceded it, then does not the historian, in effect, justify order—any order—only for the reason that it exists. Does not all order, per se, become acceptable? How can the historian escape the relativist trap? These admittedly are serious questions, and they can only be answered by saying that it is important that the historian answer them, not the witch doctor, the monk, or the scientist. His identification with his order must not be so complete as to prevent him from fulfilling his second role, which is that of critic. It is with this second task, however, that the historian often fails. He reports to the best of his ability, but he too frequently accepts what he has reported. I regret that there were not more historians on board the ships that brought to America the scientists and writers who were deserting the new Germanic order of the 1930's—that order said by its leader to be destined to endure a thousand years.

At this moment in our history, the role of the historian as critic, his willingness to face squarely the reality of his order, has taken on an urgency never before known. Every historic order, to be sure, has had premonitions of its own end. In every age there have been apocalyptic visions. But such millenarianism has always before assumed the active intervention of some supernatural force and has carried with it the idea of judgment. Our order is unique in foreseeing its own end through man's own decision and foreseeing an apocalypse without judgment, ending in nothing.

For the first time the curtain of reality is drawn wide, and every man must face chaos. It is still an alternative, but a very possible one. Should that alternative be chosen, we know from those earlier glimpses what we may expect: Forster's Marabar caves will be our home, Bosch's canvases our landscape, Kafka's trial our indiscriminate and meaningless sentence. The historian has a particular obligation to make these alternatives distinct and must, I feel, speak out against Rand Corporation studies to prove we can survive a nuclear war; must argue against fallout shelters and all other proposals that would blur our vision and would confuse reality with unreality, order with chaos. For these attempts to disguise the alternative of true nihilism with a semblance of order are worse than meaningless. They contribute to the disorder. They would put the false mask of reason on the blurred face of idiocy; they would ask chaos to keep a clean house. They would make a mockery out of the one transcendent idea that man has had, the idea of order, be it God or science, philosophy, art, or history. They could prove to be the final act of blasphemy.

Index